ICAS 2020

The Sixteenth International Conference on Autonomic and Autonomous Systems

September 27th – October 1st, 2020

ICAS 2020 Editors

Roy Sterritt, Ulster University, UK

Mark J. Balas, Texas A&M University, USA

Timothy Patten, TU Wien, Austria

Geraldo Silveira, Division of Robotics and Computer Vision, CTI, Brazil

Giulia De Masi - Zayed University, UAE

Eliseo Ferrante, Vrije Universiteit Amsterdam, the Netherlands

Printed from e-media with permission by:

Curran Associates, Inc.
57 Morehouse Lane
Red Hook, NY 12571

Some format issues inherent in the e-media version may also appear in this print version.

International Academy, Research, and Industry Association (IARIA)
412 Derby Way
Wilmington, DE 19810

Phone: (408) 893-6407
Fax: (408) 527-6351

petre@iaria.org

Additional copies of this publication are available from:

Curran Associates, Inc.
57 Morehouse Lane
Red Hook, NY 12571 USA
Phone: 845-758-0400
Fax: 845-758-2633
Email: curran@proceedings.com
Web: www.proceedings.com

Table of Contents

ICAS 2020

Forward

The Sixteenth International Conference on Autonomic and Autonomous Systems (ICAS 2020) continued a series of events covering topics related to systems automation, autonomous systems and autonomic computing.

Pervasive services and mobile computing are emerging as the next computing paradigm in which infrastructure and services are seamlessly available anywhere, anytime, and in any format. This move to a mobile and pervasive environment raises new opportunities and demands on the underlying systems. In particular, they need to be adaptive, self-adaptive, and context-aware.

Adaptive and self-managed, context-aware systems are difficult to create; they must be able to understand context information and dynamically change their behavior at runtime according to the context. Context information can include the user location, his preferences, his activities, the environmental conditions and the availability of computing and communication resources. Dynamic reconfiguration of the context-aware systems can generate inconsistencies as well as integrity problems, and combinatorial explosion of possible variants of these systems with a high degree of variability can introduce great complexity.

Traditionally, user interface design is a knowledge-intensive task complying with specific domains, yet being user friendly. Besides operational requirements, design recommendations refer to standards of the application domain or corporate guidelines.

Commonly, there is a set of general user interface guidelines; the challenge is due to a need for cross-team expertise. Required knowledge differs from one application domain to another, and the core knowledge is subject to constant changes and to individual perception and skills.

Passive approaches allow designers to initiate the search for information in a knowledge-database to make accessible the design information for designers during the design process. Active approaches, e.g., constraints and critics, have been also developed and tested. These mechanisms deliver information (critics) or restrict the design space (constraints) actively, according to the rules and guidelines. Active and passive approaches are usually combined to capture a useful user interface design.

All these points pose considerable technical challenges and make self-adaptable context-aware systems costly to implement. These technical challenges lead the context-aware system developers to use improved and new concepts for specifying and modeling these systems to ensure quality and to reduce the development effort and costs.

We take here the opportunity to warmly thank all the members of the ICAS 2020 technical program committee, as well as all the reviewers. The creation of such a high quality conference program would not have been possible without their involvement. We also kindly thank all the authors who dedicated much of their time and effort to contribute to ICAS 2020. We truly believe that, thanks to all these efforts, the final conference program consisted of top quality contributions. We also thank the members of the ICAS 2020 organizing committee for their help in handling the logistics of this event.

ICAS 2020 Chairs

ICAS 2020 Steering Committee
Roy Sterritt, Ulster University, UK
Jacques Malenfant, Sorbonne Université | LIP6 Lab, France
Mark J. Balas, Embry-Riddle Aeronautical University, USA
Claudius Stern, biozoom services GmbH - Kassel | FOM University of Applied Sciences – Essen, Germany
Radu Calinescu, University of York, UK
Petr Skobelev, Knowledge Genesis Group / Samara Technical University, Russia
Karsten Böhm, Fachhochschule Kufstein, Austria

ICAS 2020 Publicity Chair
Joseyda Jaqueline More, Universitat Politecnica de Valencia, Spain
Marta Botella-Campos, Universitat Politecnica de Valencia, Spain

ICAS 2020 Industry/Research Advisory Committee
Loris Penserini, Informatica e Società Digitale - IES, Italy
Stefanos Vrochidis, Centre for Research and Technology Hellas - Thermi-Thessaloniki, Greece
Tsuyoshi Ide, IBM T. J. Watson Research Center, USA
Rajat Mehrotra, Intelligent Automation Inc., USA
Andreas Kercek, Lakeside Labs GmbH, Austria
Satoshi Kurihara, University of Electro-Communications, Japan
Elisabetta Di Nitto, Politecnico di Milano, Italy
Karsten Böhm, Fachhochschule Kufstein, Austria
Richard Anthony, University of Greenwich, UK

ICAS 2020
Committee

ICAS 2020 Steering Committee

Roy Sterritt, Ulster University, UK
Jacques Malenfant, Sorbonne Université | LIP6 Lab, France
Mark J. Balas, Embry-Riddle Aeronautical University, USA
Claudius Stern, biozoom services GmbH - Kassel | FOM University of Applied Sciences – Essen, Germany
Radu Calinescu, University of York, UK
Petr Skobelev, Knowledge Genesis Group / Samara Technical University, Russia
Karsten Böhm, Fachhochschule Kufstein, Austria

ICAS 2020 Publicity Chair

Joseyda Jaqueline More, Universitat Politecnica de Valencia, Spain
Marta Botella-Campos, Universitat Politecnica de Valencia, Spain

ICAS 2020 Industry/Research Advisory Committee

Loris Penserini, Informatica e Società Digitale - IES, Italy
Stefanos Vrochidis, Centre for Research and Technology Hellas - Thermi-Thessaloniki, Greece
Tsuyoshi Ide, IBM T. J. Watson Research Center, USA
Rajat Mehrotra, Intelligent Automation Inc., USA
Andreas Kercek, Lakeside Labs GmbH, Austria
Satoshi Kurihara, University of Electro-Communications, Japan
Elisabetta Di Nitto, Politecnico di Milano, Italy
Karsten Böhm, Fachhochschule Kufstein, Austria
Richard Anthony, University of Greenwich, UK

ICAS 2020 Technical Program Committee

Alba Amato, Institute for High-Performance Computing and Networking (ICAR), Napoli, Italy
Mark J. Balas, Embry-Riddle Aeronautical University, USA
Ramón Barber Castaño, Universidad Carlos III de Madrid, Spain
Malek Ben Salem, Accenture Labs, USA
Julita Bermejo-Alonso, Universidad Politécnica de Madrid (UPM), Spain
Navneet Bhalla, University College London, UK
Karsten Böhm, Fachhochschule Kufstein, Austria
Kenny Bowers, Georgia Tech Research Institute, USA
Estelle Bretagne, University of Picardie Jules Verne / lab MIS (modeling, information and systems), France
Radu Calinescu, University of York, UK
Paolo Campegiani, Bit4id, Italy
Valérie Camps, Paul Sabatier University - IRIT, Toulouse, France
Elisa Capello, Politecnico di Torino and CNR-IEIIT, Italy
Dario Cazzato, Interdisciplinary Centre for Security, Reliability and Trust | University of Luxembourg, Luxembourg
Meghan Chandarana, NASA Langley Research Center, USA
Shreyansh Daftry, NASA Jet Propulsion Laboratory | California Institute of Technology, Pasadena, USA

Copyright Information

A Human-on-the-Loop Autonomy Architecture for Resident-AUV Undersea Support Infrastructure

Pedro Andrés Forero, LorRaine Duffy, and Eric Hendricks

Naval Information Warfare Center Pacific
San Diego, California 92152, USA
Emails: {pedro.a.forero; lorraine.duffy; eric.hendricks}@navy.mil

***Abstract*—The use of Resident Autonomous Underwater Vehicles (R-AUVs) is a necessary step towards increasing the safety and reliability of undersea infrastructure ranging from communication cables to oil pipelines and undersea observatories. Undersea Support Infrastructure (USI) for R-AUVs will provide docking, energy and communication services. Furthermore, it will be able to autonomously interact with R-AUVs, while enabling remote human operators to oversee, and in some cases direct, the R-AUVs and USI operations. This is particularly critical in situations where assured communications between operators and the USI are not guaranteed. This paper proposes an autonomy architecture for USIs that pursues a vertical and horizontal separation-of-concerns architecture-design approach and builds on well-documented autonomy and autonomic system design principles. Horizontal separation allows for configuration strategies and behavior policies to be defined, selected, executed and monitored by loosely coupled planning modules acting as arbitrators. Vertical separation enables decision making components to be grouped according to the timeliness of the decisions they must make. Our autonomy architecture features a dual, local and global, planning layer that provides an interface for the operator to interact with the USI, enables human-on-the-loop autonomy, and supports autonomous operations in situations where the communications between the operator and the USI are unreliable and intermittent. A use case for this architecture in the context of future at-sea inspection, maintenance, and repair services for the oil and gas industry is discussed.**

Keywords–Autonomy architecture; resident autonomous underwater vehicles; inspection, maintenance and repair; human-machine interaction.

I. Introduction

Ocean exploration and monitoring activities for both civilian and military applications are increasingly integrating sensor payloads with underwater vehicles to satisfy their need for deeper and persistent reach [17], [21], [24]. Commercially-available Autonomous Underwater Vehicle (AUV) technologies can routinely reach depths of up to 6,000 meters – the average ocean-depth has recently been estimated at 3,682 meters [6] – and conduct unattended operations for several days [21]. Furnished with advanced sensors and actuators, underwater vehicles are able to perform undersea data collection and actuation in environments previously considered too risky, costly or inaccessible for manned operations. Although challenged by the harsh environmental conditions and the intense pressure characteristic of the deeper parts of the ocean, advances in AUV design and material science will continue extending the AUVs' ability to operate deeper and longer underwater.

Despite the success of AUVs, long-term AUV deployments continue to require frequent human intervention. For instance, AUV batteries must be periodically recharged or replaced by a human operator. Coupled with the low-bandwidth acoustic channels and high-energy cost-per-bit associated with underwater acoustic communications [7], and the increasing demand for larger volumes of undersea data, the availability of limited data storage and processing capabilities onboard an AUV imposes a requirement for periodic data downloads. Not only is human intervention costly and risky, but it is also a limiting factor for the duration and operational rhythm of AUV operations. Despite these challenges, AUV capabilities in the areas of navigation, actuation, maneuverability and artificial intelligence have continued to mature [17], [21]. Indeed, the new generation of underwater vehicles combines attributes of AUVs and Remotely Operated Vehicles (ROVs) that facilitate actuation using anthropomorphic capabilities [1], [23].

Continual inspection, maintenance and repair (IMR) services for undersea infrastructure is a nascent application area for AUVs that considers the use of *Resident* AUVs (R-AUVs) [11], [15], [20]. IMR activities have been traditionally conducted by ROVs tethered via an umbilical cable, which provides power and communications, to a manned vessel or surface platform from where a human operator controls them. Pre-deployed support infrastructure will enable R-AUVs to remain unattended in proximity of the undersea infrastructure they intend to support [8], [10]. Not surprisingly, R-AUVs are expected to significantly reduce deployment and maintenance costs associated with AUV-transit in and deployment from a manned vessel, which for a typical IMR campaign can be as high as US $120,000 per day [11]. While *on-call*, R-AUVs will be able to respond quickly to IMR requests, provide support in spite of surface weather conditions, and accommodate operations in ice-covered seas. AUV docking platforms stationed several meters below the sea surface can protect R-AUVs from storms and maritime traffic. Furthermore, they can enable human operators to remotely monitor, re-task and access data collected by the R-AUVs. R-AUVS can also support the initial phases of exploration and data collection for identification of promising exploitation areas.

Beyond providing energy, communications and data storage services, Undersea Support-Infrastructure (USI) for R-AUVs offers an opportunity for introducing autonomy functions to plan, coordinate and execute operations with multiple R-AUVs. Monitoring and maintenance services for the R-AUVs themselves can be integrated as services supported by the USI directly. Due to the requirement for unmanned operations, the USI must be able to autonomously interact with and provide services to the R-AUVs. Additionally, it must allow *human-on-the-loop* operations, where a human operator remotely supervises and directs, when necessary, IMR activities. Similarly to the R-AUVs, the USI must operate autonomously while striving to accomplish the service provisioning goals and objectives defined by the operator.

This paper proposes the Human-on-the-loop Autonomy in Austere Networking Environments (HANEn) architecture, a new autonomy architecture for the USI that emphasizes planning, resource allocation and service provisioning for R-AUVs as they perform IMR activities. The operational scenario discussed herein focuses on situations where communications with a human operator are unreliable and intermittent. Similar to the MORPH architecture for self-adapting systems [4], HANEn allows for reconfiguration of subsystem parameters, and redefinition of service and behavior policies. Additionally, it features dual and cooperative Planning Layers that extend the classical three-layer architectures to accommodate the spatial dimension associated with coordinating activities across multiple USIs. Due to the inherent risks associated with undersea operations, HANEn must support fault diagnostics and management services for the USI. Furthermore, fault diagnostics services can be provided to the R-AUVs by the USI directly or as remotely-operated service managed by the operator. These services can be implemented within HANEn via the definition of appropriate configuration strategies, e.g., use redundant hardware when necessary, and behavior policies, e.g., redefine the quality-of-service provisioning provided to R-AUVs as a function of the degradation experienced by the USI hardware components.

HANEn proposes a four-layer architecture for autonomy whose fourth layer, called the Global Planning Layer, resides with the operator, outside the USI; supports multiple and concurrent USI deployments; enables planning functions to use models, policies and historical data collected from multiple USIs; and, provides an interface for the human operator to monitor and direct USIs and by extension the R-AUVs. The Local and Global Planning Layers are connected through an unreliable, low-bandwidth and high-latency communications network. One of the main implications of this separation is that the *perceived* state of the USI and its environment is not necessarily the same when seen from the Local and Global Planning Layers. Thus, modeling and inference tools become fundamental for maintaining alignment between the operator's and the USI's understanding of the state of the USI and the environment in which it operates.

The paper is organized as follows. Section II provides an overview of the HANEn Architecture. Section III describes the configuration strategy and behavior policy selection at each layer of the HANEn four-layer architecture and their interaction with the Knowledge Repositories. Section IV discusses how HANEn enables regional coordination for provisioning of IMR services to support management of oil and gas subsea infrastructure. The paper concludes in Section V.

II. HANEn Architecture Overview

In this section, the HANEn autonomy architecture is introduced. HANEn builds on the Monitor, Analyze, Plan and Execute over a Knowledge-Base (MAPE-K) model and proposes a four-layer architecture for implementing the Analyze and Plan computational modules [18]. MAPE-K defines four fundamental modules used to model the decision making process of autonomous and self-adapting systems as a control loop, namely the Monitor (M), Analyze (A), Plan (P), Execute (E) modules (see Fig. 1). Additionally, MAPE-K also features the Knowledge Repository (K) containing environment, system and goal models, inference and learning tools, and data logging and managing capabilities. Its content is available to all MAPE-K modules and layers of the decision-making hierarchy defining the Analyze and Plan modules. Our four-layer architecture introduces the Operational, Control, Local Planning and Global Planning Layers, thereby extending the three-layer architectures often used as the basis for developing autonomy architectures for self-adapting and autonomic systems with an additional planning layer [2], [4], [12], [13], [14], [16]. The Global Planning Layer can be understood as a global planning and knowledge aggregation layer bridging mutiple, otherwise disconnected, USIs as shown in Fig. 1. An overview diagram of HANEn that highlights its relationship with MAPE-K modules is shown in Fig. 2.

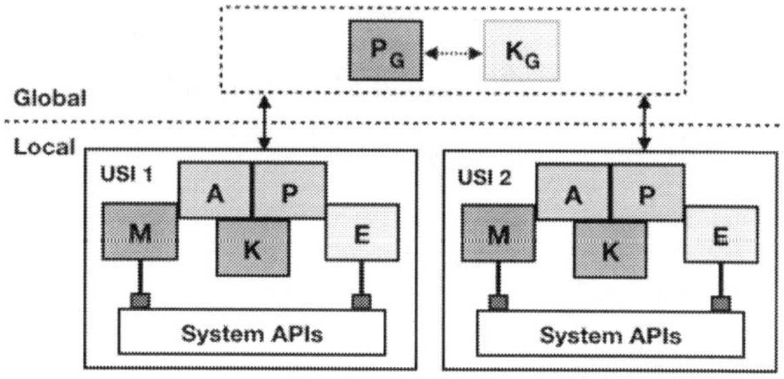

Figure 1. HANEn architecture modeled via an extended MAPE-K model featuring local M, A, P, E, and K modules interacting with the USI via its Application Programming Interfaces (APIs). It also illustrates the global Planning (P_G) and Knowledge Repositories (K_G) that enable HANEn to coordinate activities across multiple USIs.

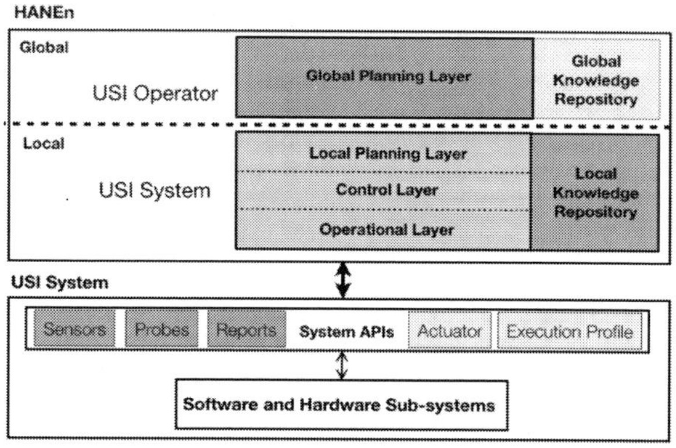

Figure 2. Block-diagram representation of the HANEn Architecture for a single operator-USI pair. Block colors used therein correspond to those used in the MAPE-K modules shown in Figure 1.

The motivation behind implementing a classical three-layer architecture for the Analyze and Plan modules within MAPE-K is the realization that decision making in any autonomous system must occur at different time scales and use different system-state definitions [2], [3], [14]. Three-layer architectures have remained relevant in the past decade as is noted by their usage for modeling recent cloud-based robotics and self adapting systems. These systems presume the availability of reliable, high-bandwidth communications between the Control Layer implemented in individual robots and the Planning Layer instantiated in a cloud computing platform [2], [22]. In that context, it is natural to implement regional Planning Layers at locations that have powerful computational resources and large sets of data and models available, rather than at individual, resource-limited robots [9]. In this case, the regional Planning Layer is continually updated with data and policy updates received from individual robots and able to support advanced, computationally-intensive inference procedures.

The four-layer architecture used by HANEn continues to separate decision making according to the timeliness and state information with which decisions must be made. This separation highlights the different *knowledge* requirements for the various levels of configuration strategy and behavior policy definition needed by the USI. The Global Planning Layer in HANEn enables the USI to use the data, models and computational resources that the USI has available via the Local (K) and Global (K_G) Knowledge Repositories, respectively (see Fig. 2). It thereby addresses the need for managing access and usage of intermittent global data and computational resources, and USI-operator directives to optimize the local and global performance of multiple USIs. Furthermore, it enables planning and execution coordination of concurrent operations among multiple USI deployments.

A brief description of HANEn and the USI systems it supports is given in the following subsections.

A. System

The USI system is the combination of controllable and observable hardware and software elements that provide support and services to the R-AUVs. It comprises all sensors and actuators that the USI uses to monitor and direct the system to provide services and execute actions. The policies and configuration options selected for the system by HANEn are constrained by the capabilities implemented in the USI and the availability of Application Programming Interfaces (APIs) to access them. From an autonomy architecture vantage point, the system provides monitoring and control mechanisms through a collection of APIs. These APIs provide access to all relevant USI subsystems. The monitoring mechanisms available in the system include the generation of status updates and event notifications, and access to raw and processed sensor data. Control mechanisms available in the system include the configuration of actuator parameters and the definition of service execution profiles.

B. Operational Layer

The Operational Layer is concerned with execution, monitoring, and enforcement of configuration and behavior policies as defined by the Plan and Control Layers. Events handled by this layer require rapid response to either maintain or recover a specific system state. The configuration strategies and behavior policies used by this layer are defined by the Control Layer. It reacts directly to data collected by the Monitor module through sensors, software probes, and status and fault reports generated by the system, and creates status and event reports for the upper layers. It also commands reconfiguration of system parameters and behavior policies via the Actuator and Execution Profile system APIs, and reports system faults and anomalies to the Control Layer.

C. Control Layer

The Control Layer is concerned with the reconfiguration of parameters and behaviors of the system components using precomputed configuration strategies and behavior policies that can be used in response to system state changes. Behavior policies can be generated via dynamic resource management and scheduling algorithms. Reconfiguration can be triggered by a request from the Planning Layer to accommodate a change in the USI goals, or a notification from the Operational Layer in response to a fault or anomaly identified in the system. Behavior reconfiguration can also be triggered by the Control Layer itself to resolve issues that would prevent the system from achieving the goals defined in the Goal Model, or capitalize on opportunities identified thru *knowledge* available in the Knowledge Repository. The latter may occur, e.g., when verifying that the assumptions under which current behaviors enacted by the Operational Layer are still valid. This layer receives new configuration strategies and behavior policies from the Local Planning Layer, and can request new configuration strategies and behavior policies when suitable ones are unavailable.

D. Local Planning Layer

The Local Planning Layer resides with the USI. It is responsible for all long-term planning activities. It defines behavior policies and corresponding system-parameter configuration strategies to support policy execution. Configuration strategies and behavior policies are chosen to satisfy the system goals defined by the operator. This layer is responsible for translating the system goals provided by the operator to a goal model that links goal satisfaction with specific system configuration and behavior requirements. Not only do goal models support the definition of long-term configuration strategies and behavior policies, but they also enable the system to identify configurations and behaviors necessary for accomplishing the system goals. The resulting set of requirements are used by this layer to define configuration strategies and behavior policies.

The Local Planning Layer relies on the state and evolution models, goal models, learning and policies database available in the local Knowledge Repository. New configuration strategies and behaviors can be triggered by requests from the Control Layer, or internally by changes in the Goal Model or the definition of new behavior policies through internal learning mechanisms. This layer checks for consistency between the behaviors and the configuration to ensure that behavior execution can be conducted as expected. Reconfiguration strategies also include safe-transition approaches to reach a given system configuration (state) given the current system configuration and behavior policies, and the environment's state.

E. Global Planning Layer

The Global Planning Layer resides with the human operator infrastructure. It includes a human-machine interface (HMI) module that the USI operator can use to monitor and manage the system remotely. When connected to the USI, it can supersede the Local Planning Layer Goal Model, configuration strategy and behavior policy definition mechanisms according to the Authority Management Functions responsible for planning decision-authority allocation. HADEn's human-on-the-loop autonomy enables the operator to demand decision-control over the system to define configuration strategies, behavior policies and force the execution of specific actions by directly interacting with the system APIs. The Authority Management Functions enable the operator to gain and relinquish control of the system via the HMI, and to reallocate decision authority over the system to the Local Planning Layer whenever the USI loses connectivity with the operator. The Global and Local Planning Layers use a collection of authority tokens to identify and track who has authority over the system. These tokens are stored in the Knowledge Repository and are managed by the Planning Layers directly.

The Global Planning Layer has access to the Global Knowledge Repository that subsumes historical data collected across a variety of USI deployments and configurations. Thus, it can, in principle, develop well-informed configuration strategies and behavior policies to enable USI and R-AUV coordination across multiple USIs, specially when compared with those developed by a single USI using its own, local Knowledge Repository. It, furthermore, can exercise case-based reasoning to transfer configurations and behaviors learned in one USI to address a similar challenge arising in a different USI.

F. Knowledge Repository

The Knowledge Repository is a resource shared by all computational blocks of HADEn. It decouples the data- and information-aggregation activities from the decision-making activities enacted by the selection of configuration strategies and behavior policies. The Knowledge Repository is responsible for logging and storage of system data and system reports. These data are used by the inference and learning blocks. The inference block uses data to update models for the environment, the USI and the R-AUVs. These models are used by the decision making layers to verify that the assumptions behind the active behavior policies are valid. Data are also used by internal learning mechanisms that attempt to develop new behavior policies. The resulting policies can be enacted by the Local Planning Layer or used to extend the Global Knowledge Repository, which is available to the USI operator. The Goal Model defined in the Knowledge Repository, together with the models of the USI, the environment and the R-AUVs, are used by the Planning and Control Layers to assess whether the requirements for goal completion are satisfied.

The Knowledge Repository is divided between the USI operator and the individual USI. In scenarios with intermittent and unreliable communications between the operator and the USI, it is not practical to synchronize the content of the Global and Local Knowledge Repositories. Instead the content of the local Knowledge Repository can be summarized via model abstractions, compressed data, report representations, and information summaries that will be sent periodically to the global Knowledge Repository residing with the USI operator, whenever communication opportunities are available.

III. Decision-Making Structure and Support

The layering approach featured by HANEn implements the separation-of-concerns design principle to manage the different time scales and information requirements of the decision

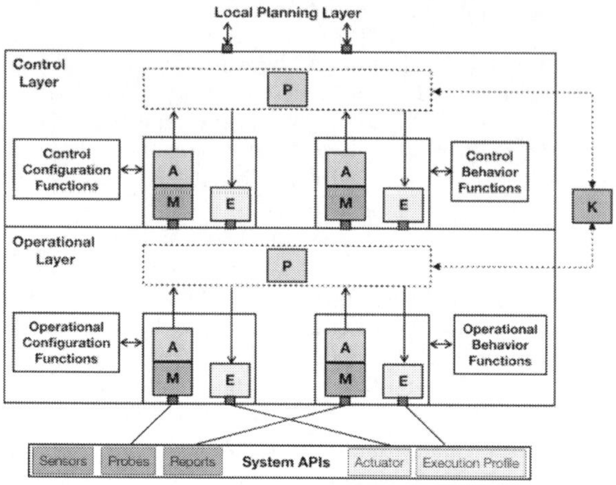

Figure 3. Internal configuration of the Operational and Control Layers, both of which have access to the Local Knowledge Repository (K). Plan (P) Modules in each layer act as arbitrators between the configuration and behavior functions to define the appropriate autonomy strategy to follow.

making processes executed within each USI, and globally across multiple USIs. When executing their internal decision making process, each layer is only concerned with requests and reports coming from the layer below, and directives in the form of new configuration strategies and behavior policies from the layer above. Additionally, each layer uses specific content and functions from the Local Knowledge Repository to verify the context in which the decision making process is taking place. The four-layer autonomy architecture used by HANEn can be modeled as a hierarchical control system implementing loosely coupled, dual MAPE-K models in the Operational and Control Layers, as shown in Figure 3, and single MAPE-K models in the Local and Global Planning Layers each having access to related, yet different, Knowledge Repositories, as shown in Figure 4.

The Operational and Control Layers are modeled via two MAPE-K models that monitor, maintain, and select the configuration strategy and behavior policy approaches used. Each Monitor and Analyze block-pair is responsible for collecting and analyzing configuration and behavior-specific data in the form of reports, requests, time-series, et cetera. Each layer implements a set of configuration and behavior functions that support the Analyze and Plan computational blocks within the layer. Per layer, the MAPE-K models share a common Planning computational block and have access to the local Knowledge Repository. In addition to deciding what configuration strategies and behavior policies to deploy, the Planning block decides how new configuration strategies and behavior policies are to be deployed and executed based on the analysis provided by the two Analyze blocks in the layer. Its role includes deciding whether the configuration strategies can support the execution of a given behavior policies, whether a change in the configuration affects the viability of the current behavior policy, and what the transition approach for new configurations and behaviors must be to avoid inadvertently driving the system configuration into an execution pitfall that would affect the ability of the system to achieve its goals.

The Local and Global Planning Layers are responsible

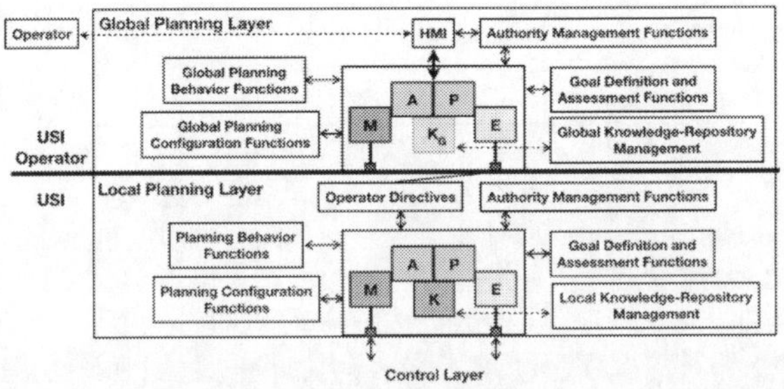

Figure 4. Internal configuration of the Global and Local Planning Layers. The Local (Global) Knowledge Repository is colored red (green) and denoted by K (K_G). Note that K and K_G do not necessarily have the same content.

for long-term planning and adaptation functions. The Local Planning Layer uses its configuration and behavior functions to define new configuration strategies and behavior policies. Updates occur whenever the USI encounters situations that cannot lead to accomplishing the USI goals given the *known* configuration and behavior strategies available in the local Knowledge Repository. This layer receives operational directives from the Operator through the Global Planning Layer, which could pass the directives directly to the USI or use its Global Knowledge Repository and up-to-date information about the USI to define a goal model for the specific USI to achieve. When directives are shared with the USI, the USI uses its Local Knowledge Repository to define a goal model that links goals with USI system requirements in a hierarchical and logical structure. The Goal Model and a set of appropriate assessment metrics are then stored and maintained in the Local Knowledge Repository. They serve as the basis for the configuration strategy and behavior policy evaluation conducted by the Control and Operational Layers.

The Global Planning Layer has similar decision-making responsibilities to those of the Local Planning Layer. It, however, features two major differences with respect to its local counterpart. First, it has access to the Global Knowledge Repository and, thus, to a larger set of information records, knowledge, and presumably more advanced data inference capabilities. This repository has records of historical data, configuration strategies, behavior policies, and models collected over time, across all USIs managed by the operator. In addition to its responsibilities with each USI, the Global Planning Layer is responsible for coordinating activities across USIs for all regional energy, data storage, communications and R-AUV services. Second, it offers an HMI for the operator to interact with the USIs. This interface allows the operator to monitor and direct individual USIs and coordinate operations across all regional USIs. The HMI uses the Global Knowledge Repository and the inference and forecasting tools available within it to present the status of a given USI and its environment to the operator. In most situations the global Knowledge Repository will not have access to the raw data captured by a USI, thus the state view offered to the operator is based on model abstractions and summary updates that an individual USI can transmit to the operator.

The Local and Global Planning Layers also share the set of authority management functions that assign and manage the *authority tokens*, defining who has authority over a given USI,

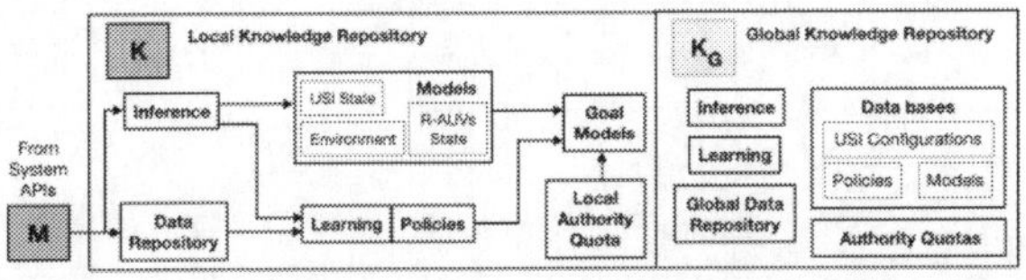

Figure 5. Internal configuration of the Local and Global Knowledge Repositories.

i.e., what Analyze and Plan computational blocks will be used by the USI to define new configuration strategies and behavior policies. The default operational mode of HANEn is configured for human-on-the-loop operations. Thus, the operator, through the Global Planning Layer, has a default supervisory role with the USI having ownership of its authority token. When the operator and the USI are connected, the operator can request an authority transfer to direct USI operations. When the authority token is assigned to the operator, the Local Planning Layer has the responsibility of monitoring its connectivity with the operator, to promptly regain authority over the USI if connectivity with the operator is lost for a predefined length of time. The Authority Quota knowledge structures in the global and local Knowledge Repositories allow the operator and the USIs to track authority ownerships. They could also define finer authority control over specific USI functions to support the implementation of adjustable autonomy strategies [5], [19].

Finally, the Planning Layers are responsible for managing the Local and Global Knowledge Repositories content, see Fig. 5. Data and model management policies are defined and enforced by the Knowledge-Repository Management block. These include data prioritization policies for exchanging data between local and global Knowledge Repositories, and data expiration policies that define when USI data logged in the Local and Global Knowledge Repositories can be archived or discarded. The Knowledge-Repository Management block is also responsible for defining behavior policies for the communication interface that connect the USI and the operator. Behavior policies include data-exchange schedules, allocation of communication resources, data summarization, data compression policies, and security postures.

IV. Regional Planning Coordination

This section discusses regional planning coordination using HANEn to support a group of USI deployments, where each USI deployment is responsible for a group of R-AUVs supporting IMR operations for an Undersea Oil and Gas Infrastructure (OGI). In this scenario, the Regional USI Operator and the OGI Manager are considered different and not necessarily co-located roles. For instance, the USI Operator could be part of an infrastructure-as-a-service provider for undersea operations, while the OGI Manager is a member of an oil and gas management company. Therefore, the scenario considered here depicts an Internet Service Provider (ISP) network connecting the USI Operator and the OGI Manager. Both the USI Operator and the OGI Manager use private networks to access and manage their infrastructure. Figure 6 shows the USIs, R-AUVs and other OGI interacting in support of an IMR mission.

Upon receiving a request from the undersea OGI Manager for periodic inspections, the regional USI Operator updates the schedule of operations for the R-AUVs available in its

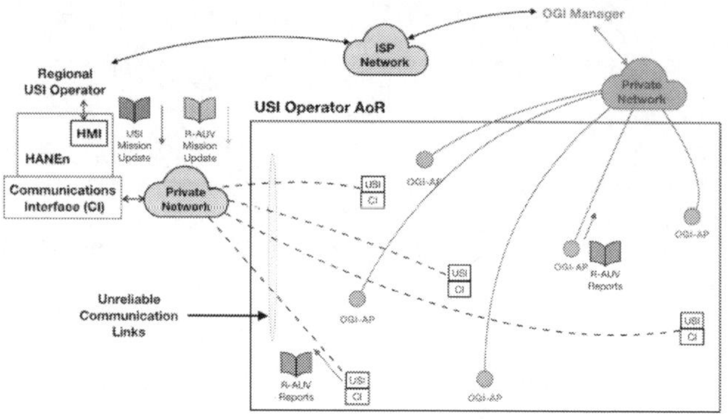

Figure 6. Sample HANEn deployment to support IMR operations for undersea OGI. The OGI is managed and monitored by the OGI Manager via OGI Access Points (OGI-APs). The regional USI Operator provides directives to the USI and R-AUVs via the HMI offered by HANEn.

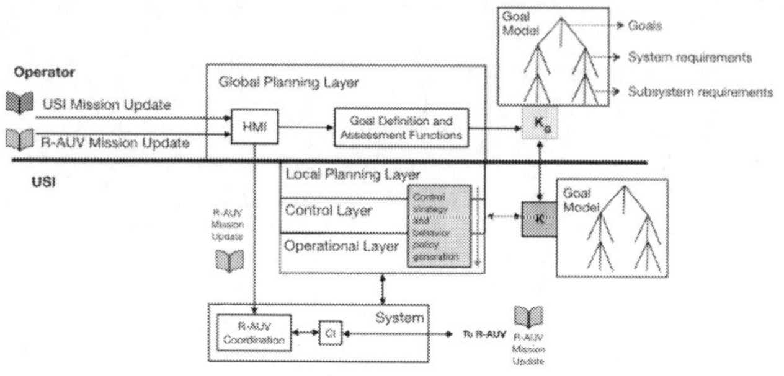

Figure 7. Goal Model generation based on a USI mission update introduced by the operator, and transfer of R-AUV mission updates via the USI.

area of responsibility (AoR). The R-AUV service schedule implicitly defines a baseline schedule of operations for the USIs in the same AoR. The USI Operator uses the HANEn HMI interface to upload USI mission updates. Then, HANEn creates an updated Goal Model within each USI that aligns with the new mission objectives. This model is created by the Global Planning Layer and stored in the Global Knowledge Repository. Then, it is transferred to an individual USI where it is maintained in their Local Knowledge Repositories. The updated Goal Model triggers a review of schedules and resource-usage profiles within each USI to verify that the currently available configuration strategies and behavior policies can support the new service profiles required by the R-AUVs given the current USI state. The operator also notifies mission and configuration updates to the R-AUVs via the USI. Updates for the R-AUVs are passed via HANEn as a *mission update file* for the R-AUV USI subsystem, which is responsible for coordinating local interactions with R-AUVs and relaying operation directives from the operator to the R-AUVs. Note that in this case the authority token remains with the USI. Figure 7 illustrates the goal-model generation and R-AUV mission update process.

After conducting their missions, R-AUVs upload data and inspection reports generated during the mission to the USI. The USI is responsible for transmitting the data gathered by the R-AUVs to the Regional USI Operator who is in turn responsible for generating an inspection report for the OGI Manager. R-AUVs also upload detailed resource utilization summaries to the USI Operator who uses them for service-billing purposes.

The OGI Manager is able to remotely monitor and manage some elements of the OGI infrastructure via strategically positioned OGI Access Points (OGI-APs). These OGI-APs enable the OGI Manager to identify and respond to anomalies and faults that require additional inspection, or on-site intervention and repair. The OGI Manager sends *urgent* service requests to the Regional USI Operator who sends updated mission directives to a selected group of R-AUVs to support the OGI Manager IMR request. Mission updates are also sent to each USI to guarantee that the updated service profile for the R-AUVs can be supported, see Figure 7.

Mission updates for the USIs and R-AUVs are transmitted over a network whose *last-mile* communications link is intermittent and unreliable. Thus, the Global Planning Layer of HANEn must carefully manage the allocation of communication resources between the operator and the USIs. These resources and their configuration are controlled directly via the local API for the Communications Interface (CI) available to the operator. The USIs have a similar management responsibility over their local CIs for managing their communications with the Regional USI Operator.

In some cases, the OGI Manager may not be able or willing to tolerate the long delay that the data collected by the R-AUVs will incur when being transmitted to the OGI Manager via the Regional USI Operator network. In this case, the latency experienced by the data aggregates both the latency due to delays and disruption in the network between the USI operator and the USIs, and the R-AUV transit time back to the USI prior to the data being delivered to it. In those cases, the R-AUVs could use the OGI-APs to upload their data and report directly to the OGI Manager. Not only could this approach reduce the overall R-AUV data latencies, but it could also give R-AUVs access to a more reliable communications infrastructure that will allow them to upload larger volumes of sensor and actuator data to the OGI Manager. Behavior policies executed on the USI Operational Layer are responsible for managing the data gathered by the R-AUVs either as backup copies of the data sent directly to the OGI Manager or as redundant data that can eventually be discarded.

V. Conclusions and Future Work

This paper proposed HANEn, a new autonomy architecture for USI supporting R-AUV missions. HANEn enables human-on-the-loop operations and is well-suited for scenarios where the communications between the operator and the USI are intermittent, and characterized by low bandwidth and high latency. USIs using HANEn can operate autonomously, while still allowing the operator to gain control over them as needed. HANEn features a four-layer autonomy architecture whose fourth layer, the Global Planning Layer, supports coordination among multiple USIs, management of regional Knowledge Repositories, and an HMI that enables observability and controllability of the USI by an operator. A key benefit achieved by the Global Planning Layer is the persistent regional USI management which is achieved by the effective use of the Global Knowledge Repository and the inference tools embedded in it. HANEn's layered architectural approach separates the decision-making processes that are conducted by the USI according to their required execution time scales. Furthermore, it separates the selection of configuration strategies and behavior policies, thereby isolating configuration and functionality concerns. The use of HANEn was discussed within the context of IMR missions for OGI.

Future work will focus on the development of a notional HANEn implementation with emphasis on the engineering aspects of the Local and Global Planning Layers, and the interaction between HANEn and the R-AUVs. As a layered architecture, HANEn could naturally extend various self-adaptive autonomy architectures, such as MORPH, and enable systems using them to coordinate activities across a common Global Planning Layer. Prior implementations of three-layer autonomy architectures can be used as a starting point for developing *local* USI autonomy. One of the major implementation challenges for HANEn lies on the *intelligent* use of the communications and networking capabilities available to connect the USI with the operator and the R-AUVs. Communications in the maritime domain are not reliable, often offer limited and variable communication bandwidths, and are sensitive to environmental conditions. Synchronization of the Local and Global Knowledge Repositories in such operating environment may be impractical if HANEn were to, e.g., attempt to synchronize raw sensor-data recordings. Our initial implementation approach relies on the use of high-resolution parametric models and bounded knowledge-graph structures that can provide sufficient information to support the reasoning and inference functions needed at the Global and Local Planning Layers of HANEn.

Finally, careful implementation of the Authority Management Functions both on the Local and Global Planning Layers is critical to avoid execution pitfalls in which the USI is unable to regain authority over some or all of its functions, even when the operator is disconnected from the USI. The Authority Management Functions are critical for HANEn to enable the operator to control the USI. Thus, they require special safeguards to be put in place to enable the Local Planning Layer to regain control over the USI. Similarly and from the operator's vantage point, authority token allocations should be resilient to instabilities in the communications path between the operator and the USI to avoid unnecessary authority token transfers and the corresponding decision-making reallocations needed as part of such transitions.

Acknowledgement

This work was funded by the Naval Innovative Science and Engineering program at the Naval Information Warfare Center Pacific.

References

[1] E. Ackerman, "The underwater transformer: Ex-NASA engineers built a robot sub that transforms into a skilled humanoid," *IEEE Spectrum*, vol. 56, no. 8, pp. 22–29, Aug 2019.

[2] A. Ahmad and M. A. Babar, "Software architectures for robotic systems," *J. Syst. Softw.*, vol. 122, no. C, pp. 16–39, Dec. 2016.

[3] R. Alami, R. Chatila, S. Fleury, M. Ghallab, and F. Ingrand, "An architecture for autonomy," *The International Journal of Robotics Research*, vol. 17, no. 4, pp. 315–337, 1998.

[4] V. Braberman, N. D'Ippolito, J. Kramer, D. Sykes, and S. Uchitel, "MORPH: A reference architecture for configuration and behaviour self-adaptation," in *Proc. of the 1st International Workshop on Control Theory for Software Engineering*, ser. CTSE 2015. New York, NY, USA: ACM, 2015, pp. 9–16.

[5] C. Calefato, R. Montanari, and F. Tesauri, "The adaptive automation design," in *Human Computer Interaction: New Developments*, K. Asai, Ed. Rijeka: IntechOpen, 2008, pp. 141–154.

[6] M. A. Charette and W. Smith, "The volume of Earth's ocean," *Oceanography*, vol. 23, pp. 112–114, June 2010.

[7] M. Chitre, S. Shahabudeen, L. Freitag, and M. Stojanovic, "Recent advances in underwater acoustic communications networking," in *IEEE OCEANS*, Sep. 15-18, Quebec City, Canada 2008, pp. 1–10.

[8] N. A. Cruz, A. C. Matos, R. M. Almeida, and B. M. Ferreira, "A lightweight docking station for a hovering AUV," in *IEEE Underwater Technology*, Feb. 21-24, Busan, South Korea 2017, pp. 1–7.

[9] D. Weyns et al., "On patterns for decentralized control in self-adaptive systems," in *Software Engineering for Self-Adaptive Systems II: International Seminar, Dagstuhl Castle, Germany, October 24-29, 2010 Revised Selected and Invited Papers*, R. de Lemos, H. Giese, H. A. Müller, and M. Shaw, Eds. Berlin, Heidelberg: Springer Berlin Heidelberg, 2013, pp. 76–107.

[10] S. Fan, C. Liu, B. Li, Y. Xu, and W. Xu, "AUV docking based on USBL navigation and vision guidance," *Journal of Marine Science and Technology*, vol. 24, no. 3, pp. 673–685, Sep 2019.

[11] M. Furuholmen, A. Hanssen, R. Carter, K. Hatlen, and J. Siesjo, "Resident autonomous underwater vehicle systems – a review of drivers, applications, and integration options for the subsea oil and gas market," in *Proc. of the 11th Offshore Mediterranean Conference*, Mar. 20-22, Ravenna, Italy 2013, pp. 387–395.

[12] D. Garlan, S.-W. Cheng, A.-C. Huang, B. Schmerl, and P. Steenkiste, "Rainbow: architecture-based self-adaptation with reusable infrastructure," *IEEE Computer*, vol. 37, no. 10, pp. 46–54, Oct 2004.

[13] D. Garlan and B. Schmerl, "Model-based adaptation for self-healing systems," in *Proc. of the First Workshop on Self-healing Systems*, ser. WOSS '02. New York, NY, USA: ACM, 2002, pp. 27–32.

[14] E. Gat, "Three-layer architectures," in *Artificial Intelligence and Mobile Robots*, D. Kortenkamp, R. P. Bonasso, and R. Murphy, Eds. Cambridge, MA, USA: MIT Press, 1998, pp. 195–210.

[15] B. Gilmour, G. Niccum, and T. O'Donnell, "Field resident AUV systems – Chevron's long-term goal for AUV development," in *IEEE/OES Autonomous Underwater Vehicles*, Sep. 24-27, Southampton, United Kingdom 2012, pp. 1–5.

[16] D. Goldberg, "Huxley: A flexible robot control architecture for autonomous underwater vehicles," in *IEEE OCEANS*, June 6-9, Santander, Spain 2011, pp. 1–10.

[17] T. Hyakudome, "Design of autonomous underwater vehicle," *International Journal of Advanced Robotic Systems*, vol. 8, no. 1, p. 9, 2011.

[18] J. O. Kephart and D. M. Chess, "The vision of autonomic computing," *Computer*, vol. 36, no. 1, pp. 41–50, Jan 2003.

[19] M. Luck, M. D'Inverno, and S. Munroe, "Autonomy: Variable and generative," in *Agent Autonomy*, H. Hexmoor, C. Castelfranchi, and R. Falcone, Eds. Boston, MA: Springer US, 2003, pp. 11–28.

[20] T. Matsuda, T. Maki, K. Masuda, and T. Sakamaki, "Resident autonomous underwater vehicle: Underwater system for prolonged and continuous monitoring based at a seafloor station," *Robotics and Autonomous Systems*, vol. 120, p. 103231, 2019.

[21] R. B. Wynn et al., "Autonomous underwater vehicles (AUVs): Their past, present and future contributions to the advancement of marine geoscience," *Marine Geology*, vol. 352, pp. 451–468, 2014, 50th Anniversary Special Issue.

[22] O. Saha and P. Dasgupta, "A comprehensive survey of recent trends in cloud robotics architectures and applications," *Robotics*, vol. 7, no. 3: 47, 2018.

[23] J. Sverdrup-Thygeson, E. Kelasidi, K. Y. Pettersen, and J. T. Gravdahl, "The underwater swimming manipulator - a bio-inspired AUV," in *IEEE/OES Autonomous Underwater Vehicles (AUV)*, Nov. 6-9, Tokyo, Japan 2016, pp. 387–395.

[24] T. Ura, "AUV "r2D4", its operation, and road map for AUV development," in *Advances in Unmanned Marine Vehicles*, ser. Control, Robotics and Sensors. Institution of Engineering and Technology, 2006, pp. 239–254.

Deep Learning Workload Analysis for Efficient Resource Allocation

Sayaka Takayama
Ochanomizu University
2-1-1 Otsuka, Bunkyo-ku
Tokyo, Japan
Email: sayaka-t@ogl.is.ocha.ac.jp

Takashi Shiraishi
Fujitsu Laboratories Ltd.
4-1-1 Kamikodanaka, Nakahara-ku
Kawasaki, Kanagawa, Japan
Email: shiraishi-ten@fujitsu.com

Shigeto Suzuki
Fujitsu Laboratories Ltd.
4-1-1 Kamikodanaka, Nakahara-ku
Kawasaki, Kanagawa, Japan
Email: shigeto.suzuki@fujitsu.com

Masao Yamamoto
Fujitsu Laboratories Ltd.
4-1-1 Kamikodanaka, Nakahara-ku
Kawasaki, Kanagawa, Japan
Email: masao.yamamoto@fujitsu.com

Yukihiro Watanabe
Fujitsu Laboratories Ltd.
4-1-1 Kamikodanaka, Nakahara-ku
Kawasaki, Kanagawa, Japan
Email: watanabe.y@fujitsu.com

Masato Oguchi
Ochanomizu University
2-1-1 Otsuka, Bunkyo-ku
Tokyo, Japan
Email: oguchi@is.ocha.ac.jp

***Abstract*—In recent years, with the prosperity of deep learning, Graphics Processing Units (GPUs) have become popular as hardware accelerators specialized for this purpose. However, compared to CPUs, which are general-purpose computing resources, GPUs are very scarce and valuable resources. Therefore, in this paper, we would like to consider some control that reduces GPU resource waste by determining GPU allocation based on the difference in application performance when using different GPUs. As a basic study, we evaluate the performance of 9 types of benchmarks executed on the framework using GPU and compare the performance when changing machine conditions. From this examination, it is judged whether the above control is possible. In addition, we estimate how much performance improvement can be expected by preferentially allocating GPUs with high performance to workloads that have a large impact on GPU performance using the data we collected. From this estimate, it is found that GPU priority control can reduce the total execution time by 8.24%.**

Keywords*–*Workload analysis; MLPerf; Zabbix; Deep learning.

I. INTRODUCTION

Graphics Processing Units (GPUs), processors designed for 3D graphics applications that require enormous computational processing, possess a large number of computing cores and memory that enables high-speed communication, and are good at parallel processing. With the prosperity of deep learning, GPUs became popular as specialized hardware accelerators. However, compared with Central Processing Units (CPUs), which are general-purpose computing resources, GPUs are very scarce and valuable computing resources. Also, deep learning does not fit well with current configuration practices and deployment models, which assume a static allocation of GPUs for each user or framework regardless of utilization, performance and scalability [1].

Therefore, we would like to consider GPU allocation control based on the difference in application performance when using different GPUs. As a basic study, we evaluated the performance of 9 benchmarks executed on a framework that uses GPUs and compared the performance on machines of different generations. From this examination, it was judged whether the above control is possible.

Also, assuming that a physical machine is fully used by one application in Docker environments, the job execution time can be determined by allocating a high-performance GPU preferentially to a workload that has a large impact on GPU performance. We estimated whether this would lead to improvement using the data we collected. As a result, it was found that the total execution time was reduced by 8.24% when GPUs were assigned according to the difference in job performance due to the difference in GPUs, compared to when GPUs were evenly assigned.

The reminder of the paper is organized as follows.

In Section II, related works about operational methods based on resource performance differences and application characteristics are introduced. The overview of the experiment for performance evaluation and comparison of each benchmark is proposed in Section IV. In Section IV, the impact of hardware on the execution of AI applications, focusing on CPUs, GPUs, and memory are described. Finally, concluding remarks are provided in Section V.

II. RELATED WORK

Operational methods based on resource performance differences and application characteristics have already been proposed. Scheduling based on the impact of power variability for specific applications, taking into account performance and power consumption variations that occur during the manufacturing process of the CPU, is the largest compared to modern scheduling policies used in production clusters. The job turnaround time has been reduced by 31% and the power supply has been reduced by up to 5.5% [2].

Also, efficiency is an important consideration for large-scale High Performance Computing centers with a wide range of different applications and heterogeneous infrastructures. For the purpose of optimizing the usage rate and job waiting time of a cluster, a method for executing job simulation of a Portable Batch System (PBS) based cluster using a historical workload has been proposed [3].

Most of the data contained in Facebook are sent to the machine learning pipeline, and the system is selectively used for training using both GPUs and CPUs and real-time inference using CPUs. Additionally, in real-time reasoning, the required resources are different because of the size of input data, and the importance of feature analysis of AI workload behavior based on machine learning is discussed in [4]. A toolkit called FBLearner has been developed for the purpose of simplifying the task of using Facebook machine learning and is processed by the CPU server and the GPU server with different resource designs according to the features of machine learning. FBLearner consists of three tools focused on different parts of the machine learning pipeline: FBLearner Feature Store, FBLearner Flow, and FBLearner Predictor. By utilizing an internal job scheduler, it allocates the resources on a shared pool of GPUs and CPUs and schedules jobs. Most of Facebook's machine learning training is performed through FBLearner.

GPU virtualization is a method for effectively using limited GPU resources. Bitfusion FlexDirect [1] is a virtualization layer that supports management of computing resources by combining multiple CPUs and GPUs into a single elastic cluster. FlexDirect is designed so that multiple workloads can be executed in parallel by slicing the GPU into a virtual GPU of any size, and achieves a significant reduction in GPU resources compared to conventional GPU solutions. Singularity [5], a Linux container for HPC developed by Lawrence Berkeley National Laboratory, implements the ability to share GPUs among multiple applications running in a virtual environment. A job scheduler is used for resource management.

CPUs and servers with automatic workload management functions to analyze the bottlenecks and allocate resources and distribute the connections have already been developed. We introduce two examples of tools and products that perform tuning based on workload. Intel's CPU architecture "Haswell" [6] executes DynamicVoltage and Frequency Scaling that switches the voltage and operating frequency according to the load on a CPU core or cluster basis. NVIDIA's "HGX-2" [7] is a server for the GPU neck jobs that has many processors and is specialized for AI workloads. Unlike a general IA server, HGX-2 can use up to 16 GPUs in a single server.

We analyze the characteristics of workload as a basic study of efficient operation technology of GPU resources.

III. Overview of the Experiment

In this study, performance evaluation and comparison of each benchmark are performed using MLPerf to analyze the hardware information at the time of the execution of application, which is a representative type of AI. We use MLPerf's nine benchmarks for performance evaluation. Zabbix [8] is used to acquire information. Information such as CPU, GPU, memory, and I/O is acquired at the time of benchmark execution by these commands for feature analysis for each benchmark. Information acquisition is performed at one minute intervals. Table IV shows the measurement conditions for each benchmark. The learning accuracy is changed to 15 only for the Recurrent Neural Network (RNN) translator (RT).

In particular, feature analysis is conducted focusing on CPU, GPU, and memory utilization. Table II shows the experimental environment.

An outline of the software used in this research is provided below.

A. MLPerf

MLPerf is an AI benchmark supported by companies, such as Google, Intel, Baidu, and NVIDIA. It aims to build a common set of benchmarks that enable the machine learning field to measure system performance for both training and inference for a variety of environments ranging from mobile devices to cloud services. This benchmark includes Image Classification (IC), Single Stage Detector (SSD), Object Detection (OD), Recommendation (RM), Sentiment Analysis (SA), Rnn Translator (RT), Translation (TL), Speech Recognition (SR), and Reinforcement (RI).

1) Time-series Data: The following introduces the hardware time-series data when MLPerf is run.

IPMI can obtain infrastructure information such as power and temperature. Figure 1 shows the time-series data for the CPU temperature. The time-series data for the CPU and GPU power consumption is shown in Figure 2. Perf can obtain the CPU utilization and memory usage that can be acquired by OS, and nvidia-smi can acquire GPU utilization. These pieces of information can be utilized for static optimal design of device resources. The obtained time-series CPU and GPU utilization data are shown in Figure 3. The CPU and GPU memory utilization time-series data are illustrated in Figure 4. Iostat can obtain how much Input and Output occurs on the disk. The results of the time-series data for the disk I/O access are shown in Figure 5. PMU can obtain the number of instructions and cache miss rate from CPU event information. These pieces of information can be used for dynamic frequency design. The time-series data of the memory intensive index in Figure 6 uses the values obtained by the following equation.

$$intensive = \frac{(local + remote)}{inst} \times 100$$

In the above equation, "local" means the number of times that the local DRAM is accessed, and "remote" means the number of time that remote DRAM is accessed because of the failure to access L3 cache memory. "inst" indicates the number of instructions.

TABLE I. MEASUREMENT CONDITIONS OF EACH BENCHMARK

Benchmark	Epoch (step, iteration)	SEED	Job Time
IC	53200 (step)	1	3:01:13
SSD	11	1	3:09:12
OD	25000 (iteration)	3	2:23:26
RM	6	1	1:09:34
SA	100	1	1:22:50
RT	1	1	2:48:18
TL	17200 (step)	1	2:59:55
SR	1	1	10:53:32
RI	4	1	5:46:00

TABLE II. ENVIRONMENT

OS	ubuntsu 16.04
Server	FUJITSU Primergy RX2540 M4
CPU	Intel Xeon Skylake 2 sockets 20 cores 2.4GHz Gold 6148 150W
GPU	NVIDIA Tesla V100 16GB
Storage M2.SSD	290GB read 0.87GB/s write 1.75GB/s
Memory	192GB DDR4 2666MHz
Python	3.50
CUDA	9.2

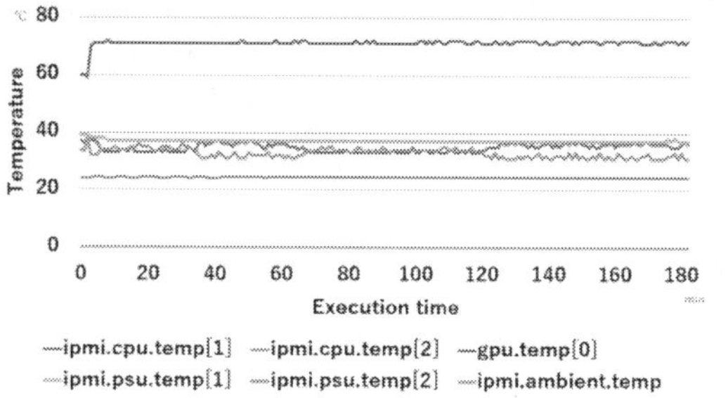

Figure 1. Temperature during the IC processing.

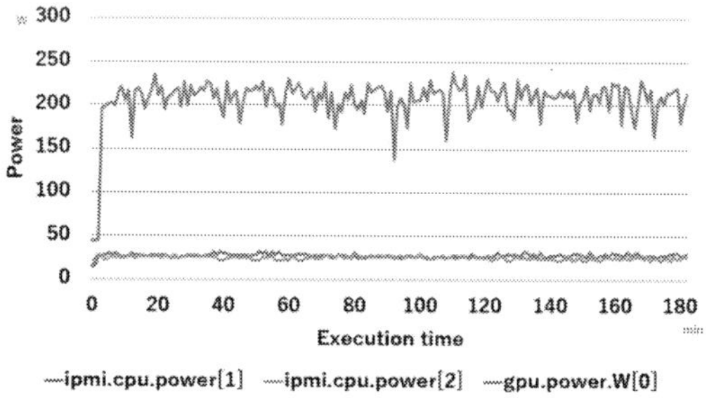

Figure 2. CPU and GPU power consumption during IC processing.

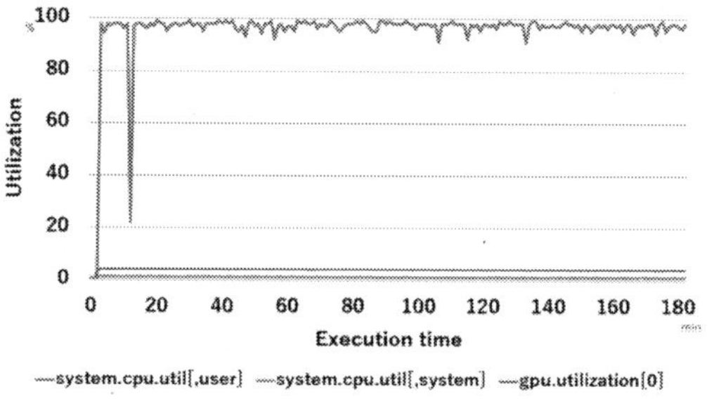

Figure 3. CPU and GPU utilization during IC processing.

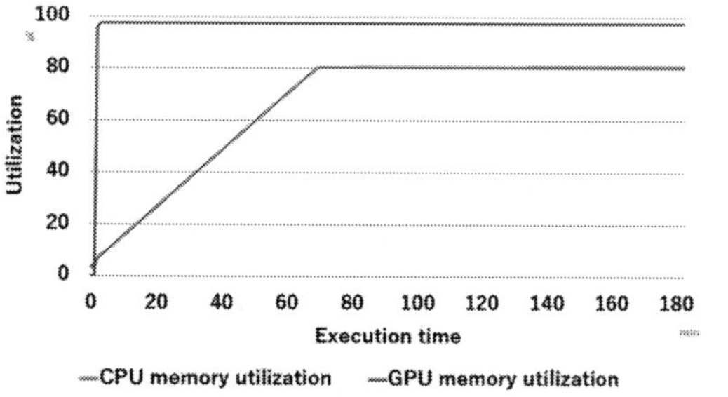

Figure 4. CPU and GPU memory utilization during IC processing.

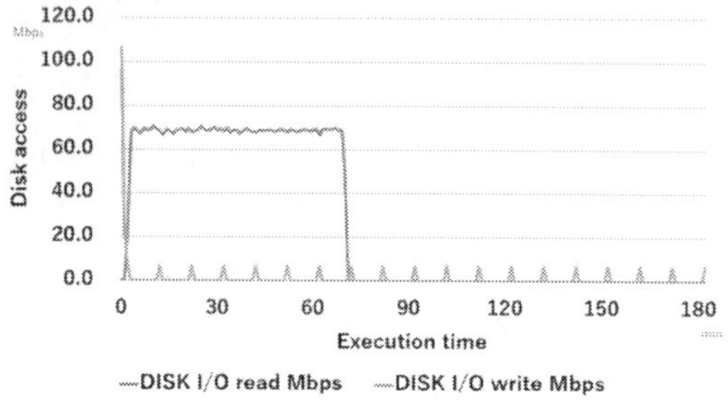

Figure 5. Disk I/O access during IC processing.

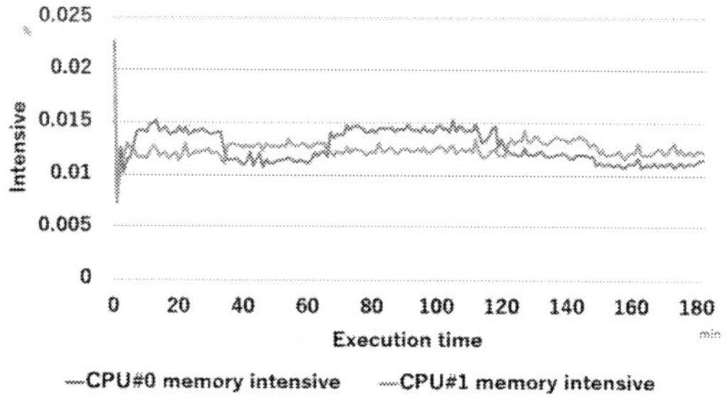

Figure 6. Intensive memory use during IC processing.

B. Zabbix

Zabbix is a flexible monitoring software and can add monitoring targets by using templates. We analyze the information that can be acquired by IPMI, Perf, nvidia-smi, and Performance Monitoring Unit (PMU) [9], which is a performance monitoring mechanism of the Intel CPU. PostgreSQL is used for data storage. We build the environment shown in Figure 7.

Since acquiring information on the benchmark execution server will influence the results, the server used for acquiring information and the server used for the execution of the benchmark are separated.

IV. Experimental Results

In this section, we investigate the impact of hardware on the execution of AI applications, focusing on CPUs, GPUs, and memory.

A. Server

We compare the results by running MLPerf on different generation servers. These servers are similar but have different performance CPUs. First, we measure the speed of disk access in the environment of Table II. Table III shows the maximum speed of disk access for each benchmark execution. The maximum disk access speed of FUJITSU Primer RX2540 M4 used in the experiment is 0.87 GB/s for reading and 1.75 GB/s for writing.

Since the maximum value of the disk access speed at the time of benchmark execution is sufficient for the server disk performance and the time required for disk access is extremely short compared to the job time, it is possible that the disk performance difference has a small impact on the benchmark.

We consider the change in the job execution time when using the server with the different CPU. For comparison, we use two servers with different specifications. the specifications of the servers used for CPU comparison are shown in Table IV.

We compared IC, SSD, OD, RM, SA, RT, TL, and RI. Table V lists the comparison results of the job times required when executing MLPerf on the environments of Table IV. We also obtained CPI information, which represents the number of the clocks required to execute one instruction, but we did not observe any major changes with the change of the server.

Figures 8 - 15 show the time-series data for the clock frequency of each thread when each benchmark is executed on each server.

The time-series data of the clock frequency for "IC" are shown in Figure 8. On Skylake, two threads had a high clock frequency and their values changed alternately. The time-series data of the clock frequency for the "SSD" are illustrated in Figure 9. There were no large differences between these graphs. The results of the time-series data for clock frequency of "OD" are shown in Figure 10. This benchmark also showed no notable change. The time-series data for the clock frequency of "RM" are shown in Figure 11. Compared with Skylake, the clock frequency on Haswell tended to be high overall. Figure 12 shows the time-series data for the clock frequency of "SA". In "SA", only a specific thread had a high clock frequency, and this was considered to be a specification that only some threads were used when the frequency decreased. The results of the time-series data for the clock frequency of "RT" are shown in Figure 13. Only the clock frequency of a specific thread remained high on Skylake. The time-series data for the clock frequency of "TL" are shown in Figure 14. On Skylake, some Specific threads showed noticeable changes, but on Haswell such changes were not observed. Figure 15 shows the time-series data for the clock frequency of "RI". The trends of the changes were similar in Skylake and Haswell, but their periods were different.

Comparing the results obtained on Skylake and Haswell, it is observed that differences in the maximum values and other details are present, but the clock frequency shows some similar changes along the time series. We concluded that the impact of the CPU on the performance of AI applications is small.

From these results, differences in servers and CPUs are considered to have little impact on AI application performance.

B. GPU

This section introduces the analysis results on how GPU performance affects the performance of each AI application.

The average GPU utilization divided by the average CPU utilization is illustrated in Figure 16. Additionally, we note that the average utilizations of GPU and CPU per socket are shown in Table VI.

Large differences were observed in processor utilization for the different applications in the family of benchmarks. Table 16 and Table VI show that the overall application tends to be GPU-necked, and that translation-based applications require a particularly large amount of GPUs. On the other hand, there are also applications in which CPU performance is considered to be important, such as RM and SSD.

We compare the results obtained by running MLPerf with different generation GPUs. the specifications of the servers used for GPU comparison are shown in Table VII.

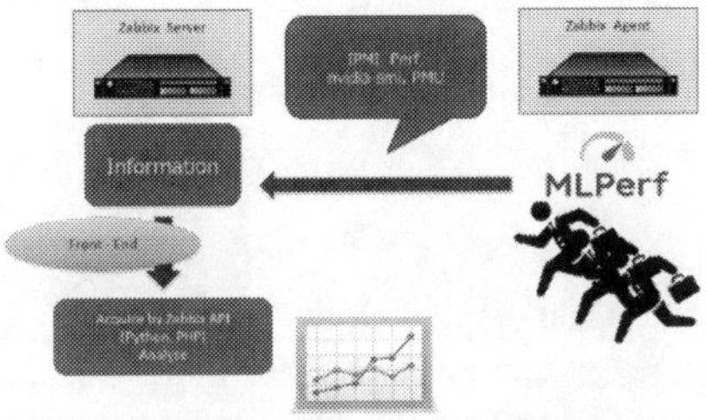

Figure 7. Zabbix environment for acquiring information.

TABLE III. DISK ACCESS SPEED

Benchmark	Read (MB/s)	Write (MB/s)
IC	73.92	111.32
SSD	6.75	10.96
OD	4.66	1.25
RM	2.67	29.26
SA	9.82	0.01
RT	29.50	0.06
TL	26.14	93.90
SR	7.10	8.05
RI	22.13	0.75

TABLE IV. ENVIRONMENTS FOR CPU COMPARISON

	Environment 1	Environment 2
OS	CentOS Linux release 7.5.1804 (Core)	ubuntsu 16.04
Server	FUJITSU Primergy CX400 M1	FUJITSU Primergy RX2540 M4
CPU	Intel Xeon Haswell 2 sockets 14 cores 2.6GHz E5-2697 145W	Intel Xeon Skylake 2 sockets 20 cores 2.4GHz Gold 6148 150W
GPU GPU	NVIDIA Tesla P100 16GB	NVIDIA Tesla P100 16GB
Storage HDD	270GB read 0.21GB/s write 1.07GB/s	290GB read 0.87GB/s write 1.75GB/s
Memory	256GB DDR4 2133MHz	192GB DDR4 2666MHz
Python	3.50	3.50
CUDA	9.2	9.2

TABLE V. COMPARISON OF THE JOB TIME - CPU

Benchmark	Haswell	Skylake	Skylake / Haswell
IC	4:36:10	4:33:04	0.99
SSD	3:56:42	3:12:18	0.81
OD	2:59:34	2:57:51	0.99
RM	1:12:00	1:09:07	0.96
SA	2:00:12	1:48:14	0.90
RT	4:06:41	4:05:28	1.00
TL	4:37:47	4:29:21	0.97
SR	-	15:07:34	-
RI	6:28:00	6:08:37	0.95

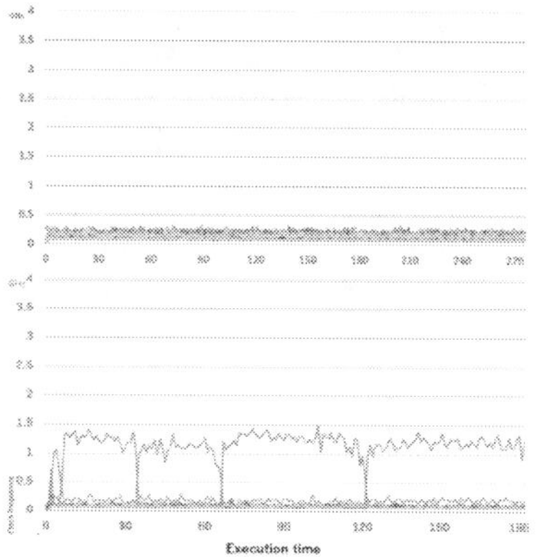

Figure 8. Time-series data for the clock frequency of IC (above:Haswell below:Skylake).

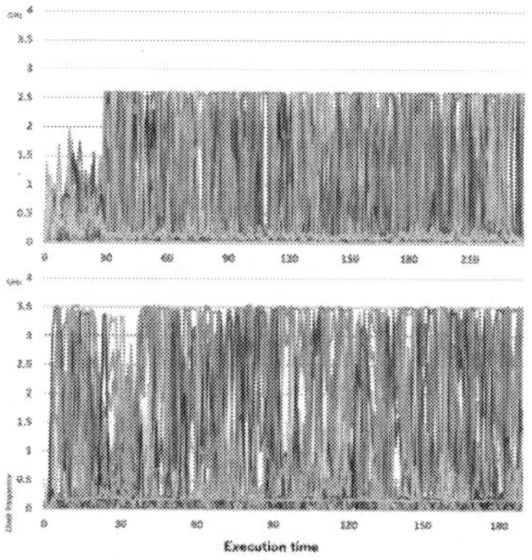

Figure 9. Time-series data for the clock frequency of SSD (above:Haswell below:Skylake).

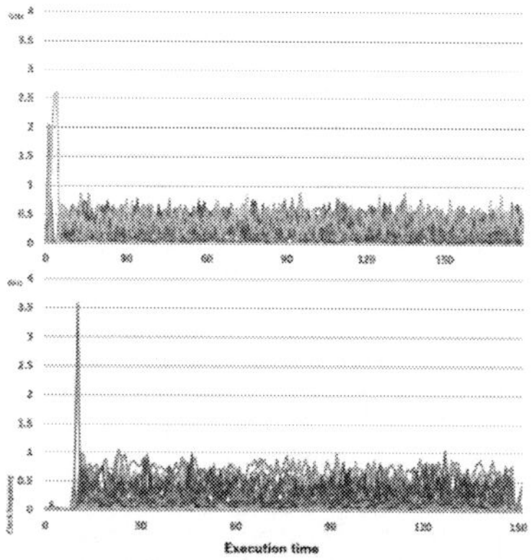

Figure 10. Time-series data for the clock frequency of OD (above:Haswell below:Skylake).

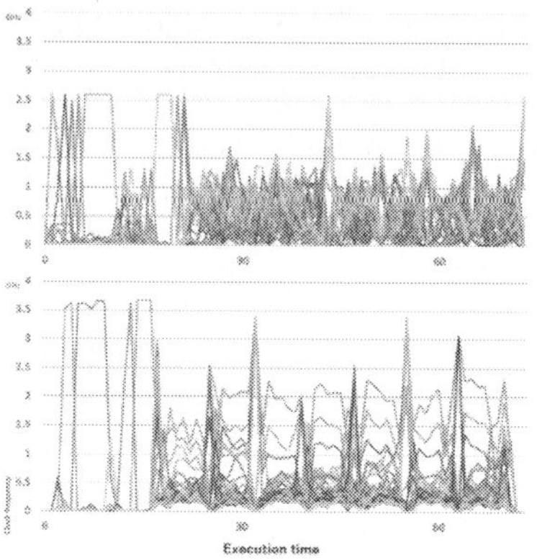

Figure 11. Time-series data for the clock frequency of RM (above:Haswell below:Skylake).

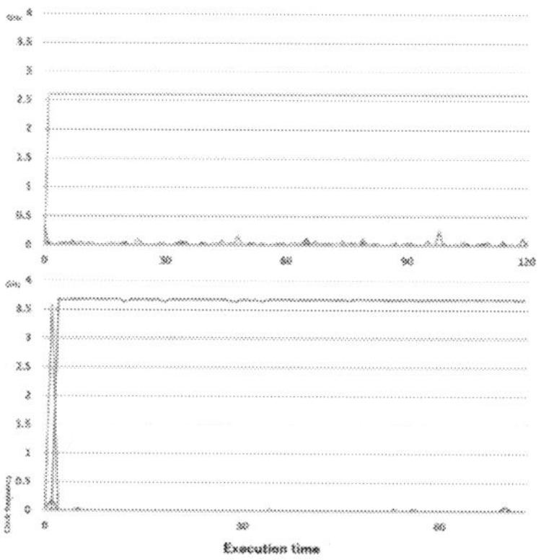

Figure 12. Time-series data for the clock frequency of SA (above:Haswell below:Skylake).

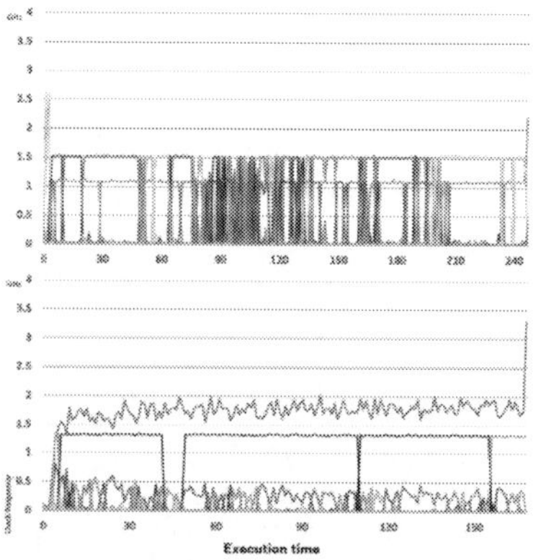

Figure 13. Time-series data for the clock frequency of RT (above:Haswell below:Skylake).

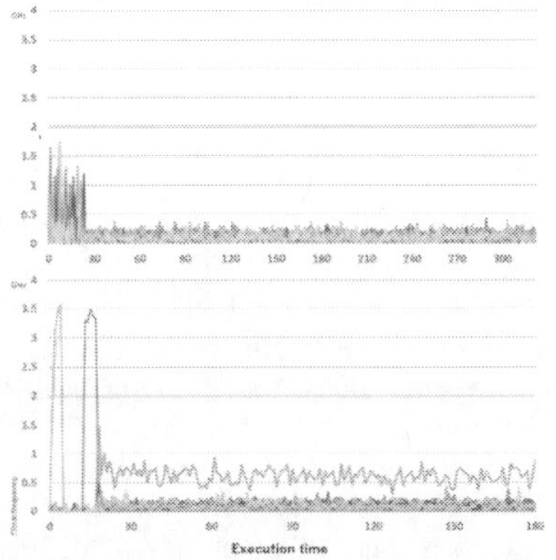

Figure 14. Time-series data for the clock frequency of TL (above:Haswell below:Skylake).

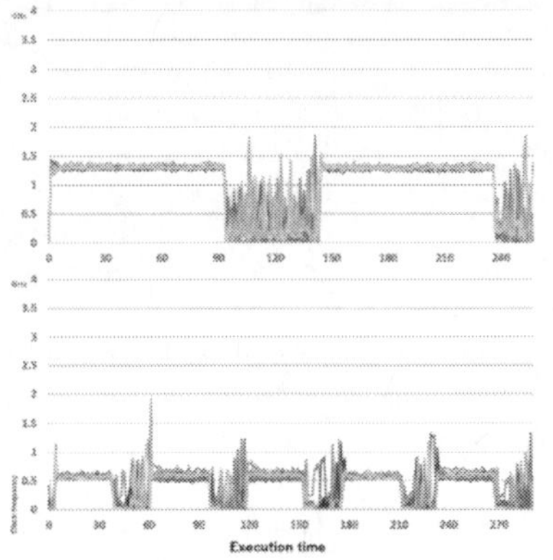

Figure 15. Time-series data for the clock frequency of RI (above:Haswell below:Skylake).

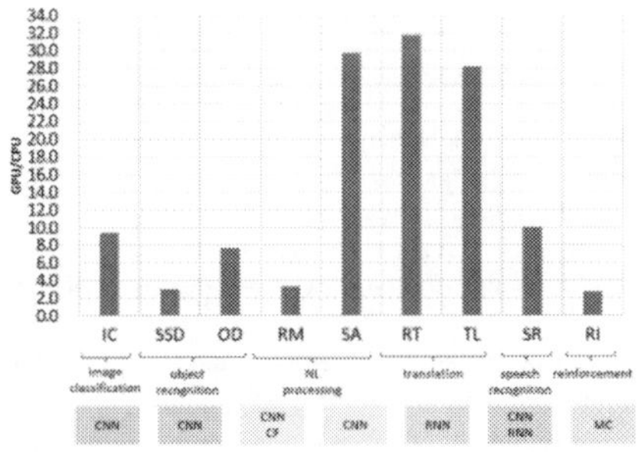

Figure 16. Average GPU/CPU utilization.

TABLE VI. GPU AND CPU AVERAGE UTILIZATION

Benchmark	CPU (%)	GPU (%)
IC	5.1	95.4
SSD	9.9	59.8
OD	4.9	74.5
RM	6.7	44.3
SA	1.4	82.0
RT	1.5	95.5
TL	1.5	83.9
SR	3.2	65.1
RI	11.4	62.7

TABLE VII. ENVIRONMENTS FOR GPU COMPARISON

	Environment 1	Environment 2
OS	ubuntsu 16.04	ubuntsu 16.04
Server	FUJITSU Primergy RX2540 M4	FUJITSU Primergy RX2540 M4
CPU	Intel Xeon Skylake 2 sockets 20 cores 2.4GHz Gold 6148 150W	Intel Xeon Skylake 2 sockets 20 cores 2.4GHz Gold 6148 150W
GPU	NVIDIA Tesla P100 16GB	NVIDIA Tesla V100 16GB
Storage HDD	290GB read 0.87GB/s write 1.75GB/s	290GB read 0.87GB/s write 1.75GB/s
Memory	192GB DDR4 2666MHz	192GB DDR4 2666MHz
Python	3.50	3.50
CUDA	9.2	9.2

TABLE VIII. GPU SPEC

	P100	V100
Core	3584	5120
MHz	1300	1455
FP16	18.636	119.19
FP32	9.318	14.90
FP64	4.659	7.45
Memory Bandwidth	720	900

Table VIII shows the specifications of the GPUs V100 and P100 used in this experiment.

Table IX lists the comparison of job times obtained when running each benchmark on different GPUs. Compared to the average GPU utilization data presented in Table VI, the change in the job time when changing the GPU is larger for the benchmarks with higher average GPU utilization.

The present result suggested that a job with a high GPU utilization shows a high job performance improvement effect due to changes in the GPU performance, and the difference in the job performance due to the changes in the CPU performance is small.

C. Memory

Figure 17 shows the maximum value of the memory utilization of each benchmark. Compared with the memory utilization of a CPU, the memory use of a GPU is remarkably large in this experiment. This is because the capacity of GPU memory is insufficient for the data size required by applications. Additionally, both the class "IC" and the class "TL" have high GPU utilization but show a large difference in

TABLE IX. COMPARISON OF JOB TIME - GPU

Benchmark	P100	V100	V100 / P100
IC	4:33:04	3:01:13	0.66
SSD	3:12:18	3:09:12	0.98
OD	2:57:51	2:23:26	0.81
RM	1:09:07	1:09:34	1.01
SA	1:48:14	1:22:50	0.76
RT	4:05:28	2:48:18	0.68
TL	4:29:21	2:59:55	0.67
SR	15:07:34	10:53:32	0.72
RI	6:08:37	5:46:00	0.93

the CPU memory utilization. This difference is caused by the data set type.

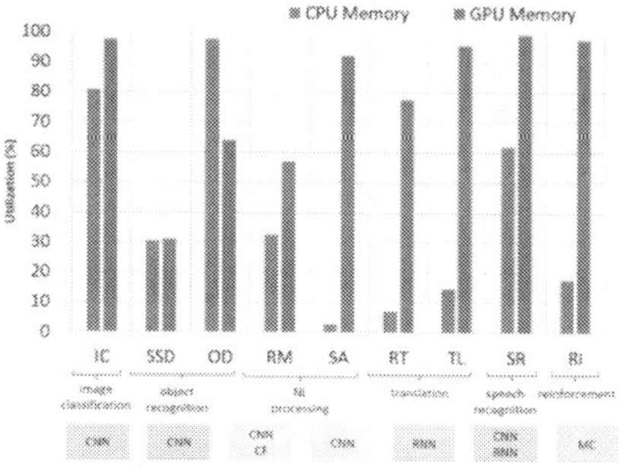

Figure 17. Memory utilization.

In this experimental environment and experimental conditions, the amount of total memory is sufficient for the operation of the application, and the effect on job performance is considered to be small.

D. GPU Priority Assignment

From the results of comparing job execution times when changing the GPU in Table VIII, we estimate the improvement in job time by GPU priority assignment.

In a Docker environment, it is assumed that one application fully uses a physical machine. Each machine that handles nine MLPerf benchmarks is assigned one of 10 P100 and 10 V100 as GPU resources, and process the same number of each benchmark in this assumption. Table X shows the comparison of the total execution time when a new GPU is preferentially assigned to a benchmark where the improvement in job execution time due to GPU performance was significant (Proposed Method) and the time when a GPU is evenly assigned (Evenly Assigned).

TABLE X. COMPARISON OF TOTAL EXECUTION TIME

Number of Jobs	Proposed Method (h:m:s)	Evenly Assigned (h:m:s)	Reduce (%)
200	74:30:00	81:11:27	8.241
400	149:00:00	162:22:54	8.241
600	223:30:00	243:34:21	8.241
800	298:00:00	324:45:48	8.241
1000	372:30:00	405:57:15	8.241
10000	3724:42:00	4059:32:33	8.248

Regardless of the number of jobs to be processed, improvement in job performance was confirmed at an almost constant rate. In the research works on task scheduling algorithm, the previous study [10] has shown that overall execution time was reduced by 1.2% - 8% over one-step and predictive average interval scheduling policies based on more accurate information prediction. Also, it was observed that the proposed algorithm resulted in 9.47% in terms of overall execution time of task completion in previous reseach [11]. These research works focus on the task scheduling of different target from ours.

From the simulation results, the control method proposed in this study is expected to reduce the total execution time by 8.24%, which can lead to efficient operation of limited GPU resources.

However, from the viewpoint of fairness of allocation among applications, the order of job processing should not necessarily be determined only by the type of benchmark, the order of job processing should not be determined only by the type of benchmark.

V. Conclusion and Future Work

In this paper, the efficient operation technology of GPU resources has been investigated using the difference of job performance caused by the difference of GPU performance. As a basic study, we evaluated the characteristics of 8 types of benchmarks executed on a framework that uses GPUs and compared performance on machines of different generations.

As a result of job performance analysis when GPUs of different generations were used, it was found that there is a big difference in job performance caused by the difference of GPU performance for each benchmark.

Assuming a Docker environment where old GPUs and new GPUs coexist, the execution time of the case where GPUs were evenly assigned was estimated and compared with that of the case where new GPUs were preferentially assigned to benchmarks with large differences in job performance due to differences in GPUs. The total execution time was reduced by 8.24%. This suggests that the above control leads to efficient operation of limited GPU resources. In the future, we would like to construct a system that actually controls the operation of the GPU.

VI. ACKNOWLEDGMENTS

This work is partially based on a collaborative research agreement between Ochanomizu University and Fujitsu Laboratories.

References

[1] bitfusion, "Bitfusion flexdirect virtualization technology white paper," bitfusion, Tech. Rep., November 2017.

[2] Chasapis et al., "Power efficient job scheduling by predicting the impact of processor manufacturing variability," in Proceedings of the ACM International Conference on Supercomputing. ACM, 2019, pp. 296–307.

[3] G. Zitzlsberger, B. Jansík, and J. Martinovič, "Job simulation for large-scale pbs based clusters with the maui scheduler," Big Data Analytics, Data Mining and Computational Intelligence 2018, Theory and Practice in Modern Computing 2018, p. 137.

[4] K. Hazelwood et al., "Applied machine learning at facebook: A datacenter infrastructure perspective," IEEE HPCA2018, 2018, pp. 620–629.

[5] L. B. N. Laboratory, "Singularity," https://singularity.lbl.gov/, retrieved: April, 2020.

[6] Intel, "Haswell," https://ark.intel.com/ja/products/codename/42174/Haswell.html, retrieved: April, 2020.

[7] NVIDIA, "HGX-2," https://www.nvidia.com/en-us/data-center/hgx/, retrieved: April, 2020.

[8] Zabbix, "Zabbix," https://www.zabbix.com/documentation/4.2/manual, retrieved: April, 2020.

[9] Intel, Intel 64 and IA-32 Architectures Software Developer's Manual Volume 3B :Order Number 253669-067US., 2018, pp. 19.3–19–24, 19.46–19.58, https://software.intel.com/en-us/articles/intel-sdm.

[10] L. Yang, J. M. Schopf, and I. Foster, "Conservative scheduling: Using predicted variance to improve scheduling decisions in dynamic environments," in Proceedings of the 2003 ACM/IEEE conference on Supercomputing. ACM, 2003, p. 31.

[11] Y. K. Ashish Kumar Mishra, Dhirendra K. Yadav and N. Jain, "Improving reliability and reducing cost of task execution on preemptible vm instances using machine learning approach," The Journal of Supercomputing, vol. 75, no. 4, 2019, pp. 2149–2180.

Contingent Planning Using Counter-Examples from a Conformant Planner

Sebastien Piedade*, Alban Grastien†, Charles Lesire*, Guillaume Infantes‡
*ONERA, Toulouse, France
Emails: sebastien.piedade@onera.fr, charles.lesire@onera.fr
†Australian National University, Canberra, Australia
Email: alban.grastien@anu.edu.au
‡Jolibrain, Toulouse, France
Email: guillaume.infantes@jolibrain.com

Abstract—**Decision-making for autonomous robots in real world applications has to manage uncertainties in order to efficiently accomplish a mission. Some planning methods deal with uncertainty by improving the robustness of the plan embedded in the robot. In this paper, we propose a novel approach to one of these methods, contingent planning. Most of the existing approaches are limited by the computation complexity and the quality of the solutions they return. To deal with these limitations, we propose to limit the number of observations in the plan as observations involve an important cost in computation time and energy. The originality of our approach is that our contingent planner uses an underlying conformant planner, i.e., a planner that is not allowed to make observations, to compute conformant subplans and insert observations between conformant subplans only when a conformant plan cannot be computed. We evaluate this approach by comparing its results with respect to Contingent-FF (Contingent Fast-Forward), a well known contingent planner, on a set of benchmarks. This comparison reveals that, even if our approach has some limitations, as it is not complete, it works quite effectively in terms of solution quality on classic benchmarks of the planning community.**

Keywords–contingent planning; autonomous decision-making; uncertainty.

I. Introduction

In our world, where disasters are more and more frequent, fast and effective victims rescue has become a major issue. While robots are already used by first responders in such situations to access difficult terrains or hazardous areas, the next step would be to use autonomous robots, that would be able to adapt to the situation in order to provide a fast and efficient response. This need for autonomous robotics in search and rescue has been emphasized by [1] and [2]. This capability to adapt to the environment requires us to embed into the robot platform some decision-making processes able to reason about uncertain states of the environment, as stated by [3] while reporting about the use of robots in earthquake responses.

In this paper, we propose an algorithm for planning under uncertainty that settles in the contingent planning paradigm: uncertainty is represented by sets of possible states, and the objective is to find a conditional plan, i.e., a graph of actions containing branches allowing an online decision making influenced by the results of observations of some unknown parts of the environment.

Most of the existing approaches are limited by the complexity of the plan computation and the quality of the solutions they return. One of the ways to deal with these limitations is to limit the number of observations in the plan. In fact, especially in autonomous robots missions, observations have an important cost in computation time and energy. Conformant planning [4]–[7] consists in dealing with the uncertainty of the environment by computing a plan working for every possible initial state without making any observation. Being able to solve a problem without observation is an advantage that we find interesting to study, especially as existing contingent approaches do not use a background conformant planner and its advantages.

The originality of our approach is precisely that we use in the background a conformant planner iteratively, by asking it to solve subproblems. If the conformant planner cannot find a conformant plan, then we use counter-examples returned by this planner to insert observations in-between the conformant plans obtained for such subproblems. In this version of the approach, we try to perform the observation as close as possible from the failing action of a failing plan, assuming the fact that an observation could potentially be more efficient close to the issue. The approach described in this paper has some limitations. In fact, our approach is not yet complete, but it worked quite effectively so far in terms of solution quality on classic benchmarks of the planning community.

The rest of the paper is structured as follows. In Section 2, we present some related works on planning under uncertainty. In Section 3, we present some background and notation about the problem formalisation. In Section 4, we describe and evaluate theoretically our algorithm. In Section 5, we compare our approach with respect to Contingent-FF, and we present some results on some academic benchmarks. Finally, in Section 6, we conclude this paper.

II. Related Works

Various planning methods exist to handle uncertainty. We can separate these methods in different types depending on how uncertainty is defined. Replanning is a method consisting in computing a first plan without handling uncertainties and replanning if an event occurs during the execution of the plan [8] [9]. Fast-Forward Replan (FF-Replan) [9] is one of these methods in which the probabilities of the problem are determinized and a plan is computed with a classical planning method. If an unexpected state occurs during the execution of the plan, then the planner replans in the same determinization of the problem. When uncertainty can be represented as probabilities on state transitions or action non-deterministic effects, probabilistic planning is commonly used. Among these probabilistic methods we can cite Markov Decision Processes (MDPs) [10] that model the problem as a fully observable stochastic system. The solution for a MDP is an optimal policy mapping the best action to each state of the MDP. This optimal policy can be found by various methods, like dynamic programming [11] and some of its variants like Value iteration method or Policy iteration [12]. When the problem is only partially observable, Partially Observable MDPs (POMDPs) [13] are used instead of MDPs. POMDPs introduce a belief over the environment state which is updated by some observations. This belief is updated by a function over state transition probabilities and observation probabilities. Some solving methods for MDPs and POMDPs follow a forward search approach generally making some sampling from the initial belief, then computing only a partial policy [14]–[16]. Chanel et al. [17] have also proposed an architectural approach to compute partial policy online in bounded time by making assumptions on the current belief.

When uncertainty is expressed as a set of possible initial states of the system, symbolic planning methods can be used. If the agent is not able to perform any observation, conformant planning can be used to solve the planning problem [4]–[7]. The plan returned by a conformant planner is generally an action sequence. Conformant Fast-Forward (Conformant-FF) [4] is a conformant planner that explores the belief space using heuristic functions based on a relaxation of the problem actions, by ignoring the delete lists of their effects. Conformant-FF then uses the Fast-Forward (FF) planner to compute a relaxed plan for each search state. Conformant Planner via Counter-Example and Sampling (CPCES) [7] is another conformant planner that computes a conformant plan using only a subset of the initial states, which allows CPCES to reduce the problem to classical planning.

If the planning problem is (partially) observable, contingent planning can be used to solve the problem. Contingent planning [18]–[20] consists in computing a conditional plan containing branches allowing an online decision making influenced by the results of some observations of the system. The conditional plan returned by a contingent planner is generally represented as a decision tree. Contingent Fast-Forward (Contingent-FF) [18] is a contingent planner that uses the same belief space representation as Conformant-FF. In Contingent-FF, the search space is an And-Or tree and the returned plan is a sub-tree where all leaves are goal states. Belief states are represented through action-observation sequences.

The approach proposed in this paper is part of the contingent planning approaches. Indeed, in the kind of application like search and rescue missions by autonomous robots, designing a model of the complete problem by a (PO)MDP is hard, as most of the uncertainty distributions are either unknown, or with the occurence of rare events. Online Replanning methods are not really suitables for autonomous robots missions as the cost of computing a new plan during the execution has an important computation and energy cost. Conformant planning has lots of advantages, but conformant plans do not always exist for autonomous robots problems, as some observations must be done to decrease the uncertainty. However, the approach we propose can be seen as a contingent meta-planner that uses a conformant planner to compute conformant plans for subproblems when such a conformant plan exists and add observations in between the conformant subplans when observations are needed. Therefore, our approach can be useful for missions in which we need to limit the number of observations.

III. BACKGROUND

In this section, we introduce some background and notations that we use later to present our approach. First, we introduce notations to describe the problem, including a description of states and operators. Second, we introduce some notations about belief representation, that we use in our approach to manage uncertainty. In these definitions, all actions are assumed to be deterministic and the uncertainty is assumed to lie in the initial situation only. Note that it has been proven that non-deterministic effects can be eliminated by introducing artificial initial uncertainty [21].

A. Problem definition

The following notations are adapted from [22] [23].

Definition 1 (Planning Problem). A planning problem $\mathbb{P}$ is defined by a tuple $(\mathcal{L}, \mathcal{O}, I, G)$ where:

- $\mathcal{L} = \{p_1, ..., p_n\}$ is a finite set of proposition symbols; a state s is then represented by a set of propositions that hold, i.e., that are true, in s; propositions that do not hold in s are assumed to be false; we denote $\mathcal{W} = 2^{\mathcal{L}}$ as the set of all possible world states;
- $\mathcal{O}$ is a finite set of *operators*, partitioned into the set of *actions* A and the set of *observations* O; each operator $op \in \mathcal{O}$ is defined by a precondition $pre(op) \subseteq \mathcal{L}$ and a set of effects *eff(op)*;
- $I \subseteq \mathcal{W}$ is the set of possible initial states;
- $G \subseteq \mathcal{L}$ is the set of propositions defining the goal.

Definition 2 (Action Application). An action $a \in A$ is *applicable* in state $s \in \mathcal{W}$ if and only if its preconditions hold in s, i.e.,

$$pre(a) \subseteq s \tag{1}$$

Each effect e of a (i.e., $e \in \mathit{eff}(a)$) is defined by a triple $con(e) \subseteq \mathcal{L}, add(e) \subseteq \mathcal{L}, del(e) \subseteq \mathcal{L}$, where:

- $con(e)$ are the conditions in which e is applied (unconditional effects are defined by $con(e) = \emptyset$);
- $add(e)$ are the propositions that will be added to the state after applying e;
- $del(e)$ are the propositions that will be deleted from the state after applying e.

If a is applicable in s, then $T(s, a)$ is the transition function such that:

$$\begin{aligned} T(s,a) = s - & \bigcup_{e \in \mathit{eff}(a) \text{ s.t. } con(e) \subseteq s} del(e) \\ \cup & \bigcup_{e \in \mathit{eff}(a) \text{ s.t. } con(e) \subseteq s} add(e). \end{aligned} \tag{2}$$

We assume that the problem actions are not self-contradictory, i.e., when applying action a in state s, for two effects $e, e' \in \mathit{eff}(a)$, if $p \in add(e)$ and $p \in del(e')$, then $con(e)$ and $con(e')$ are not both satisfied in state s. We have $con(e) \cup con(e') \not\subseteq s$. Consequently, we also assume that for each effect e, $add(e) \cap del(e) = \emptyset$.

Definition 3 (Observation Application). An observation $o \in O$ is applicable in state $s \in \mathcal{W}$ if and only if its preconditions hold in s (see (1)). The effects o are defined by a proposition ($\mathit{eff}(o) \in \mathcal{L}$) that is observed when applying o, i.e., whose truth value is known after applying o. The application of an observation o in state s has no effect over the state s, i.e.,

$$T(s, o) = s \tag{3}$$

The application of an observation o has no effect on the world state, but it will have an effect on the belief the agent has on the current state. Notations and definitions about belief reasoning are described below. Note that we assume that an observation o observes only one proposition at a time, without loss of generality.

B. Belief reasonning

As classically done in planning under uncertainty, we model the uncertain knowledge about the current state as a *belief* represented by a set of all the possible states (consistent with the actions/observations done so far). The following notations are taken or adapted from [23] [24].

Definition 4 (Belief State). The current belief $\mathcal{B} = \{s_1, \ldots, s_n\} \subseteq \mathcal{W}$ is the set of possible current states $s_1, \ldots, s_n$. The initial belief $\mathcal{B}_0$ corresponds to the possible initial states I of the problem.

Definition 5 (Action Application on a Belief). An action $a \in A$ is applicable in belief $\mathcal{B}$ if and only if a is applicable for each possible state in $\mathcal{B}$, i.e., iff:

$$\forall s \in \mathcal{B}, pre(a) \subseteq s \tag{4}$$

The effect of applying action a in $\mathcal{B}$ then results in a belief $\mathcal{B}'$ such that:

$$\mathcal{B}' = \{T(s,a), \text{ s.t. } s \in \mathcal{B}\} \tag{5}$$

where $T(s,a)$ is computed according to (2). By extension, the effect of applying a in $\mathcal{B}$ can be noted as $T(\mathcal{B}, a)$.

Definition 6 (Observation Application on a Belief). An observation $o \in O$ is applicable in belief $\mathcal{B}$ if and only if o is applicable for each possible state in $\mathcal{B}$ (see (4)). Let $\nu(o)$ be the observation result, i.e., the observed truth value of the effects of o. We denote $\nu^+(o) \subseteq \mathcal{L}$ as the set of observed propositions that hold in the current state, and $\nu^-(o) \subseteq \mathcal{L}$ the set of observed propositions that do not hold. The application of observation o in belief $\mathcal{B}$ does not modify the state itself, as described in Def. 3, but results in a new belief $T(\mathcal{B}, o)$ such that:

$$T(\mathcal{B}, o) = \{s, \text{ s.t. } s \in \mathcal{B} \wedge \nu^+(o) \subseteq s \\ \wedge \nu^-(o) \cap s = \emptyset\} \tag{6}$$

As we assume that an observation observes only one proposition p (see Def. 3), either $\nu^+(o)$ or $\nu^-(o)$ is empty, the other being equal to p. Also, note that (6) would work for observations whose effect has multiple propositions.

C. Conditional Plan

A conditional plan can be represented as a graph of operators, leading an initial belief to a resulting belief (then having a flow network structure). Branchings in this graph correspond to results of observations, depending whether the observed properties hold or not in the current belief.

Definition 7 (Conditional Plan). Given a problem $\mathbb{P} = (\mathcal{L}, \mathcal{O}, I, G)$, a conditional plan is inductively defined by the following facts:

- The empty plan ε is a conditional plan;
- (op) is a conditional plan $\forall op \in \mathcal{O}$;
- if π_1 and π_2 are conditional plans, then $\pi_1;\pi_2$ is a conditional plan representing the sequence of π_1 and π_2;
- if π_1, π_2 are conditional plans and $o \in O$ is an observation, then the plan **if** o **then** π_1 **else** π_2 is a conditional plan representing that, according to the result of observation o, π_1 is executed if the observed proposition is true, otherwise π_2 is executed.

A conditional plan π is *executable* in a belief $\mathcal{B}$ if its root operator is applicable in $\mathcal{B}$, and if all operators in π are applicable in the belief corresponding to the result of their previous operators. We denote $T(\mathcal{B}, \pi)$ as the result of applying an executable conditional plan in belief $\mathcal{B}$. Using a similar inductive definition, we formally say that a conditional plan π is executable in a belief $\mathcal{B}$ if:

- $\pi = (op)$, $op \in \mathcal{O}$ such that op is applicable in $\mathcal{B}$ (see Eq. 4); then $T(\mathcal{B}, \pi) = T(\mathcal{B}, op)$;
- $\pi = \pi_1; \pi_2$, with π_1 applicable in $\mathcal{B}$ and π_2 applicable in $T(\mathcal{B}, \pi_1)$; then $T(\mathcal{B}, \pi) = T(T(\mathcal{B}, \pi_1), \pi_2)$;
- $\pi =$ **if** o **then** π_1 **else** π_2, with o applicable in $\mathcal{B}$, π_1 is applicable in $\mathcal{B}^+$ and π_2 is applicable in $\mathcal{B}^-$, where $\mathcal{B}^+$ (resp. $\mathcal{B}^-$) $= T(\mathcal{B}, o)$ when $\nu^+(o)$ (resp. $\nu^-(o)$) $= eff(o)$; the result of applying π is then $T(\mathcal{B}, \pi) = T(\mathcal{B}^+, \pi_1) \bigcup T(\mathcal{B}^-, \pi_2)$.

A conditional plan π executable in I and that leads to G (i.e., $G \in T(I, \pi)$) is a *solution* to problem $\mathbb{P}$. We can notice that the definition of a plan in classical formalism is equivalent to the three first points of Def. 7.

IV. Contingent Planning Algorithm

The proposed approach settles on the use of a conformant planner that is asked to solve subproblems. To be used in our approach, the conformant planner must return either the conformant plan it has found, but also, in case no conformant plan exists, a counter-example (i.e., an initial state that caused the failure) and information about why the planner is failing on this counter-example, in the form of a plan (i.e., a sequence of actions) that fails for this counter-example.

Based on such a conformant planner, the principle of our approach is to give a problem to solve to the conformant planner and, in case of failure, use the counter-example and the failing plan to determine which observation to perform, and when, and then split the problem into subproblems taking this observation into account to reduce the uncertainty on the subproblems, and then ask the conformant planner to solve these subproblems. This process is used iteratively on the subproblems if the conformant planner fails in finding a solution. In this version of the approach, we try to perform the observation as close as possible from the failing action of the failing plan returned by the conformant planner, assuming the fact that an observation could potentially be more efficient close to the plan issue. As a conformant planner, we use CPCES [7], which fulfills our assumption: it provides a counter-example and a failing plan in case of failure. Note that we could use any conformant planner returning the same kind of information, and for conformant planners that would instead return for instance a proposition that makes the solver fail, we could integrate it with slight modification of the algorithm, without reconsidering the approach.

In subsection A. of this section, we present the CPCES algorithm and the data it provides. Then, we present and describe the main algorithm of our approach, before analysing some properties.

A. CPCES

CPCES [7] is a conformant planner that follows an iterative approach, in which a deterministic planner, namely FF [25], is used to find a plan π (an action sequence) for a subset of the initial belief, and then the validity of this plan on the complete initial belief is checked by solving a boolean satisfiability (SAT) problem with Z3 [26]. If the plan is not valid, Z3 provides a counter-example γ, i.e., a possible initial state for which the plan is not valid. This counter-example is integrated into the initial subset, and FF is asked to solve it again. This process is used iteratively, starting from one single state of the belief, until either a valid plan is found, or FF finds no plan for the subset, in which case the counter-example and the previous plan found by FF are returned.

Figure 1 contains the CPCES algorithm taken from [7] and adapted to the notations introduced in the previous section. FF is called to compute a new plan in line 9 and Z3 is used to check the plan validity in line 4.

Input: $\mathbb{P} = (\mathcal{L}, A, I, G)$
Output: π, γ
1: $\mathcal{B} := \emptyset$
2: $\pi := \varepsilon$
3: **loop**
4:   check validity of π
5:   **if** π is a solution for $\mathbb{P}$ **then**
6:     **return** $\pi, \emptyset$
7:   let γ be a counter-example
8:   $\mathcal{B} := \mathcal{B} \cup \{\gamma\}$
9:   compute a new plan π' for $\mathbb{P}' = (\mathcal{L}, A, \mathcal{B}, G)$
10:   **if** no such π' exists **then**
11:     **return** π, γ
12:   $\pi := \pi'$

Figure 1. CPCES Algorithm

B. Contingent planner

Input: $\mathbb{P} = (\mathcal{L}, \mathcal{O}, I, G)$
Output: π_c
1: $\pi, \gamma :=$ conformantPlanner($\mathbb{P}$)
2: **if** $\gamma = \emptyset$ **then**
3:   **return** π
4: $\mathcal{B}_o, o :=$ findObservation$(I, \mathcal{O}, \pi, \gamma)$
5: $\pi_o :=$ ContingentPlanning$((\mathcal{L}, \mathcal{O}, I, \mathcal{B}_o))$
6: $\mathcal{B}^+ := T(\mathcal{B}_o, o)$ *with* $\nu^+(o) =$ *eff(o)*
7: $\pi_p :=$ ContingentPlanning$((\mathcal{L}, \mathcal{O}, \mathcal{B}^+, G))$
8: $\mathcal{B}^- := T(\mathcal{B}_o, o)$ *with* $\nu^-(o) =$ *eff(o)*
9: $\pi_n :=$ ContingentPlanning$((\mathcal{L}, \mathcal{O}, \mathcal{B}^-, G))$
10: **return** (π_o ;**if** o **then** π_p **else** π_n)

Figure 2. Contingent Planning Procedure

Figure 2 illustrates our main contingent plan computation algorithm. This algorithm takes as input the contingent problem $\mathbb{P}$ and returns a contingent plan π_c. We first ask a conformant planner (in our implementation, CPCES, as described in Alg. 1) to compute a conformant plan π (line 1). If such a conformant plan exists, (line 2), we return this plan. Otherwise, the conformant planner returns a counter-example γ and a plan π that fails for this counter-example. From these pieces of information, we look for an observation to include in the plan. The findObservation function (further detailed in Alg. 3) returns an observation o and a belief $\mathcal{B}_o$ in which this observation could be performed (line 4).

Finally, we call our algorithm again on the subproblems corresponding to: reaching the belief states in which to perform the observation from the initial state (line 5), and reaching the goal from both cases where the belief has been updated after a positive observation (line 7) and a negative observation (line 9). We finally return a plan made of the subplan to reach $\mathcal{B}_o$ followed by a branching conditionned by the observation result (line 10).

Input: $I, \mathcal{O}, \pi, \gamma$
Output: $(\mathcal{B}_o, o)$
1: $beliefList := [I]$
2: $\mathcal{B} := I$
3: **for** a in π **do**
4:   **if** a applicable in γ **then**
5:     $\gamma := T(\gamma, a)$
6:     $\mathcal{B} := T(\mathcal{B}, a)$
7:     $beliefList := beliefList + \mathcal{B}$
8:   **else**
9:     let $unsatPre$ be the unsatisfied preconditions of a
10:     **break**
11: **for** p in $unsatPre$ **do**
12:   let o be an observation for p in $\mathcal{O}$
13:   **for** $\mathcal{B}_o$ in $beliefList$ **do**
14:     **if** o applicable in $\mathcal{B}_o$ **then**
15:       **return** $(\mathcal{B}_o, o)$
16: **return** $(\mathcal{B}, None)$

Figure 3. findObservation Algorithm

Figure 3 describes the findObservation algorithm. This algorithm is used to determine which observation o we need to perform to discriminate the counter-example γ from the other possible states and in which belief $\mathcal{B}_o$ we need to perform the observation. The inputs are the set of operators $\mathcal{O}$, the failing plan π previously computed by the conformant plan and the counter-example state γ. The outputs are the observation o we need to perform and the belief $\mathcal{B}_o$ in which we need to perform the observation o.

We first look for the action a in π that is not applicable in γ (lines 4 to 7) by iteratively applying each action of the plan to the counter-example γ (line 5). We also keep track of the beliefs computed by the application of each action of π to the initial belief (lines 6 and 7). Once the failing action has been found, we get the set of propositions $unsatPre$ in the preconditions of a that does not hold in the state γ (line 9). We can notice that $unsatPre$ will never be empty because there is necessarily a failing action in the failing plan π returned by the conformant planner. Each proposition of $unsatPre$ is a potential observable proposition allowing to discriminate the counter-example and the other states in which this proposition does not hold from the other possible states. We then try to find an observation able to observe one of these propositions in one of the beliefs computed in the belief list (lines 11 to 15). We scan the possible observations in $\mathcal{O}$ to find an observation performing an observation effect over the value of the proposition p (line 12).

Finally, we verify if the observation o is applicable in one of the computed beliefs in $beliefList$ (lines 13 to 15). If o is applicable in the current belief $\mathcal{B}_o$, then we return $\mathcal{B}_o$ and o. In the other case, we verify if the observation o is applicable in one of the previously computed beliefs in $beliefList$. If o is not applicable in any belief of $beliefList$, then we try to find another observation able to observe another proposition p of $unsatPre$. If there is no observation able to discriminate the counter-exemple, then we return $None$, meaning that there is no possible observation.

C. Theoretical evaluation

Our method is sound because, if there is a solution to the problem, then the plan found is a contingent or conformant solution to the problem under the assumption that the conformant planner used is sound. If there is no solution, then the method terminates returning a no solution message that does not appear in the algorithms above. The algorithm always terminates because, if there is a contingent solution, then the size of the search space is convergent due to the splitting of the search space after each observation. If there is a conformant solution, then it is returned directly after the first call of CPCES, and if there is no solution, the algorithm terminates with an exit message. Our method is not complete, particularly because there is no backtracking. We are currently working on a version including backtracking, but it will be a second version of the algorithm.

V. Results

We have evaluated our algorithm by comparing its performance with respect to Contingent-FF on a set of benchmarks provided by Contingent-FF. The results are given on Table I. Computation times are given in seconds. TO indicates that the computation timed out after 5 min. NO indicates that the planner did not find an applicable observation. *Size* gives the number of actions in the plan, *depth* the maximal depth of the plan, and *observations* the number of observations. For our approach, we also compute the depth of the *shortest* path of the plan. This comparison is especially interesting given that Contingent-FF uses the same PDDL (Planning Domain Description Language) input language as our method. For this evaluation, we limited the computation time of the two approaches to 5 minutes, and we used the heuristic option of Contingent-FF that provided the fastest results (otherwise, the solver times out on most of the benchmarks). The results are given on Table I.

First, we can notice that for some benchmarks we find the same results as Contingent-FF, except for computation time, namely *ebtcs, grid p2, egrid p2, elogistics p1 and p3*. Sometimes neither Contingent-FF nor our approach are able to find a solution, like in *egrid p3* and *p4*, where our approach does not succeed to find an applicable observation and Contingent-FF times out.

We can notice in Table I that Contingent-FF has clearly better results in *blocks* where our approach finds plans with the same number of observations, but with a bigger size and a longer depth. In *erovers* $p4$, we obtain the same result in size as Contingent-FF, but our approach computes a longer plan in depth. Moreover, in *erovers p6*, Contingent-FF finds a solution with less observations, even if our solution is shorter.

We can observe in Table I that our approach is better than Contingent-FF in benchmarks where a conformant solution exists, namely *btcs, grid, rovers, logistics*. In that case, as we rely on CPCES, we find a conformant plan whereas Contingent-FF includes observations in its solution. Moreover, it generally results in finding a shorter plan, except for *logistics* and *btcs* where Contingent-FF finds a plan with a shorter depth. In problems like *elogistics p5, p7* and *erovers p2 and p8*, we find plans having the same number of observations than Contingent-FF, but the plans we find are shorter in size and depth. Moreover, our approach succeeds in solving *egrid p5* problem, while Contingent-FF times out.

One of the only drawbacks of our approach with respect to Contingent-FF is the computation time needed to solve some of the problems. First, we can notice these computation times have the same order of magnitude than Contingent-FF and do not seem to grow exponentially when increasing the size of the problems. Second, this computation time partly comes from the fact that we use CPCES as a "black-box" conformant planner, itself considering FF as a "black-box" planner. This induces a lot of access to files for writing/reading problems for these solvers during our process, while Contingent-FF does all the computation in memory. Our approach is not complete, which implies that in some problems we cannot find any applicable observations. In fact, in the current version of the approach, there is no backtracking in the failing plan computation and in the observation computation process. Our approach does not succeed when no observation is applicable in any belief computed from the application of the failing plan computed by CPCES. However, an interesting fact we can notice in these results is that our approach is better on benchmarks *rovers, logistics and elogistics*, which are closer to autonomous robots problems in which we need to navigate and explore an environment in order to pick or analyze some items.

A simulation of an autonomous robot scenario is currently in development. This simulation will allow us to evaluate the performance of our approach and see the behavior of the robot during the plan execution.

VI. Conclusion

In this paper, we have proposed a new contingent planner with an original approach, as we use a conformant planner to find conformant subplans when possible. Our approach consists in asking CPCES, a conformant planner, to solve a problem. If no conformant plan exists for this problem, CPCES returns a counter-example and a failing plan for this counter-example. We use this information to first add an observation in the plan to reduce the uncertainty related to this counter-example, and second to decompose the problem into subproblems with less uncertainty. These subproblems are sent to CPCES again to find a conformant plan, and the process iterates until a complete conditional plan has been found.

We compared our approach with Contingent-FF on a set of benchmarks and, despite the fact that we generally have higher computation time, we get some concluding results. First, on benchmarks where a conformant solution exists, we

TABLE I. RESULTS OF A COMPARISON WITH CONTINGENT-FF ON SOME BENCHMARKS.

Problem	Contingent Planning with counter-examples					Contingent-FF			
	time (s)	size	depth	shortest	observations	time (s)	size	depth	observations
blocks/p3	0.94	6	4	3	1	0.00	6	4	1
blocks/p7	5.6	89	16	10	7	0.05	**55**	**9**	7
blocks/p11	6.4	169	29	20	7	0.43	**117**	**18**	7
blocks/p15	8.05	244	39	27	7	3.20	**163**	**25**	7
btcs/p10	0.76	19	19	19	**0**	0.02	19	10	9
btcs/p30	2.36	59	59	59	**0**	0.8	59	30	29
btcs/p50	8.13	99	99	99	**0**	9.79	99	50	49
btcs/p70	24.11	139	139	139	**0**	57.31	139	70	69
ebtcs/p10	6.21	19	10	2	9	0.01	19	10	9
ebtcs/p30	22.73	59	30	2	29	0.42	59	30	29
ebtcs/p50	56.8	99	50	2	49	4.93	99	50	49
ebtcs/p70	156.11	139	70	2	69	29.10	139	70	69
grid/p2	3.61	9	9	9	0	0.01	9	9	0
grid/p3	4.05	**19**	**19**	19	**0**	9.78	174	43	15
grid/p4	21.24	**45**	**45**	45	**0**	227	464	68	17
grid/p5	18.64	**31**	**31**	**31**	**0**	TO	-	-	-
egrid/p2	3.96	9	9	9	0	0.01	9	9	0
egrid/p3	NO	-	-	-	-	TO	-	-	-
egrid/p4	NO	-	-	-	-	TO	-	-	-
egrid/p5	73.24	**185**	**31**	**23**	**7**	TO	-	-	-
rovers/p2	0.38	**8**	**8**	8	**0**	0.00	13	10	1
rovers/p4	0.52	**13**	**13**	13	**0**	0.00	23	14	3
rovers/p6	0.86	**23**	**23**	23	**0**	0.11	448	66	11
rovers/p8	0.65	**23**	**23**	23	**0**	0.03	170	83	3
erovers/p2	1.09	**11**	**9**	5	1	0.00	13	10	1
erovers/p4	3.39	23	17	5	3	0.00	23	**14**	3
erovers/p6	15.52	**144**	**27**	21	11	0.09	346	48	**7**
erovers/p8	3.34	**44**	**21**	15	3	0.01	95	36	3
logistics/p1	0.39	**9**	9	9	**0**	0.01	10	7	1
logistics/p3	0.49	**14**	14	14	**0**	0.01	18	8	2
logistics/p5	0.58	**29**	29	29	**0**	0.054	172	26	7
logistics/p7	0.75	**31**	31	31	**0**	0.2	247	27	11
elogistics/p1	1.07	10	7	4	1	0.00	10	7	1
elogistics/p3	1.8	18	8	5	2	0.00	18	8	2
elogistics/p5	9.02	**138**	**22**	20	7	0.12	172	26	7
elogistics/p7	10.63	**185**	26	21	11	0.13	247	26	11

always find a conformant plan. Second, on most of the other benchmarks, we either get solutions with less observations, or with less actions in the plan. Moreover, ou approach is better on benchmarks close to autonomous robots problems in which we need to navigate and explore uncertain environments.

Future works consist first in improving the completeness of our method by performing a backtracking in the failing plan computation and in the observation computation process if we fail to find an observation applicable in a belief computed from the current failing plan. Second, we would like to apply our method to autonomous robots problems closer to reality with navigation and exploration by implementing it on a real robot.

REFERENCES

[1] A. Birk and S. Carpin, "Rescue robotics a crucial milestone on the road to autonomous systems," Advanced Robotics, vol. 20, no. 5, 2006, pp. 595–605.

[2] R. R. Murphy et al., "Search and rescue robotics," Springer handbook of robotics, 2008, pp. 1151–1173.

[3] H. Kitano and S. Tadokoro, "Robocup rescue: A grand challenge for multiagent and intelligent systems," AI magazine, vol. 22, no. 1, 2001, pp. 39–39.

[4] J. Hoffmann and R. I. Brafman, "Conformant planning via heuristic forward search: A new approach," vol. 170, no. 6-7. Elsevier, 2006, pp. 507–541.

[5] D. Bryce, S. Kambhampati, and D. E. Smith, "Planning graph heuristics for belief space search," Journal of Artificial Intelligence Research (JAIR), vol. 26, 2006, pp. 35–99.

[6] A. Albore, M. Ramirez, and H. Geffner, "Effective heuristics and belief tracking for planning with incomplete information," in International Conference on Automated Planning and Scheduling (ICAPS), Freiburg, Germany, June 2011, pp. 2–9.

[7] A. Grastien and E. Scala, "Intelligent belief state sampling for conformant planning." in IJCAI, 2017, pp. 4317–4323.

[8] U. Kuter, D. Nau, E. Reisner, and R. Goldman, "Using classical planners to solve nondeterministic planning problems," in Proceedings of the Eighteenth International Conference on International Conference on Automated Planning and Scheduling, 2008, pp. 190–197.

[9] S. W. Yoon, A. Fern, and R. Givan, "Ff-replan: A baseline for probabilistic planning." in ICAPS, vol. 7, 2007, pp. 352–359.

[10] M. L. Puterman, Markov decision processes: discrete stochastic dynamic programming. John Wiley & Sons, 2014.

[11] R. Bellman, "Dynamic programming," Science, vol. 153, no. 3731, 1966, pp. 34–37.

[12] Mausam and A. Kolobov, "Planning with markov decision processes: An ai perspective," Synthesis Lectures on Artificial Intelligence and Machine Learning, vol. 6, no. 1, 2012, pp. 1–210.

[13] L. P. Kaelbling, M. L. Littman, and A. R. Cassandra, "Planning and acting in partially observable stochastic domains," Artificial intelligence, vol. 101, no. 1-2, 1998, pp. 99–134.

[14] E. Hansen and S. Zilberstein, "LAO*: A heuristic search algorithm that finds solutions with loops," Artificial Intelligence Journal (AIJ), vol. 129, no. 1-2, 2001, pp. 35–62.

[15] F. Teichteil-Königsbuch, U. Kuter, and G. Infantes, "Incremental plan aggregation for generating policies in MDPs," in International Conference on Autonomous Agents and MultiAgent Systems (AAMAS), Toronto, Canada, May 2010, pp. 1231–1238.

[16] H. Kurniawati, D. Hsu, and W. S. Lee, "SARSOP: Efficient Point-Based POMDP Planning by Approximating Optimally Reachable Belief Spaces," in Robotics: Science and Systems (RSS). Zurich, Switzerland, July 2008.

[17] C. P. C. Chanel, A. Albore, J. THooft, C. Lesire, and F. Teichteil-Königsbuch, "Ample: an anytime planning and execution framework for dynamic and uncertain problems in robotics," Autonomous Robots, vol. 43, no. 1, 2019, pp. 37–62.

[18] J. Hoffmann and R. Brafman, "Contingent planning via heuristic forward search with implicit belief states," in Proc. ICAPS, vol. 2005, 2005.

[19] A. Albore, H. Palacios, and H. Geffner, "A translation-based approach to contingent planning," in International Joint Conference on Artificial Intelligence (IJCAI), Providence, RI, USA, July 2009.

[20] B. Bonet, H. Palacios, and H. Geffner, "Automatic derivation of memoryless policies and finite-state controllers using classical planners," in International Conference on Automated Planning and Scheduling (ICAPS), Thessaloniki, Greece, September 2009, pp. 34–41.

[21] A. Albore, H. Palacios, and H. Geffner, "Compiling uncertainty away in non-deterministic conformant planning," in European Conference on Artificial Intelligence (ECAI), Lisbon, Portugal, August 2010, pp. 465–470.

[22] M. Ghallab, D. Nau, and P. Traverso, Automated Planning: theory and practice. Elsevier, 2004.

[23] A. Albore and H. Geffner, "Acting in partially observable environments when achievement of the goal cannot be guaranteed," in Proc. of ICAPS Workshop on Planning and Plan Execution for Real-World Systems. Citeseer, 2009.

[24] P. E. U. de Souza, C. P. C. Chanel, and F. Dehais, "Momdp-based target search mission taking into account the human operator's cognitive state," in 2015 IEEE 27th International Conference on Tools with Artificial Intelligence (ICTAI). IEEE, 2015, pp. 729–736.

[25] J. Hoffmann, "Ff: The fast-forward planning system," AI magazine, vol. 22, no. 3, 2001, pp. 57–57.

[26] L. De Moura and N. Bjørner, "Z3: An efficient smt solver," in International conference on Tools and Algorithms for the Construction and Analysis of Systems. Springer, 2008, pp. 337–340.

On Metabolic Complex Networks for Entropic Robust Autonomy

Chris Nowak
Defence Science & Technology Group
Sydney, Australia
e-mail: chris.nowak.5@gmail.com

Darryn Reid
Defence Science & Technology Group
Adelaide, Australia
e-mail: darryn.reid@dst.defence.gov.au

Abstract—**Autonomous systems are expected to be robust: they should be resilient to perturbations arising both from the external environment and from within the system itself. In other words, they should maintain a state of dynamic equilibrium, or homeostasis, within known limitations. By framing autonomous systems as metabolic systems, which can be understood as systems with flows and transformations that are capable of functioning well in a complex environment, it is demonstrated how a homeostatic control mechanism could be designed to enable such systems to self-adapt to the changing environment. To illustrate these ideas, they are applied to the problem of designing robust autonomous supply networks; their homeostatic control mechanisms and catalysts are identified.**

Keywords–Robust Autonomy; Resilience to Perturbations; Metabolism; Homeostasis & Allostasis; Transformations; Capability, Function & Behaviour; Self-adaptation; Curvature; Entropy.

I. Introduction

This paper is concerned with achieving robustness of autonomous systems, meaning the ability to absorb perturbations arising both exogenously—from the environment—and endogenously—from the system itself—within known limits. Using supply networks as an example for analysis, we frame the problem of robustness as "metabolic" complex networks to obtain a set of homeostatic control mechanisms. Illustrating the generality of this approach, this set of homeostatic controls should be capable of scaling irrespective of the complexity of any supply network instance.

Complex networks [1][2] are understood as networks that exhibit *complex behaviours*; complex networks are neither *regular,* nor *random*—and these networks behave in interesting (not regular, not random) ways. The real world, both natural and man-made, *creates* complex networks—and they either behave and function well, or get replaced by new versions which work better. The Internet is a complex network where new computers connect themselves (neither regularly, nor randomly) to the already existing network. It is debatable whether the Internet is a *scale-free network* [3], but the Internet does build itself up using the *preferential attachment* [2] mechanism (used to explain scale-free networks): new nodes prefer to attach themselves to *hubs*, i.e., nodes which are already well connected. Naturally, networks with hubs form. And they have one important advantage of being resilient to random attacks, and one important disadvantage of being vulnerable to targeted attacks. The following question presents itself: how can networks function well?

The question of functioning well implies a range of more specific questions. How is the network supposed to function? Can we measure how well it is functioning now? Can we predict how well it will be functioning in the future? Does the network need to be adaptive, situation-aware (of the environment and self), autonomous? Should the network be self-modifying, and given the library of *plans* that the network has, should it be able to modify the plans, or create new ones? But also: is it that the ability to manage and execute plans is the most important capability of the network? This paper suggests that it is *not.*

This paper suggests that *plans* are *secondary*—and *perturbations* are *primary concerns.* The functioning of a biological organism is primarily about handling perturbations, such as changes of temperature, sugar or pH level—it is the perturbations which dictate which plans are to be selected and executed. It is claimed here that complex systems with non-trivial behaviours should be *metabolic*: they should detect perturbations and employ *homeostatic control mechanisms* in order to maintain a *dynamic equilibrium* state (in which they can function well). The recommended "metabolic perspective" facilitates a conceptual shift from "plans first" to "perturbations first" and indicates that a complex system should: detect and measure perturbations, evaluate their effects on the way the system itself functions and whether it has been pushed out of the equilibrium state, and select and employ appropriate homeostatic (or allostatic) control mechanisms to return to the previous stable state (or move to a new stable state, respectively). This approach suggests that, given a complex system, to *understand* the system we should focus not on plans (or mechanisms of functioning), but on how the system handles perturbations and maintains homeostasis—because not only biological organisms do that, but so do infrastructure systems, cities, ecosystems, and a variety of other complex systems.

Given this stance, the long term goal is to analyse complex networks (which are discrete models of real-world systems) from the metabolic perspective by mapping perturbations to homeostatic and allostatic control mechanisms that can execute plans ensuring that the dynamic equilibrium states are maintained (as in these states the networks function well). Such a research program would be applicable to many complex systems domains—it just adds the metabolic perspective to the complex networks research program. Given that our models would be complex networks, both problems and solutions could be formulated in abstract ways, namely in terms of network topology, node and link attributes, and flows (all of them dynamic). One would expect that multiple real-world problems would share the same abstract problem and its solution. It is also important to be able to *measure* how well the given network functions; recent complex network research indicates that *curvature* based measures [4]–[5] seem to provide appropriate and powerful tools. The framework requires a conceptual—or ontological—shift; the ontology sketched in Section VII (and Appendix B) provides a step in this direction. The contribution of this paper is mostly conceptual: it proposes an ontology emphasising perturbations and homeostasis, it provides a discussion on measuring the health of networks, and it employs a supply network example to demonstrate the applicability of metabolic notions to non-biological systems. It should be noted that socio-technical systems have been seen as "metabolic systems" before, for instance in the case of urban systems [6][7]—however, metabolism there is being associated with the management of resource flows, and not explicitly with perturbations and homeostatic control.

A discussion on robust autonomy is presented in Section II, with *robustness* understood as *resilience to perturbations.* Section III considers communities, health and functions, indicating that, in a simple case, a community can be healthy and functioning well when it is well-connected. In such a case, it is also clear what the meaning and nature of *network curvature* is: well connected networks (such as cliques) have positive curvature, while other networks (such as trees) have negative curvatures, and, hence, making the network better connected would increase its curvature [8][5]. *Metabolic Complex Networks (MCN)* are described in Section IV, starting with metabolic cycles, and extending to metabolic pathways (networks of connecting transformations) which explain what functions the system can perform. Subsection IV-A focuses on two component systems, analysing them from two perspectives: firstly, by associating the *health* of the network (understood as its ability to function well) with the number of arrows connecting the network's nodes, and secondly, by considering the presence of *sinks* and *sources* as *attributes* of the network (and using the Formal Concept Analysis (FCA) framework [9] to construct a lattice ordering on networks). Then, a supply network scenario is analysed in Section V, and evacuation scenarios are (briefly) discussed in Section VI. The importance of Section VI comes from the fact that an evacuation network should be seen as composed of multiple *interdependent* supply networks (and, in general, networks can consist of many *interdependent* networks). Ontologies for robotics are considered in Section VII; this section explicitly states that Dennett's *intentional stance* [10] should be extended by adding the *metabolic level* above Dennet's physical, design and intentional levels. Further work is described in Section VIII and Section IX concludes this work.

II. Robust autonomy

The problem of robustness for autonomous systems as addressed herein consists of the following features:

- an *autonomous system* ω has an (overall) *capability* c_ω to perform its (overall) *function* f_ω; we will say that the system is *functioning* when it is performing its function f_ω;
- for the system to be functioning, it must maintain its dynamic equilibrium, i.e., *homeostasis* or *allostasis,* because outside of the equilibrium state the system's functioning is either difficult or impossible.

Thus, we distinguish two fundamental behavioural regimes, homeostasis and allostasis; the ability to manifest both with respect to various kinds of perturbations yields the desired robustness, while the limitations of allostasis provide explicit bounds on robustness:

- homeostasis, when understood in a less restrictive way, allows moving to an *alternative* dynamic equilibrium state rather than returning to the original equilibrium state; this is referred to as *allostasis;*
- *homeostatic and allostatic control mechanisms* allow the system—in the presence of perturbations—to continue performing its original function, or switch to performing an alternative function, respectively;
- homeostatic/allostatic control mechanisms are triggered by *perturbations;* however, it is beneficial for the system to *detect* the perturbations as early as possible, and even to predict the potential for perturbations of various kinds; perturbations need to be *handled,* i.e., *processed* after being detected or predicted.

Regarding systems' *capabilities,* we distinguish the following:

1) capability to perform normal functions;
2) capability to maintain homeostasis and allostasis;
3) capability to handle perturbations;
4) capability to handle plans.

The above constitutes a description of *robust autonomy* as "functioning + handling perturbations." Note that plan monitoring (related to performing function f_ω, with possible slight *homeostatic* variations) and plan modifying (switching from $f'_\omega = f_\omega$ to an *allostatic* $f''_\omega \neq f_\omega$) can be continuously performed while executing functions related to capabilities (1–3); therefore, (4) can be seen as a meta-level homeostatic/allostatic control mechanism. [Plan monitoring is not the focus here.]

It is also of importance to assess how well systems function. One way of achieving this is through *curvature-based methods* [11], cf. Section III. Robustness, curvature and entropy have been linked [4], and so entropic curvature-based measures could be applied to assess systems' *robustness.* Hence, when entropy (and related notions) are applied to autonomous systems, we could talk about *Entropic Robust Autonomy (ERA).*

We suggest introducing entropy and related concepts along the following lines. The assessment of the robustness of a system in terms of its ability within known limits to absorb various kinds of perturbations implies the need for an order parameter or set of order parameters: an order parameter provides a mechanism of abstraction from the myriad of details and thereby yields distinction between different modes in the environment and, correspondingly, different regimes of autonomous system behaviour. Here, we are concerned especially with distinguishing homeostatic and allostatic behavioural regimes in response to various kinds of perturbation. Entropy and related notions provide order parameters that promise to provide robust stable measures or estimates to determine these change points. Moreover, such estimates do not imply detailed predictions about system or environment state evolution; as a means of abstraction, we may rely on predictions about bounds on overall behaviour. Note that it is argued in [12] that the heart of the problem with autonomy is its need to deal with *uncertainty*.

III. Communities, Health and Functions

If a network represents a society—or a social group—then one might want to detect communities within the society, where the communities are strongly connected subgroups. Communities are often being detected in order to perform *sentiment analysis* [8]; however, we can also associate communities with *functionalities*. If a society (a social group) is to perform some *functions*, it might need to delegate sub-functions to specialised communities (sub-groups of the whole social group). Given that communities are strongly connected sub-groups, we can associate "strong connectedness" with "health" and say that what is being detected are "healthy sub-groups." Then, forming healthy communities is a part of maintaining a healthy society, where "health" can be understood as "capability"—communities have capabilities to perform their functions, in this way building up the total capability of the society. Topological graph theory based methods allow us to detect communities (assess sub-groups' health), but entropic curvature-based (geometric) methods are also used [5][8] (figures presented in [8] show how the geometric (curvature) transformation of the network can be performed). It should be noted that a community might start to deteriorate by losing connections, which could create *sink-only* and *source-only* nodes—this leads to the analysis of Section IV-A.

Using an entropic measure essentially means mapping the raw system model with all of its full complexities into a different, smaller model, where what comes out are regimes of behaviour rather than masses of possible behaviour. That is, the simplification is through functional abstraction, rather than component abstraction by merely grouping components together. In essence, this is what a method of using the entropic curvatures would give us here: the abstraction amounts to a mapping between the problem space into a smaller one whereby the many details are collapsed down into the regimes of behaviour with respect to the kinds of perturbations the environment or the autonomous system itself can impose on the autonomous system.

IV. Metabolic Complex Networks

Complex networks are networks that are neither regular, nor random [1]–[3][14][15]. *Metabolic networks* are networks that can handle metabolic flows; Figure 1 shows some biological metabolic pathways [13][16].

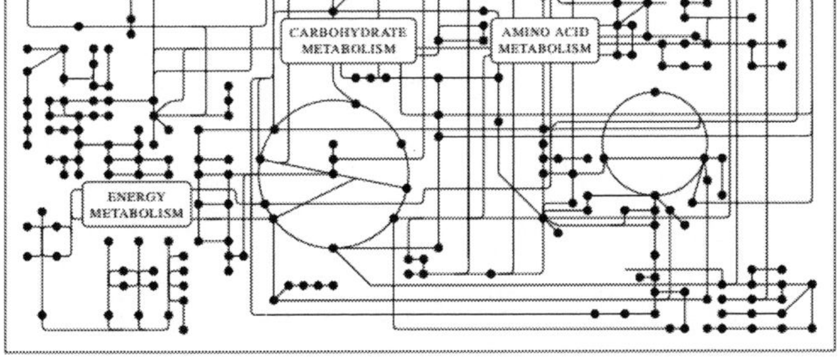

Figure 1. Metabolic pathways (FIGURE 15–1 in [13], page 570).

In a simple case, the system accepts an *input pattern* and *transforms* it to an *output pattern*. For instance, Figure 2 shows a *metabolic cycle:* a system that accepts the recurring (a, b, c, d) *input patterns* and *transforms* them—using the appropriate recurring patterns (t_1, t_2, t_3, t_4) of *transformations*—into the recurring *output patterns* (e, f, g, h). Metabolic cycles are simple examples of metabolic pathways which are, in general, sequences of connecting transformations (in the case of biological systems, transformations can take the form of *chemical reactions*). Figure 1 shows the *metabolic pathways* of a eukaryotic cell (further information on *pathways* can be found in [13] (FIGURE 15–1), [16] and on the websites [17]–[18]).

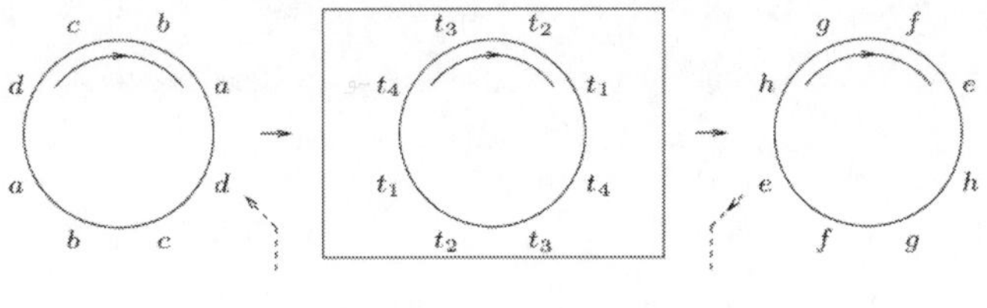

Figure 2. Metabolic cycles.

Assuming that a metabolic system ω is a complex network, the following sets need to be considered:

Θ	nodes (they accept inputs and produce outputs)
I	inputs (they are accepted by nodes)
O	outputs (they are produced by nodes)
Δ	transformations (transf. a node's inputs to outputs)
Φ	flows (a flow is an output connecting to an input)
Σ	streams (selections of metabolic inputs/outputs)
Υ	pathways (flow sequences associated with functions)
Γ	catalysts (facilitate transformations; not consumed)
Ψ	homeostatic control mechanisms (ensure stability)
Λ	allostatic control (alternative equilibrium states)
Ξ	interdependent networks (sources of perturbations)
Π	perturbations (coming from env. or other systems)

Hence, if we analysed a metabolic network ω, we would analyse it as $\omega(\Theta, I, O, \Delta, \Phi, \Sigma, \Upsilon, \Gamma, \Psi, \Lambda, \Xi, \Pi)$—which is more than $G = (V, E) = (\Theta, \Phi)$—i.e., we would analyse its: nodes, inputs, outputs, transformations, flows, streams, pathways, catalysts, homeostatic and allostatic control mechanisms, related interdependent networks, and perturbations. The ultimate goal of *metabolic analysis* is to understand ω as a *metabolic system* (with the elements just listed) capable of *functioning* and *handling perturbations* by *self-adapting* to the environment. We are interested in knowing the limits of self-adaptation, where we expect to be able to characterise these limits in terms of the appropriate entropy measure.

Recall that a node has inputs and outputs; a single input is accepted by a specific node; a single output is produced by a specific node; a node transforms its inputs into its outputs (and, therefore, a transformation (of a node) is an (inputs, outputs (of the node)) pair); a single flow (from ϑ_a to ϑ_b) is a single output (from ϑ_a) connecting to (or "becoming") a single input (to ϑ_b). Further, catalysts are expected to be associated with homeostatic and allostatic control mechanisms; homeostatic control mechanisms ensure that the system returns to its stable state; allostatic control mechanisms move the system to stable but possibly new states. Further, a stream can be an arbitrary selection of inputs and outputs, but would normally be considered as a starting point to a pathway investigation; pathways are the goals of the analysis—they identify functionalities and ensure functioning (corresponding to the identified functionalities) while maintaining a state of dynamic equilibrium and, therefore, *functioning while handling perturbations*. Finally, (external) perturbations come from the system's environment, i.e., from systems external to the system in question (but internal perturbations are also possible). As each perturbation must have its *source*, we claim that the sources of the perturbations are other networks, namely *interdependent networks*.

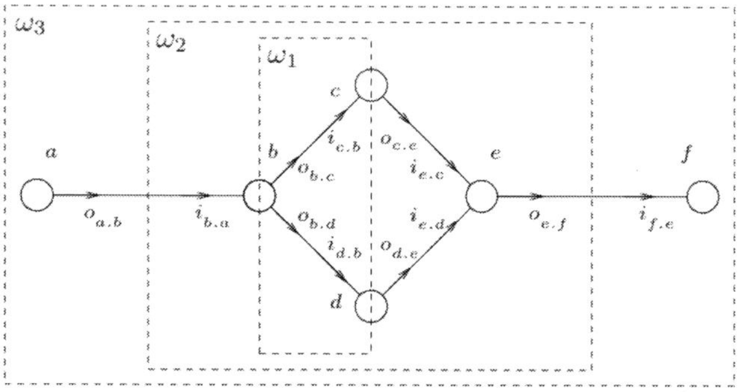

Figure 3. Metabolic systems ω_1, ω_2 and ω_3.

Figure 3 shows systems ω_1, ω_2 and ω_3. We can list these systems' nodes, inputs and outputs: $\omega_3(\Theta_3, I_3, O_3) = \omega_3(\{a, b, c, d, e, f\}, \{i_{b.a}, i_{c.b}, i_{d.b}, i_{e.c}, i_{e.d}, i_{f.e}\}, \{o_{a.b}, o_{b.c}, o_{b.d}, o_{c.e}, o_{d.e}, o_{e.f}\})$; $\omega_2(\Theta_2, I_2, O_2) = \omega_2(\{b, c, d, e\}, \{i_b, i_{c.b}, i_{d.b}, i_{e.c}, i_{e.d}\}, \{o_{b.c}, o_{b.d}, o_{c.e}, o_{d.e}, o_e\})$; $\omega_1(\Theta_1, I_1, O_1) = \omega_1(\{b, c, d\}, \{i_{c.b}, i_{d.b}\}, \{o_{b.c}, o_{b.d}\})$. System ω_3 is isolated: it has neither inputs, nor outputs connecting it to the environment (or systems immersed in the environment); all inputs and outputs of ω_3 are internal. We also note that node a is a *source-only* node, and that node f is a *sink-only* node. But ω_3 has *flows* and *transformations:* a flow from node a to node b, denoted $\varphi_{a.b}$, is the output $o_{a.b}$ connecting to the input $i_{b.a}$, i.e., $\varphi_{a.b} = o_{a.b}.i_{b.a}$; and a transformation of node b, denoted δ_b, is the pair, with the first element of the pair being the inputs I_b of b and the second element being the output O_b of b; given that $I_b = \{i_{b.a}\}$ and $O_b = \{o_{b.c}, o_{b,d}\}$ we have that $\delta_b = I_b.O_b = \{i_{b.a}\}.\{o_{b.c}, o_{b,d}\}$. Regarding system ω_2 (which has, comparing to ω_3, lost some nodes and their inputs and outputs), it has one input (to ω_2) from the environment, namely i_b (rather than $i_{b.a}$, as we have dropped node a), and one ouput (from ω_2) to the environment, namely o_e (rather than $o_{e,f}$, as we have dropped node f). This allows us to say that the *stream* flowing through ω_2 is the input i_b (to ω_2) transformed (by ω_2) to the output o_e (from ω_2). Regarding system ω_1, it has lost (comparing to ω_2) only one node e, but we set ω_1 boundaries in such a way that we only consider flows from b to c and from b to d—consequently, we consider neither inputs to b, nor outputs from c or d, and thus also do not consider the nodes' transformations. We will analyse ω_1 network—as a *supply network*—in Section V.

A. Two component systems

This section considers a system with two components A and B; in the environment, there are also other systems C, D, E and F which can connect to A and B, cf. Figure 4. If all the arrows shown in Figure 4 are present, then the binary code for this network will consist of six 1s representing that all six arrows j_1–j_6 are present; the code for this network can be found in row (1), column (a) of Table I. [It should be noted that neither *one component systems*, nor *three component systems* are considered here. The case of a one component system is trivial, as there would only be two possible arrows and four (2^2) possible networks: a system that receives an input from the environment and produces an output to the environment, a system that is a sink only system, a system that is a source only system, and an isolated system (without any arrows). The case of a three component systems would require considering twelve arrows (six arrows between the three nodes, and two arrows between each of the three nodes and the environment) and 2^{12} possible networks (although multiple networks would be have the same topology). Although such three (or more) component networks could be analysed in an analogous way to two component systems discussed in this section, a multi-component system would probably be initially partitioned into two subsystems (and therefore treated as a two component system), with simple interdependence between the components. For a specific multi-component network, the connectivity between the components could be simple, and given the network, in many cases there would only be a limited number of alternative topologies to which the network could transform. Multiple case studies should allow building a library of functioning complex networks, with different real world networks sharing the same abstract model; for instance, a particular food distribution network could be functioning in an exactly the same way as a particular information distribution network.]

Different connection topologies are determined by subsets of the set (of arrows) $J = \{j_1, \ldots, j_6\}$. Table I shows *binary codes* (indicating presence and absence of arrows in the given network) for systems with different subsets of J (and Figure 5 shows the corresponding systems). It is straightforward to order the resulting systems by the subset relation on the sets of directed edges present in the systems' topologies.

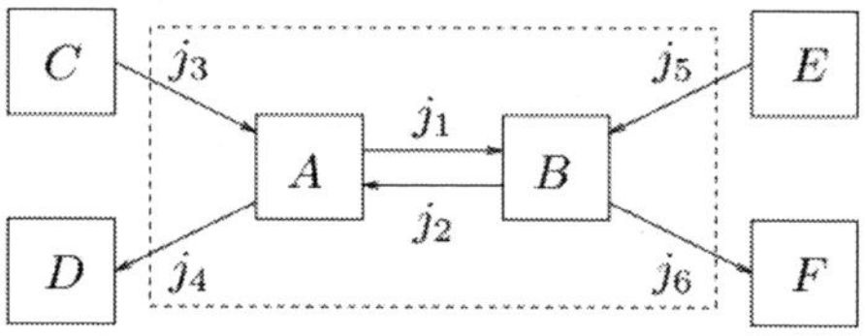

Figure 4. $S_{a_1} = S_{111111}$ with code $c_{a_1} = 111111$ indicating $\{j_1, \ldots, j_6\}$.

Table I consists of cells $(a, 1), \ldots, (h, 6)$ corresponding to the systems of Figure 5 and, therefore, these systems could be named $a_1, \ldots, h_6$. Hence, in Figure 5, the top system could be labelled a_1, the bottom system could be labelled h_6, and so on. Only some of these labels are used in Figure 5, but all labels can easily be derived from the correspondence between the nodes of Figure 5 and the cells of Table I (we will also use

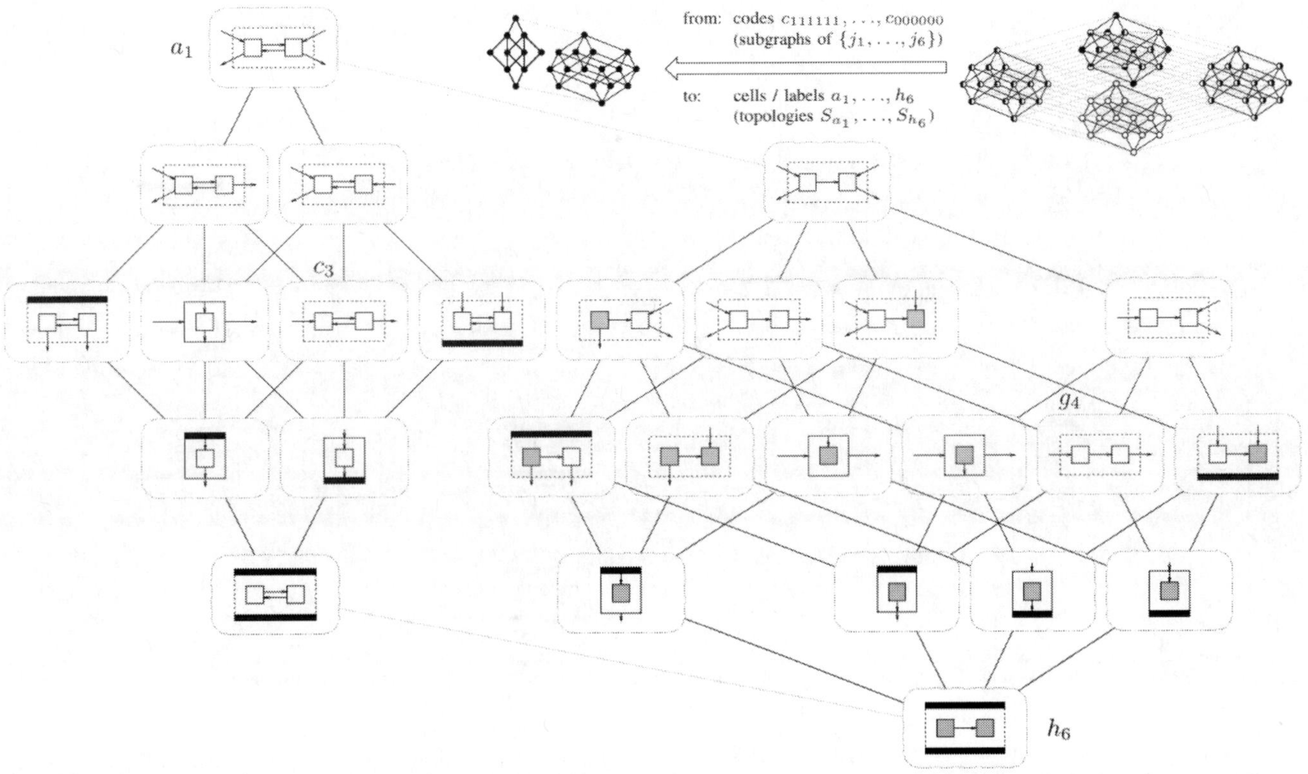

Figure 5. Ordering on $\boldsymbol{S}_J = \{S_{a_1}, \ldots, S_{h_6}\}$ with codes of Table I (the systems' labels—only a_1, c_3, g_4, h_6 are shown here—can be derived from Table I).

these labels for the systems presented in Figure 6). The ordered set $(\mathcal{P}(J), \subseteq)$) induces, in an obvious way, the order on $\boldsymbol{S}_J = \{S_{a_1}, \ldots, S_{h_6}\}$, as shown in Figure 5. It is the ordering of Figure 5 which places, for instance, the network a_1 (the best connected network which has the code 111111 indicating that all arrows are present) at the top of the ordered set, and the network h_6 (the least connected network which has two codes 100000 and 010000 indicating that the network topology is the topology of exactly one arrow between the components A and B of Figure 4; the topology with an arrow from A to B is equivalent to the topology with an arrow from B to A) at the bottom of the ordered set. This is why the code 111111 has been placed at the topmost row (row 1) of Table I and the codes 100000 and 010000 have been placed at the bottom-most row (row 6—or more precisely, rows 6a and 6b): it is the ordering of Figure 5 that has been used when placing the network codes in Table I.

$\boldsymbol{S}_J$ is the set of all posssible *connection topologies* (for a two component system). An alternative way of ordering $\boldsymbol{S}_J$ can be produced if we treat the systems in $\boldsymbol{S}_J$ as "objects" and consider some "properties" these systems have, rejecting the idea (which induced the ordering of Figure 5) that adding arrows makes the network "better" (cf. the paragraph below which discusses $g_4\uparrow$). Using the framework of *Formal Concept Analysis (FCA)* [9], we can form an *FCA context* K in which the systems in $\boldsymbol{S}_J$ are *FCA objects*, and some properties are used as *FCA properties*. Note that the FCA objects are (listing all FCA object): $\boldsymbol{S}_J = \{S_{a_1}, S_{a_2}, S_{b_2}, S_{h_2}, S_{a_3}, S_{b_3}, S_{c_3}, S_{d_3}, S_{e_3}, S_{f_3}, S_{g_3}, S_{h_3}, S_{a_4}, S_{b_4}, S_{c_4}, S_{d_4}, S_{e_4}, S_{f_4}, S_{g_4}, S_{h_4}, S_{a_5}, S_{e_5}, S_{f_5}, S_{g_5}, S_{h_5}, S_{h_6}\}$, i.e., $\text{card}(\boldsymbol{S}_J) = 26$. We need to determine what properties of systems in $\boldsymbol{S}_J$ should be considered.

TABLE I. CODES 111111, ..., 010000 AND CELLS (LABELS) $a_1, \ldots, h_6$.

	(a)	(b)	(c)	(d)	(e)	(f)	(g)	(h)
(1)	11 11 11							
(2a)	11 11 01	11 11 10						10 11 11
(2b)	11 01 11	11 10 11						01 11 11
(3a)	11 01 01	11 11 00	11 10 01	11 10 10	10 01 11	10 11 01	10 11 10	10 10 11
(3b)		11 00 11	11 01 10		01 11 01	01 01 11	01 10 11	01 11 10
(4a)	11 01 00	11 10 00	10 01 01	10 01 10	10 11 00	10 00 11	10 10 01	10 10 10
(4b)	11 00 01	11 00 10	01 01 01	01 10 01	01 00 11	01 11 00	01 01 10	01 10 10
(5a)	11 00 00				10 01 00	10 00 01	10 00 10	10 10 00
(5b)					01 00 01	01 01 00	01 10 00	01 00 10
(6a)								10 00 00
(6b)								01 00 00

We introduce the following definitions (note that we assume that there is at least one connection between the (two) components of the system).

Definition 1: (sink/source systems)
Let M be a two component system,

- if a component of M has only inputs, then this component is a *sink-only* system;
- if a component of M has only outputs, then this component is a *source-only* system;
- if M has a component that is a sink-only system, then

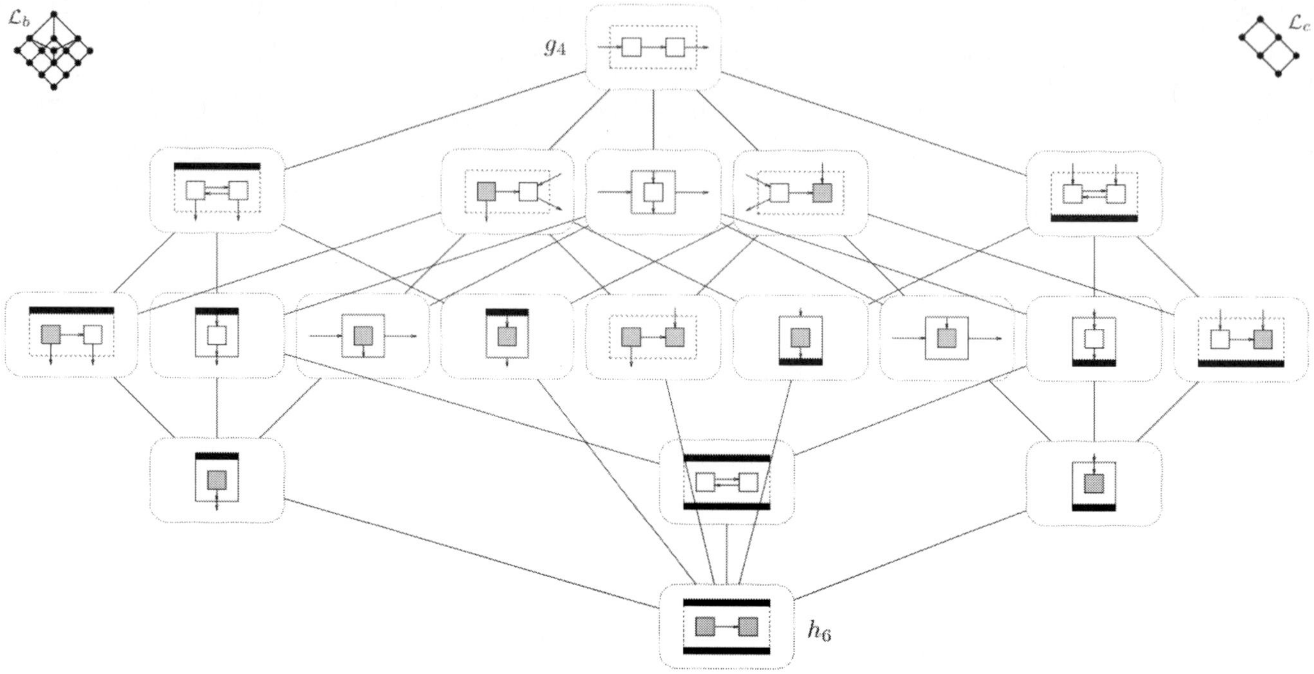

Figure 6. FCA concept lattice $\mathcal{L} = (\boldsymbol{S}_F, \leqslant)$ for context K of Table II (labels are collected in Table III; further comments are at the end of Section IV-A).

M is a *partial sink* system;

- if M has a component that is a source-only system, then M is a *partial source* system;
- if M—w.r.t. the environment—has only inputs, then M is a *total sink* system;
- if M—w.r.t. the environment—has only outputs, then M is a *total source* system;
- if a component of M is disconnected from the environment, then M is a *partially closed* system;
- if M—w.r.t. the environment—has neither inputs nor outputs, then M is a *totally closed* system.

TABLE II. AN FCA CONTEXT K.

	$n_\circ$	$n_\bullet$	$r_\circ$	$r_\bullet$	$c_\circ$
g_4					
b_3					×
a_3				×	
d_3		×			
a_4				×	×
b_4		×			×
a_5		×		×	×
e_3			×		
g_3	×				
c_4			×	×	
d_4	×		×		
e_4	×				×
f_4			×		×
h_4	×	×			
e_5	×			×	
f_5			×	×	×
g_5		×	×		
h_5	×	×			×
h_6	×	×	×	×	×

Using the symbols $n_\circ$, $n_\bullet$, $r_\circ$, $r_\bullet$, $c_\circ$, $c_\bullet$, for the predicates *partial sink*, *total sink*, *partial source*, *total source*, *partially closed*, *totally closed*, respectively, we have that $c_\bullet(S) \leftrightarrow n_\bullet(S) \wedge r_\bullet(S)$ (i.e., $c_\bullet$ can be expressed using $n_\bullet$ and $r_\bullet$). Hence, we use $n_\circ, n_\bullet, r_\circ, r_\bullet$ and $c_\circ$ as *properties* of systems and, therefore, employ the set $\{n_\circ, n_\bullet, r_\circ, r_\bullet, c_\circ\}$ as the set of *FCA properties*. The FCA context K of Table II associates the elements of $\boldsymbol{S}_J$ with properties in $\{n_\circ, n_\bullet, r_\circ, r_\bullet, c_\circ\}$.

Given the FCA context K of Table II, the corresponding *FCA concept lattice* $\mathcal{L}$ can be derived, and provides an ordering on *FCA concepts*—and, therefore, also an ordering on FCA objects, i.e., on systems of $\boldsymbol{S}_J$. The lattice $\mathcal{L}$ is shown in Figure 6 (given an FCA context, its FCA lattice can be constructed using the portal `latviz.loria.fr`). As mentioned before, we could use the labels $a_1, \ldots, h_6$ (corresponding to cells $(a, 1), \ldots, (h, 6)$ of Table I), to label the systems presented in Figure 6; these labels being collected in Table III. [Note that Table III provides labels for the nodes of the lattice of Figure 6 in a similar way as Table I provides labels for the nodes of the ordering of Figure 5.]

TABLE III. LABELS FOR THE FCA CONCEPT LATTICE OF FIGURE 6.

				g_4				
	a_3		e_3	b_3	g_3		d_3	
c_4	a_4	f_4	e_5	d_4	g_5	e_4	b_4	h_4
	f_5			a_5			h_5	
				h_6				

Notice (cf. Figure 5) that $g_4{\uparrow} = \{x \mid x \geq g_4\} = \{g_4, f_3, h_3, h_2, c_3, a_2, b_2, a_1\}$ and all the corresponding systems have none of the properties in $\{n_\circ, n_\bullet, r_\circ, r_\bullet, c_\circ\}$ (i.e., they are all *good* w.r.t. $\{n_\circ, n_\bullet, r_\circ, r_\bullet, c_\circ\}$) and, therefore, g_4

is included in Table II as the only representative of $g_4\uparrow$—this is why the set of systems reduced from $\mathrm{card}(\boldsymbol{S}_J) = 26$ to $19 = \mathrm{card}(\boldsymbol{S}_F)$, where $\boldsymbol{S}_F = \boldsymbol{S}_J \setminus \{S_j \mid j \in g_4\uparrow \setminus \{g_4\}\}$.

Figure 6 presents an FCA *concept lattice* $\mathcal{L}$ (for context K of Table II) with nodes being metabolic systems, and links indicating the health ordering, where the health of system ω is related to the set of its FCA properties $A_\omega \subseteq \{n_\circ, n_\bullet, r_\circ, r_\bullet, c_\circ\}$ (see Table II and Figure 6). Alternative sets of FCA properties and contexts could be used—consider the following contexts: (a) $A_a = \{n_\circ, n_\bullet, r_\circ, r_\bullet, c_\circ\}$ and context $K_a = K$ of Table II; (b) $A_b = A_a$ but K_b conforms to $n_\bullet \to n_\circ$ and $r_\bullet \to r_\circ$; (c) $A_c = \{n_\circ \vee r_\circ, n_\bullet \vee r_\bullet, c_\circ\}$ with K_c a modification of K_b. Note that Figure 6 shows the concept lattice $\mathcal{L}_a = \mathcal{L}$ for $K_a = K$, while the small inset lattices show FCA concept lattices $\mathcal{L}_b$ and $\mathcal{L}_c$ for the contexts K_b and K_c, respectively. The FCA objects $\boldsymbol{S}_F = \{S_{g_4}, \ldots, S_{h_6}\}$ form a lattice $\mathcal{L} = (\boldsymbol{S}_F, \leqslant)$, with "$\leqslant$" being the ordering relation. We expect the following: if $S_1 \leqslant S_2$ then $\mu(S_1) \leq \mu(S_2)$, where "μ" is a *numeric* (entropic, curvature based) measure on $\boldsymbol{S}_F$. [For additional information on FCA analysis of $\boldsymbol{S}_F$, cf. Appendix A.]

V. Supply Networks as Metabolic Networks

We consider a small supply network $\{b, c, d\}$ (which could be seen as a part of a larger network $\{a, b, c, d, f, g\}$); this supply network is shown in Figure 7, its self-adapting behaviour in Figure 8, and the list of nodes' *attitudes* in Table IV.

It will be demonstrated that the supply network of Figure 7 will, while adapting to the changing environment, exhibit a complex behaviour—note that it is the complex behaviour of the network that should be associated with the word "complex" in the term "complex network." For some research on using complex networks for supply chains, see [19][20].

We have specific values for the sets $\Theta, I, O, \Delta, \Phi, \Sigma, \Upsilon, \Gamma, \Psi, \Lambda, \Xi, \Pi$. We have $\Theta = \{\vartheta_b, \vartheta_c, \vartheta_d\}$ or simply $\Theta = \{b, c, d\}$. $I = \{i_{c.b}, i_{d.b}\}$. $O = \{o_{b.c}, o_{b.d}\}$. $\Delta = \varnothing_\Delta = \varnothing$ (because for node b we only consider its outputs (but not inputs), and for c and d we only consider their inputs (but not outputs)). $\Phi = \{\varphi_{b.c}, \varphi_{b.d}\}$. $\Lambda = \varnothing_\Lambda = \varnothing$ (it seems we will not have allostatic control mechanisms—but we will have some homeostatic ones). Σ and Υ would not be considered, given that all we have is flows from b to c and from b to d—however, if the system ω_2 of Figure 3 was considered, we could take $\Sigma = \{i_b.o_e\}$ and search for *pathways* Υ associated with the *streams* of Σ. Then, $\Xi = \varnothing_\Xi = \varnothing$ (because no interdependent networks are considered; but we would have interdependent networks, if we modeled *evacuation scenarios*, cf. Section VI). Π could be taken to be the flows $\Phi = \{\varphi_{b.c}, \varphi_{b.d}\}$—imposed by b on c and d (but earlier, possibly imposed on b by a).

Γ (catalysts) and Ψ (homeostatic control mechanisms)—omitted above—are the interesting ones, and we now analyse ω's *homeostatic control mechanisms* and *catalysts*. Figure 8 is almost self-explanatory: it demonstrates that both c and d will need to *split* (forming $\{c_1, c_2\}$ and $\{d_1, d_2\}$, respectively); then, c_2 and d_2 will need to *merge* in order to maximise efficiency while maintaining effectiveness.

Table IV shows (at lines 05–11) how nodes c and d calculate their *effectiveness* and *efficiency*. At line 13, c splits an ineffective node (namely, node c), and d splits an inefficient node (namely, node d). After the splits, we get (apart from

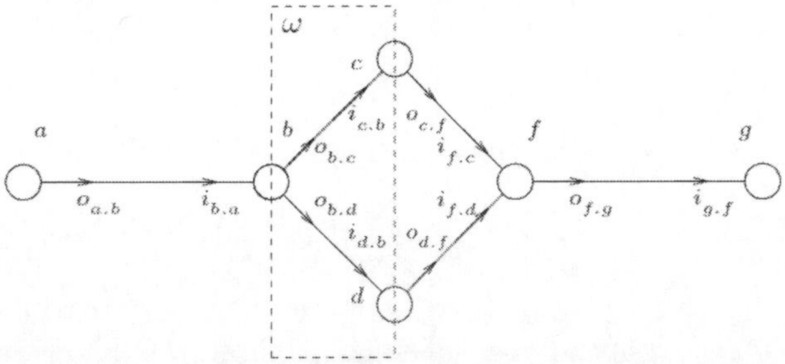

Figure 7. A metabolic supply network ω with nodes $\{b, c, d\}$.

effective and efficient nodes c_1 and d_1) an ineffective node c_2 (with 0 capability) and an inefficient node d_2 (with 0 flow). At line 25 (after a short negotiation) nodes c_2 and d_2 decide to *merge*, forming node e. It happens that e is both effective and efficient (if it was not, it would act in a way analogous to either c or d, and we would be left with an unmatched node with either 0 capability, or 0 flow, respectively); therefore, e accepts the flow of 2—the resulting system is, in this case, effective and efficient. The discussion demonstrates that the supply network can handle perturbations by using *homeostatic control mechanisms* of *split* and *merge*. Namely, we get the following. $\Psi = \{\psi_{\mathrm{split}}, \psi_{\mathrm{merge}}\}$ (more precisely, we get two types of *splits:* $\psi^{\mathrm{ineffect}}_{\mathrm{split}}$ (splitting an *ineffective* node), and $\psi^{\mathrm{ineffic}}_{\mathrm{split}}$ (splitting an *inefficient* node); regarding the merge operation $\psi_{\mathrm{merge}} = \psi^{\mathrm{c0f0}}_{\mathrm{merge}}$ *ineffective* nodes with 0 capability are merged with *inefficient* nodes with 0 flow). Regarding the catalyst, we have $\Gamma = \{\gamma_{\mathrm{ee}}\}$, and γ_{ee} should be understood as an *effectiveness and efficiency filter* that triggers the *split* and *merge* homeostatic control mechanisms. What the nodes *believe, intend,* and what (*split* and *merge*) operations they perform is shown in Table IV; however, some details—such as those related to *controlling, commanding, delegating, influencing* and *reporting*—are not included. Briefly: node c can *influence* node d by making d aware of c's beliefs or intentions; it can *command* node d by explicitly issuing a command (cf. line 23 in Table IV); or, finally, it can *control* other nodes (cf. lines 02–04 in Table IV). Work is underway on large scale supply networks self-adapting to perturbations, as described here.

Regarding *pathways* Υ, for ω of Figure 7, we have $\Upsilon = \varnothing$ (or rather $\Upsilon = \{\omega\}$). However, for large supply networks, it could easily be the case that pathways—corresponding to specific *functionalities*—could be identified (for instance, in food supply networks, we could identify pathways of *refrigerated* supplies). Regarding *interdependent networks* Ξ and *perturbations* Π we have $\Xi = \varnothing$ and $\Pi = \varnothing$. However, when evacuation scenarios are considered, they bring interdependent networks, cf. Section VI.

VI. Evacuation Scenarios

A simple evacuation scenario involving *people, buses* and *fuel* is presented in Figure 9.

The scenario of Figure 9 involves three *interdependent networks:* ω_P is a network consisting of three nodes, $\Theta_P = \{\vartheta^b_P, \vartheta^c_P, \vartheta^d_P\}$ with *flows of people;* ω_B is a network consisting of three nodes, $\Theta_B = \{\vartheta^b_B, \vartheta^c_B, \vartheta^d_B\}$ with

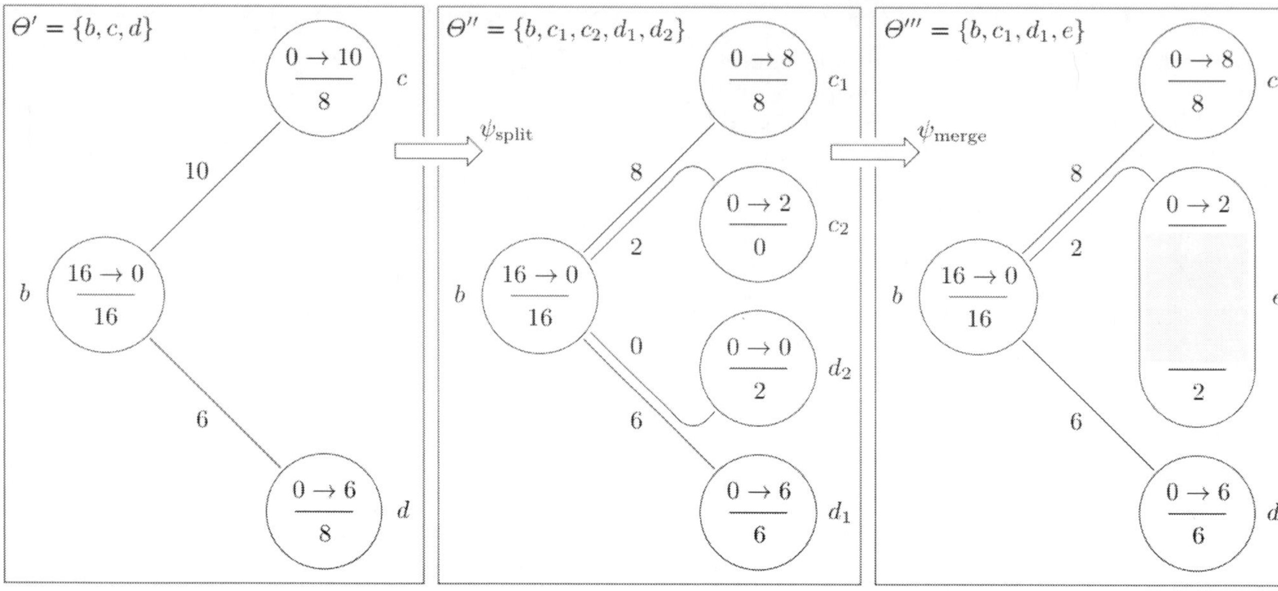

Figure 8. Self-adapting metabolic complex network $\omega(\Theta, I, O)$ with $\Theta' = \{b, c, d\}$, $\Theta'' = \{b, c_1, c_2, d_1, d_2\}$ and $\Theta''' = \{b, c_1, d_1, e\}$.

flows of buses; ω_F is a network consisting of three nodes, $\Theta_F = \{\vartheta_F^b, \vartheta_F^c, \vartheta_F^d\}$ with *flows of fuel.* The network ω_P can *request services* from ω_B—in order to evacute people, ω_P needs services that ω_B can provide; however, what is important is that the request for services obtained by ω_B can be seen as *perturbations* that ω_B has to handle. Similarly, the network ω_B can *request services* from ω_F—in order to run buses, ω_B needs services (namely: fuel) that ω_F can provide; again, it is important to note that the request for services obtained by ω_F can be seen as *perturbations* that ω_F has to handle.

This scenario will be further analysed in our future work—but the point we can make now is that we can see *perturbations* as interactions between *interdependent networks.*

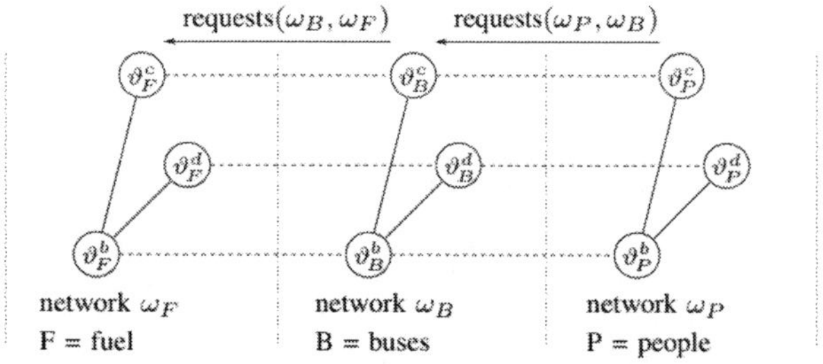

Figure 9. Evacuation scenario.

VII. Ontologies for robotics

There is a push for building autonomous systems, and autonomous robots. Given that autonomous robots' capabilities are becoming more complex, there is an urgent need to clarify such concepts as *capability, function, behaviour* and *structure.* Such analysis, however, could be performed at different levels, with capabilities (and the related functions and behaviours) being associated with some identified *conceptual levels.* Dennett [10] suggested the *intentional stance,* explaining that when conceptualising and analysing the world we might do so at different levels; he suggested a *physical level,* a *design (or functional) level,* and an *intentional level.* At the physical level, we use physics and physical properties (such as colour and size) to describe and understand the world. At the design level, we abstract away from physics and use such relations as *transform, move, attach, emit, sense, interpret* and *inform* (such relations have been employed in the Consensus system [21]). Using intentional level we ascribe *beliefs* (and other *attitudes*) to systems, for instance, we might say that a thermostat-controlled air-conditionning system has a belief "it's too hot in here" [22] (we should see such a system as an autonomous system capable of handling the temperature *perturbations*). Dennett has also mentioned a "person level"—but maybe "autonomy level" would be more appropriate, with *metabolic autonomy* understood as the capability to handle (various types of) perturbations. If Dennett's scheme was extended by adding the metabolic autonomy level, then the required concepts would include *pathways, homeostasis* and *perturbations.* Such an extension might be necessary if we want our robots to be robustly autonomous (i.e., resilient to perturbations).

The metabolic approach provides the highest level of the conceptualisation: we could consider a *metaphysical level* for *space, time, matter* (without physical boundaries), then Dennett's *physical, design* and *intentional level.* At the intentional level, we can have beliefs and intentions of single agents, but we can also have attitudes—and transfers of attitudes (including *influences* and *delegations*)—at the social level (of groups of agents). Finally, we have a *metabolic autonomy level* (with pathways, homeostatic control and perturbations). The following list provides some *conceptual relations* at those levels:

1) *metaphysical:* spatially / temp. connects, orients;
2) *physical:* temperature, size, rigidity, toxicity;
3) *design:* senses, moves, transforms, interprets;

TABLE IV. SELF-ADAPTING METABOLIC COMPLEX NETWORK $\omega(\Theta, I, O)$ MODIFYING ITS NODES AND FLOWS.

```
    intends(a,  intends(b,  flow([b,{c,d}], [t1,t2], 16)))
[t1,t2]
    intends(b,  flow([b,{c,d}], [t1,t2], 16))
    intends(b,  intends(c, flow([b,c], [t1,t2], 10))) % ............................... push([b,c], 10)
    intends(b,  intends(d, flow([b,d], [t1,t2],  6))) % ............................... push([b,d],  6)
        intends(c, flow([b,c], [t1,t2], 10))          intends(d, flow([b,d], [t1,t2], 6))
        believes(c, capability(c, 8))                 believes(d, capability(d, 8))
        believes(c, state-curr(c, t1, 0))             believes(d, state-curr(d, t1, 0))
        believes(c, state-next-flw(c, t2, 10))        believes(d, state-next-flw(d, t2, 6))
        believes(c, state-next-cap(c, t2,  8))        believes(d, state-next-cap(d, t2, 6))
        believes(c, state-next-max(c, t2,  8))        believes(d, state-next-max(d, t2, 8))
        believes(c, effective(c, [t1,t2], 8/10))      believes(d, effective(d, [t1,t2], 6/6))
        believes(c, efficient(c, [t1,t2], 8/8))       believes(d, efficient(d, [t1,t2], 6/8))
        believes(c, ineffective(c, [t1,t2]))          believes(d, inefficient(d, [t1,t2]))
        splits-ineffective-node(c, [c, [c1, c2]])     splits-inefficient-node(d, [d, [d1, d2]])
        intends(c,  flow([b,c1], [t1,t2], 8))         intends(d, flow([b,d1], [t1,t2], 6))
        intends(c,  flow([b,c2], [t1,t2], 2))         intends(d, flow([b,d2], [t1,t2], 0))
        believes(c1, effective-efficient(c1)*)        believes(d1, effective-efficient(d1)*) % pull([c1,b], 8)
        believes(c2, ineffective(c2, [t1,t2]))        believes(d2, inefficient(d2, [t1,t2])) % pull([d1,b], 6)
        believes(c2, capability(c2, 0))               believes(d2, capability(d2, 2)
        intends(c2,  flow([b,c2], [t1,t2], 2))        intends(d2, flow([b,d2], [t1,t2], 0))
        believes(c2,t1,effective(c2,[t1,t2],0))       believes(d2, t1, effective(d2, [t1,t2], 1))
        believes(c2,t1,efficient(c2,[t1,t2],1))       believes(d2, t1, efficient(d2, [t1,t2], 0))
        believes(c2,t1,ineffective-w0c(c2,[t1,t2])) believes(d2, t1, inefficient-w0f(d2, [t1,t2]))
        commands(c2,d2,offer(flow(c2,d2,t*,2)))
                                                      accepts (d2, c2, offer(flow(c2,d2,t*,2)))
        agrees(c2, t1, merge([c2,d2],e,[t1,t2]))      agrees(d2, t1, merge([c2,d2],e[t1,t2]))
            merges-0-cap-nodes-with-0-flw-nodes([c2,d2], [[c2, d2], e])
            believes(e, capability(e,       2))
            intends(e,  flow([b,e, [t1,t2], 2)) .......................................% pull([e,b],  2)
```

4) *intentional:* believes, intends, obligates, influences;
5) *metabolic:* perturbs, homeo-allostatically controls.

[For information on the conceptualisation cf. Appendix B.]

We could consider the following examples of metabolic streams at the above five levels: (1) streams of gravitational forces; (2) flows of water through a city; (3) streams of aircraft's radar readings transformed into movement maneuvers; (4) streams of beliefs, intentions, influences and obligations during a country's elections; (5) streams of modifications to city's infrastructure systems' homeostatic control mechanisms. It should be noted that many conceptual relations can be found at multiple levels in the above conceptualisation—consider e.g., *connects, senses* or *strikes* (with a *weapon*). It should also be noted that a metabolic system, in order to keep functioning (or keep living) should be continuously monitoring the environment in order to detect and handle all perturbations that have the potential to push the system out of the equilibrium state—it seems that this process of monitoring and handling perturbations constitutes the system's top-level goal. To test, verify and progress with such a framework, multiple case studies should be performed (such case studies could vary widely w.r.t. both domains and scale).

We are also interested in *non-monotonic ontology evolution,* cf. the last paragraph of Section VIII.

VIII. FUTURE WORK

There is a growing need to design and build robust autonomous systems; some domains, research areas and mathematical tools related to autonomy are listed in Table V.

TABLE V. DOMAINS AND TOOLS FOR AUTONOMY.

curvature & entropy	Forman-Ricci Ollivier-Ricci	$\overset{d \leftarrow c}{\longleftarrow}$	Ricci curvature (on manifolds)
maths	geometry		geometry
measures	■ generic entropy/curvature-based measures ↓ ■ specific performance measures (cf. generic meas.) ↑		
concepts	robustness resil. to pert.	$\overset{?}{\longleftarrow}$	robustness
	↕ perturbations	≡	↕ perturbations
	self-adaptation	≡	self-adaptation
	autonomy	≡	autonomy
maths sub-area area	graph th. & topology complex networks networks	$\overset{appr}{\longrightarrow}$	diff. equations complex dyn. sys. dynamical systems
domain	discrete		continuous

However, there is no consensus on the concepts of autonomy or robustness; sometimes robustness is considered to be a property that a system is said to possess if it does not fail some *proposed performance tests.* Autonomy is usually understood as ability to function without external control—but it has to be added that this ability should survive certain *changes (perturbations)* occurring in the complex (dynamic, uncertain) environment. Robustness, understood as *resilience to perturbations,* is closely related to self-adaptation; and it is the notion of perturbations that links robustness with adaptation—as indicated in the *concept rows* of Table V.

TABLE VI. TWO COMPONENT SYSTEMS: LABELS, CODES, GRAPHS AND TOPOLOGIES (PART 1 OF 3).

(1) label l	(2) code c	(3) graph $J_c\ (\subseteq J)$	(4) topology T_l	(5) topology T_l^c	(6) topology T_l^m
g_4	10 10 01 01 01 10	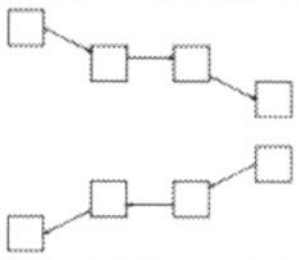	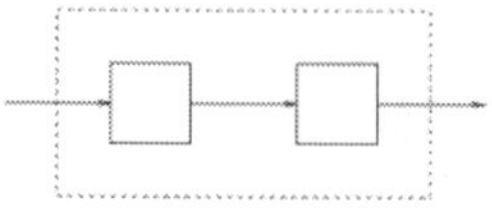	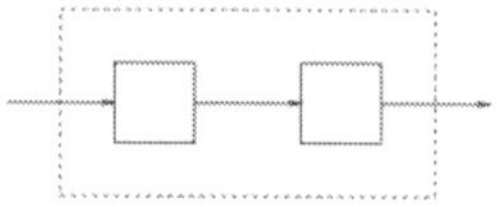	
a_3	11 01 01	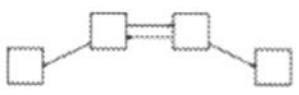	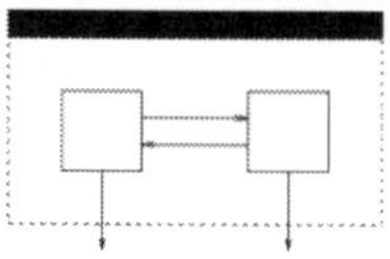	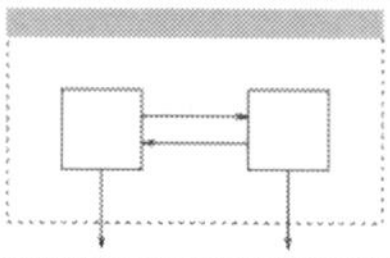	
e_3	10 01 11 01 11 01	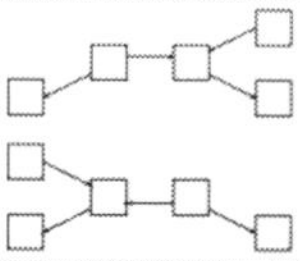	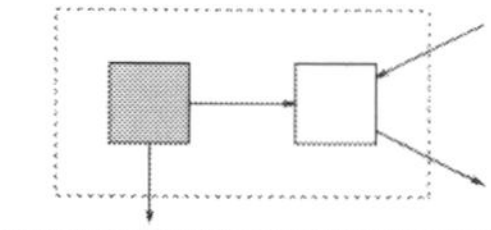	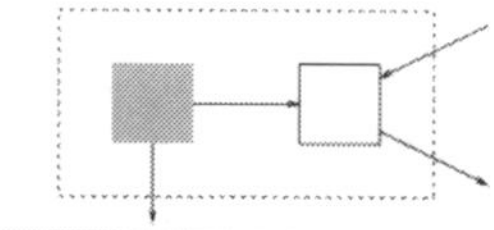	
b_3	11 11 00 11 00 11	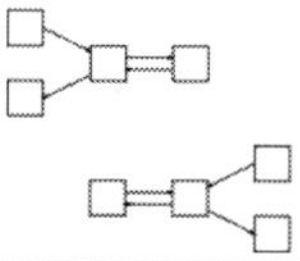	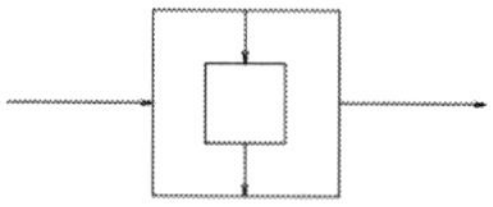	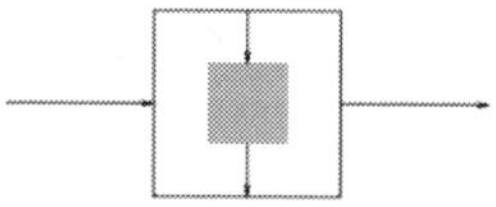	
g_3	10 11 10 01 10 11	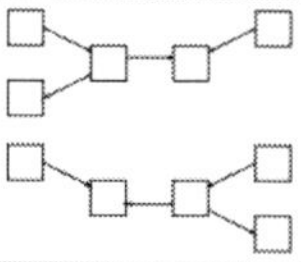	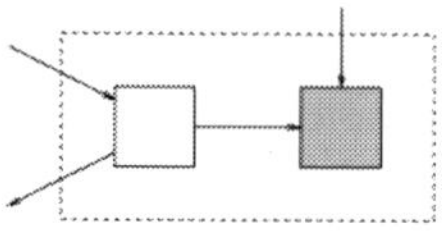	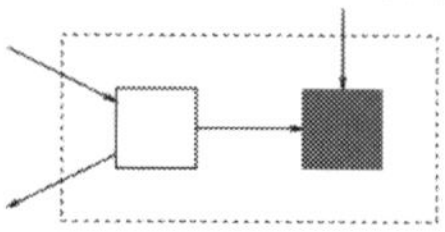	
d_3	11 10 10	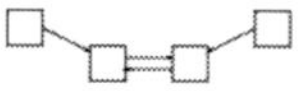	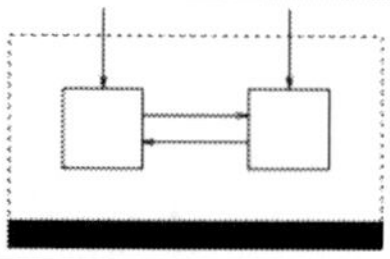	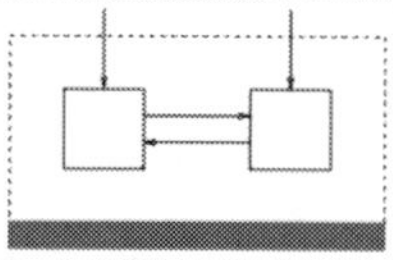	
c_4	10 01 01 01 01 01	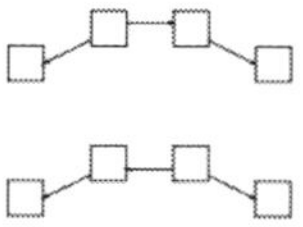	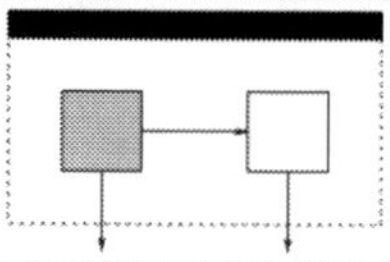	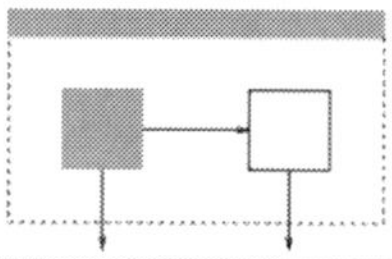	

Given a functioning system ω, it seems appropriate to say that: *autonomous*$(\omega) \leftrightarrow$ *self-adaptable*$(\omega) \leftrightarrow$ *robust*(ω). Furthermore, *robustness* has been linked to *curvature* and *entropy* [4]; therefore, entropic curvature-based measures could be applied to assess systems' *robustness.* It should be noted that curvatures are geometric notions; they have been recently considered appropriate for quantifying functionality and robustness of networks [4]. The top part of Table V shows that *discretisations* (changing from *continuous* to *discrete*) have been applied to Ricci curvature to produce (discrete) Forman-Ricci and Ollivier-Ricci curvatures. The second line of Table V, labelled *measures,* indicates that a promising line of research should investigate: (a) entropy/curvature based measures that should apply to systems in general; (b) performance/functionality related measures for specific systems (such as *supply networks*); (c) relating general entropic measures (of (a)) to specific performance measures (of (b)) for selected classes of systems.

We also have work underway looking at *non-monotonic ontology evolution.* Ontologies have traditionally been developed monotonically in the sense of them being built by additively including additional concepts. This assumes that the problem is fixed and we can build, eventually, a full and correct account of the universe of discourse. This does not suffice for a changing problem environment where we have to adapt. The insight is that what is required is a set of bounding conditions within which we allow non-monotonic ontology change; these bounding conditions would be related to regimes of behaviour picked out by order parameters as mechanisms of abstraction.

IX. CONCLUSION

This paper provides a description of the *Metabolic Complex Networks (MCN)* framework and an analysis of *supply networks* from the perspective of the MCN framework; the obtained set of *homeostatic control mechanisms* $\Psi = \{\psi_{\text{split}}, \psi_{\text{merge}}\}$ is appropriate. Research on adaptive supply networks [7][19][20][23]–[24] and large scale implementation (using Python and NetworkX) are underway.

The essential components of the framework are:

TABLE VII. TWO COMPONENT SYSTEMS: LABELS, CODES, GRAPHS AND TOPOLOGIES (PART 2 OF 3).

(1) label l	(2) code c	(3) graph J_c ($\subseteq J$) / (4) topology T_l / (5) topology T_l^c / (6) topology T_l^m
a_4	11 01 00 11 00 01	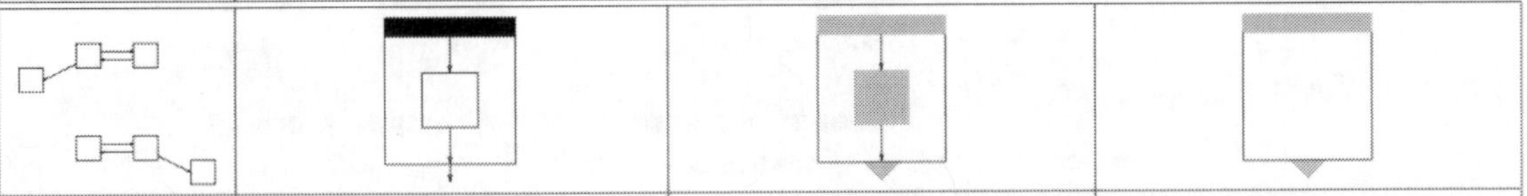
f_4	10 00 11 01 11 00	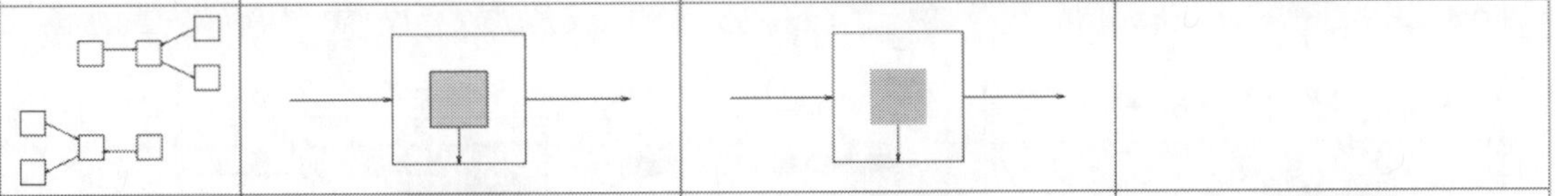
e_5	10 01 00 01 00 01	
d_4	10 01 10 01 10 01	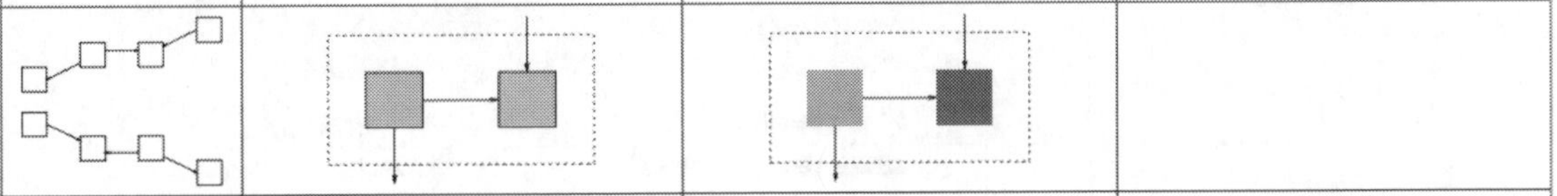
g_5	10 00 10 01 10 00	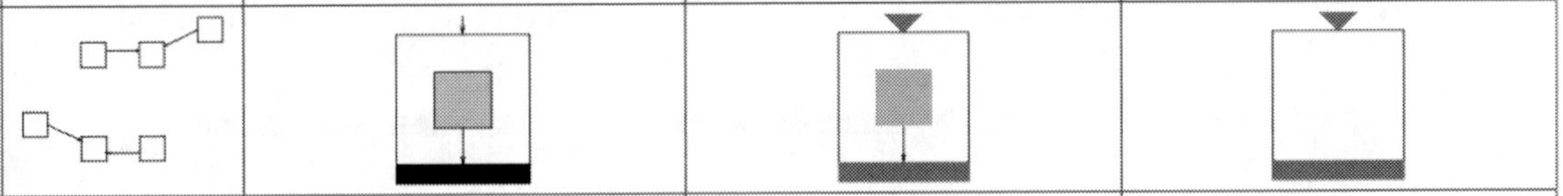
e_4	10 11 00 01 00 11	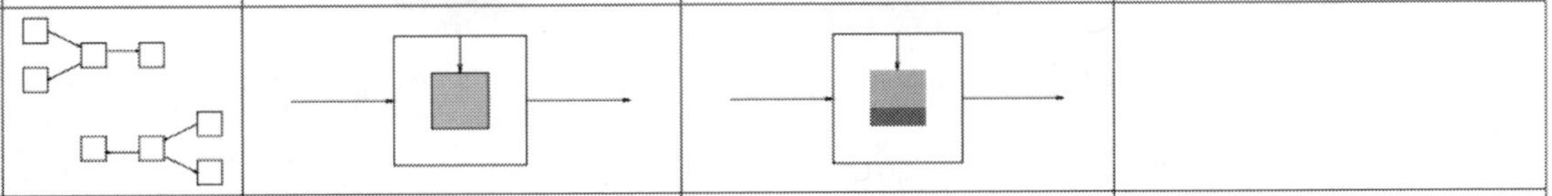
b_4	11 10 00 11 00 10	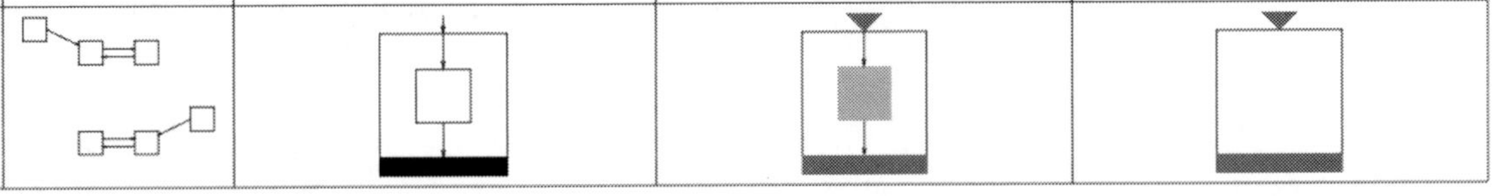

I. ONTOLOGY: conceptual understanding of the domain;
II. METABOLISM: homeostatic handling of perturbations;
III. CURVATURE: entropic quantifying of robustness.

Future work—sketched in Section VIII—will focus on a metabolic analysis of evacuation operations expanded by an entropic analysis of robustness of the selected systems.

ACKNOWLEDGMENT

La démarche de chercher à comprendre les réseaux complexes comme des systèmes métaboliques est née lors du séjour du premier auteur à Rouen, en France, en décembre 2018 et janvier 2019. Merci à Thérèse et Daniel Caillemet pour la création d'un environnement métabolique excellent, impossible à trouver ailleurs.

APPENDIX

A. *FCA analysis of two component systems*

This appendix provides details on the FCA analysis of Section IV-A. Tables VI–VIII show labels, codes and ways to visualise the systems and facilitate the construction of FCA contexts (colours *magenta/orange/cyan* indicate *sink/source/closed* ($n_\circ/r_\circ/c_\circ$), respectively). In Tables VI, VII and VIII, the following columns are used: (1) label l, with labels $a_1, \ldots, h_6$ corresponding to the cells $(a, 1), \ldots, (h, 6)$ of Table I; (2) code c, identifying the subset J_c of J—these codes have been collected in Table I; (3) graph J_c ($\subseteq J$), showing input–output connections between the two components of the system and the environment—note that Figure 4 shows the graph J_{111111} (of system S_{111111}) for code $c = 111111$; (4) topology T_l, representing the connection topology of graph J_c, with the association between the label l and the code c provided in Table I (note that multiple codes can be associated with a single label, as multiple graphs can have the same connection topology); these topologies have been shown in Figures 5 and 6; (5) topology T_l^c, visualising topology T_l differently, using colour; (6) topology T_l^m, a modification of T_l^c.

The contexts K_b and K_c mentioned in Section IV-A are provided in Tables IX and X; their concept lattices $\mathcal{L}_b$ and $\mathcal{L}_c$ were provided in Figure 6.

TABLE VIII. TWO COMPONENT SYSTEMS: LABELS, CODES, GRAPHS AND TOPOLOGIES (PART 3 OF 3).

(1) label l	(2) code c	(3) graph J_c ($\subseteq J$)	(4) topology T_l	(5) topology T_l^c	(6) topology T_l^m
h_4	10 10 10	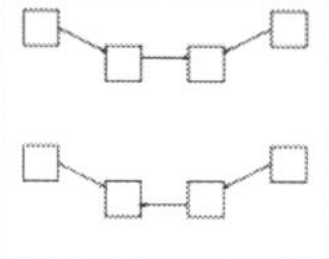	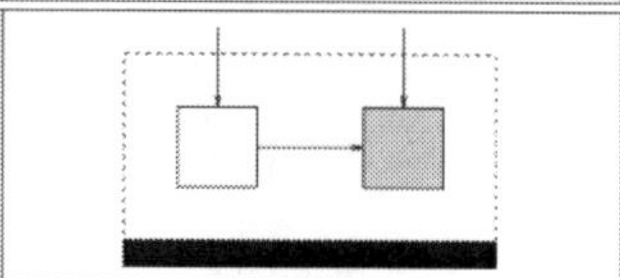	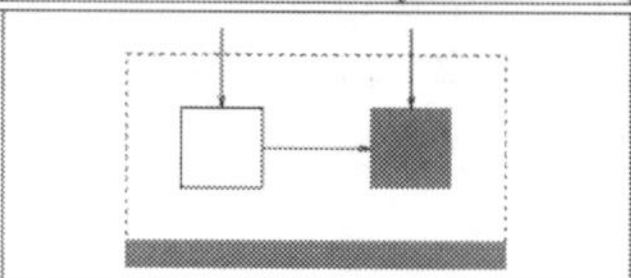	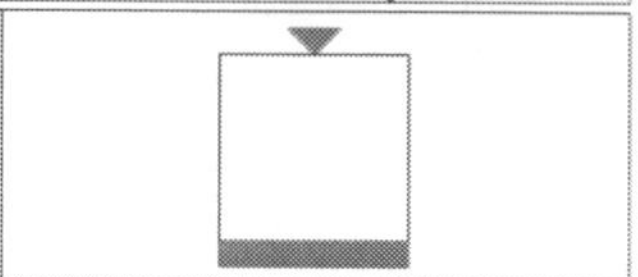
	01 10 10				
f_5	10 00 01	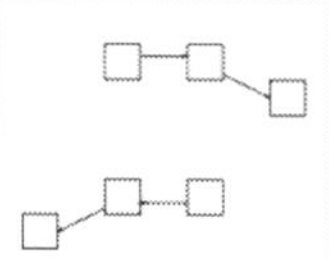	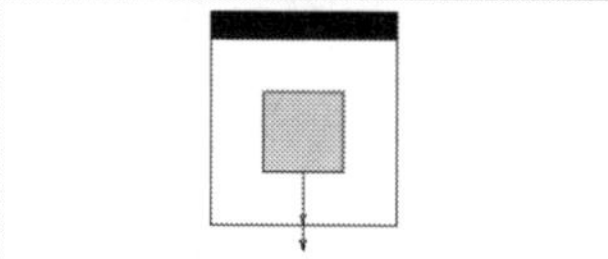	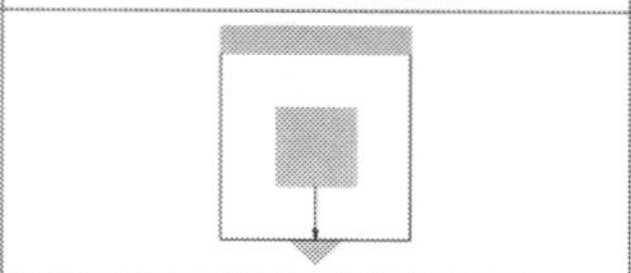	
	01 01 00				
a_5	11 00 00	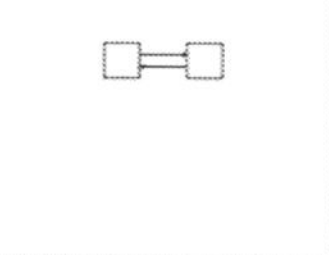	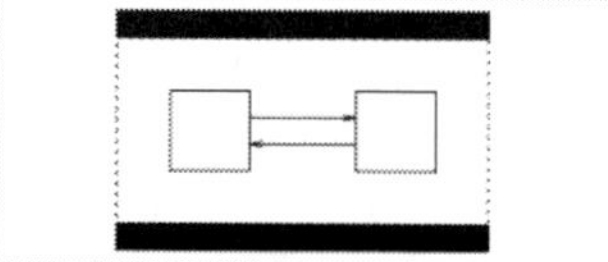	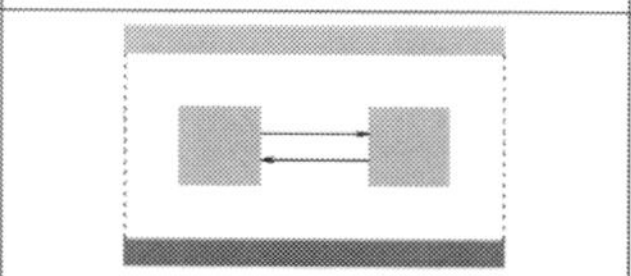	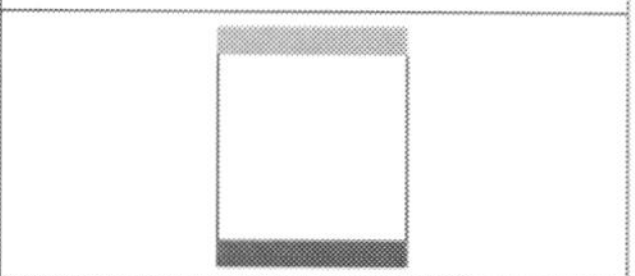
h_5	10 10 00	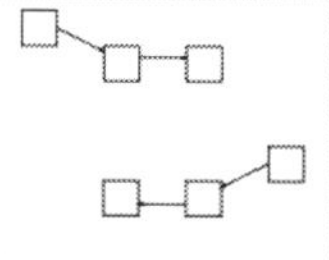	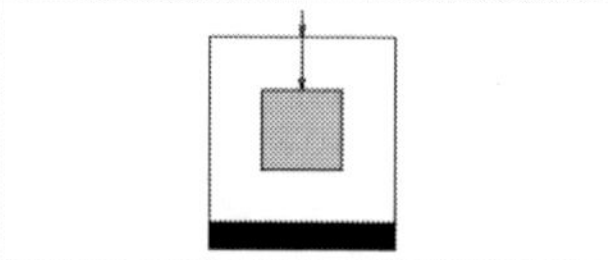	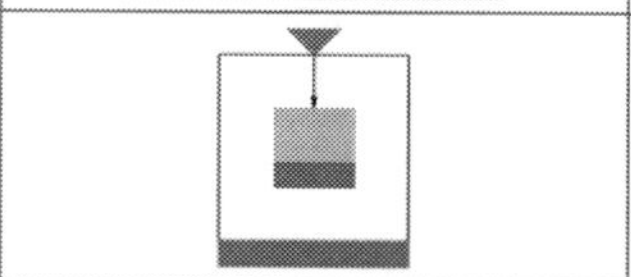	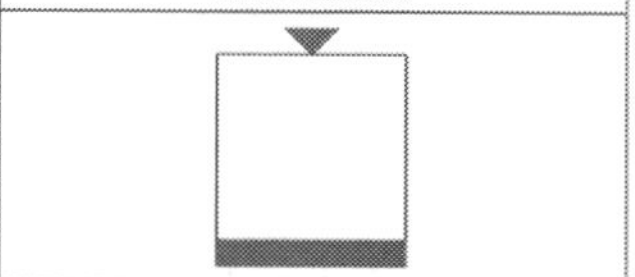
	01 00 10				
h_6	10 00 00	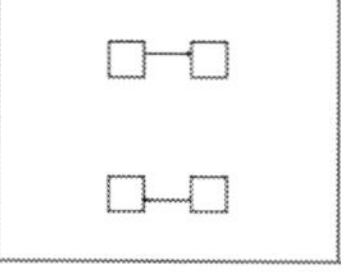	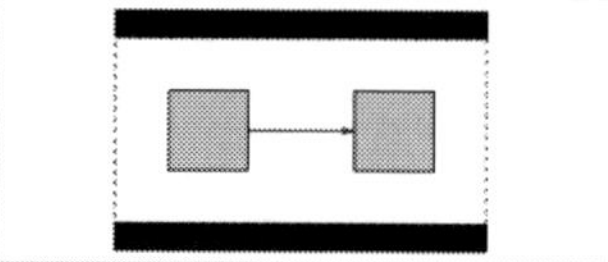	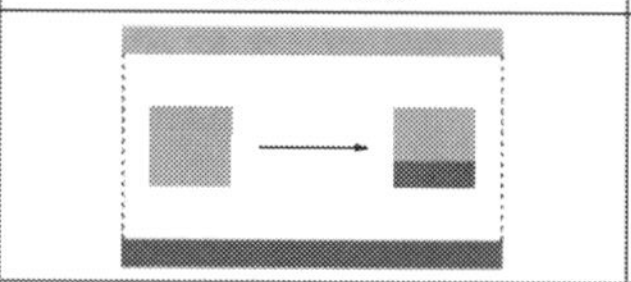	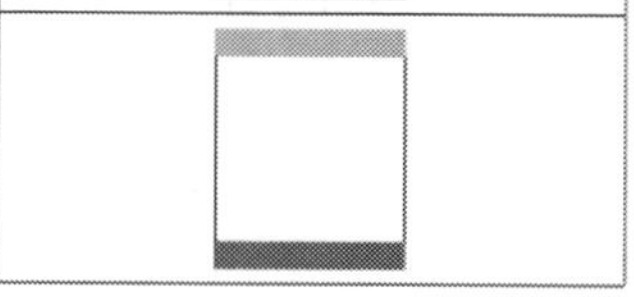
	01 00 00				

TABLE IX. AN FCA CONTEXT K_b.

	$n_\circ$	$n_\bullet$	$r_\circ$	$r_\bullet$	$c_\circ$
g_4					
b_3					×
a_3			×	×	
d_3	×	×			
a_4			×	×	×
b_4	×	×			×
a_5	×	×	×	×	×
e_3			×		
g_3	×				
c_4			×	×	
d_4	×		×		
e_4	×				×
f_4			×		×
h_4	×	×			
e_5	×		×	×	×
f_5			×	×	×
g_5	×	×	×		×
h_5	×	×			×
h_6	×	×	×	×	×

TABLE X. AN FCA CONTEXT K_c.

	$n_\circ \vee r_\circ$	$n_\bullet \vee r_\bullet$	$c_\circ$
g_4			
b_3			×
a_3	×	×	
d_3	×	×	
a_4	×	×	×
b_4	×	×	×
a_5	×	×	×
e_3	×		
g_3	×		
c_4	×	×	
d_4	×		
e_4	×		×
f_4	×		×
h_4	×	×	
e_5	×	×	×
f_5	×	×	×
g_5	×	×	×
h_5	×	×	×
h_6	×	×	×

B. *Conceptualising metabolic systems*

Regarding the conceptualisation, the following list of *conceptual relations* was presented in Section VII.

1. *metaphysical:* spatially / temporally connects, orients;
2. *physical:* temperature, colour, weight, rigidity, toxicity;
3. *design:* senses, moves, transforms, interprets, informs;
4. *intentional:* believes, intends, obligates, influences;
5. *metabolic:* perturbs, homeo-allostatically controls.

We list selected *concepts* and *relations* for the above five levels.

1) metaphysical level
   a) `process, spatial, temporal`
   b) `connects, meets`
   c) `distance, between`
2) physical level
   a) `temperature` (+ physical props/rels)
   b) `toxicity` (+ chemical props/rels)

3) design level
   a) `transforms`
   b) `damages, repairs, enables`
   c) `attaches, moves`
   d) `emits, senses`
   e) `interprets, informs`
4) intentional level
   a) `believes, desires, intends`
   b) `permits, obligates`
   c) `influences, controls`
   d) `delegates`
5) metabolic level
   a) `perturbs`
   b) `detects-perturbation`
   c) `handles-perturbation`
   d) `homeostatically-controls`
   e) `allostatically-controls`

In the remainder of this appendix, we provide further comments on the above ontological concepts and relations by listing some frameworks and examples. For instance, (1b) clarifies that *connects* and *meets* are the primitive relations of the *Region Connection Calculus (RCC)* framework [25] and of Allen's *interval algebra* [26], respectively, while (3a) lists three examples of *transformation:* biological metamorphosis, cellular respiration ($\rightarrow$) & photosynthesis ($\leftarrow$), and transformation of mercury (Hg) into gold (Au).

Metaphysical level (1)—existence, space, time
(1b) `connects` [25] and `meets` [26]
(1c) *qualitative distance* (e.g., `near` and `far`) [27]
(1c) `between`: cf. *[Paris/1915, Berlin/1910, Moscow/1905]*
Physical level (2)—the domain of *physics* and *chemistry*
(2a) physical properties: temperat., colour, mass, size, texture
(2b) chemical properties: toxicity, flammability, chem. stabil.
Design level (3)—above the level of physics and chemistry
(3a) `transforms`: *metamorph.*, $C_6H_{12}O_6 \leftrightarrow CO_2$, $Hg \rightarrow Au$
Intentional level (4)—attitudes (information, pro, normative)
(4a) `believes, intends`: cf. $B_i \neg\alpha \wedge B_i I_j B_i \alpha$ [28]
(4b) `permits`: cf. $P_{k,i}\,[\text{protects}(i,i)] \leftarrow I_j\,[\text{kills}(j,i)]$
(4c) `influences`: *"Ann influences Ben to control Craig"*
Metabolic level (5)—functioning despite *perturbations*
(5a) `perturbs`: cf. earthquake, flood, socio-techn. systems
(5b) `detects perturb.`: cf. earthquake warning system
(5c) `handles perturb.`: cf. flood mitigation dams
(5d) `homeostatically controls`: cf. air-cond. system
(5e) `allostatically controls`: social adaptation [29].

References

[1] S. H. Strogatz, "Exploring complex networks," *Nature*, vol. 410, pp. 268–276, 2001.
[2] X. F. Wang and G. Chen, "Complex Networks: Small-World, Scale-Free and Beyond," *IEEE Circuits and Systems Magazine*, pp. 6–20, 2003.
[3] A.-L. Barabási and E. Bonabeau, "Scale-free networks," *Scientific American*, vol. 288, pp. 50–59, 2003.
[4] A. R. Tannenbaum et al., "Graph curvature and the robustness of cancer networks," 2015, arXiv 1502.04512.
[5] J. Sia, E. Jonckheere, and P. Bogdan, "Ollivier-Ricci curvature-based method to community detection in complex networks," *Scientific Reports*, vol. 9, pp. 1–12, 2019.
[6] M. Magoni, "Resilience thinking and urban metabolism in spatial planning: which possible integrations," *City, Territory and Architecture*, vol. 4, pp. 1–8, 2017.
[7] P. G. Flikkema and M. Vigil-Hayes, "Self-adaptive and resilient urban networking infrastructure for disasters and smart city services," in *IEEE International Conference on Big Data*, pp. 4074–4079, 2017.
[8] C.-C. Ni, Y.-Y. Lin, F. Luo, and J. Gao, "Community Detection on Networks with Ricci Flow," *Scientific Reports*, vol. 9, pp. 1–12, 2019.
[9] B. Ganter and R. Wille, *Formal Concept Analysis. Mathematical Foundations*. Springer, 1996.
[10] D. C. Dennett, *The Intentional Stance*. The MIT Press, 1987.
[11] A. Samal et al., "Comparative analysis of two discretizations of Ricci curvature for complex networks," *Scientific Reports*, vol. 8, pp. 1–16, 2018.
[12] D. J. Reid, "An Autonomy Interrogative," in *Foundations of Trusted Autonomy* (H. A. Abbass, J. Scholz, and D. J. Reid, eds.), pp. 365–391, Springer, 2018.
[13] D. L. Nelson and M. M. Cox, *Lehninger Principles of Biochemistry*. W. H. Freeman and Company, 2008.
[14] A.-L. Barabási and R. Albert, "Emergence of scaling in random networks," *Science*, vol. 286, pp. 509–512, 1999.
[15] D. J. Watts and S. H. Strogatz, "Collective dynamics of "small-world" networks," *Nature*, vol. 393, pp. 440–442, 1998.
[16] S. Okuda et al., "KEGG Atlas mapping for global analysis of metabolic pathways," *Nucleic Acids Research*, vol. 36, no. 1, pp. W423–W426, 2008.
[17] P. V. Sengbusch, *Metabolic Pathways*, 1998 (accessed January 26, 2020). https://s3.lite.msu.edu/res/msu/botonl/b_online/ e19_1/metabol.htm.
[18] *Biochemical Pathways, Part 1: Metabolic Pathways*. F. Hoffmann-La Roche AG, 2020 (accessed January 26, 2020). http://biochemical-pathways.com/#/map/1.
[19] E. J. S. Hearnshaw and M. M. J. Wilson, "A complex network approach to supply chain network theory," *International Journal of Operations & Production Management*, vol. 33, pp. 442–469, 2013.
[20] S. I. Mari, Y. H. Lee, and M. S. Memon, "Complex network theory-based approach for designing resilient supply chain networks," *International Journal of Logistics Systems and Management*, vol. 21, pp. 365–384, 2015.
[21] D. A. Lambert, A. Saulwick, and K. Trentelman, "Consensus: A comprehensive solution to the Grand Challenges of Information Fusion," in *Proceedings of the 18th International Conference on Information Fusion*, pp. 908–915, 2015.
[22] J. Searle, *Minds, brains and science*. Harvard University Press, 1985.
[23] S. S. N. Perera, M. G. H. Bell, and M. C. J. Bliemer, "Modelling supply chains as complex networks for investigating resilience: an improved methodological framework," in *37th Australasian Transport Research Forum*, pp. 1–16, 2015.
[24] A. Surana, S. Kumara, M. Greaves, and U. N. Raghavan, "Supply-chain networks: a complex adaptive systems perspective," *International Journal of Production Research*, vol. 43, pp. 4235–4265, 2005.
[25] D. A. Randell, Z. Cui, and A. G. Cohn, "A spatial logic based on regions and connection," in *3rd Int. Conf. on Knowledge Representation and Reasoning* (B. Nebel, C. Rich, and W. Swartout, eds.), pp. 165–176, Morgan Kaufmann, 1992.
[26] J. F. Allen, "Maintaining knowledge about temporal intervals," *Communications of the ACM*, vol. 26, no. 11, pp. 832–843, 1983.
[27] D. Hernández, E. Clementini, and P. D. Felice, "Qualitative distances," in *Spatial Information Theory A Theoretical Basis for GIS. COSIT 1995* (A. U. Frank and W. Kuhn, eds.), pp. 45–57, Springer, 1995.
[28] W. van der Hoek and M. Wooldridge, "Towards a logic of rational agency," *L. J. of the IGPL*, vol. 11, pp. 133–157, 2003.
[29] J. Schulkin, "Social allostasis: Anticipatory regulation of the internal milieu," *Frontiers in Evolutionary Neuroscience*, vol. 2, pp. 1–15, 2011.

Novel Modular Self-Reconfigurable Robot for Pipe and Plant Inspection

Sergio Leggieri

Department of Advanced Robotics,
Italian Institute of Technology,
Genova, Italy 16163
Department of Management, Information
and Production Engineering,
University of Bergamo,
Dalmine, Italy 24044
Email: sergio.leggieri@iit.it
Email: sergio.leggieri@unibg.it

Carlo Canali, Ferdinando Cannella
and Darwin Caldwell

Department of Advanced Robotics,
Italian Institute of Technology,
Genova, Italy 16163
Email: carlo.canali@iit.it
Email: ferdinando.cannella@iit.it
Email: darwin.caldwell@iit.it

***Abstract*—In the last decades, the trend of replacing humans with robots has increased enormously, especially in repetitive or dangerous tasks such as inspection and maintenance. Various inspection robots have been developed so far, but usually those systems are designed for addressing very specific operations. The spread of such devices is mainly limited by the lack in adaptability to different tasks, and by the design restrictions of these robots. Instead, modular and self-reconfigurable robots have proven superior performance in different scenarios. Here, the idea of developing a modular, self-reconfigurable robot for inspection is discussed. The system consists of two modular vehicles with docking modules for reassembling into a snake robot. Thanks to its structure, it overcomes the challenges posed during pipe and plant inspections.**

Keywords–inspection robot; modular robots; self-reconfigurable mobile robot.

I. Introduction

Although robots are becoming very popular in industry, nowadays most of the inspection and maintenance operations on structures and equipments are still largely carried out by human operators. Human-based inspection, however, may not be the optimal solution in terms of costs and time. Preparatory work is often required before starting the operations to access the machinery or the assets and to ensure safety standard for the workers. The reliability and repeatability of the results is another major concern when inspections are performed by humans.

To address the challenges mentioned above, robotic devices have been developed in the last years to perform inspection, especially in industrial plants and in pipeline networks, where major challenges need to be overcome to deal with various problems that could be encountered. For example, the geometrical features of the asset to be inspected may be very demanding, setting sharp constraints in the design of the robots. The environment, where the machinery and the equipments reside, can be very harsh due to the presence of dirt, mud, hazardous substances, staircases, or unexpected obstacles. Finally, even the robot deployment, in some cases, can be a risky operation for humans.

Considering all these issues, a novel modular self-reconfigurable robot is proposed hereafter. Such system is intended to perform inspection of pipelines and industrial plants, travelling autonomously within the environments to reach its targets. Moreover, this system can self-reconfigure into a snake robot to deal with the most advanced tasks.

This paper is organized as follows: Section II presents related works on inspection robots and snake robots; Section III describes the system, analyzing its main features and providing graphical representations of it; Section IV concludes the paper and provides information about next steps in the robot development.

II. Related Works

Within industrial plants, the inspection can be divided into two main groups: inspection of specific machinery and general inspection and monitoring. For machinery, many robots have been developed, such as [1][2]. These robots are very specialized devices, expressly designed for addressing inspection of specific machinery. However, these systems may result ineffective even for different models of the same asset. For general inspection, robots, such as [3]-[5], have been developed. These latter systems show a great flexibility to deal with different scenarios. Such robots consist in assemblies of different robotic devices like mobile platforms with robotic arms on top.

In pipe inspection, usually, robots have to deal with highly constrained environments. In addition to the passive systems whose motion ability is guaranteed by fluid flow, the active systems can be categorized according to the locomotion methods, as in [6][7]. Some of these robots have standard structure, with wheels or tracks for moving and cameras as visual feedback. However, their use can be quite limited. In the same manner, other devices have just one or two modules, but are equipped with complex mechanisms for adapting to pipe networks [8]. In recent years, however, the trend has shifted toward the design of versatile robots with many articulated modules [7].

Since the ’70s, many snake robots have been developed, such as [9]-[12]. These robots can move in complex environments coordinating the motion of their parts, using the well-known gaits called lateral undulation and side-winding, see [13]. Due to their slender bodies made of redundant modules, snake-like robots are extremely suitable in performing inspection in constrained environments, as described in [14]-[16].

The unchallenged mobility and adaptability of these robots, however, come at the cost of a high mechanical complexity and a demanding motion control.

III. The System

Modularity and self-reconfigurability are key features for designing multipurpose robots [17][18]. Some robots that have proven to exhibit good performance in surveillance and search and rescue missions are described in [19]-[22]. Here, the robot design is based on these examples, but it introduces important novelties in its mechanical structure and features, which are described throughout this section.

The system consists of two independent vehicles that can self-reconfigure into a snake robot through their docking modules. The vehicles are intended for performing most of the inspection tasks by themselves, so the motion control of individual robots involves only few modules and joints. Nonetheless, the vehicles can deal with complex scenarios or particularly demanding tasks by coupling together and self-reconfiguring into a snake robot. In this way, the mechanical and control complexities of the system increase, but the robot can exploit its redundant kinematics to overcome obstacles, walk through difficult terrains, or climb vertical pipe segments.

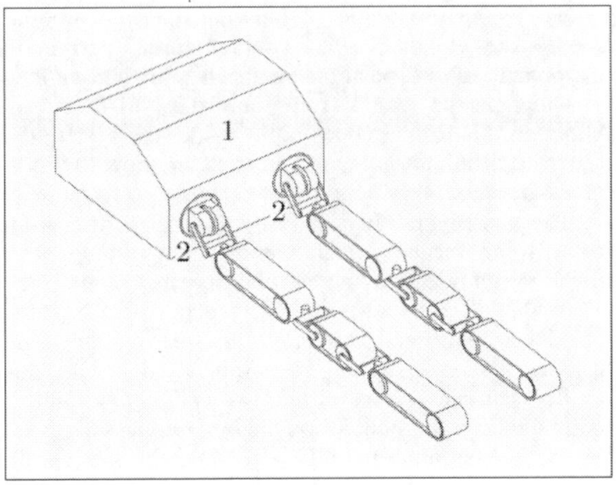

Figure 1. Representation of two vehicles docked at the base for recharging: 1 main base; 2 docking module interfaces.

The complete system includes also a main base. This base is meant for recharging purposes, but eventually it can be used also as a platform for travelling long distances and for deploying the vehicles in proximity of the point of interest. Finally, it is reasonable to assume that, after docking the two vehicles, the main base can use them as manipulators widening the possible fields of application of this system. A graphical representation of the entire system is given in Figure 1.

A. The vehicles

Both vehicles consist of three main modules and a docking module at one extreme, as shown in Figure 2. The modules are connected through active joints that form two specular inter-modules kinematic chains with respect to the central segment. Each docking module is then connected to the front of each vehicle through another kinematic chain.

The vehicle utilizes a combination of active/passive tracks for locomotion. The extreme modules contain all the required electronics and the control boards for actuating the two motors that drive the tracks. The central module has a passive track, it stores the batteries, the sensors for inspection and the pitch joints of the inter-modules kinematic chains. Each inter-modules chain consists of one pitch joint, a link and an active Cardan joint.

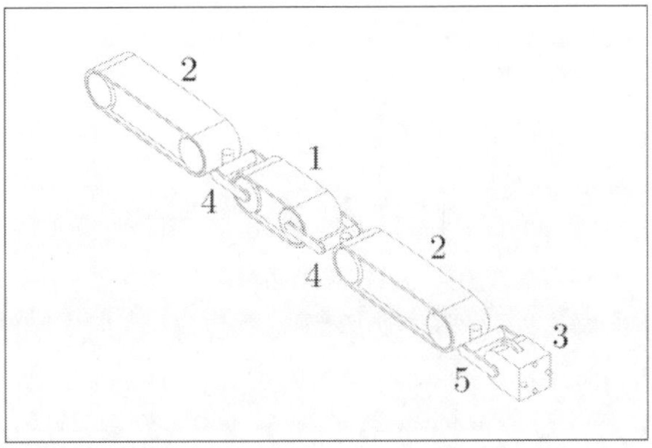

Figure 2. Representation of the vehicle: 1 central module; 2 extreme modules; 3 docking module; 4 inter-modules kinematic chains; 5 docking module kinematic chain.

This kinematics allows the vehicle to steer by rotating its extremes on the horizontal plane, as discussed in the next subsection. On the sagittal plane, the same kinematics allows the robot to adapt to slopes or gaps, overcome obstacles, and climb stairs. By defining proper gaits, the vehicles can perform lateral movements or turn on the spot using its modules as limbs. Moreover, the central part can be displaced vertically to push against pipe walls increasing the grip on its tracks to possibly move in vertical pipes as well.

The docking module kinematics is similar to the one previously described, but the joints are arranged in reverse order: an active Cardan joint, a link and a pitch joint. This sequence is chosen to preserve the symmetry between modules once the two vehicles join together and form the snake robot. The symmetry is crucial for implementing typical snake gaits such as lateral undulation, side-winding, sinus-lifting. In snake robot form, the system can travel easily over rough terrains, can overcome large obstacles and can lift part of its body, as shown in Figure 3.

B. Vehicle kinematics and maneuverability

A preliminary kinematic analysis has focused only on the vehicle, while the docking module and its connecting kinematics have been neglected. Nevertheless, this analysis provides useful information for identifying crucial parameters for the robot design.

The inter-modules kinematics has been computed using the Denavit-Hartenberg convention [23]. As shown in Figure 4, the floating base frame $\{O_b\}$ is located in the central module. Local frames $\{O_{ri}\}$ and $\{O_{li}\}$ are attached on each ith link of the chain, and the additional subscripts $\mathtt{r}$ and $\mathtt{l}$ represent the right and left chain, respectively.

In Table I, the D-H parameters of the right kinematic chain are summarized. The first row represents the fixed transformation from the base frame $\{O_b\}$ to the first joint

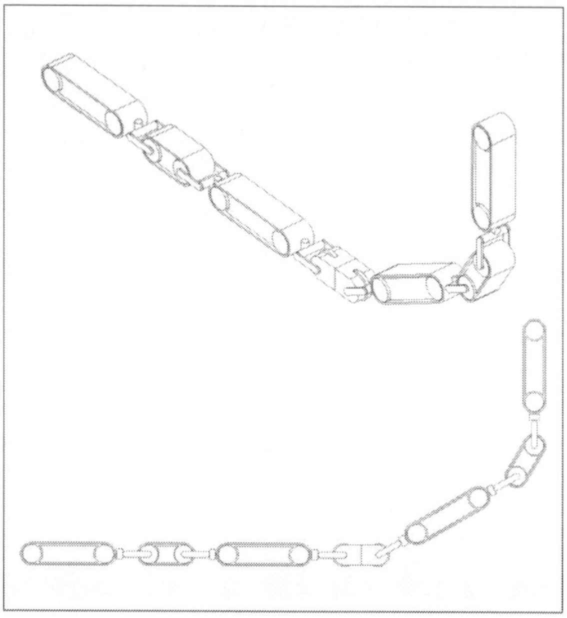

Figure 3. Representation of two vehicles coupled together to form a snake robot. In this mode, the robot can raise segments of the body to overcome obstacles or reach high points.

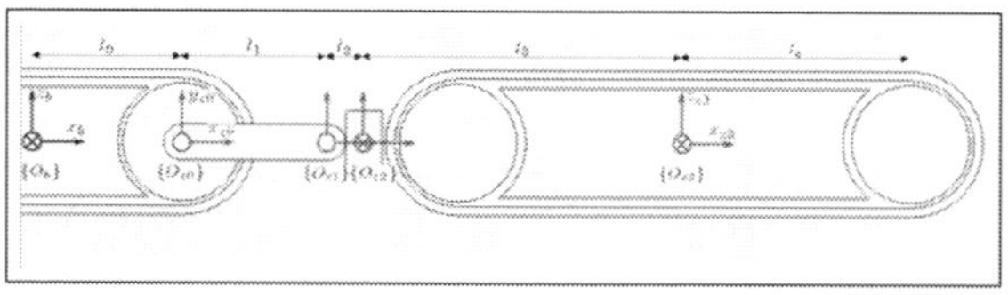

Figure 4. Schematic representation of the right kinematic chain. In black, the base frame $\{O_b\}$. In red, the local frames $\{O_{ri}\}$.

TABLE I. D-H PARAMETERS FOR THE RIGHT KINEMATIC CHAIN

Frames	a_i	α_i	d_i	θ_i
$\{O_b\} \rightarrow \{O_{r0}\}$	l_0	$\pi/2$	0	0
$\{O_{r0}\} \rightarrow \{O_{r1}\}$	l_1	0	0	q_{r1}
$\{O_{r1}\} \rightarrow \{O_{r2}\}$	l_2	$-\pi/2$	0	q_{r2}
$\{O_{r2}\} \rightarrow \{O_{r3}\}$	l_3	0	0	q_{r3}

frame $\{O_{r0}\}$, which is translated by l_0 along the x axis and rotated by $\pi/2$ about the same axis. The successive rows describe the translation and rotation transformations defined by the joint variables d_i and θ_i along and about the z axis. The parameters a_i and α_i represent the translation and rotation along and about the x axis. So, l_i is the length of the ith link, while q_{ri} is the angle of the ith joint. Here, the Cardan joint is modeled as two distinct joints with local frames $\{O_{r1}\}$ and $\{O_{r2}\}$, which are shifted by a distance l_2.

Computing the homogeneous matrices from these transformations allows to describe positions and orientations of all the local frames with respect to the base frame $\{O_b\}$. The homogeneous matrix A^b_{r3} of the last frame $\{O_{r3}\}$ serves to identify the robot workspace. The corresponding position vector $\mathbf{p}^b_{r3}$ of the last frame is:

$$\mathbf{p}^b_{r3} = \begin{bmatrix} l_0 + l_1 c_{r1} + l_2 c_{r12} + l_3 c_{r12} c_{r3} \\ l_3 s_{r3} \\ l_1 s_{r1} + l_2 s_{r12} + l_3 s_{r12} c_{r3} \end{bmatrix} \quad (1)$$

Here, l_0, l_1, l_2 and l_3 are the link lengths; c and s refer to the cosine and sinus functions; the subscript $r3$ stands for the joint angle q_{r3}; and the subscript $r12$ represents the sum $q_{r1} + q_{r2}$.

Focusing on the third component of the vector $\mathbf{p}^b_{r3}$, it is possible to compute the maximum height H that the extreme module can reach, as follows:

$$H = \frac{h}{2} - \frac{h}{2c_{r12}} + l_1 s_{r1} + l_2 s_{r12} + (l_3 + l_4) s_{r12} c_{r3} \quad (2)$$

Here, the first term is half the central module height h; the second is the projection of half the extreme module height h onto the global z axis. The remaining part is the third component of the position vector $\mathbf{p}^b_{r3}$ to whom it is added l_4, which is the length from frame O_{r3} to the front wheel. Although this formula does not consider the system dynamics, it gives preliminary information to define how the link lengths affect the maximum height H.

The maneuverability analysis provides further information for defining further design parameters. Although the mono-tread design reduces the number of motors in the vehicle and makes it less sensitive with respect to debris, this feature introduces additional challenges in steering the system. For instance, the skid-steering technique used in caterpillars can not be used here. However, the two active yaw joints allow to rotate the extreme modules on the horizontal plane, as shown in Figure 5. Assuming that all the modules lay on this plane and have uniform tangential velocity v, it is possible to evaluate the curvature radius r_c of the system as follows:

$$r_c = \frac{l_3 + \frac{(l_0+l_1+l_2)}{\cos q_{r3}}}{\tan q_{r3}} \quad (3)$$

So, the angular rate ω of the central module is:

$$\omega = \frac{v}{r_c} \quad (4)$$

Equations (2) – (4) depend on the link lengths of the robot. So, increasing the lengths l_1, l_2, l_3 and l_4 ensures to reach and overcome higher obstacles, but, in addition, it increases the curvature radius of the vehicle, thus limiting its maneuverability in constrained environments. Such dualism reinforces the idea of designing a modular, self-reconfigurable robot.

C. The docking module

Various technologies and mechanisms [24]-[27] have been developed for connecting autonomously two or more robotic modules. Some coupling devices are based on activation and de-activation of shape-memory alloys, [24][25], others are based on actuated mechanisms [26][27]. Since these latter seem to provide a good trade-off between connection robustness and power consumption, the vehicles utilize docking devices based on a novel actuated mechanism that is described hereafter.

The docking modules, at the extremes of the vehicles, have passive wheels in place of tracks. Each frame stores the batteries and a gearbox driven by a single motor. The gearbox

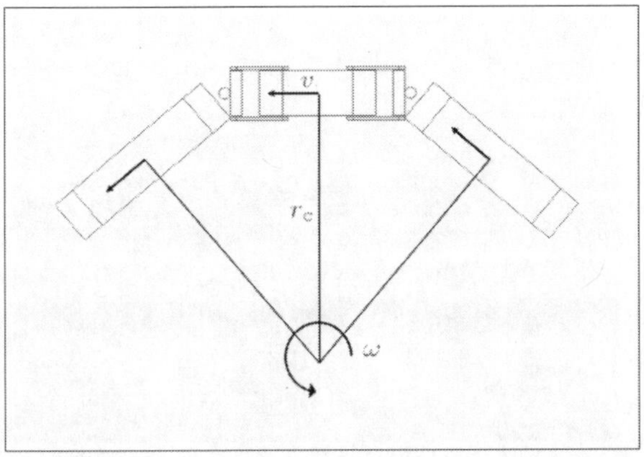

Figure 5. Representation of the vehicle in the C-shape configuration adopted to steer.

consists of three sprockets: one in the middle, driven by motor; and two lateral with a fixed screw each. The outer faces of each module are complementary, and on each surface there are two tampered pins and two threaded sockets. Hence, one docking module is rotated by $\pm 90\,\mathrm{deg}$ around the global x axis with respect to the other one. When the vehicles get in contact, the motors drive the gearboxes. The lateral gears, besides rotating, slide along the central sprocket pulling out the bolts that tighten to the complementary threaded sockets. Each docking module also includes a camera for vision, a set of infrared transmitters and receivers, and sliding contacts.

D. The main base

The design of the main base is not completely defined yet. However, the primary purpose of this system is to recharge the vehicles. On the base, there are two docking interfaces, which have the same coupling mechanism as the docking modules. These interfaces are driven by roll joints, in such a way that the docking ports in the base can be re-aligned to properly match the configuration of docking modules on the vehicles, as shown in Figure 1.

The roll joints can also rotate the vehicles, which can be used as robotic arms, as in Figure 6. Moreover, it is under consideration the possibility of mounting wheels or tracks on the base. This additional feature can be useful to deploy the vehicles near the point of interest, especially when the inspection has to be performed in very wide areas.

IV. Conclusion and Future Work

The system described in this work aims at replacing human operators in performing inspection in inaccessible or risky environments, such as pipelines or industrial plants. Modularity and self-reconfigurability are considered as key features to fulfill this purpose.

The proposed device consists of two modular mono-tread vehicles with active joints. The novel mono-tread design reduces the chances to get stuck on debris, but, in turn, it introduces some maneuverability limitations. These drawbacks have been identified and discussed, analyzing the vehicle kinematics and maneuverability. Notably, the motion control of the system, in this configuration, involves only a few modules and joints.

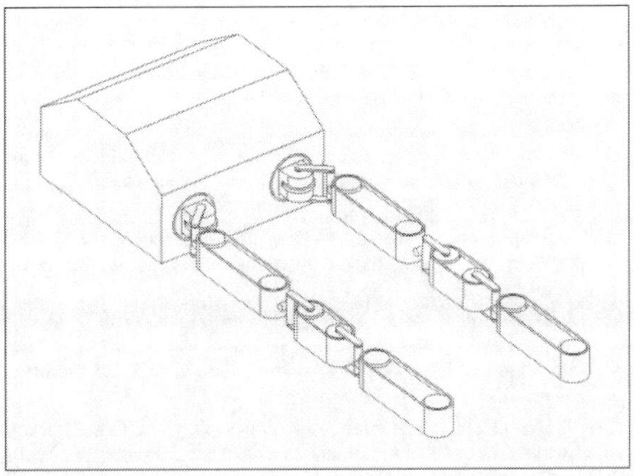

Figure 6. Representation of the vehicles used as manipulator. Once coupled, the roll joints within the base rotate the vehicles in the double arms configuration.

The docking modules, based on the novel mechanism discussed, allow the vehicles to reconfigure into a snake robot or to connect to the main base. As a snake robot, the motion control increases in complexity, but the system can perform advanced operations, such as crossing rough terrains, lifting part of the body or travelling through difficult pipe segments.

The project is still at an early stage, with ongoing simulations to evaluate the performance of such system and to define its design parameters. The definition of dynamic models for the robot as vehicle and as snake is another crucial step toward the development of the proposed system.

References

[1] E. Zwicker, W. Zesch, and R. Moser, "A modular inspection robot platform for power plant applicationst," in 2010 1st International Conference on Applied Robotics for the Power Industry, Oct. 2010, pp. 1–6.

[2] G. Caprari et al., "Highly compact robots for inspection of power plants," Journal of Field Robotics, vol. 29, Gen. 2012, pp. 47–68.

[3] J. Steele et al., "Development of an Oil and Gas Refinery Inspection Robot," ASME International Mechanical Engineering Congress and Exposition, Proceedings (IMECE), vol. 4, Nov. 2014, pp. 1–10.

[4] I. Maurtua et al., "MAINBOT Mobile Robots for Inspection and Maintenance in Extensive Industrial Plants," Energy Procedia, vol. 49, 2014, pp. 1810–1819.

[5] S. Soldan, J. Welle, T. Barz, A. Kroll, and D. Schulz, Towards Autonomous Robotic Systems for Remote Gas Leak Detection and Localization in Industrial Environments. Springer Tracts in Advanced Robotics, Springer, Berlin, Heidelberg, Jan. 2014, pp. 233–247, in Yoshida, K. and Tadokoro, S., Field and Service Robotics, ISBN: 978-3-642-40685-0.

[6] J. Mirats-Tur and W. Garthwaite, "Robotic Devices for Water Main In-Pipe Inspection: A Survey," Journal of Field Robotics, vol. 27, Jul. 2010, pp. 491–508.

[7] G. Mills, A. Jackson, and R. Richardson, "Advances in the Inspection of Unpiggable Pipelines," Robotics, vol. 6, Nov. 2017, p. 36.

[8] J. Park, D. Hyun, W. Cho, T. Kim, and H. Yang, "Normal-Force Control for an In-Pipe Robot According to the Inclination of Pipelines," IEEE Transactions on Industrial Electronics, vol. 58, Dec. 2011, pp. 5304–5310.

[9] S. Hirose, "Snake-like locomotors and manipulators," Biologiclly Inspired Robots, 1993.

[10] M. Mori and S. Hirose, "Development of active cord mechanism ACM-R3 with agile 3D mobility," in Proceedings 2001 IEEE/RSJ International Conference on Intelligent Robots and Systems. Expanding the Societal

Role of Robotics in the Next Millennium (Cat. No.01CH37180, Mar. 2001, pp. 1552–1557.

[11] C. Wright et al., "Design and architecture of the unified modular snake robot," in 2012 IEEE International Conference on Robotics and Automation, May 2012, pp. 4347–4354.

[12] P. Liljebäck, K. Y. Pettersen, and Ø. Stavdahl, "A snake robot with a contact force measurement system for obstacle-aided locomotion," in 2010 IEEE International Conference on Robotics and Automation, Jun. 2010, pp. 683–690.

[13] S. Hirose and M. Mori, "Biologically Inspired Snake-like Robots," in 2004 IEEE International Conference on Robotics and Biomimetics, Sep. 2004, pp. 1–7.

[14] H. Schempf, E. Mutschler, A. Gavaert, G. Skoptsov, and W. Crowley, "Visual and nondestructive evaluation inspection of live gas mains using the Explorer family of pipe robots," Journal of Field Robotics, vol. 27, May 2010, pp. 217–249.

[15] J. Borenstein, M. Hansen, and A. Borrell, "The OmniTread OT-4 Serpentine Robot I Design and Performance," Journal of Field Robotics, vol. 24, Jul. 2007, pp. 601–621.

[16] S. A. Fjerdingen, P. Liljebäck, and A. A. Transeth, "A snake-like robot for internal inspection of complex pipe structures (PIKo)," in 2009 IEEE/RSJ International Conference on Intelligent Robots and Systems, Oct. 2009, pp. 5665–5671.

[17] J. Liu, X. Zhang, and G. Hao, "Survey on Research and Development of Reconfigurable Modular Robots," Advances in Mechanical Engineering, vol. 8, Aug. 2016, pp. 1–21.

[18] S. Chennareddy, A. Agrawal, and A. Karuppiah, "Modular Self-Reconfigurable Robotic Systems: A Survey on Hardware Architectures," Journal of Robotics, vol. 2017, Mar. 2017, pp. 1–19.

[19] H. Zhang, G. Zong, and Z. Deng, A Reconfigurable Mobile Robots System Based on Parallel Mechanism. IntechOpen, Apr. 2008, chapter 16, pp. 347–362, in Wu, H., Parallel Manipulators, towards New Applications, ISBN: 978-3-902613-40-0.

[20] W. Wei and T. Huilin, "Reconfigurable multi-robot system kinematic modeling and motion planning," in 2011 6th IEEE Conference on Industrial Electronics and Applications, Jun. 2011, pp. 1672–1677.

[21] H. B. Brown, J. M. Vande Weghe, C. A. Bererton, and P. K. Khosla, "Millibot trains for enhanced mobility," IEEE/ASME Transactions on Mechatronics, vol. 7, no. 4, Dec. 2002, pp. 452–461.

[22] P. Ben-Tzvi, A. A. Goldenberg, and J. Zu, "Design and Analysis of a Hybrid Mobile Robot Mechanism With Compounded Locomotion and Manipulation Capability," Journal of Mechanical Design, vol. 130, Jul. 2008.

[23] B. Siciliano and O. Khatib, Eds., Springer handbook of robotics. Springer, Berlin, Heidelberg, 2016, ISBN: 978-3-540-23957-4.

[24] A. Castano, A. Behar, and P. Will, "The Conro modules for reconfigurable robots," IEEE/ASME Transactions on Mechatronics, vol. 7, Dec. 2002, pp. 403–409.

[25] H. Kurokawa et al., "M-TRAN II: metamorphosis from a four-legged walker to a caterpillar," in 2003 IEEE/RSJ International Conference on Intelligent Robots and Systems (IROS 2003) (Cat. No.03CH37453), Nov. 2003, pp. 2454–2459.

[26] D. Li, H. Fu, and W. Wang, "Ultrasonic based autonomous docking on plane for mobile robot," in 2008 IEEE International Conference on Automation and Logistics, Sep. 2008, pp. 1396–1401.

[27] H. Kurokawa et al., "Distributed self-reconfiguration of M-TRAN III modular robotic system," The International Journal of Robotic Research, vol. 27, Mar. 2008, pp. 373–386.

A Novel System for Grasping and Handling Flat and Deformable Objects

Claudio Gloriani

ISA - Department of Engineering and Applied Sciences
University of Bergamo
Dalmine, Italy
Email: claudio.gloriani@unibg.it

ADVR - Advanced Robotics
Italian Institute of Technology
Genova, Italy
Email: claudio.gloriani@iit.it

Isiah Zaplana and Ferdinando Cannella

ADVR - Advanced Robotics
Italian Institute of Technology
Genova, Italy
Email: Isiah.Zaplana@iit.it

Email: Ferdinando.Cannella@iit.it

Mariapaola D'Imperio and Emanuela Cepolina

ADVR - Advanced Robotics
Italian Institute of Technology
Genova, Italy
Email: Mariapaola.DImperio@iit.it

Email: Emanuela.Cepolina@iit.it

***Abstract*—For the automated industry, it is important to develop a new mechatronics system, which is able to grasp and manipulate deformable objects in a reliable way. This paper discusses an idea for developing a concept of gripper exploiting the physical proprieties of the objects to be manipulated such as, for example, fabrics textile, sheets of paper or, in general, Flat and Deformable Objects (FDOs). The idea is to build a gripper prototype, which uses two rotational wheels, microspines placed on the fingertips, in order to buckle and lift up the flat material. The methodology and the type of gripper used will be described in detail.**

Keywords–Flat and Deformable Objects; Grasping; Robotic Manipulation; Friction; Buckling; Microspines; Rotational Hand.

I. INTRODUCTION

Manipulation and grasping of rigid objects is a mature field in robotics, but the study of deformable objects is not so extensive in the robotics community. Unfortunately, deformable objects are extremely difficult to manipulate because they have infinite degrees of freedom [1]. The automation industry has faced this problem and in particular how to manipulate Flat and Deformable Objects (FDOs) such as, for example: garments, fabrics textile, cloths, which require strong skills in handling and, for this reason, are performed mainly by humans [2]. The majority of industries have a great need for simple, reliable, versatile and low cost grippers for grasping and handling these kinds of objects. So, endowing robots able to manipulate FDOs for some specific industry has a great advantage in economic terms. For instance, using these kind of systems reduces the labor cost [3][4] and the physical burden on workers [5][6]. The idea starts from some papers which deal with manipulation of FDOs using a parallel gripper that has two rotational wheels on the fingertips [7] and exploits some ideas used to pick up textile fabrics from layers described [8] and [9]. The choice of using microspine in the gripper is given by the fact that the study in [10] provided very reliable results for grasping and handling flat and deformable materials. The different approach used in this paper exploits an intrusive method using microspines, but also also a non-intrusive method exploiting the friction of the wheels; it is also possible to combine them together. The main purpose of this research is to increase the reliability of the grip of an FDO, but at the same time to make it adaptable. This concept of gripper exploits friction between the rotational wheels, placed on the top of the fingertips, and the flat material to be manipulated in order to transfer the frictional force which is parallel to the plane of the FDO (see Figure 1). This frictional force is proportional to the force contact of the wheel and also depends on the friction coefficient. This kind of gripper is very useful when it is necessary to pick up, for example, a piece of textile fabric from layers. A big inspiration for making the new gripper comes from an interesting work [11] where, in the Jet Propulsion Laboratory (JPL), a lightweight robot which is able to climb rough surface using wheels with microspines has been developed. The interactions between microspines and asperities of the rough surface generate the movement of the robot and, therefore, the idea is to exploit this principle in order to grasp textile fabrics or other FDOs. The material of the wheels that will be used in the novel gripper is one that guarantees a good grip and also works with smooth surfaces.

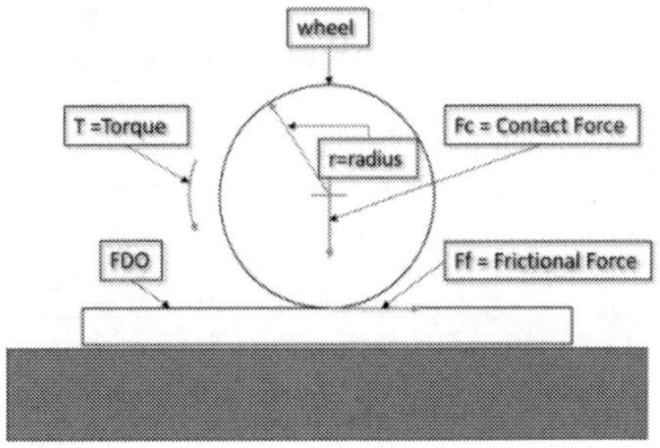

Figure 1. Frictional Force transmitted to the FDO.

II. Description of the Novel Gripper

The gripper is currently at conceptual stage and still a work in progress, but, in the future, it will be completely developed. Figure 4 shows the longitudinal section of the novel gripper in a simplified version in which it is possible to identify the main components for understanding better its working principle. This gripper will be mounted on the end effector of a robotic arm taking advantage of its degrees of freedom for spatial movement. The grasping system chosen is a parallel gripper, widely used for handling in industries, which is simple to build, but very reliable and useful for pinching the object to be manipulated. The gripper will have these basic, but important components:

- A Body
- Two Fingers
- Two wheels
- Microspines

The Body is a structural part of the gripper where components such as, for example, electrical wirings, sensors, actuators and all others movable parts ae mounted. The Two Fingers are mounted in the Body and they are moved thanks to a screw (see Figure 4) which is actuated with a single electrical motor. In this way, it is possible to slide in parallel the two fingers on the Body. At the fingertips, two rotational wheels are placed, each one actuated with an electrical motor. The new concept of gripper is all in the development of the wheels which it will be the key to grasp every FDOs. Inside these two wheels there are placed 12 microspines distributed every $\frac{\pi}{6}$ radians (see Figure 4) which can be extended or retracted rotating the reel where the wires of the microspines are wrapped. The wire of each microspine follows a logarithmic spiral path, inside a hole of the wheel, which has the Cartesian coordinates expressed in the following parametric form:

$$\begin{cases} x(\theta) = r(\theta)(\cos(\theta)) \\ y(\theta) = r(\theta)(\sin(\theta)) \end{cases}$$

where θ is the angle expressed in radians and $r(\theta) = r_0 e^{b\theta}$ is its polar equation. The terms of the polar equation are: r_0 which is the radius where the logarithmic curve starts and b is a parameter for determining the rate of increase of the spiral. The parameter b is expressed in radians because $b = \cot(\psi)$, where ψ is the angle between $r(\theta)$ and the respective tangent of the curve. Figure 3 shows an example when $\psi = 70^{\circ}$ and the interesting aspect is that this angle remains constant so it means that it does not depend on the values of θ and r_0. Figure 2 shows different paths as the ψ angle changes. The variable θ is very useful in order to compute the total length of the spiral. These aspects are very important because it is possible to test the microspines with different angles and lengths in order to have an optimal interaction with the FDO to be grasped and manipulated (as shown in Figure 6). The use of this kind of gripper is particularly interesting when the FDOs considered are textile fabrics or general materials with rough surfaces. It is also possible to manage non rough FDOs as, for example, sheets of paper using wheels in rubber's material, or only their contact surfaces, in order to exploit its high coefficient of friction. In the next section, we explain two methods for picking up FDOs using the gripper described.

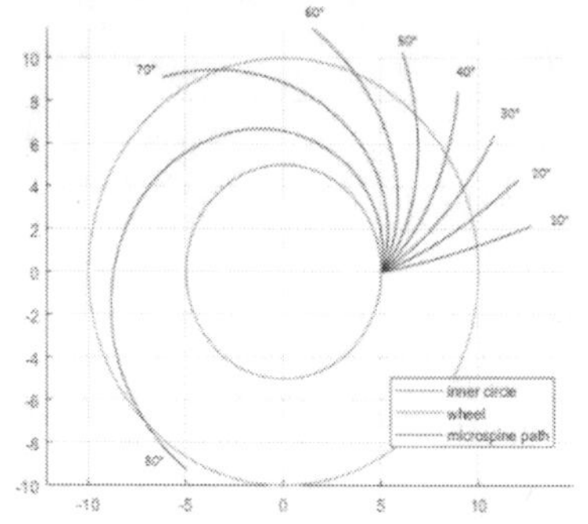

Figure 2. Example of different logarithmic spiral path as the ψ angle changes.

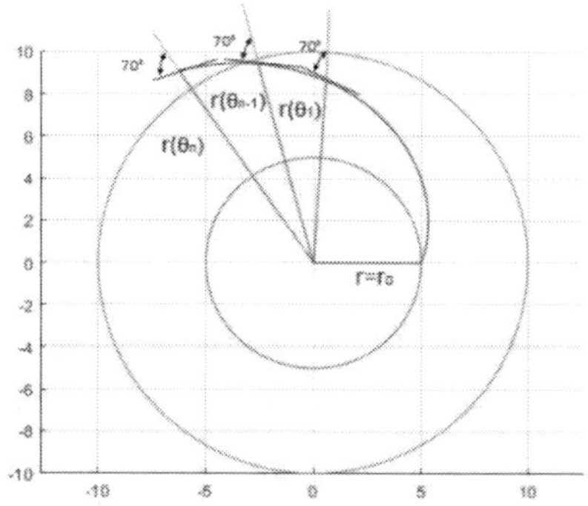

Figure 3. Equiangular spiral path.

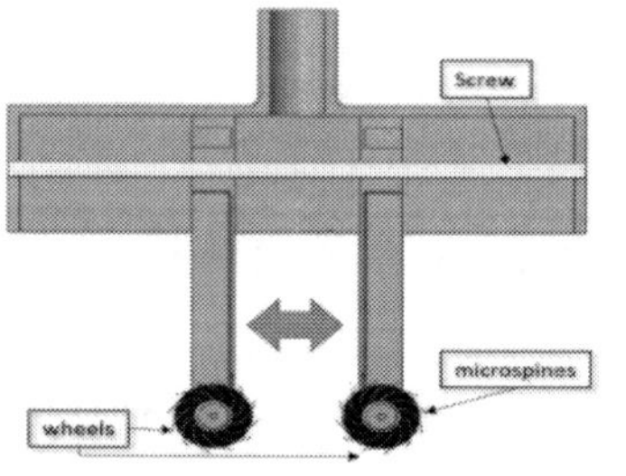

Figure 4. Longitudinal section of the novel gripper.

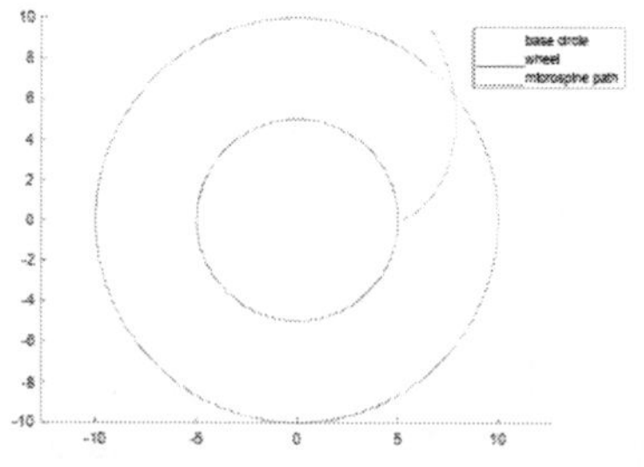

Figure 5. Generation of a single microspine's path.

III. Methodology used in the Novel gripper for grasping

In this section, we explain two different approaches for grasping FDOs using the gripper described in Section II. The first method is very useful when it is not possible to grasp the FDOs at the boundary. Before starting any operation, the thickness of the FDO should be known to be able to manipulate it in order to regulate the right length of the microspines which have to penetrate into the material, as shown in Figure 6. This kind of gripper is studied also for picking up the material from a layer of materials. However, if there is a risk of damaging the FDO by using the microspines, these can be retracted in order to work only with the rubber of the wheels in order to exploit the frictional force generated between the two contact surfaces. The grasping procedure is quite simple and could be synthesized in these few points:

1) Gripper approaching
2) Grasping action
3) Manipulation

In the first point, using a robotic arm, the gripper is moved above the object and its two fingers are opened at an appropriate distance. After that, the wheels are moved down until the wheels lightly touch the FDO and, therefore, a large contact force is not required. In the second procedure, the two wheels are activated to rotate at the same speed in order to allow the microspines to penetrate into the FDO. This action lifts and, at the same time, folds the FDO, as shown in Figure 7. The buckling generated from the torque of the wheels depends on the material considered and it is related to the flexibility of the FDO. Therefore, if the object is too rigid, it will be impossible to use this method. The second method, shown in Figure 8, is quite similar to the first one, but there is a difference with the grasping point of the material. Such point is placed quite near to the boundary. This can be an advantage when it is impossible to grasp it in a different place and, furthermore, it is possible to engage less material during the grasping. The choice of methodology depends on the task that needs to be performed.

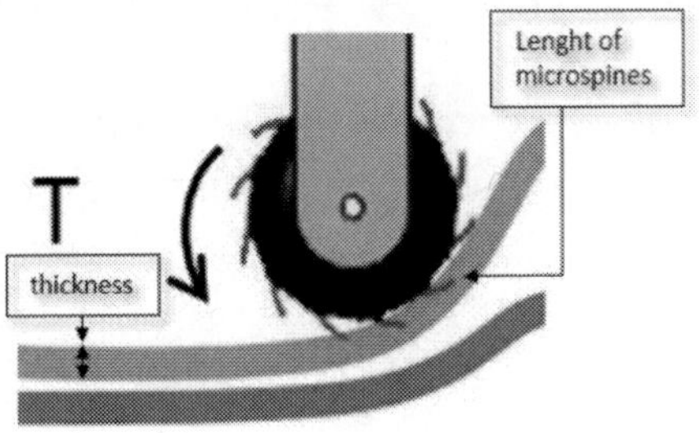

Figure 6. Detail of the interaction between wheels and FDO.

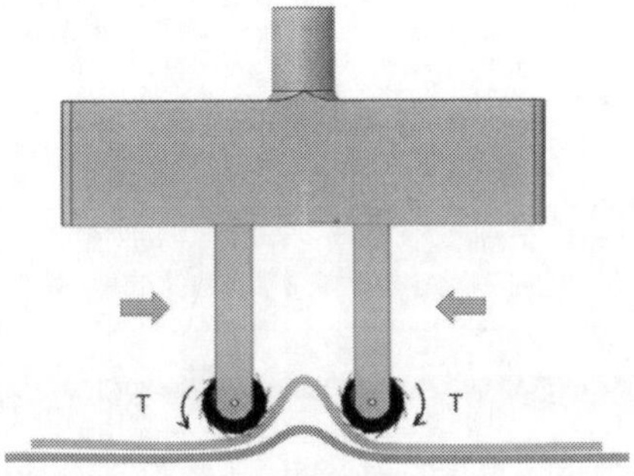

Figure 7. First method in order to Buckle and lift up the FDO.

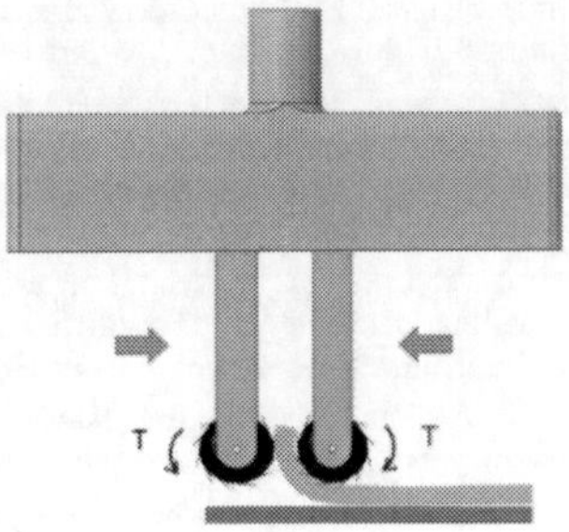

Figure 8. Second method in order to Buckle and lift up the FDO.

IV. Conclusion and Future Works

In this work, we have explained different methodologies that will be used in our gripper for grasping and manipulating Flat and Deformable Objects (FDOs). In particular, we focused on the study of the geometry for realizing the microspines. In the future, we will also study other important aspects such as, for example, the choice of the proper microspines material, its size, etc. This is just a preliminary idea of a gripper and, in the future, it will be studied and developed more, adding all the necessary components useful to produce a prototype able to work in a reliable way. After that, it will be tested in a real scenario using different kinds of FDOs in order to check its performance.

REFERENCES

[1] F. Guo, Huan Lin, and Y. Jia, "Squeeze grasping of deformable planar objects with segment contacts and stick/slip transitions," in 2013 IEEE International Conference on Robotics and Automation, May 2013, pp. 3736–3741.

[2] P. N. Koustoumpardis, K. X. Nastos, and N. A. Aspragathos, "Underactuated 3-finger robotic gripper for grasping fabrics," in 2014 23rd International Conference on Robotics in Alpe-Adria-Danube Region (RAAD), 2014, pp. 1–8.

[3] S. Tokumoto, Y. Fujita, and S. Hirai, "Deformation modeling of viscoelastic objects for their shape control," in Proceedings 1999 IEEE International Conference on Robotics and Automation (Cat. No.99CH36288C), vol. 1, May 1999, pp. 767–772.

[4] R. Buckingham, A. Graham, H. Arnarson, P. Snaeland, and P. Davey, "Robotics for de-heading fish - a case study," Industrial Robot: An International Journal, vol. 28, 08 2001, pp. 302–309.

[5] J. Acker and D. Henrich, "Manipulating deformable linear objects: characteristic features for vision-based detection of contact state transitions," in Proceedings of the IEEE International Symposium onAssembly and Task Planning, 2003, July 2003, pp. 204–209.

[6] M. Rambow, T. Schauß, M. Buss, and S. Hirche, "Autonomous manipulation of deformable objects based on teleoperated demonstrations," in 2012 IEEE/RSJ International Conference on Intelligent Robots and Systems, Oct 2012, pp. 2809–2814.

[7] T. Kabaya and M. Kakikura, "Research on a service robot for housekeeping —handling of clothes—," Transactions of the Japan Society of Mechanical Engineers Series C, vol. 64, 01 1998, pp. 1356–1361.

[8] E. Ono, K. Kitagaki, and M. Kakikura, "On friction picking up a piece of fabric from layers," vol. 4, 01 2005, pp. 2206 – 2211.

[9] E. Ono and Kunikatsu Takase, "On better pushing for picking a piece of fabric from layers," in 2007 IEEE International Conference on Robotics and Biomimetics (ROBIO), Dec 2007, pp. 589–594.

[10] A. Karakerezis, Z. Doulgeri, and V. Petridis, "A gripper for handling flat non-rigid materials," in Automation and Robotics in Construction XI: Proceedings of the Eleventh International Symposium on Automation and Robotics in Construction (ISARC), D. A. Chamberlain, Ed. Brighton, UK: International Association for Automation and Robotics in Construction (IAARC), May 1994, pp. 593–601.

[11] K. Carpenter, N. Wiltsie, and A. Parness, "Rotary microspine rough surface mobility," IEEE/ASME Transactions on Mechatronics, vol. 21, no. 5, Oct 2016, pp. 2378–2390.

Integration of Landmark Detection and Low-cost Sensors for Vehicle Localization in Challenging Environments

Yu Hsiang Wang
Electrical Engineering
National Cheng Kung University
Tainan, Taiwan
e-mail: ex4587@gmail.com

Jyh Ching Juang
Electrical Engineering
National Cheng Kung University
Tainan, Taiwan
e-mail: 8202019@gs.ncku.edu.tw

Muhammad Rony Hidayatullah
Electrical Engineering
National Cheng Kung University
Tainan, Taiwan
e-mail: mronyh97@gmail.com

***Abstract*—A seamless vehicle localization capability with high accuracy and integrity is essential for the safe operation of automated vehicles. This study integrates a map-matching based detection scheme and a low-cost Global Navigation Satellite System (GNSS) and Inertial Measurement Unit (IMU) system to enhance the localization capability in a challenging environment. Existing vehicle navigation systems typically use a GNSS/IMU navigation suite to provide position, velocity, and attitude. Such a navigation suite is subject to the error characteristics of the IMU and the operating environment of the GNSS. If the GNSS signals are affected for a long period of time and the quality of the IMU is not well calibrated, erroneous navigation results may occur. It is noted that a challenging environment is featured with some landmarks such as traffic lights. The significant visual feature can be detected robustly by using a deep learning model in a whole day time, which means the availability of the proposed method is better than previous vision-based localization schemes. The paper investigates the fusion of a low-cost GNSS receiver, IMU, vehicle odometer, monocular camera, and an HD map to render seamless navigation. The system is implemented in a vehicle and tested at Taiwan CAR Lab. The effectiveness of the proposed scheme is demonstrated.**

Keywords-autonomous vehicle; computer vision; vehicle localization; high definition map; sensor fusion.

I. INTRODUCTION

With the development of intelligent transportation systems, automated driving or self-driving has attracted worldwide attention for its potential in enhancing vehicle safety, improving transportation efficiency, and introducing business opportunities. Precise localization is an essential component of autonomous vehicles. A high-accuracy and high-integrity localization result leads to high-performance path planning, decision-making, and motion control behaviors. Typically, the localization is implemented by using a Global Navigation Satellite System receiver, which results in acceptable performance in the absence of signal obstruction. However, the availability of GNSS-based localization suffers from signal blocking, multipath effect, and atmospheric signal distortions. The integration of the GNSS receiver and Inertial Navigation System (INS) has become an important vehicle navigation suite as GNSS and INS are complementary and can be intelligently fused to render continuous location and attitude information. The use of GNSS Real Time Kinematic (RTK) technique [1] can further improve accuracy. Another technique is Normal Distribution Transform (NDT) [2] using the lidar to estimate the location by matching the point cloud. Although both of these two methods can achieve centimeter-level accuracy localization, they cost a lot.

To reduce the localization error of a low-cost GNSS/INS, it is required to develop another technique to achieve enough localization accuracy in a dense urban environment. Map-matching based localization systems by using visual features and point cloud are widespread. The concept of map-matching based methods is to detect road elements such as poles, traffic signs, and road markings via perception sensors and find the correspondences of landmarks to help deduce the actual vehicle's position. Map-matching based localization approaches can be generally divided into three categories: (1) The Kalman filter-based localization estimates the vehicle position by matching features on an image with map information. Pink *et al.* [3] proposed to estimate the vehicle's location by using a stereo camera rig to match the visual measurement to a digital feature map. Weiss *et al.* [4] used lidar features associated with precise landmark maps to deduce the vehicle's location based on an Extended Kalman Filter (EKF). (2) Monte-Carlo signal-level localization methods use the raw data to update the state without doing feature extraction. Mattern *et al.* [5] used a coherency value derived from the structure tensor to directly update the image. (3) The last localization approach category is feature extraction based Monte-Carlo localization. Within the Monte-Carlo localization approach, Schindler *et al.* [6] deduced the position by integrating perception information from a monocular camera and laser scanner and associated the landmarks in the high-precision digital map.

Recently, the "High-Definition Map (HD Map)" [7] has become a major research topic to help satisfy the high accuracy demand in Advanced Driver Assistance Systems, as well as the self-driving industry. In contrast with previous digital maps, an HD map includes more precise road geometry, slope, and new features for vehicle localization and perception. In other words, an HD map with highly detailed three-dimensional information can make the vehicle operate more wisely. Apart from using an HD map to improve vehicle localization performance, it can be utilized to enhance detection accuracy by projecting

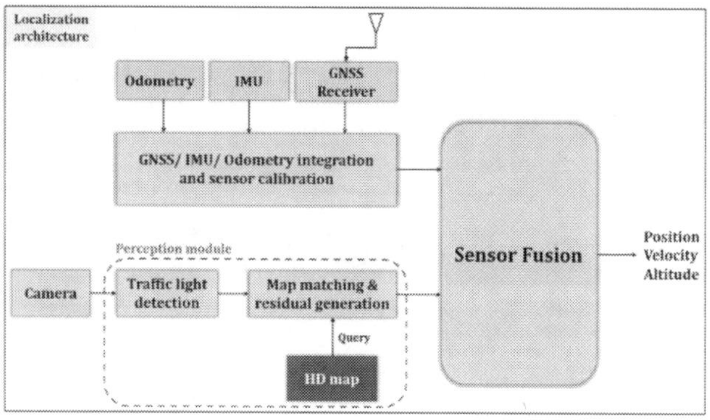

Figure 1. Overview of the self-localization approach.

the information of landmarks stored in the map. Taking advantage of this feature, this paper focuses on integrating an HD map with landmark features, such as traffic lights, to develop a map-matching based localization system. There are several reasons to target traffic lights as the landmark features on an image. First, owing to the detection of road features by using a monocular camera, the quality of the image is sensitive to illumination, exposure, and weather. Traffic lights have significant vision characteristics on an image that can make perception systems get more robust detection results. Second, compared to other road features, traffic lights have long-term stability which is more reliable in terms of its position information on the map. Third, an HD map can constitute prior information for generating region of interest on an image that can improve traffic light recognition and reduce false positives.

Considering the background described above, the main purpose of this paper is to fuse different sensors based on Kalman filter and combine an HD map to overcome the difficulty of vehicle localization inside tunnels. Moreover, in view of the whole system architecture, Region Of Interest (ROI) projection querying from the map is used not only to estimate observations, but also to help recognize traffic lights.

The rest of the paper is structured as follows. In Section II, we describe the idea of our system, which is a vision-aided loosely coupled framework. Section III describes how to obtain correction information by image processing. Section IV goes into the multi-sensor fusion based on an EKF for vehicle localization. Section V demonstrates the experimental results. Finally, we conclude the work in Section VI.

II. System Overview

An overview of the proposed localization architecture is illustrated in Figure 1. The main idea of the approach to determine the vehicle position is based on the Kalman Filter. The integration of GNSS and INS has been well investigated in the literature. Different integration strategies have been exploited and analyzed with different levels of IMU [8][9]. According to the type of operating systems and applications, a specific strategy can be

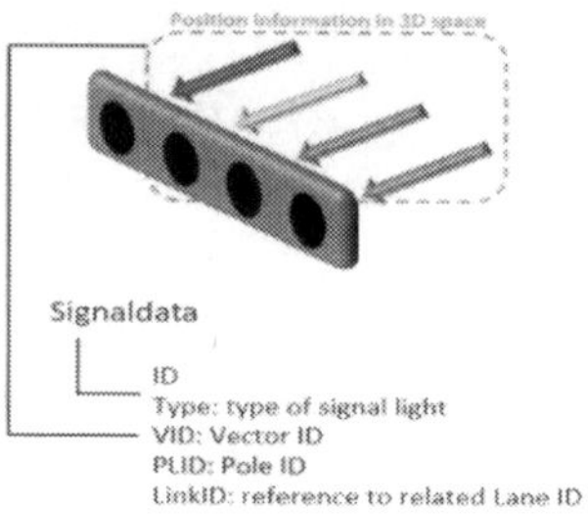

Figure 2. Traffic light information in an HD map.

chosen. Due to the simplicity of implementation and robustness, the loosely coupled integration has been chosen in this paper. The robustness lies in the fact that if one of the systems fails, navigation can still be provided by another sensor [10]. To enhance the capacity and reliability of the localization system for a complex environment, a visual feature-aided method is added to the loosely coupled integration.

The whole framework can be regarded as having two phases. One phase uses the common GPS/INS/Odometry integration strategy. The positions and velocities of the vehicle derived by GNSS signal processing are merged as updates of the INS estimates via a Kalman filter. The other phase uses an observation model for providing correction information by associating the traffic light measurement from the monocular camera with the corresponding information in the high-definition map. Therefore, the system exploits Traffic Lights (TLs) in the testing field as visual features. To detect traffic lights robustly against similar objects, such as a backlight of a vehicle or an external light source, the usage of the HD map as the prior knowledge to generate ROIs can not only drastically reduce false positive detection results, but also can be used to identify the status of the traffic light. In this context, we focus on elaborating on the development of the map-matching based scheme, which improves the capability of the detector and the accuracy of low-cost devices for navigation.

III. Image Processing

To generate correction information for updating the status of the vehicle's location, the detected landmark features should be matched to the corresponding information in the HD map. In Section III, the integration process of the monocular camera and the HD map are introduced, as follows.

A. Landmark Projection

Establishing an explicit coordinate system is a very important step to a multi-sensor fusion methodology. In this paper, the process of mapping the information from the HD map to the image plane is achieved by the coordinate transformation. The coordinate conversions include three different kinds of coordinate systems which are world coordinate, vehicle coordinate, and sensor coordinate, respectively. The HD map provides location information with WGS-84 coordinate, while the navigation frame (n-frame) is the North East Down (NED) Cartesian coordinate. Hence, the conversion between WGS-84 and NED local coordinate system can be written as the following formula (1):

$$P_{NED} = R^T (P_{ECEF} - P_{Ref}) \quad (1)$$

where P_{NED} is a 3D position in a NED coordinate system, converted from P_{ECEF} ECEF position with respect to reference ECEF position P_{Ref} . Each signal data of a traffic light in the HD map consists of a pole and light bulbs presented in vectors aligned with the center position of bulbs, as shown in Figure 2. For practical utilization of landmark features, mainly front orientated traffic lights will be projected in an image. The origin of the camera frame is the lens optical center and the optical axis is the z-axis of the camera frame. According to the current position of the vehicle, the monocular camera can extract 3D information of traffic lights from the HD map, and only the light markers which are contained in the line-of-sight of the camera will be mapped to the image plane via coordinate transformations (2).

$$P^c = R_n^c P^n + T_n^c \quad (2)$$

where P^n represent the traffic light position in the navigation frame, and derived the point of the traffic light in the camera frame P^c by rotation and transformation from the navigation frame to the camera frame. Conversion from navigation frame to vehicle frame (body frame) is according to the position and the orientation of the vehicle. Because the monocular is mounted on the vehicle, thus, the relationship between the body frame and camera frame is right the extrinsic parameters of the camera model, which can be obtained by offline camera calibration. By finishing the camera calibration, both intrinsic and extrinsic parameters can be known. Eventually, the re-projection process is done by being derived with intrinsic parameters. The pixel coordinates are denoted as u and v. The two-dimensional image plane can be denoted as (3)

$$u = \frac{f_x \cdot x_C}{z_C} + c_x, \; v = \frac{f_y \cdot y_C}{z_C} + c_y \quad (3)$$

B. Traffic Light Recognition

Vision-based traffic light recognition methods have been widely investigated by using feature-learning models [11], which can detect targets within ROIs. However, only a vision-based method has a lot of challenges such as the influence of weather conditions, varying illumination, viewpoints, and so on. Owing to the rapid development of deep neural networks, a deep model can classify and localize objects accurately.

In 2019, H. Law and J. Deng proposed the CornerNet [12] which detects an object with a pair of key points. Due to objects detected as paired keypoints, the design of using anchor boxes as single-stage detectors was modified. After the novel approach of keypoints,

Figure 3. Model inference at a different time of a day.

(a) (b)

Figure 4. (a) The projection of traffic lights' center points. (b) ROI generation according to the projection from the map.

CenterNet [13], detecting objects as axis-aligned boxes, uses keypoint estimation to search center points of objects and then optimizes the objective function to regress to all other object properties, such as object size and location. Owing to its faster inference time and higher accuracy, it is applied to recognize TLs in different illumination of a day time shown in Figure 3.

Although using a deep network to detect TLs, false-positives might be generated because of external light sources or the influence of illumination variation. Various approaches extending localization and map information as prior knowledge for traffic light recognition have been proposed [14]. Therefore, we adopt CenterNet to detect targets that should be verified as true TLs in ROIs generated by the HD map. It shows that utilizing the map as prior information can dramatically reduce noise that disturbs the model shown in Figure 4(b).

C. Data Association

When the deep learning model detects lighted marks in certain sections, there may be more than one traffic light in an image. To obtain the re-projection errors as correction information, the detection results from the deep neural network and re-projection of corresponding TLs from the map should be matched correctly. The distance $y(\tilde{d}_k, \hat{d}_k)$ between the detection $\tilde{d}_k^{\,i}$ and the projection $\hat{d}_k^{\,j}$ of the traffic light at epoch k is hereby

Figure 5. Data association between detection results and projection (gray virtual box).

formulated as a combination of the Mahalanobis distance [15] according to their positions (4):

$$y(\tilde{d}_k, \hat{d}_k) = \alpha \cdot \delta d_k^{iT} S_k^{-1} \delta d_k^i + (1-\alpha) \cdot \frac{\omega_d^2}{\sigma_d^2} \quad (4)$$

where $\delta d_k^{\,i}$ is Euclidean distance of $\tilde{d}_k^{\,i} - \hat{d}_k^{\,j}$, S_k is the covariance of $\delta d_k^{\,i}$, ω_d is the width of the bounding box of the detected TL, while σ_d is the width of projection, and the additional factor α is used to weight the impact of the position and width of a TL. If the Mahalanobis distance of each detected TL is lower than the threshold, the re-projection errors between detection and projection results can be regarded as residuals for updating the status of the vehicle shown in Figure 5. Finally, the correction information can be utilized by the visual measurement model for EKF, which will be introduced in Section IV.

IV. Sensor Fusion For Localization

In our work, the Extended Kalman filter has been chosen to accomplish the self-localization for the vehicle. In state formulations, the state equation at each epoch is propagated with the INS dynamic model and updates each state with measurements from multi-sensors.

A. State Model

An INS with fifteen states was developed and the complete state is denoted as:

$$X = [p^n \ v^n \ \rho \ b_a \ b_g]^T \quad (5)$$

where p^N is the vehicle position in the navigation frame, v^N is the velocity of the vehicle, ρ is attitude including roll, pitch, and yaw angle, b_a is the bias of the accelerometer, b_g is the bias of the gyroscope. The nominal-state kinematics corresponding to the system without noises or perturbations can be denoted as (6)

$$\begin{aligned} \dot{p}^n &= v^n \\ \dot{v}^n &= R_b^n \cdot f_{ib}^b - (2\Omega_{ie}^n + \Omega_{en}^n) \cdot v^n + g^n \\ \dot{R}_b^n &= R_b^n (\Omega_{ib}^b - \Omega_{ie}^b) \end{aligned} \quad (6)$$

where f_{ib}^b represents the acceleration of the vehicle in b-frame, R_b^n is the rotation matrix from body frame to navigation frame, $(2\Omega_{ie}^n + \Omega_{en}^n) \cdot v^n$ represents the Coriolis acceleration and g^n is the gravitational acceleration given by gravity model. Ω_{ib}^b is the skew-symmetric matrix of the angular velocity in b-frame. Ω_{ie}^b is the skew-symmetric matrix of the angular velocity of the Earth's rotation. The state model is formulated in discrete-time corresponding to the real system. The prediction stage consists of predicting the state using knowledge of the previous epoch, as (7)

$$X_{k+1}^- = A_{k+1} X_k^+ + \Gamma_{k+1} w_k \quad (7)$$

where A_{k+1} is the state transition matrix at epoch k. w_k is the process noise transformed by Γ_{k+1} to body frame.

$$P_{k+1}^- = \Phi_{k+1} P_k^+ \Phi_{k+1}{}^T + Q_k \quad (8)$$

where the transformation matrix Φ_{k+1} can be approximately as $\Phi_{k+1} = I + F \cdot dt$ by using the first order of the Taylor series.

B. GNSS/Odometry Measurement Model

For the common loosely-coupled integration, the GNSS measurement model can be calculated by:

$$z_k = \begin{bmatrix} r_{GNSS}^n - r_{INS}^n \\ v_{GNSS}^n - v_{INS}^n \end{bmatrix} \quad (9)$$

where r_{GNSS}^n and v_{GNSS}^n are the position and velocity derived by GNSS in n-frame. r_{INS}^n and v_{INS}^n are position and velocity that derived by INS mechanism in n-frame. The observation matrix for updating the GNSS measurement can be derived as (10)

$$H_k = \begin{bmatrix} I_{3\times3} & 0_{3\times3} & 0_{3\times9} \\ 0_{3\times3} & I_{3\times3} & 0_{3\times9} \end{bmatrix} \quad (10)$$

The Odometry measurement is written as follows:

$$z_k = \left[speed_{Odometry}^n - speed_{INS}^n \right] \quad (11)$$

$$speed_{Odometry}^n = \frac{1}{2} \cdot r_{wheel} \cdot (\omega_{rl} + \omega_{rr}) \quad (12)$$

$$speed_{INS}^n = \sqrt{v_n^2 + v_e^2 + v_d^2} \quad (13)$$

where ω_{rl} and ω_{rr} are the angular velocities of the left and right wheels, respectively. r_{wheel} is the radius of the wheels and the observation model can be written as (14)

$$H_k = \begin{bmatrix} 0_{1\times3} & \frac{v_n}{speed_{INS}^n} & \frac{v_e}{speed_{INS}^n} & \frac{v_d}{speed_{INS}^n} & 0_{1\times9} \end{bmatrix} \quad (14)$$

C. Visual Measurement Model

The re-projection result of the landmark, changing with the camera's pose, can be described as the observation model denoted as (15).

$$\hat{d}_k = h(\hat{X}_k^+) \quad (15)$$

where h is the measurement function that extracts the nearby traffic lights to convert to the measurement at k epoch. The residual between the visual measurement and the predicted value can be given in (16).

$$\delta d_k = \tilde{d}_k - \hat{d}_k = H_k \delta X_k + v_k \quad (16)$$

where $H_k = \left.\frac{\partial h}{\partial X}\right|_{X=\hat{X}_k^+}$ is the Jacobians of the estimated measurement with respect to the state vector and v_k is the observation noise that correlated with R_k. Based on the knowledge of 3D reconstruction optimization algorithm, Bundle adjustment [16], the relationship between the error on image and the camera pose can be derived by minimizing the re-projection error described as (17)

$$\delta d_k^* = \arg\min_{\delta d_k} \frac{1}{2}\sum_{i=1}^{n} \left\| \tilde{d}_k^i - \hat{d}_k^i \right\| \quad (17)$$

$$\hat{d}_k^i = \frac{1}{s} \cdot K \cdot [R \mid T]_n^c \cdot P^n \quad (18)$$

where s is the scale factor. K is the intrinsic parameters of the camera model, obtained by camera calibration [17], and P^n is the landmark position in the map. By linearizing the error with the first order of the Taylor series, the corresponding Jacobian matrix can be derived as (19)

$$H_k = K_c DC \cdot \begin{bmatrix} -I_{3\times3} & 0_{3\times3} & [\hat{P}^c \times] & 0_{3\times6} \end{bmatrix} \quad (19)$$

where

$$K_c = \begin{bmatrix} fy & 0 \\ 0 & fx \end{bmatrix} \quad (20)$$

,

$$D = \begin{bmatrix} d_{11} & d_{12} \\ d_{21} & d_{22} \end{bmatrix} \quad (21)$$

where

$d_{11} = 1 + k_1 r^2 + k_2 r^4 + 2 p_1 x_c' + 4 p_2 x_c'$

$d_{12} = 2 p_1 x_c'$

$d_{21} = 2 p_1 y_c'$

$d_{22} = 1 + k_1 r^2 + k_2 r^4 + 2 p_2 x_c' + 4 p_1 y_c'$,

C is the partial derivative of the re-projection error with respect to the position in camera coordinate:

$$C = (1/(\hat{z}_c)^2) \begin{bmatrix} \hat{z}_c & 0 & -\hat{x}_c \\ 0 & \hat{z}_c & -\hat{y}_c \end{bmatrix} \quad (22)$$

$\left[\hat{P}^c \times\right]$ is the skew-symmetry matrix of the landmark position in camera coordinate k.

Once there exist traffic lights in an image, the residuals calculated by the difference between the detection result and the re-projection mentioned in Section III can be used to correct the localization error. The Kalman gain at k epoch can be calculated as (23)

$$K_k = P_{k+1}^- H_k^T * [H_k P_{k+1}^- H_k^T + R_k]^{-1} \quad (23)$$

Therefore, the state vector can be updated (24).

$$X_{k+1}^+ = X_{k+1}^- + K_k \cdot \delta d_k \quad (24)$$

The Kalman filter calculates the updated covariance P_{k+1}^- after getting the state estimation, which will be used in the next time step.

$$P_{k+1}^+ = [I - K_k H_k] P_{k+1}^- \quad (25)$$

There might be multiple traffic lights in an image at the same time. To get the measurements that can truly correct the localization errors, the two closest TLs, which are not affected significantly by the geometry distortion of the camera, are chosen as visual measurements to update the state vector. Each measurement is used to update the state estimation and re-calculate the Kalman gain once again. By selecting the specific traffic lights as measurements, the observation values are more reliable and can avoid the bad correction while detection results mismatch the corresponding information in the HD map.

V. EXPERIMENTAL RESULTS

In this section, the evaluation of the proposed method was verified at the Taiwan CAR Lab test facility where various environmental complexities simulate street conditions in Taiwan. The HD map in the testing field was produced by the High Definition Maps Research Center at National Cheng Kung University. In our work, the point 22.99665875N° , 120.222584889E° is set as the origin of the local tangent plane coordinate system and we chose the driving route including different types of traffic lights and a tunnel. Let the vehicle drive counterclockwise to test the capacity of the map-matching based localization system.

A. System configuration

As shown in Figure 6, the level of centimeter localization result from NDT, with lidar VLP 16, is set as the reference. The locating signals are received by the antenna to the GNSS receiver. Except for GMSL camera connected to Nvidia Drive PX2, the other on-board sensors are connected to Industrial PC. The monocular camera is rigidly coupled to the vehicle. The camera optical axis is aligned to the driving direction that can collect the front view image data. The specification of the sensors is shown in Table I. Based on Robot Operating System (ROS), we integrated these two computing core platforms - IPC and Nvidia Drive PX2- to develop our approach.

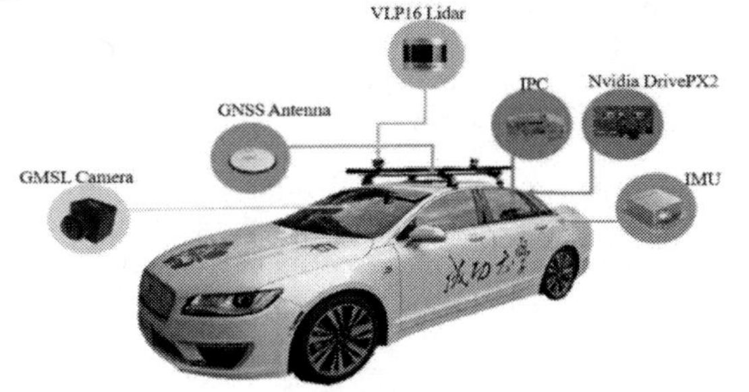

Figure 6. Lincon MKZ with high-performance computing cores and sensors.

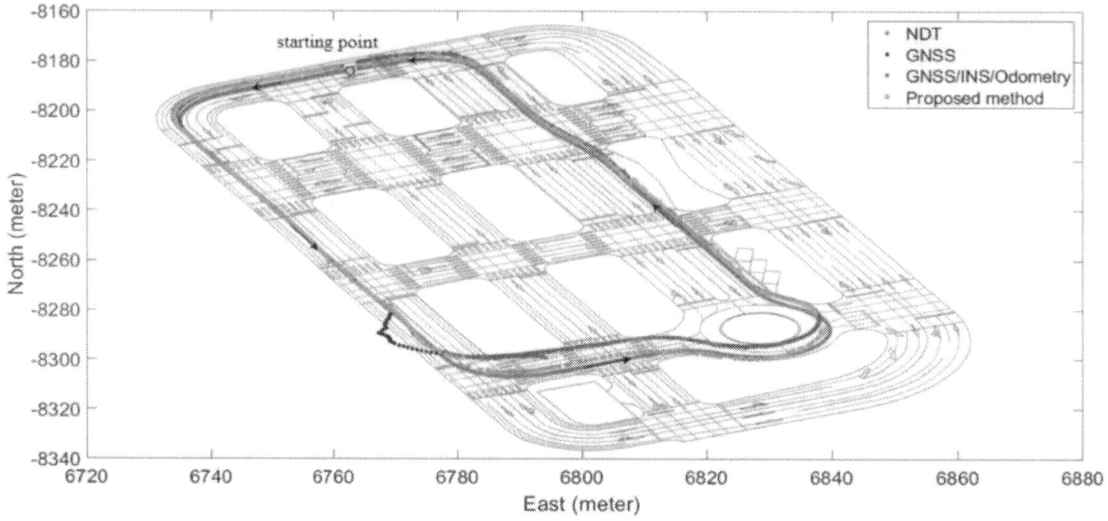

Figure 7. The overall localization results show on the high-definition map. The *x*-*y* axis represents the local tangent plane coordinates: east and north respectively. Violet: NDT as the reference. Blue: Only GNSS localization. Red: Integrated GNSS with INS. Green: Corrected localization error by fusing with landmark features in an image and the corresponding information in the HD map.

TABLE I. TABLE TYPE STYLES

Sensor	Model	Type	Parameter
GNSS receiver	HDM2024 EVK	Positioning Accuracy	2.5 m
		Velocity Accuracy	0.1 m/s
		Time Accuracy	25 ns
		Velocity Limit	515 m/s
Camera	GMSL	Resolution	1928x1208
		Optical format	1/2.7 inch
		Field Of View	60 degree

B. *Localization results*

In this experiment, the maximum localization error happened when the vehicle drove into the tunnel because of the signal outage. The condition of positioning gradually recovered while leaving the tunnel. As the situation mentioned above, the localization system can not only rely on GNSS; otherwise, it will cause fatal accidents for the vehicle. To reduce the localization error, the inertial navigation system can be used to enhance the consistency of updating the position.

Although the fusion of GPS, IMU, and Odometry can provide more reliable navigation solutions that allow the vehicle to drive within the lane, the vehicle still drove against the traffic shown in Figure 7. Owing to the characteristics of the integration of these sensors based on an EKF, the localization estimation had more confidence in the solution from IMU when the vehicle lost signal from GNSS. The drawback of error accumulations from IMU for a period led the vehicle to drive on the wrong side of the road. The proposed method can obtain visual measurements by using the monocular camera to overcome the problems of the conventional GNSS/INS integration approach.

Figure 8. (a) The mask represents the tunnel section in the HD map. (b) The residual between the detection result and the re-projection of the traffic light indicated in (a).

Since the camera is sensitive to the light intensity variation, it was hard to detect the traffic light when the vehicle departed from the tunnel that changed the view from low illumination to high exposure. Compared to the conventional vision learning-based methods, the powerful deep learning model can get more robust detection results against the quality of the image. Therefore, the challenge of varying illumination can be overcome to obtain the correction information for adjusting the state of the vehicle effectively.

Figure 8(a) shows that it is a big challenge for the localization system because of the GNSS/INS localization performance degradation when the vehicle was going to drastically turn left. The residual between the visual measurement detected by the deep model and the re-projection shown in Figure 8(b) can provide significant correction information to help correct the localization error, especially the outcome in the east direction in Figure 9(b). The localization errors in North and East direction are calculated as Table II, which shows that the improvement of the localization accuracy is greater than fifty percent.

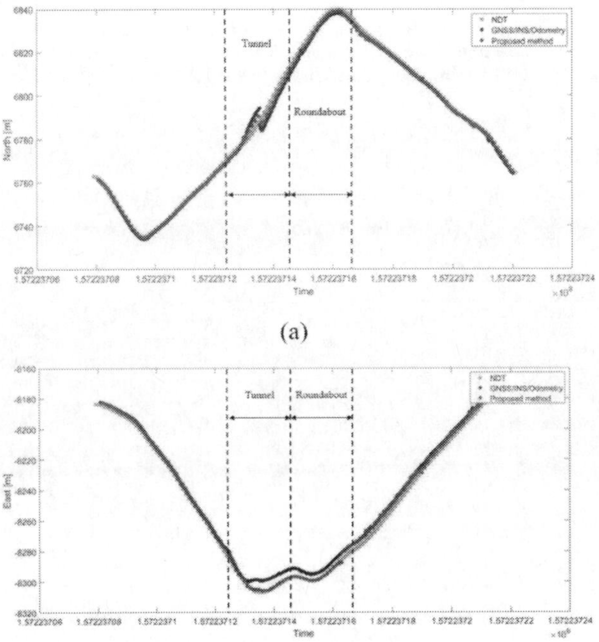

(a)

(b)

Figure 9. Localization in each direction (a) Localization in North direction. (b) Localization in East direction.

TABLE II. TABLE TYPE STYLES

	GNSS	GNSS/IMU/Odometry	Proposed method
North error [m]	4.22	4.10	1.85
East error [m]	2.65	1.99	1.32

In addition, the proposed method can provide the vehicle's attitude information. Figure 10 refers to the heading angle comparison. It can be seen that the heading drifted due to GNSS signal-degraded when the vehicle passed through the tunnel. Owing to the loosely coupled integration using IMU, the heading angle is corrected. In particular, the correction information generated by the camera and HD map can be used to dramatically improve the heading.

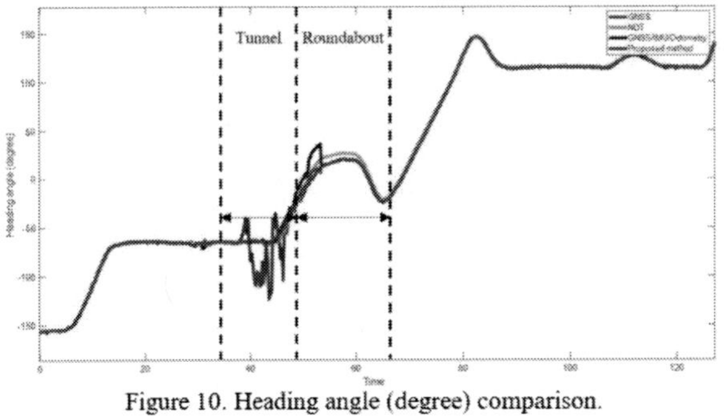

Figure 10. Heading angle (degree) comparison.

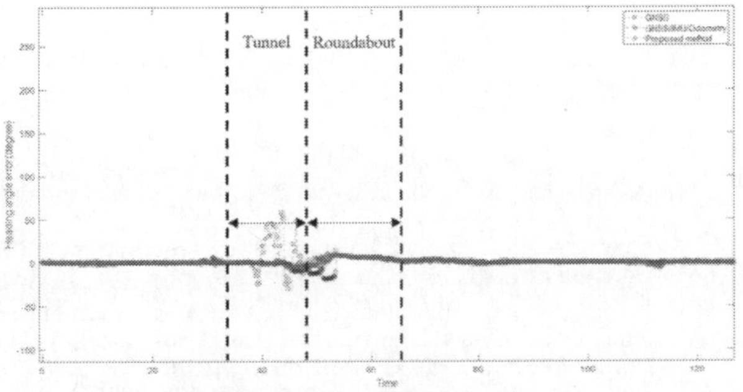

Figure 11. Heading angle (degree) error.

Further comparing to the ground truth, the heading errors are depicted in Figure 11. The heading errors can be averagely reduced below 5 degrees.

VI. CONCLUSION AND FUTURE WORK

The map-matching based localization scheme demonstrated in this work shows that the integration of visual features and an HD map can dramatically improve a low-cost GNSS, IMU and Odometry integration. This paper is aimed to solve the problem when the GNSS/INS/Odometry localization system fails to locate a reliable position under some circumstances, especially in a tunnel. The experimental results show that even the localization drifts caused by the GNSS signal outage and IMU error accumulation, as long as landmark features can be extracted by the monocular camera, then the residuals computed by the re-projection error in an image can effectively correct the positioning error. Moreover, the proposed method can provide a more accurate vehicle heading angle.

Although the availability of the proposed method is subject to intersections, the strong visual features of traffic lights can make it up in a challenging environment. The integration of traffic light recognition and an HD map can not only reduce the false-positive detection results, but also provide useful correction information for the system update. Besides, the camera calibration is a very important prerequisite for the visual observation model, because the change of each direction or orientation will significantly affect the projection result. Therefore, further researches may pay attention to on-line camera calibration to avoid long-term drifting of the camera parameters. To overcome the limitation that TLs can be only detected at intersections, other road features in an image should be considered such as lane lines, traffic signs and pole-like objects, which can provide more useful information for vehicle localization.

In conclusion, the map-matching based system using traffic lights as visual features can significantly improve an integration strategy with low-cost devices for vehicle localization. Moreover, the availability of a vision-aided loosely coupled framework can be enhanced and it can be improved by solving the problems mentioned above.

ACKNOWLEDGMENT

This research was funded by the Ministry of Science and Technology, Taiwan, grant number MOST 108-2218-E-006-052.

REFERENCES

[1] R. J. Keller, M. E. Nichols, and A. F. Lange, "Methods and apparatus for precision agriculture operations utilizing real time kinematic global positioning system systems," ed: Google Patents, 2001.

[2] P. Biber and W. Straßer, "The normal distributions transform: A new approach to laser scan matching," in *Proceedings 2003 IEEE/RSJ International Conference on Intelligent Robots and Systems (IROS 2003)(Cat. No. 03CH37453)*, 2003, vol. 3: IEEE, pp. 2743-2748.

[3] O. Pink, F. Moosmann, and A. Bachmann, "Visual features for vehicle localization and ego-motion estimation," in *2009 IEEE Intelligent Vehicles Symposium*, 2009: IEEE, pp. 254-260.

[4] T. Weiss, N. Kaempchen, and K. Dietmayer, "Precise ego-localization in urban areas using laser scanner and high accuracy feature maps," in *IEEE Proceedings. Intelligent Vehicles Symposium,* 2005: IEEE, pp. 284-289.

[5] N. Mattern and G. Wanielik, "Camera-based vehicle localization at intersections using detailed digital maps," in *IEEE/ION Position, Location and Navigation Symposium*, 2010: IEEE, pp. 1100-1107.

[6] A. Schindler, "Vehicle self-localization with high-precision digital maps," in *2013 IEEE Intelligent Vehicles Symposium Workshops (IV Workshops)*, 2013: IEEE, pp. 134-139.

[7] F. Poggenhans *et al.*, "Lanelet2: A high-definition map framework for the future of automated driving," in *2018 21st International Conference on Intelligent Transportation Systems (ITSC)*, 2018: IEEE, pp. 1672-1679.

[8] A. Solimeno, "Low-cost INS/GPS data fusion with extended Kalman filter for airborne applications," *Masters of Science, Universidade Technica de Lisboa,* 2007.

[9] M. G. Petovello, *Real-time integration of a tactical-grade IMU and GPS for high-accuracy positioning and navigation*. Citeseer, 2003.

[10] S. Godha, "Performance evaluation of low cost MEMS-based IMU integrated with GPS for land vehicle navigation application," *UCGE report,* no. 20239, 2006.

[11] A. Mogelmose, M. M. Trivedi, and T. B. Moeslund, "Vision-based traffic sign detection and analysis for intelligent driver assistance systems: Perspectives and survey," *IEEE Transactions on Intelligent Transportation Systems,* vol. 13, no. 4, pp. 1484-1497, 2012.

[12] H. Law and J. Deng, "Cornernet: Detecting objects as paired keypoints," in *Proceedings of the European Conference on Computer Vision (ECCV)*, 2018, pp. 734-750.

[13] X. Zhou, D. Wang, and P. Krähenbühl, "Objects as points," *arXiv preprint arXiv:1904.07850,* 2019.

[14] M. Hirabayashi, A. Sujiwo, A. Monrroy, S. Kato, and M. Edahiro, "Traffic light recognition using high-definition map features," *Robotics and Autonomous Systems,* vol. 111, pp. 62-72, 2019.

[15] R. De Maesschalck, D. Jouan-Rimbaud, and D. L. Massart, "The mahalanobis distance," *Chemometrics and intelligent laboratory systems,* vol. 50, no. 1, pp. 1-18, 2000.

[16] B. Triggs, P. F. McLauchlan, R. I. Hartley, and A. W. Fitzgibbon, "Bundle adjustment—a modern synthesis," in *International workshop on vision algorithms*, 1999: Springer, pp. 298-372.

[17] A. Dhall, K. Chelani, V. Radhakrishnan, and K. M. Krishna, "LiDAR-camera calibration using 3D-3D point correspondences," *arXiv preprint arXiv:1705.09785,* 2017.

Achieving Trustworthy Autonomous Systems through Autonomic and Apoptotic Computing

Keynote at ICAS 2020

Roy Sterritt
School of Computing, Faculty of Computing, Engineering and the Built Environment.
Ulster University
Newtownabbey, Northern Ireland
email:r.sterritt@ulster.ac.uk | ORCID 0000-0002-4035-9363

***Abstract*— This paper considers the issue of trust in Autonomous Systems. This is a challenge as these systems are already deployed across many industrial sectors in specialised and controlled conditions with little focus on trustworthiness. When unexpected or uncontrolled situations are introduced into the environment, with a probable high level of interaction with people, the resulting potential for unexpected and/or undesirable results is significant. This paper reflects upon the Autonomic Computing (self-managing) paradigm, and the Apoptotic Computing (pre-programmed death as a safety mechanism) paradigm by presenting some of our research utilizing both, as a potential contribution to achieve Assured and Trustworthy Autonomous Systems.**

Keywords—Autonomic Computing; Apoptotic Computing; Autonomous Systems; Trustworthy Autonomy; Assured Autonomy; Autonomy.

I. INTRODUCTION

Autonomous systems are already developed and deployed across industrial sectors in specialised and controlled conditions with little focus on trustworthiness [1]. When autonomous systems are used in an uncontrolled environment, where there is a high level of interaction with people and a much larger number of variables, the resulting potential for unexpected and/or undesirable results is non-negligible [1]. These unanticipated events could have a very significant negative impact on the acceptability and thus compromise widespread deployment of autonomous systems [1]. For society to use and benefit from autonomous systems, people need to trust them. This means that the autonomous systems need to function as expected for their purpose, and they need to be designed and tested to ensure that they work consistently and safely and that they are appropriately developed within a legal, ethical and social context. Trust will only be enabled through technical advances conducted in specific societal circumstances [1]. To ensure that autonomous systems can be trusted, and ultimately adopted by society, fully integrated advances in both technical, and social sciences and humanities research are needed [1]. For example, research in logic, autonomy and intelligence and engineering (robotics and vehicles) is needed, but these technical developments must be carried out in the context of fundamental social sciences and humanities research across psychology, sociology, economics, ethics, philosophy, law, political science, international studies, innovation management and science and technology studies. The engagement of multiple disciplines in this endeavour, alongside regulators and the public, is key to ensuring that autonomous systems are developed to be used in real-world situations [1].

The hypothesis presented in this paper is that Trustworthy Autonomous Systems (TAS) can be (partially) achieved through Autonomic Computing extended with Apoptotic Computing.

The rest of the paper is structured as follows. In Section 2, the Autonomic Computing and Autonomic Communications paradigms are recapped, then, in Section 3, the Apoptotic Computing paradigm is summarised before presenting some of our research utilising both in Section 4. Section 5 then concludes the paper with some observations.

II. AUTONOMIC COMPUTING AND COMMUNICATIONS

In 2001, IBM researchers predicted that by the end of the decade the IT industry would need up to 200 million workers, equivalent to the entire US labor force, to manage a billion people and millions of businesses using a trillion devices connected via the Internet. Only if computer-based systems became more autonomic—that is, to a large extent self-managing—could we deal with this growing complexity, and they accordingly issued a formal challenge to researchers [2]. Over the two decades since Autonomic Computing has become a paradigm allowing the advanced automation of system management. In effect, it is a specialisation of autonomous systems – the autonomy of the management of the system itself.

The vision of autonomic computing represents a surprising combination of revolution and retrenchment. By focusing on total costs of ownership for enterprise systems, Kephart and Chess [3] highlighted the central impact that IT systems can have on the core economics of modern businesses. Indeed, the deployment, maintenance, and evolution of enterprise systems often require enormous efforts by extremely valuable staff, whose successes add little visible business value but are nevertheless vital and whose failures can be catastrophic for the whole enterprise. Autonomic computing, in its broadest sense, seeks to reduce the need for such heroic efforts and their consequential risks.

The most widely recognized elements of autonomic systems are the so-called self-* properties: For systems to be self-managing they should be self-configuring, self-healing, self-optimizing, and self-protecting and exhibit self-awareness, self-situation (environment and context awareness), self-monitoring, and self-adjustment [4]-[6]. Despite their seeming simplicity, these goals mask a complex interaction between the behaviors of systems and their goals, users, and relationships with the external environment. We can only optimize a system against some external criteria, so self-optimization implies that these criteria are made available in some way to the management system. Moreover, composition and analysis of systems probably imply that the criteria be explicit, symbolic, and machine-readable rather than embedded implicitly into algorithms [7].

In thinking of systems rather than simply of machines, we must also consider communications a component of the problem space [4], the most notable omission from Kephart's and Chess's vision. Mikhail Smirnov [8] propounded the notion of Autonomic Communications, not only based on IBM Autonomic Computing, but David Clark and colleagues' call for a knowledge plane for the Internet [9], and which became an active research topic in itself [10], especially in Europe, where it has received considerable support from the EU's Framework programs. Considering communications as well as computing naturally leads to an exploration of the interplay of these different aspects [7].

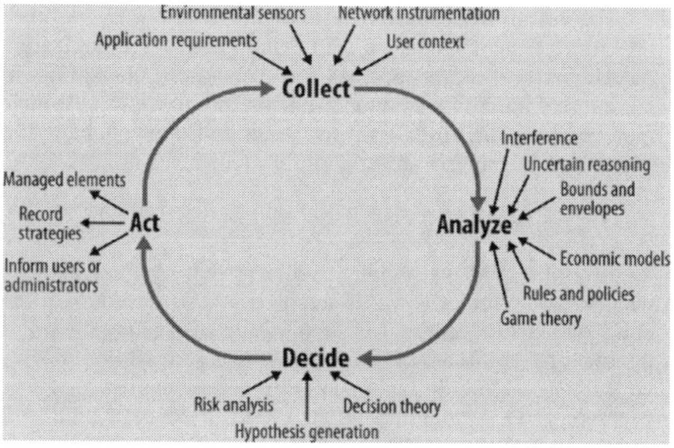

Figure 1. Collect-Analyze-Decide-Act control loop [7][10]

As Figure 1 shows [10][7], providing self-monitoring and self-control suggests the application of control theory—expressing a control action derived from a system's observed behavior against a model of intended or expected behavior. Researchers have successfully applied such techniques to, for example, power management, to achieve clear closed form representations. However, it is less clear whether the techniques can be applied more broadly in areas where the control domain changes dynamically and provide an assured or trusted autonomy.

III. APOPTOTIC COMPUTING

Apoptotic Computing and Apoptotic Communications are inspired by the apoptosis mechanism in biological systems. This mechanism provides security for the overall system by having a pre-programmed death and indeed a death by default at, for instance, the cellular level. It has been argued that this approach should be included in our modern ubiquitous/pervasive computer-based systems.

The Apoptotic Computing project, first started back in 2002 [11]-[15], involves working towards the long-term goal of developing Programmed Death by Default for Computer-Based Systems to provide for this foreseen future. It is essentially biologically-inspired by the Apoptosis mechanisms in multicellular organisms. It may be considered as a sub-area of Bio-Inspired Computing, Natural Computing or Autonomic Systems (providing the self-destruct property) [16][17].

With biological systems, it is believed that a cell knows when to commit suicide because cells are programmed to do so – self-destruct (sD) is an intrinsic property. This sD is delayed due to the continuous receipt of biochemical retrieves. This process is referred to as apoptosis [18], pronounced either as APE-oh-TOE-sis or uh-POP-tuh-sis and means for 'to fall off' or 'drop out', used by the Greeks to refer to the Fall/Autumn dropping of leaves from trees, i.e., loss of cells that ought to die in the midst of the living structure [19]. The process has also been nicknamed 'death by default' [20], where cells are prevented from putting an end to themselves due to constant receipt of biochemical 'stay alive' signals. The key aspect of apoptosis is that the cell's self-destruction takes place in a programmed and controlled way; the suicidal cell starts to shrink, decomposes internal structures and degrades all internal proteins. Thereafter, the cell breaks into small membrane-wrapped fragments (drop-off) that will be engulfed by phagocytic cells for recycling. Necrosis, is the un-programmed death of a cell, involving inflammation and toxic substances leaking to the environment [21].

Further investigations into the apoptosis process [18] have discovered more details about the self-destruct program. Whenever a cell divides, it simultaneously receives orders to kill itself. Without a reprieve signal, the cell does indeed self-destruct. It is believed that the reason for this is self-protection, as the most dangerous time for the body is when a cell divides, since if just one of the billions of cells locks into division the result is a tumour, while simultaneously a cell must divide to build and maintain a body. The suicide and reprieve controls have been compared to the dual-key on a nuclear missile [19]. The key (chemical signal) turns on cell growth but at the same time switches on a sequence that leads to self-destruction. The second key overrides the self-destruct [19].

Apoptotic Computing takes its inspiration from the biological apoptosis, and can be implemented as part of the self-management of Autonomic Computing. The following sections will discuss some of the research conducted into these.

IV. AUTONOMIC AND APOPTOTIC COMPUTING CASE STUDIES

As has been stated, the hypothesis presented in this paper, is that TAS can be (partially) achieved through Autonomic Computing extended with Apoptotic Computing.

We consider to truly achieve Autonomy, design and development of Autonomous Systems benefits from separation of concerns, namely splitting the advanced automation of the task/mission/user oriented goal of the system from the advanced automation of the management and running of the actual system. The former represents self-governance/autonomy of the system (and what users focus in on) and the later represents self-management/autonomicity. A simple example of such is self-driving (autonomous) cars. The user perception is cars that drive themselves; which represents the task/mission/goal, the split in roles is that the autonomic system takes care of is the actual management of the system, are the sensors, actuators, algorithms, and processors working correctly? Requiring re-configuring to improve performance or reflex reactions of self-protection and self-healing if a tire blows out. Division of labor into Autonomous and Autonomic layers in the design and development effort should enable a more trustworthy system. The autonomicity can be added to provide assurance at the system, application and/or component level.

A. System level Trust and Assurance Cases

Motivated by an incident at a Smart (elderly care) Home where a resident with dementia left the building undetected, unaccompanied and not dressed for the external elements. Thankfully, the older resident was found quickly, but a google search on this incident found cases where similar events occurred nationally, where the care home (or fold) has Smart technology yet dementia residents leave undetected and unfortunately were not found before hypothermia set in resulting in death. In our case, the issue was a faulty fire alarm, where for safety the fire doors cannot be locked from the inside but are alarmed for when opened. The faulty alarm had not been detected. This obviously raises trustworthy issues for this type of autonomous system. We researched how autonomic computing helps provide assurance in this scenario.

In this research, an approach to ensuring fault tolerance in intelligent environments for the elderly through the provision of mobile sensor substitution (via a robot) in the event of the detection of anomalous static (smart home) sensor behaviour was investigated. One stream focused on the monitoring of an external door in an intelligent care home environment. A mobile robot equipped with an array of ultrasonic sensors is dispatched to monitor the door state and report a change in state to a central server. For each door state, there are consistent changes in the sensor readings identified in the course of the experiments carried out within this work. The use of ultrasonic sensors provides a viable substitution option that can assist a central system in deciding whether a care assistant or maintenance engineer is required to resolve the anomalous static sensor behaviour.

A robot to investigate static sensors and then act as "watchbot" filling in for the defected door sensor with its sonar sensors until a technician can arrive (potentially days later) and replace the faulty sensor may seem like a "sledge-hammer to crack a nut" solution but there was a wider context to this autonomic solution that the robot would also be proactively testing the sensors around the smart-home as well as determining conflict in sensor readings such as has the elderly person fallen at the front door or is it a parcel/dog lying on the sensor mat constantly alarming to the system? Figure 2 depicts a high-level overview of the autonomic solution providing trustworthiness and assurance to the autonomous system (smart home). Note NASM and EHSM in the figure stand for Normal Activity State Machine and Error Handling State Machine which were FSMs designed with novel built-in adaptability. More details can be found in [23]- [25].

Another critical autonomous system we researched from an autonomic perspective, adding assurance and trustworthiness at the system level, was a biometric enabled prison/correctional institute system [26]. This system was already extensively robust (in a FTC–fault tolerant computing way) with a watchdog/sentential polling components in the system. Yet, we investigated better (autonomic) ways of designing the system to provide more proactive than reactionary fault tolerance [27] to then attempt to move towards next-gen prison systems [28][29] beyond high granularity of prisoner tracking (essentially knowing which area they have biometrically entered/exited) to a much finer grained self-management of the system, ensuring a trustworthy system for inmates, staff and visitors [30].

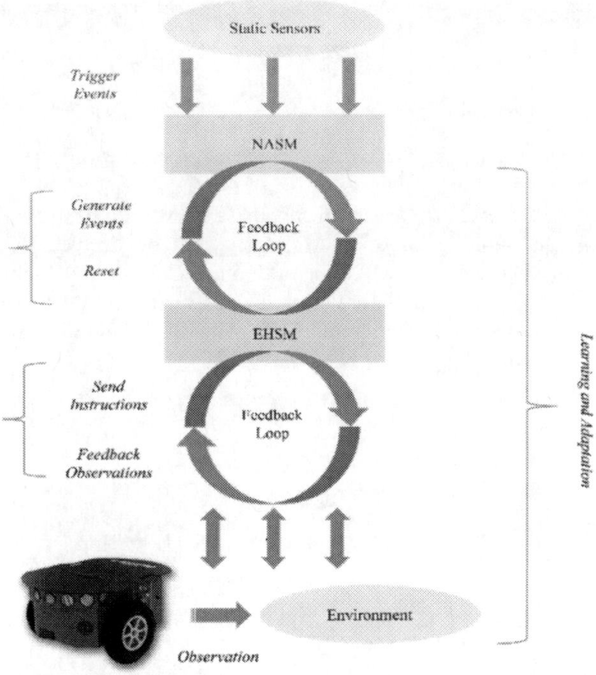

Figure 2. Autonomic Robot ensuring TAS in a Elderly care Smart Home [23].

We have extensively discussed in the literature the research with NASA into how Autonomic Computing can provide assurance for Swarm-Based Space Exploration Systems (most notably ANTS – Autonomous Nano Technology Swarms – concept mission), for instance [31]. The following section though will highlight how this also provided assurance at the application and component (or even Nano) level.

B. Application and Component level Trust and Assurance Cases

Autonomic Computing can provide assurance at all levels of an autonomous system through its feedback control self-management. Apoptotic Computing, with its pre-programmed death tends to provide assurance at the component level and possibly the application level (rarely would one want a system level self-destruct (apoptotic) mechanism).

We have researched introducing apoptotic measures into Agent-Based Systems, Autonomic (Self-managing and adaptive) Systems and Swarm Based Space Exploration Systems as highlighted earlier [11]-[17]. At an application level, we have applied this to Robotics (Apoptotic Robotics) [32]. In the wider view of this stream of research, Autonomic

Robotics, we have carried out several case studies investigating self-* healing strategies and a confirmatory case study;

- Robot Wheel Alignment Fault [33][34]
- Robot Sonar Sensor Faults [35]
- Robot Battery Degradation Fault [36]
- Stereo Vision Camera Fault – Confirmatory Case Study [37]

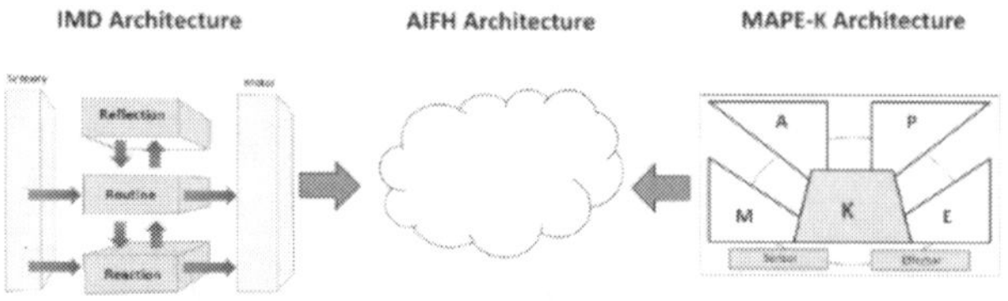

Figure 3. Towards an Autonomic Robotics Architecture.

The lessons learnt from these case studies enabled an Autonomic Robotics Architecture to be derived from IMD (Robotics) and MAPE (Autonomic Computing) architectures (Figure 3 and Figure 4), which is also referred to as AIFH: Autonomic Intelligent Fault Handling architecture. More detail can be found in [37][38].

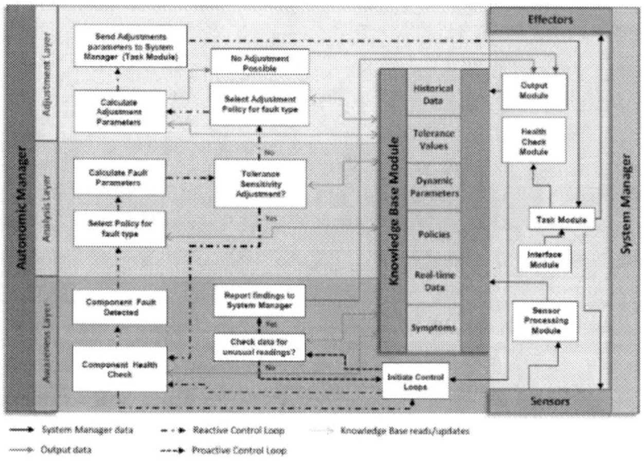

Figure 4. Autonomic Architecture for Fault Handling in Mobile Robots

More recently, we have been investigating it with application to CubeSats/NanoSats/PicoSats.

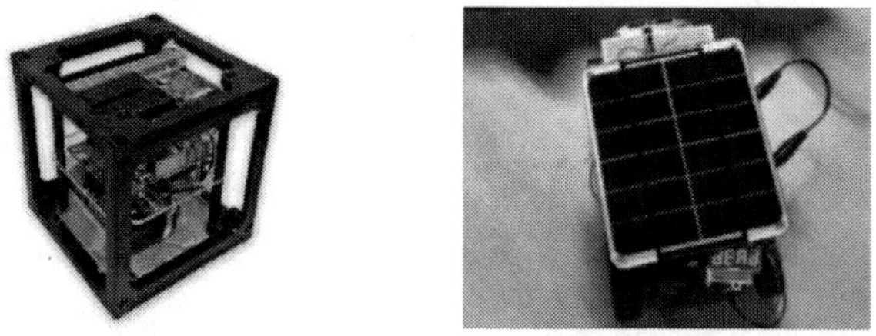

Figure 5. Autonomic and Apoptotic CubeSat research.

In the first instance, the research was to build in the apoptotic pre-programmed death (component level) to the CubeSat in an attempt to prevent adding to the proliferation of Space Debris/Space Junk (Figure 5) [39].

In the second instance, with a broader perspective, this research has widened into developing a "Cubesat Autonomicity Capability Model (CACM)" as a roadmap for future autonomic cubesat development including autonomic cooperation in constellations, thus addressing trust at the system level once again, while having a "killswitch" (Apoptotic Computing) pre-

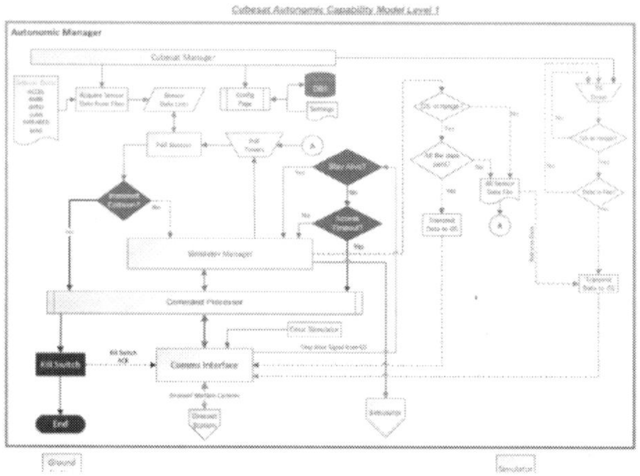

Figure 6. Part of CubeSat Autonomic Capability Model (CACM) – Level 1

programmed at the component level [40][41], for instance, Figure 6.

V. CONCLUSION

The hypothesis presented in this paper, was that Trustworthy Autonomous Systems (TAS) and Assured Autonomous Systems can be (partially) achieved through Autonomic Computing extended with Apoptotic Computing.

The research carried out in the noughties on Autonomic and Apoptotic Computing with NASA GSFC, briefly recapped here, started in the first instance as expanding on the NASA Formal Approaches to Swarm Technologies (FAST) project which was funded by the NASA Office of Systems and Mission Assurance (OSMA) through its Software Assurance Research Program (SARP). The concern that was attempting to address here was the future concept missions of potentially 1000s of autonomous adaptive craft and how can you assure their operation. The apoptotic (pre-programmed nano-craft death) became the ultimate assurance with autonomic paradigm ensuring the trustworthy self-management of the mission assets. This work lead to 16 patents [43], such as [44].

This assurance and trustworthy via autonomic and apoptotic computing theme carried on throughout reflection on our other research; from elderly care smart homes to prison systems, robotics and returning to space with cubesats and the derivation of a generic architecture and a capability model. Yet the larger, more difficult task of combining these point solutions into wider autonomous systems remains. More consideration must be given to integrating solutions, and to choosing solutions from the range of possibilities— to *trustworthy and assured autonomous and autonomic systems engineering*, in other words. Without the development of such an approach, we will simply rediscover the risks of feature interaction at a higher level, and in a way that is so dynamic as to be resistant to debugging and testing. We are confident, however, that the foundation exists to construct a systems theory and practice from which we can engineer trustworthy autonomous solutions for the next generation of enterprise and sensor systems.

ACKNOWLEDGMENT

The author is supported by the Ulster University's Computer Science Research Institute and School of Computing. Some of the research described in this paper is patented by Roy Sterritt (Ulster University) and Mike Hinchey (Lero—the Irish Software Research Centre, formerly NASA GSFC) through NASA and assigned to the US government. Thanks to all colleagues and in particular my PhD students who have done a lot of the heavy lifting, in particular during the tens.

REFERENCES

[1] EPSRC, "Trustworthy Autonomous Systems Nodes –Outline funding call", ver.9, Oct. 2019

[2] P. Horn, "Autonomic Computing: IBM's Perspective on the State of Information Technology," 15 Oct. 2001, IBM Research.

[3] J. O. Kephart and D. M. Chess, "The Vision of Autonomic Computing," Computer, Jan. 2003, pp. 41-50.

[4] R. Sterritt, "Towards Autonomic Computing: Effective Event Management," Proc. 27th Ann. NASA Goddard Software Eng. Workshop (SEW 02), IEEE CS Press, 2002, pp. 40-47. doi: 10.1109/SEW.2002.1199448

[5] R. Sterritt and D. W. Bustard, "Towards an autonomic computing environment," 14th International Workshop on Database and Expert Systems Applications, 2003. Proceedings., Prague, Czech Republic, 2003, pp. 694-698. doi: 10.1109/DEXA.2003.1232103

[6] R. Sterritt, Innovations Syst Softw Eng (2005) 1: 79. doi: 10.1007/s11334-005-0001-5

[7] S. Dobson, R. Sterritt, P. Nixon and M. Hinchey, "Fulfilling the Vision of Autonomic Computing," in Computer, vol. 43, no. 1, pp. 35-41, Jan. 2010. doi: 10.1109/MC.2010.14

[8] M. Smirnov, Autonomic Communication: Research Agenda for a New Communications Paradigm, tech. report, Fraunhofer FOKUS, 2004.

[9] D. D. Clark, C. Partridge, J. C. Ramming, and J. T. Wroclawski "A Knowledge Plane for the Internet," Proc. 2003 Conf. Applications, Technologies, Architectures, and Protocols for Computer Comm. (Sigcomm 03), ACM Press, 2003, pp. 3-10.

[10] S. Dobson et al., "A Survey of Autonomic Communications," ACM Trans. Autonomous and Adaptive Systems, vol. 1, no. 2, 2006, pp. 223-259.

[11] R. Sterritt and M. G. Hinchey, "Apoptosis and Self-Destruct: A Contribution to Autonomic Agents?", Proceedings of Third NASA Goddard/IEEE Workshop on Formal Approaches to Agent-Based Systems (FAABS III), Washington DC, April 26-27, 2004, in "LNAI 3228", SpringerVerlag, pp. 262-270, doi: 10.1007/978-3-540- 30960-4_18

[12] R. Sterritt and M. G. Hinchey, "Engineering Ultimate Self-Protection in Autonomic Agents for Space Exploration Missions", Proceedings of IEEE Workshop on the Engineering of Autonomic Systems (EASe 2005) at 12th Annual IEEE International Conference and Workshop on the Engineering of Computer Based Systems (ECBS 2005), Greenbelt, MD, USA, , 3-8 April, 2005, pp. 506-511 doi: 10.1109/ECBS.2005.36

[13] R. Sterritt and M. G. Hinchey, "From Here to Autonomicity: Self-Managing Agents and the Biological Metaphors that Inspire Them", Proceedings of Integrated Design & Process Technology Symposium (IDPT 2005), Beijing, China, 13-17 June, pp. 143-150

[14] R. Sterritt and M. G. Hinchey, "BiologicallyInspired Concepts for Autonomic Self-Protection in Multiagent Systems", Proceedings of 3rd International Workshop on Safety and Security in Multi-Agent Systems (SASEMAS 2006) at AAMAS 2006, Hakodate, Japan, 8-12 May 2006, doi: 10.1007/978-3-642-04879-1_22

[15] R Sterritt and M. G. Hinchey, "SPAACE IV: Self-Properties for an Autonomous & Autonomic Computing Environment – Part IV A Newish Hope", Proceedings of AA-SES-IV: 4th IEEE International Workshop on Autonomic and Autonomous Space Exploration Systems (at SMCIT), Pasadena, CA, USA, June 2009, in "Proceedings of the Seventh IEEE International Conference and Workshops on Engineering of Autonomic and Autonomous Systems (EASe 2010)", IEEE CS Press, pp. 119-125, doi: 10.1109/EASe.2010.29

[16] R. Sterritt, "Apoptotic computing: Programmed death by default for computer-based systems," in Computer, vol. 44, no. 1, pp. 59-65, Jan. 2011. doi: 10.1109/MC.2011.5

[17] R. Sterritt and M. G. Hinchey, " Apoptotic Computing: Programmed Death by Default for Software Technologies," in "Software Technology: 10 Years of Innovation in IEEE Computer: 10 Years of Innovation, First,", Wiley, 2018, doi: 10.1002/9781119174240.ch5

[18] J. Klefstrom, E. W. Verschuren, and G. I. Evan, "c-Myc Augments the Apoptotic Activity of Cytosolic Death Receptor Signaling Proteins by Engaging the Mitochondrial Apoptotic Pathway", J. Biol Chem,. 277:43224-43232, 2002.

[19] J. Newell, "Dying to live: why our cells self destruct," Focus, Dec. 1994.

[20] Y. Ishizaki, L. Cheng, A. W. Mudge, and M. C. Raff, "Programmed cell death by default in embryonic cells, fibroblasts, and cancer cells," Mol. Biol. Cell, 6(11):1443-1458, 1995.

[21] M. Sluyser, (ed.) "Apoptosis in Normal Development and Cancer". Taylor & Francis, London, 1996

[22] G. Brady, R. Sterritt and G. Wilkie, "An Investigation into the Viability of a Mobile Ultrasonic Array as a Sensor Substitute in an Autonomic Intelligent Environment," 2013 IEEE International Conference on Systems, Man, and Cybernetics, Manchester, 2013, pp. 577-582, doi: 10.1109/SMC.2013.104

[23] G. Brady, R. Sterritt, and G.Wilkie, "An adaptive approach to self-healing in an intelligent environment," in Proceedings for ADAPTIVE 2014, The Sixth International Conference on Adaptive and Self-Adaptive Systems and Applications, IARIA, May 2014. ISBN 978 1 61208 341 4

[24] G. Brady, R. Sterritt, G. Wilkie, (2015). Mobile Robots and Autonomic Ambient Assisted Living. Paladyn, Journal of Behavioral Robotics, 6(1), 205-217, doi: 10.1515/pjbr-2015-0013

[25] G. Brady, "Autonomic Robot for Assisted Living: Supporting Smart Environment Occupants through Sensor Substitution", PhD diss., Ulster University, 2016.

[26] P. O'Hagan, E. Hanna and R. Sterritt, "Addressing the Corrections Crisis with Software Technology," in Computer, vol. 43, no. 2, pp. 90-93, Feb. 2010. doi: 10.1109/MC.2010.29

[27] R. Sterritt, G. Garrity, E. Hanna, and P. O'Hagan, "Autonomic Agents for Survivable Security Systems", Proceedings of 1st IFIP Workshop on Trusted and Autonomic Ubiquitous and Embedded Systems (TAUES 2005) at EUC'05, in "LNCS 3823", Springer, December 6-9 2005.

[28] C. L. Mulholland, R. Sterritt, P. O'Hagan, and E. Hanna, (Mar 2008) "Tagging and Tracking System for Prisons and Correctional Facilities – A Design Roadmap", Proceedings of Fifth IEEE International Workshop on Engineering of Autonomic and Autonomous Systems (EASe 2008), Belfast, Northern Ireland, 31st March - 4th April, IEEE CS Press, pp 143-153

[29] C. McFarland, R. Sterritt, P. O'Hagan and E. Hanna, "Interfacing with Next Generation Tagging and Tracking Systems for Prisons and Correctional Facilities," 2010 Seventh IEEE International Conference and Workshops on Engineering of Autonomic and Autonomous Systems, Oxford, 2010, pp. 43-50, doi: 10.1109/EASe.2010.14

[30] C. McFarland, R. Sterritt, D. W. Bustard, S. I. McClean, and P. O'Hagan, "AARCTIC: Autonomic Analytics Research for Corrections Technology, Institutional and in the Community", 11th IEEE International Conference and Workshops on the Engineering of Autonomic & Autonomous - APL, Laurel, Maryland, USA. Sep 2014.

[31] R. Sterritt, M. Hinchey, C. Rouff, J. Rash and W. Truszkowski, "Sustainable and autonomic space exploration missions," 2nd IEEE International Conference on Space Mission Challenges for Information Technology (SMC-IT'06), Pasadena, CA, 2006, 8 p, doi: 10.1109/SMC-IT.2006.78

[32] R. Sterritt, "Apoptotic Robotics: Programmed Death by Default," 2011 Eighth IEEE International Conference and Workshops on Engineering of Autonomic and Autonomous Systems, Las Vegas, NV, 2011, pp. 107-113. doi: 10.1109/EASe.2011.21

[33] M. Doran, R. Sterritt, and G. Wilkie, "Autonomic Wheel Alignment for Mobile Robots". At: 11th IEEE International Conference and Workshops on the Engineering of Autonomic & Autonomous , APL, Laurel, Maryland, USA. IEEE CS. 6 p., 2014

[34] M. Doran, R. Sterritt, and G. Wilkie, Autonomic Self-Adaptive Robot Wheel Alignment. Adaptive 2016: The Eighth International Conference on Adaptive and Self-Adaptive Systems and Applications pp. 27-33.

[35] M. Doran, R. Sterritt, and G. Wilkie, Autonomic Sonar Sensor Fault Manager for Mobile Robots. ICACCE 2017 : 19th International Conference on Autonomic Computing and Computer Engineering London, UK, Mar 2017

[36] M. Doran, R. Sterritt, and G. Wilkie, Autonomic Management for Mobile Robot Battery Degradation. ICACCE 2018 : 20th International Conference on Autonomic Computing and Computer Engineering - London, UK, May 2018

[37] M. Doran, R. Sterritt, and G. Wilkie, 'Autonomic Architecture for Fault Handling in Mobile Robots', Innovations in System and Software Engineering, a NASA Journal, Springer Publications, 26 p., ISSE-D-19-00010R1, Apr. 2020. doi:10.1007/s11334-020-00361-8

[38] M. Doran, "Autonomic Architecture for Fault Handling in Mobile Robots", PhD diss., Ulster University, 2020.

[39] R. Palmer and R. Sterritt, "Autonomic & Apoptotic Computing Prototype; Providing Pre-Programmed Death of Cubesats for Avoiding Space JUNK", 2019 IEEE International Conference on Space Mission Challenges for Information Technology (SMC-IT), Pasadena, CA, USA, 2019, pp. 78-86, doi: 10.1109/SMC-IT.2019.00015

[40] C. Gama, R. Sterritt, G. Wilkie, and G Hawe, Towards a Cubesat Autonomic Capability Model (CACM): A Road Map. At 2017 6th International Conference on Space Mission Challenges for Information Technology (SMC-IT 2017), Alcala de Henares, Sept. 2017

[41] C. Gama, R. Sterritt, G. Wilkie, and G Hawe, "Towards a Cubesat Autonomicity Capability Model A Roadmap for Autonomicity in Cubesats", The Tenth International Conference on Adaptive and Self-Adaptive Systems and Applications (ADAPTIVE 2018), Feb. 2018.

[42] R. Sterritt, G. Wilkie, C. Saunders, M. Doran, C. Gama, G. Hawe, and L. McGuigan, "Inspiration for Space 2.0 from Autonomic-ANTS (Autonomous NanoTechnology Swarms) Concept missions" 17th BIS Reinventing Space Conference, 12-14 November 2019, Belfast, Northern Ireland.

[43] NASA, R. Sterritt et al. Patents, https://pure.ulster.ac.uk/en/persons/roy-sterritt/publications/?type=%2Fdk%2Fatira%2Fpure%2Fresearchoutput%2Fresearchoutputtypes%2Fpatent%2Fpatent. [retrieved : July 2020]

[44] NASA, R. Sterritt and M. G. Hinchey, Autonomic and Apoptopic Systems in Computing, Robotics, and Security. [US Patent 8983882], 17th March 2015.

Reduction of Decoherence in Quantum Information Systems Using Direct Adaptive Control of Infinite Dimensional Systems

Mark J. Balas
Mechanical Engineering Department
Texas A&M University
College Station, Texas, USA
mbalas@tamu.edu

***Abstract*— Quantum systems are inherently infinite dimensional. In particular quantum computers will use quantum systems as gates to store and manipulate information. But such systems suffer from decoherence which is caused by the quantum gate becoming entangled with its environment and losing information into that quantum environment. Feedback control has the promise of reducing this decoherence, but the feedback must be adaptive in the sense that it can perform its control tasks with very little information about the details of the quantum system itself. This paper is concerned with providing a framework for adaptive control of infinite dimensional quantum systems. The quantum system is described as a linear continuous-time infinite-dimensional plant on a complex Hilbert space with persistent disturbances of known waveform but unknown amplitude and phase caused by fluctuations in the external quantum environment. We show here that there is a stabilizing direct model reference adaptive control law with disturbance rejection and robustness properties. The plant is described by a closed, densely defined linear operator, which is the Hamiltonian of the quantum system that generates a continuous semigroup of bounded operators on the complex Hilbert space of states. There is no state or disturbance estimation used in this adaptive approach. We show that adaptive control can produce convergence of a quantum system to a Decoherence-Free Subspace. Our research direction continues on using our developing research in adaptive control of infinite dimensional systems to explore how these feedback control ideas in conjunction with quantum gates and quantum error correction can reduce decoherence in quantum information and computing.**

Keywords - Quantum Systems; Adaptive Control; Infinite-Dimensional Systems.

I. INTRODUCTION

Quantum systems are inherently infinite dimensional. In particular quantum computers will use quantum systems as gates to store and manipulate information. But such systems suffer from decoherence which is caused by the quantum gate becoming entangled with its environment and losing information into that quantum environment. Feedback control has the promise of reducing this decoherence, but the feedback must be adaptive in the sense that it can perform its control tasks with very little information about the details of the quantum system itself. This paper is concerned with providing a framework for adaptive control of infinite dimensional quantum systems.

The quantum system is described as a linear continuous-time infinite-dimensional plant on a complex Hilbert space with persistent disturbances of known waveform but unknown amplitude and phase caused by fluctuations in the external quantum environment. We show here that there is a stabilizing direct model reference adaptive control law with disturbance rejection and robustness properties. The plant is described by a closed, densely defined linear operator, which is the Hamiltonian of the quantum system that generates a continuous semigroup of bounded operators on the complex Hilbert space of states. There is no state or disturbance estimation used in this adaptive approach.

Our overall direction is on using our developing research in adaptive control of infinite dimensional systems to explore how these feedback control ideas in conjunction with quantum gates and quantum error correction can reduce decoherence in quantum information and computing.

Let X be an infinite dimensional separable complex Hilbert space with inner product (x, y) and corresponding norm $\|x\| \equiv \sqrt{(x,x)}$.

Consider the Linear Infinite Dimensional Plant with *Persistent Disturbances*:

$$\begin{cases} \frac{\partial}{\partial t}x(t) = Ax(t) + Bu(t) + \Gamma\, u_D(t) \\ x(0) \equiv x_0 \in D(A) \subseteq X \\ Bu \equiv \sum_{i=1}^{m} b_i u_i \\ y(t) = Cx(t) + Eu_D(t) \\ y_i \equiv (c_i, x(t)), i = 1...m \end{cases} \quad (1)$$

where $x \in D(A)$ is the plant state, $b_i \in D(A)$ are actuator influence functions, $c_i \in D(A)$ are sensor influence functions, $u, y \in \Re^m$ are the control input and plant output m-vectors respectively, u_D is a disturbance with known basis functions φ_D. The persistent disturbances u_D will enter the plant through the state channels Γ and the output channels E.

In order to accomplish disturbance rejection in a direct

adaptive scheme, we will make use of a definition, given in [4] and [7], for persistent disturbances:

Definition: A disturbance vector $u_D \in R^q$ is said to be persistent if it satisfies the disturbance generator equations:

$$\begin{cases} u_D(t) = \theta z_D(t) \\ \dot{z}_D(t) = F z_D(t) \end{cases} \text{or} \begin{cases} u_D(t) = \theta z_D(t) \\ z_D(t) = L\varphi_D(t) \end{cases} \quad (2)$$

where F is a marginally stable matrix and $\varphi_D(t)$ is a vector of known functions forming a basis for all the possible disturbances. This is known as "a disturbance with known waveform but unknown amplitudes". We can easily show that an operator L exists to relate the persistent disturbances to a known basis vector $\varphi_D(t)$, but the adaptive controller will not need to know the actual L.

The *objective* of control in this paper will be to cause the output $y(t)$ of the plant to regulate asymptotically:

$$y \xrightarrow[t\to\infty]{} 0 \quad (3)$$

and this control objective will be accomplished by a *Direct Adaptive Control Law* of the form:

$$u = G_e y + G_D \varphi_D \quad (4a)$$

The direct adaptive controller will have adaptive gains given by:

$$\begin{cases} \dot{G}_e = -yy^* \gamma_e; \gamma_e > 0 \\ \dot{G}_D = -y\varphi_D^* \gamma_D; \gamma_D > 0 \end{cases} \quad (4b)$$

Note that the output feedback gains are directly adapted and no estimation or identification of plant information is used in the control law.

II. Ideal Trajectories

We define the Ideal Trajectories for (1) the following way:

$$\begin{cases} x_* = S_1 z_D \\ u_* = S_2 z_D \end{cases} \text{with } z_D \in \Re^{N_D} \quad (5)$$

where the ideal trajectory $x_*(t)$ is generated by the ideal control $u_*(t)$ from

$$\begin{cases} \dfrac{\partial x_*}{\partial t} = Ax_* + Bu_* + \Gamma u_D \\ y_* = Cx_* + Eu_D = 0 \end{cases} \quad (6)$$

If such ideal trajectories exist, they will be linear combinations of disturbance state, and they will produce exact output tracking in a disturbance-free plant (8).

By substitution of (5) into (6), we obtain the *Model Matching Conditions*:

$$\begin{cases} AS_1 + BS_2 = S_1 F + \underbrace{H_1}_{\Gamma\theta} \\ CS_1 = H_2 = -E\theta \end{cases} \quad (7)$$

where $S_1 : \Re^{N_D} \to D(A) \subset X, S_2 : \Re^{N_D} \to \Re^M$.

Because (S_1, S_2) are both of finite rank, they are bounded linear operators on their respective domains.

A Special Case occurs when E=0 and $Range(\Gamma) \subseteq Range(B)$. Then there exists S2 such that $BS_2 + \Gamma\theta = 0$ and S1=0. In this case the full system state x becomes disturbance-free, but in general we really only want to make the output y disturbance-free.

III. Normal Form

We need two lemmas:

Lemma 1: If CB is nonsingular then $P_1 \equiv B(CB)^{-1}C$ is a (non-orthogonal) bounded projection onto the range of B, R(B), along the null space of C, N(C) with $P_2 \equiv I - P_1$ the complementary bounded projection, and $X = R(B) \oplus N(C)$, as well as $D(A) = R(B) \oplus [N(C) \cap D(A)]$.

Proof of Lemma 1: See [17].

Now for the above pair of projections $(P_1.P_2)$ we have

$$\begin{cases} \dfrac{\partial P_1 x}{\partial t} = P_1 \dfrac{\partial x}{\partial t} = \underbrace{(P_1AP_1)}_{A_{11}} P_1 x + \underbrace{(P_1AP_2)}_{A_{12}} P_2 x + \underbrace{(P_1B)}_{B} u \\ \dfrac{\partial P_2 x}{\partial t} = P_2 \dfrac{\partial x}{\partial t} = \underbrace{(P_2AP_1)}_{A_{21}} P_1 x + \underbrace{(P_2AP_2)}_{A_{22}} P_2 x + \underbrace{(P_2B)}_{=0} u \\ y = \underbrace{(CP_1)}_{C} P_1 x + \underbrace{(CP_2)}_{=0} P_2 x \end{cases}$$

which implies

$$\begin{cases} \dfrac{\partial P_1 x}{\partial t} = A_{11}P_1 x + A_{12}P_2 x + Bu \\ \dfrac{\partial P_2 x}{\partial t} = A_{21}P_1 x + A_{22}P_2 x \\ y = CP_1 x = Cx \end{cases}$$

Because

$$y = Cx = C(B(CB)^{-1}C)x = CP_1 x$$

$$\text{and } P_1 x = B(CB)^{-1}Cx = B(CB)^{-1}y$$

$$\text{and } CP_2 = C - CB(CB)^{-1}C = 0$$

$$\text{and } P_2 B = B - B(CB)^{-1}CB = 0.$$

Lemma 2: If CB is nonsingular, then there exists and invertible, bounded linear operator $W \equiv \begin{bmatrix} C \\ W_2 P_2 \end{bmatrix} : X \to \tilde{X} \equiv R(B) x l_2$ such that

$\bar{B} \equiv WB = \begin{bmatrix} CB \\ 0 \end{bmatrix}$, $\bar{C} \equiv CW^{-1} = \begin{bmatrix} I_m & 0 \end{bmatrix}$, and $\bar{A} \equiv WAW^{-1}$.

This coordinate transformation puts (1) into normal form

$$\begin{cases} \dot{y} = \bar{A}_{11}y + \bar{A}_{12}z_2 + CBu \\ \dfrac{\partial z_2}{\partial t} = \bar{A}_{21}y + \bar{A}_{22}z_2 \end{cases} \quad (8)$$

where the subsystem: $(\bar{A}_{22}, \bar{A}_{12}, \bar{A}_{21})$ is called the zero dynamics of (1) and

$\bar{A}_{11} \equiv CA_{11}B(CB)^{-1} = CAB(CB)^{-1}; \bar{A}_{12} \equiv CAW_2^*$;

$\bar{A}_{21} \equiv W_2A_{21}B(CB)^{-1}; \bar{A}_{22} \equiv W_2A_{22}W_2^*$

and $W_2 : X \to l_2$ by $W_2x \equiv \begin{bmatrix} (\theta_1, P_2x) \\ (\theta_2, P_2x) \\ (\theta_3, P_2x) \\ \cdots \end{bmatrix}$ is an isometry from $N(C)$ into l_2.

Proof of Lemma 2: See [17].

Now we have the following theorem about the *Existence of Ideal Trajectories*:

Theorem 1: Assume CB is nonsingular. Then

$$\sigma(F) = \sigma_p(F) \subset \rho(\bar{A}_{22}) \equiv \{\lambda \in C / (\lambda I - \bar{A}_{22})^{-1} : l_2 \to l_2 \text{ is a bounded linear operator}\}$$

(or $\sigma_p(F) \cap \sigma(\bar{A}_{22}) = \varphi$ where $\sigma(\bar{A}_{22}) \equiv [\rho(\bar{A}_{22})]^c$),

if and only there exist unique bounded linear operator solutions (S_1, S_2) satisfying the Matching Conditions (7).

Proof: See [17].

It is possible to relate the point spectrum $\sigma_p(\bar{A}_{22}) \equiv \{\lambda / \lambda I - \bar{A}_{22} \text{ not 1-1}\}$ to the set Z of transmission (or blocking) zeros of (A, B, C).

Similar to the finite-dimensional case [16], we can see that

$$Z \equiv \left\{ \begin{array}{l} \lambda / V(\lambda) \equiv \begin{bmatrix} \lambda I - A & B \\ C & 0 \end{bmatrix} : \\ D(A)x\Re^m \to Xx\Re^m \text{ linear operator is not 1-1} \end{array} \right\}$$

Lemma 3: $Z = \sigma_p(\bar{A}_{22}) \equiv \{\lambda / \lambda I - \bar{A}_{22} \text{ is not 1-1}\}$ is called the point spectrum of $\bar{A}_{22}$. So, the transmission zeros of the infinite-dimensional open-loop plant (A, B, C) are the point spectrum of its zero dynamics $(\bar{A}_{22}, \bar{A}_{12}, \bar{A}_{21})$.

Proof of Lemma 3:

From

$$\bar{V}(\lambda) = \begin{bmatrix} \lambda I - \bar{A} & \bar{B} \\ \bar{C} & 0 \end{bmatrix} = \begin{bmatrix} W^{-1} & 0 \\ 0 & I \end{bmatrix} \underbrace{\begin{bmatrix} \lambda I - A & B \\ C & 0 \end{bmatrix}}_{V(\lambda)} \begin{bmatrix} W & 0 \\ 0 & I \end{bmatrix}$$

we obtain $\begin{bmatrix} \lambda I - \bar{A} & \bar{B} \\ \bar{C} & 0 \end{bmatrix}$ not 1-1 if and only if $\begin{bmatrix} \lambda I - A & B \\ C & 0 \end{bmatrix}$ not 1-1.

But, using normal form from Lemma 2,

$$\bar{V}(\lambda) \equiv \begin{bmatrix} \lambda I - \bar{A} & \bar{B} \\ \bar{C} & 0 \end{bmatrix} = \begin{bmatrix} \lambda I - \bar{A}_{11} & -\bar{A}_{12} & CB \\ -\bar{A}_{21} & \lambda I - \bar{A}_{22} & 0 \\ I_m & 0 & 0 \end{bmatrix}$$

And, therefore, $0 = \bar{V}(\lambda)h = \bar{V}(\lambda)\begin{bmatrix} h_1 \\ h_2 \\ h_3 \end{bmatrix}$, if and only if

$h_1 = 0; h_3 = (CB)^{-1}\bar{A}_{12}h_2; (\lambda I - \bar{A}_{22})h_2 = 0.$

So, $h \neq 0$, if and only if $h_2 \neq 0$. Therefore $\begin{bmatrix} sI - \bar{A} & \bar{B} \\ \bar{C} & 0 \end{bmatrix}$ is not 1-1 if and only if $\lambda \in \sigma_p\ (\bar{A}_{22})$.

This completes the proof of Lemma 3.

Using Lemma 3 and Theorem 1, we have the following *Internal Model Principle*:

Corollary 1: Assume CB is nonsingular and $\sigma(\bar{A}_{22}) = \sigma_p(\bar{A}_{22}) = \sigma_p(P_2AP_2)$ where $\bar{A}_{22} \equiv W_2^*P_2AP_2W_2$. There exist unique bounded linear operator solutions (S_1, S_2) satisfying the Matching Conditions (7) if and only if $\sigma(F) \cap Z = \varphi$, i.e., no eigenvalues of F can be zeros of the open-loop plant (A, B, C).

Note: $\lambda I - \bar{A}_{22}$ is not 1-1 if and only if there exists $x \neq 0$ such that $P_2x \neq 0$ and

$$\begin{aligned} 0 &= (\lambda I - \bar{A}_{22})W_2P_2x \\ &= (\lambda \underbrace{W_2W_2^*}_{I} - W_2PAP_2W_2^*)W_2P_2x \\ &= [W_2(\lambda I - P_2AP_2)W_2^*]W_2P_2x \end{aligned}$$

if and only if $W_2(\lambda I - P_2AP_2)W_2^*$ is not 1-1 on $N(C)$.

But W_2 is an isometry on $N(C)$.

Therefore $\sigma_p(\bar{A}_{22}) = \sigma_p(P_2AP_2)$.

IV. Stability of the Error System

The error system can be found from (1), (2) and (6): Define $e \equiv x - x_*$ and $\Delta u \equiv u - u_*$, this implies

$$\begin{cases} \dfrac{\partial e}{\partial t} = Ae + B\Delta u \\ y = y - 0 = \Delta y \equiv y - y_* = Ce \end{cases} \tag{9}$$

Now we consider the definition of Strict Dissipativity for infinite-dimensional systems and the general form of the "adaptive error system" to prove stability. The main theorem of this section will later be utilized to assess the convergence and stability of the adaptive controller with disturbance rejection for linear diffusion systems.

Noting that there can be some ambiguity in the literature with the definition of strictly dissipative systems, we modify the suggestion of Wen in [8] for finite dimensional systems and expand it to include infinite dimensional systems.

Definition 1: *The triple (A_c, B, C) is said to be* ***Strictly Dissipative (SD)*** *if A_c is a densely defined ,closed operator on $D(A_c) \subseteq X$ a complex Hilbert space with inner product (x, y) and corresponding norm $\|x\| \equiv \sqrt{(x,x)}$ and generates a C_0 semigroup of bounded operators $U(t)$,and (B,C) are bounded finite rank input/output operators with rank M where $B: R^m \to X$* and *$C: X \to R^m$. In addition there exist symmetric positive bounded operator P and Q on X such that*

$0 \le p_{\min}\|e\|^2 \le (Pe,e) \le p_{\max}\|e\|^2; 0 \le q_{\min}\|e\|^2 \le (Qe,e) \le q_{\max}\|e\|^2$

i.e. P,Q are bounded and coercive, and

$$\begin{cases} \mathrm{Re}(PA_c e, e) \equiv \frac{1}{2}[(PA_c e, e) + \overline{(PA_c e, e)}] \\ = \frac{1}{2}[(PA_c e, e) + (e, PA_c e)] \\ = -(Qe, e) \le -q_{\min}\|e\|^2; e \in D(A_c) \\ PB = C^* \end{cases} \tag{10}$$

where W^* is the adjoint of the operator W.

We also say that (A, B, C) is *Almost Strictly Dissipative (ASD)* when there exists $G_* mxm$ gain such that (A_c, B, C) is SD with $A_c \equiv A + BG_*C$. Note that if $P = I$ in (10)by the Lumer-Phillips Theorem [10], p405, we would have $\|U_c(t)\| \le e^{-\sigma t}; t \ge 0; \sigma \equiv q_{\min} > 0$.

Henceforth, we will make the following set of assumptions:

Hypothesis 1: *Assume the following:*

1) There exists a gain G_e^* such that the triple $(A_C \equiv A + BG_e^*C, B, C)$ is SD, i.e. (A, B, C) is ASD.

2) A is a densely defined ,closed operator on $D(A) \subseteq X$ and generates a C_0 semigroup of bounded operators $U(t)$,

3) φ_D is bounded.

From (5), we have $u_* = S_2 z_D$ and using (4a), we obtain:

$$\begin{aligned} \Delta u &\equiv u - u_* = (G_e y + G_D \varphi_D) - (S_2 \underbrace{z_D}_{L\varphi_D}) \\ &= G_e^* y + \Delta G_e y + \Delta G_D \varphi_D = G_e^* e_y + \Delta G \eta \end{aligned} \tag{11}$$

where

$\Delta G \equiv G - G_*; G \equiv \begin{bmatrix} G_e & G_D \end{bmatrix}; G_* \equiv \begin{bmatrix} G_e^* & S_2 L \end{bmatrix}; G_D^* \equiv S_2 L;$

and $\eta \equiv \begin{bmatrix} y \\ \varphi_D \end{bmatrix}$.

From (4), (9), and (11), the *Error System* becomes

$$\begin{cases} \dfrac{\partial e}{\partial t} = \underbrace{(A + BG_e^* C)}_{A_c} e + B\Delta G \eta = A_c e + B\rho; \\ e \in D(A); \rho \equiv \Delta G \eta \\ e_y = Ce \\ \Delta \dot{G} = \dot{G} - \dot{G}_* = \dot{G} = -e_y \eta^* \gamma \end{cases} \tag{12}$$

where $\gamma \equiv \begin{bmatrix} \gamma_e & 0 \\ 0 & \gamma_D \end{bmatrix} > 0$.

Since B, C are finite rank operators, so is $BG_e^* C$. Therefore $A_c \equiv A + BG_e^* C$ which has $D(A_c) = D(A)$, and generates a C_0 semigroup $U_c(t)$ because A does, see [9]Theo 2.1 p 497. Furthermore, by Theo 8.10 p 157 in [11], $x(t)$ remains in $D(A)$ and is differentiable there for all $t \ge 0$. This is because $F(t) \equiv B\rho = B\Delta G \eta$ is continuously differentiable in $D(A)$.

We see that (12) is the *feedback interconnection* of an infinite-dimensional linear subsystem with $e \in D(A) \subseteq X$ and a finite-dimensional subsystem with $\Delta G \in \Re^{mxm}$. This can be written in the following form using $w \equiv \begin{bmatrix} e \\ \Delta G \end{bmatrix} \in D \equiv D(A) x \Re^{mxm} \subseteq \bar{X} \equiv X x \Re^{mxm}$:

$$\begin{cases} \dfrac{\partial w}{\partial t} = w_t = f(t, w) \equiv \begin{bmatrix} A_c e + B\rho(t) \\ -e_y \eta^* \gamma \end{bmatrix} \\ w(t_0) = w_0 \in D \text{ dense in } \bar{X} \equiv X x \Re^{mxm} \end{cases} \tag{13}$$

The inner product on $\bar{X} \equiv X x \Re^{mxm}$ can be defined as $(w_1, w_2) \equiv \left(\begin{bmatrix} x_1 \\ \Delta G_1 \end{bmatrix}, \begin{bmatrix} x_2 \\ \Delta G_2 \end{bmatrix} \right) \equiv (x_1, x_2) + tr(\Delta G_2 \Delta G_1^*)$, which will make it a Hilbert space also.

Now, we present a new version of Barbalat-Lyapunov for systems on an infinite dimensional Hilbert space:

Theorem 2 (Lyapunov-Barbalat):

Let $w(t) = w(t, t_0, w_0) \in D$ and $V(t, w)$ satisfy:

$$\begin{cases} \alpha \|w\|^2 \leq V(t, w) \leq \beta \|w\|^2 \\ \dot{V}(t, w) \equiv \dfrac{\partial V(t, w)}{\partial t} + \dfrac{\partial V(t, w)}{\partial w} f(t, w) \leq -S(w) \leq 0 \end{cases}$$

for all $w \in D$. Then, $w(t)$ is bounded in $\bar{X}$. Furthermore, if the following are true:

1) $S(w) \geq \mu \|\aleph w\|^2 \; \forall w \in D; \mu > 0$; with $\aleph$ a bounded operator on $D \subseteq \bar{X} \equiv X x \Re^{mxm} \to X$ such that $(\aleph w)_t = \aleph w_t$.

2) $\mathrm{Re}(\aleph w, \aleph f(t, w))$ is bounded on bounded sets of $w \in D$, then $\aleph w(t) \xrightarrow[t \to \infty]{} 0$.

Proof: See Appendix I in [17].

For this proof, we will need the following version of Barbalat's Lemma; see [15] pp210-211:

Lemma 4: We say $f(t)$ is a *uniformly continuous* function on $(0, \infty)$ when for all $\varepsilon > 0$ there exists $\delta = \delta(\varepsilon) > 0$, such that $|f(t_2) - f(t_1)| < \varepsilon \; \forall |t_2 - t_1| < \delta$. If $f(t)$ is a real, *uniformly continuous* function on $(0, \infty)$ with $\int_0^\infty f(t) dt < \infty$, then $f(t) \xrightarrow[t \to \infty]{} 0$.

Now we can prove the stability and convergence of the direct adaptively controlled error system (12):

Theorem 3: Under Hypothesis 1and $\mathrm{Re}(A_c e, e)$ bounded on bounded sets of $e \in D(A)$, we will have state and output tracking of the reference model: $e \xrightarrow[t \to \infty]{} 0$, and since C is a bounded linear operator: $e_y = y - y_m = Ce \xrightarrow[t \to \infty]{} 0$ with bounded adaptive gains $G \equiv \begin{bmatrix} G_e & G_m & G_u & G_D \end{bmatrix} = G_* + \Delta G$.

Proof: See Appendix II in [17].

V. Convergence to a Subspace

In many cases, and especially in quantum information systems, e.g. [2], it is desirable to have all state trajectories converge to appropriate well-behaved subspaces. In the Quantum systems situation, the appropriate subspace is a "decoherence-free subspace" as described in [20]-[22]. These subspaces are finite-dimensional, Hamiltonian - invariant subspaces of the Schrodinger partial differential equation representing the quantum dynamics of the information system. In such a subspace S the decoherence effects of the environment are removed, i.e. the Schrodinger dynamic group is unitary on S and thus preserves the energy in all states in the decoherence-free subspace. Therefore, within S, quantum information can be handled with quantum gates that do not lose information through decoherence.

In this section, we will deal with the general problem of adaptively controlling the states of a linear infinite-dimensional system to converge to a prescribed subspace. The prescribed subspace S will be an A-invariant subspace of the state space X in (1) with $\dim S \equiv N < \infty$. Consequently S is closed and $X = S \oplus S^\perp$.

Let $P_N \equiv$ orthogonal projection onto S along $S^\perp$, with $P_R \equiv I - P_N$ the complementary bounded projection. We define Convergence to a Subspace S of a trajectory $x(t)$ as $d(x(t), S) \xrightarrow[t \to \infty]{} 0$,

or equivalently $P_R x(t) \equiv (I - P_N) x(t) \xrightarrow[t \to \infty]{} 0$.

So, for the above pair of projections (P_N, P_R), we have $P_N P_R = 0$ and $AP_N = P_N A$, $AP_R = P_R A$, because S is A-invariant, and the linear infinite dimensional system (1) decomposes into

$$\begin{cases} \dfrac{\partial P_N x}{\partial t} = P_N \dfrac{\partial x}{\partial t} = \underbrace{(P_N A P_N)}_{A_N} P_N x + \underbrace{(P_N A P_R)}_{A_{NR}} P_R x + \underbrace{(P_N B)}_{B_N} u \\ \dfrac{\partial P_R x}{\partial t} = P_R \dfrac{\partial x}{\partial t} = \underbrace{(P_R A P_N)}_{A_{RN}} P_N x + \underbrace{(P_R A P_R)}_{A_R} P_R x + \underbrace{(P_R B)}_{B_R} u \\ y = \underbrace{(C P_N)}_{C_N} P_N x + \underbrace{(C P_R)}_{C_R} P_R x \end{cases} \quad (14)$$

Let $x_N \equiv P_N x$ and $x_R \equiv P_R x$,

which yields to $\begin{cases} \dfrac{\partial x_N}{\partial t} = A_N x_N + A_{NR} x_R + B_N u \\ \dfrac{\partial x_R}{\partial t} = A_{RN} x_N + A_R x_R + B_R u \\ y = C_N x_N + C_R x_R \end{cases}$.

Since S is A-invariant, we have $A_{NR} = P_N A P_R = P_N P_R A = 0$ and similarly $A_{RN} = 0$.

$$\Rightarrow \begin{cases} \dfrac{\partial x_N}{\partial t} = A_N x_N + B_N u \\ \dfrac{\partial x_R}{\partial t} = A_R x_R + B_R u \\ y = C_N x_N + C_R x_R \end{cases}$$

By choosing actuators $\{b_1, ..., b_M\}$ and sensors $\{c_1, ..., c_M\}$ in $S^\perp$, we can have $B_N = P_N B = 0$ and $C_N = C P_N = 0$.

$$\Rightarrow \begin{cases} \dfrac{\partial x_N}{\partial t} = A_N x_N \\ \dfrac{\partial x_R}{\partial t} = A_R x_R + B_R u \\ y = C_R x_R \end{cases}$$

Theorem 4: If (A_R, B_R, C_R) is ASD (i.e. $C_R B_R > 0$ and $C_R(sI - A_R)^{-1} B_R$ is minimum phase, then the direct adaptive controller (4a) and (4b) will produce $\|x_R = P_R x\| \xrightarrow[t\to\infty]{} 0$ (convergence to the subspace S) $\forall x_0 \in D(A)$ with bounded adaptive gain $G(t)$ (and will mitigate persistent disturbances if they are present in the (A_R, B_R, C_R) subsystem).

VI. Application: Adaptive Control of Hamiltonian Quantum Systems

In general, the dynamics of quantum systems are described by the Schrodinger wave equation on a complex Hilbert space [18]-[19]. We will apply the above direct adaptive controller on the following single-input/single-output Cauchy problem which represents *a feedback-controlled quantum system* with one control actuator and one sensor:

$$\begin{cases} \dfrac{\partial x}{\partial t} = Ax + b(u+u_D), x(0) \equiv x_0 \in D(A) \\ y = (c,x), \text{ with } b = c \in D(A) \end{cases} \quad (15)$$

where *A is the Hamiltonian operator for the quantum system* which is self-adjoint, has compact resolvent, and generates a C_0 semigroup.

From the compact resolvent property, we have that every state in the Hilbert space can be represented as $x = \sum_{k=1}^{\infty} c_k \phi_k$, where ϕ_k are the orthonormal eigenstates of A and are the so-called pure states of the system. Thus x is in general a *mixed state* where $\sum_{k=1}^{\infty} |c_k|^2 = 1$, and the $|c_k|^2$'s are the probabilities that the measured state is the pure state ϕ_k.

Consequently, there exists G_* such that $A_c \equiv A + BG_*C$ satisfies $\operatorname{Re}\lambda_k \le -\mu < 0, \forall \lambda_k \in \sigma_p(A_c)$, which implies that

$$\operatorname{Re}(A_c x, x) \equiv \frac{1}{2}[(A_c x, x) + \overline{(A_c x, x)}] = \frac{1}{2}[(A_c x, x) + (x, A_c x)] \\ = -(Qx, x) \le -\mu \|x\|^2 ; x \in D(A_c)$$

Also, since $b = c$ we have $C^* = B$. Therefore, we have that (A, B, C) is ASD with $P = I$.

From $\operatorname{Re}(A_c x, x) \le -\mu \|x\|^2, \forall x \in D(A)$ we clearly have $\operatorname{Re}(A_c x, x)$ bounded on bounded sets of $x \in D(A)$.

For this application we will *assume the disturbances are sinusoidal with frequency 1 rad/sec* (but this is not a restriction as long as φ_D is bounded:

$$\begin{cases} u_D = \begin{bmatrix} 1 & 0 \end{bmatrix} z_D \\ \dot{z}_D = \begin{bmatrix} 0 & 1 \\ -1 & 0 \end{bmatrix} z_D \end{cases}$$

implies that $F = \begin{bmatrix} 0 & 1 \\ -1 & 0 \end{bmatrix}; \theta_D = \begin{bmatrix} 1 & 0 \end{bmatrix}; \varphi_D \equiv \begin{bmatrix} \sin t \\ \cos t \end{bmatrix}$, and implies that $u = G_e y + G_D \varphi_D$ with $\begin{cases} \dot{G}_e = -yy^* \gamma_e \\ \dot{G}_D = -y\varphi_D^* \gamma_D \end{cases}$.

So, since $B = \Gamma$, there is a gain $S_2 = -\theta$ such that $BS_2 + \Gamma\theta = B(-\theta + \theta) = 0$, which implies that $S_1 = 0$, and this is the special case of (7). Finally, $E = 0$, and the eigenvalues of F are $\pm j$, but the zeros of *(A, B, C)* are real; so the matching conditions are satisfied and ideal trajectories exist. Therefore, we satisfy the hypothesis of Theo. 3 and we have, via the direct adaptive controller, state regulation $x \xrightarrow[t\to\infty]{} 0$ and output regulation $y \xrightarrow[t\to\infty]{} 0$ with bounded adaptive gains $G \equiv \begin{bmatrix} G_e & G_D \end{bmatrix}$ in the presence of sinusoidal persistent disturbances.

We note that quantum control would more likely be done with a master equation involving density operators rather than the usual Schrodinger equation in (15); also, the interaction with the environment would be modelled by an appropriate Lindblad operator. But the above gives a start at a framework for adaptive quantum control.

VII. Conclusions

In Theorem 1, we showed conditions under which ideal trajectories exist for a linear infinite-dimensional system to be capable of rejecting a persistent disturbance in the output of the plant. In Theorem 3 we used an extension of Barbalat-Lyapunov result for linear dynamic systems on infinite-dimensional Hilbert spaces under the hypothesis of almost strict dissipativity for infinite dimensional systems, to show that direct adaptive control can regulate the state and the output of a linear infinite-dimensional system in the presence of persistent disturbances without using any kind of state or parameter estimation. In Theorem4, we began the development of adaptive control causing a quantum system to converge to a decoherence -free subspace where quantum error-correction can operate. The control of a simple quantum system is described by a general Schrodinger wave equation with external disturbances using a single actuator and sensor and direct adaptive output feedback.

These results give a basic framework for direct adaptive control of quantum systems. They are meant as a beginning for the use of adaptive control in this context. They show that adaptive control does not require deep knowledge of specific properties or parameters of the system to accomplish decoherence reduction. But there are still many technical issues to overcome.

References

[1] A. Pazy, Semigroups of Linear Operators and Applications to partial Differential Equations, Springer 1983.

[2] D. D'Alessandro, Introduction to Quantum Control and Dynamics, Chapman & Hall, 2008.

[3] Balas, M., R. S. Erwin, and R. Fuentes, "Adaptive control of persistent disturbances for aerospace structures", AIAA GNC, Denver, 2000.

[4] R. Fuentes and M. Balas, "Direct Adaptive Rejection of Persistent Disturbances", Journal of Mathematical Analysis and Applications, Vol 251, pp 28-39, 2000.

[5] R. Fuentes and M. Balas, "Disturbance accommodation for a class of tracking control systems", Proceedings of AIAA GNC, Denver, Colorado, 2000.

[6] R. Fuentes and M. Balas, "Robust Model Reference Adaptive Control with Disturbance Rejection", Proc. ACC, 2002.

[7] M. Balas, S. Gajendar, and L. Robertson, "Adaptive Tracking Control of Linear Systems with Unknown Delays and Persistent Disturbances (or Who You Callin' Retarded?)", Proceedings of the AIAA Guidance, Navigation and Control Conference, Chicago, IL, Aug 2009.

[8] J. Wen, "Time domain and frequency domain conditions for strict positive realness", IEEE Trans Automat. Contr., vol. 33, no. 10, pp.988-992, 1988.

[9] T. Kato, Perturbation Theory for Linear Operators, Springer, 1980.

[10] M. Renardy and R. Rogers, An Introduction to Partial Differential Equations, Springer, 1993

[11] R. Curtain and A. Pritchard, Functional Analysis in Modern Applied Mathematics, Academic Press, 1977.

[12] M. Balas, "Trends in Large Space Structure Control Theory: Fondest Hopes, Wildest Dreams", IEEE Trans Automatic Control, AC-27, No. 3, 1982.

[13] M. Balas and R. Fuentes, "A Non-Orthogonal Projection Approach to Characterization of Almost Positive Real Systems with an Application to Adaptive Control", Proc. of American Control Conference, 2004.

[14] P. Antsaklis and A. Michel, A Linear Systems Primer, Birkhauser, 2007.

[15] V. M. Popov, Hyperstability of Control Systems, Springer, Berlin, 1973.

[16] T. Kailath, Linear Systems, Prentice-Hall, 1980, pp. 448-449.

[17] M. Balas and S. Frost, "Robust Adaptive Model Tracking for Distributed Parameter Control of Linear Infinite-dimensional Systems in Hilbert Space", Acta Automatica Sinica, 2014, 1(3), 92-96.

[18] P.A.M. Dirac, The Principles of Quantum Mechanics 4th edition, Oxford University Press, 1930.

[19] J. Von Neumann, Mathematical Foundations of Quantum Mechanics, Princeton University Press, 1955.

[20] P. Zanardi and M. Rasetti, "Error Avoiding Quantum Codes", http://arxiv.org/abs/quant-ph/9710041v1

[21] D. A. Lidar, I. L. Chuang and K. B. Whaley, "Decoherence Free Subspaces for Quantum Computation", http://arxiv.org/abs/quant-ph/9807004v2

[22] D. A. Lidar and K. B. Whaley," Decoherence-Free Subspaces and Subsystems", http://arxiv.org/abs/quant-ph/0301032v1

Data-Assisted Distributed Stabilization of Interconnected Linear Multiagent Systems without Persistency of Excitation

Vahid Rezaei and Margareta Stefanovic

Department of Electrical and Computer Engineering
University of Denver
Denver, CO 80208, USA
Emails: a.v.rezaei [at] gmail.com & Margareta.Stefanovic [at] du.edu

Abstract—**Stability of large-scale systems has been commonly achieved using centralized and decentralized control configurations. Several graph theoretic protocols have recently been developed for the distributed stabilization of partially unknown interconnected multiagent systems, when an upper bound on the unknown interconnection allocation matrices is provided to the control designer. The need for such an upper bound can be relaxed using adaptive control ideas. However, due to the inaccurate parameter estimation in the absence of the persistency of excitation for all agents' regressors, the use of traditional adaptive control ideas will only ensure the boundedness of all trajectories. We develop a data-assisted distributed protocol which operates under a new condition, collective finite excitation, in order to overcome this challenge. Despite the completely unknown interconnection allocation matrices, we prove the exponential estimation of all interconnection matrices and exponential convergence of all state trajectories of the interconnected multiagent systems to the origin.**

Keywords–Distributed Control; Decoupling Control; Finite Excitation; Interconnected Systems; Multiagent Systems.

I. INTRODUCTION

Along the advances in low-cost, low-dimension embedded sensing, computation, and communication systems, graph theoretic approaches have received significant attention in the consensus of Multi Agent Systems (MASs). Initial studies focused on the simple integrators or completely known agents [1]. Recently, the consensus for MASs with completely known interconnections among agent dynamics [2] and local or agent-level modeling uncertainties ([3] and [4]) has also been studied. In particular, [4] discusses that the consensus on zero is a nontrivial problem for MASs with modeling uncertainties.

Parallel to these efforts, the concept of multilayer control using graph theoretic approaches was proposed [5]. Egerstedt [6] considered the use of graph theory to capture the architectural aspect of cyber-physical systems for a completely known MAS of interconnected integrator agents. However, based on [7], we know that the cyber and physical layers of cyber-physical systems might be subject to various abnormalities.

With a focus on the modeling uncertainties over the physical (agent) layer, [8] proposed a graph theoretic decoupling framework in order to stabilize an interconnected MAS subject to the nonlinear modeling uncertainties. However, that result is based on the locally (interconnection-free) stable agents, and the control layer topology is identical to the completely known agent layer topology. Rezaei and Stefanovic [9] reformulated the solution approach in order to capture the architectural aspect of cyber-physical systems, yet the result was limited to a special agent layer interconnection topology. This issue was addressed in [10], however, it was based on a symmetric control layer topology. Rezaei et al. [11] designed several structurally nonsymmetric control layers for interconnected single and double integrator agents, and [12] developed two design procedures to build structurally nonsymmetric control layers for interconnected MASs subject to both matched and unmatched nonlinear modeling uncertainties. Nevertheless, all of these robust formulations require the knowledge about an upper bound on the norms of the unknown terms, and may end in a level of inherent conservatism (see section 4 in [12]).

Adaptive control ideas provide an appropriate framework to handle a wider range of modeling uncertainties in dynamical systems including networked systems. While the traditional adaptive control methods have been reported in several studies (e.g., see [13] for synchronization and [14] for consensus in MASs), the need for the Persistency of Excitation (PE) [15] might be problematic when the control signal depends on the estimation of the unknown parameters [16]. This might be serious challenge when dealing with an MAS. This is because the poor transient performance of each non-PE agent can easily propagate via the (networked) distributed controller which, consequently, degrades the performance of the entire MAS.

Motivated by the aforementioned observations, [17] proposed a cooperative PE condition to be satisfied by a group of agents (vs. each individual agent of an MAS). However, similar to the conventional PE condition, that cooperative PE condition must be satisfied in all (future) time windows. Yuan et al. [18] reported a cooperative Finite Excitation (FE) condition for the adaptive consensus in non-interconnected MASs. Further, [19] designed a cooperative FE condition for the stabilization of interconnected MASs. That method is based on a series of low-pass filtered signals and the control layer is symmetric. (See [19] for a more comprehensive survey of the literature.)

As discussed in [12], the use of an adaptive decoupling approach may reduce the conservatism that inherently comes with any robust control techniques. Therefore, motivated by the findings in [19] and inspired by [20] (for single dynamical systems), we develop a new data-assisted distributed protocol to stabilize a class of linear time-invariant interconnected MASs subject to the matched modeling uncertainties. The control layer is built by two sublayers: A decoupling sublayer to cancel the effect of the interconnections, and a cooperation layer to stabilize the interconnected MAS even when the non-interconnected agents are unstable or to shape the closed-loop time response. The new data-assisted approach relies on the use of a few data collection matrices to satisfy a collective

FE condition which enables us to potentially improve the performance of the multilayer interconnected MAS using an appropriate criterion from the literature of matrix algebra. We theoretically prove that, under the proposed collective FE condition, all estimated interconnection allocation matrices exponentially converge to their actual values and, similarly, all state trajectories of the multilayer interconnected MAS converge to the origin. We also characterize the boundedness of all trajectories during the transient time.

We overview the required notation and definitions in Section II, provide the main theoretical developments in Section III, and summarize the paper in Section IV.

II. Notation and Definitions

$A \succ B$ ($\succcurlyeq$) means $A - B$ is a positive (semi) definite matrix. $\mathbf{0}$ denotes a matrix of all zeros, diag$\{.\}$ a (block) diagonal matrix of the scalars (matrices) in $\{.\}$, col$\{x_i\}$ an aggregated column vector, $\|.\|$ the (induced) 2-norm of a vector (matrix), and vec$(A) \in \mathbb{R}^{mn}$ is a vectorization of $A \in \mathbb{R}^{m \times n}$.

We consider three graph topologies: $\mathscr{G}_a$ to represent the physical interaction of agents' dynamics over the agent layer, $\mathscr{G}_d$ a communication topology to compensate for the effect of interconnections on agents' dynamics using a data-assisted strategy over a decoupling layer, and $\mathscr{G}_c$ a communication topology for the controllers' communication over a cooperation layer. We allow the existence of selfloops over all layers where, by a selfloop, we refer to an edge outgoing from and returning to the same node without passing though any other nodes. Since the standard definitions of adjacency and Laplacian matrices do not admit selfloops [21], we redefine them in the rest of this section.

An agent layer digraph $\mathscr{G}_a$ with N nodes is characterized by an adjacency matrix $\mathscr{A}_a = [a^a_{ij}] \in \mathbb{R}^{N \times N}$ where $a^a_{ij} \neq 0$ if the ith agent is affected by the jth agent's dynamics for $i, j \in \{1, 2, ..., N\}$, and $a^a_{ij} = 0$ otherwise. Unlike the standard definition, $j = i$ is acceptable and each a^a_{ij} is a real valued scalar with either positive or negative sign. $\mathscr{N}_i^a$ represents the set of ith agent's neighbors over $\mathscr{G}_a$ which may include the number i as well (selfloop). *We introduce $\mathscr{S}_a$ as the set of nodes affected by some neighbor agents over the agent layer (including themselves through the selfloops).*

The control layer is divided into two separate (sub-) graphs with N nodes: $\mathscr{G}_c$ and $\mathscr{G}_d$. We do not discuss the communication topology $\mathscr{G}_d$ for the data-assisted decoupling control, because it is the same as $\mathscr{G}_a$. A cooperation layer digraph $\mathscr{G}_c$ with N nodes is characterized by a modified Laplacian matrix $\mathscr{H}_c = \mathscr{L}_c + \mathscr{S}_c \in \mathbb{R}^{N \times N}$. $\mathscr{L}_c \in \mathbb{R}^{N \times N}$ is a standard Laplacian matrix for a digraph $\mathscr{G}_c'$, with non-negative edge weights a^c_{ij}, to be obtained by removing all selfloops from $\mathscr{G}_c$: $\mathscr{L}^c_{ij} = -a^c_{ij}$, $\mathscr{L}^c_{ii} = \sum_{j \in \mathscr{N}_i^c} a^c_{ij}$, and $\mathscr{N}_i^c$ characterizes the ith agent's (controller) neighbors over $\mathscr{G}_c'$. Also, $\mathscr{S}_c = \text{diag}\{s^c_i\} \in \mathbb{R}^{N \times N}$ is a diagonal matrix to represent selfloops: $s^c_i > 0$ when there is a selfloop around the ith controller, and $s^c_i = 0$ otherwise. These selfloops and directed one-way communications between the control nodes create a *structurally nonsymmetric control layer*.

A typical three-layer (closed-loop) interconnected MAS is depicted in Figure 1. Both $\mathscr{G}_a$ (thus, $\mathscr{G}_d$) and $\mathscr{G}_c$ can be disconnected; however, all control nodes in each connected component of $\mathscr{G}_c$ must have access (direct path) to at least one node with a selfloop.

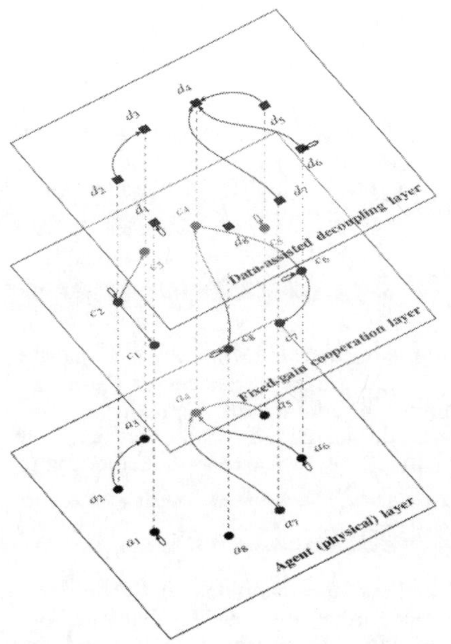

Figure 1. Example of a closed-loop distributed stabilization framework with separate agent and control layers. Top two layers form the control layer. Legend: a_i are agent nodes, c_i are fixed-gain cooperation nodes, d_i are data-collection (data-assisted control) nodes.

III. Main Results

A. Problem statement

We consider a MAS of N agents with the following interconnected dynamics:

$$\dot{x}_i(t) = Ax_i(t) + B\big(u_i(t) + C_i \sum_{j \in \mathscr{N}_i^a} a^a_{ij} x_j(t)\big) \tag{1}$$

where $x_i \in \mathbb{R}^{n_x}$ denotes the ith agent's state variable, $u_i \in \mathbb{R}^{n_u}$ control input, $A \in \mathbb{R}^{n_x \times n_x}$ and $B \in \mathbb{R}^{n_x \times n_u}$ system matrices, $C_i \in \mathbb{R}^{n_u \times n_x}$ interconnection matrix, and $\mathscr{N}_i^a$ the set of ith agent's neighbors over the agent (or physical) layer graph $\mathscr{G}_a$. We assume the pair (A, B) is stabilizable and the control allocation matrix B is full column rank (This stabilizability assumption is milder than the associated controllability one and, according to assumption 3.1.2 in [22], is required in order to have a solvable problem). For all affected agents $i \in \mathscr{S}_a$, the interconnection matrices C_i are completely unknown to the control layer designer which means the fixed-gain distributed stabilization ideas of [10] and [11] are no longer applicable for the distributed stabilization problem of this paper:

$$\lim_{t \to \infty} x_i(t) = \mathbf{0} \qquad \forall i \in \{1, 2, ..., N\} \tag{2}$$

which must be achieved (exponentially) by all agents.

B. Design foundation

We propose a distributed stabilization protocol with two components:

$$u_i(t) = u_{ci}(t) + u_{di}(t) \qquad \forall i \in \{1, 2, ..., N\} \tag{3}$$

where $u_{ci} \in \mathbb{R}^{n_u}$ denotes the ith agent's cooperation input signal over a cooperation layer $\mathscr{G}_c$, to be developed in Subsection III-C, and $u_{di} \in \mathbb{R}^{n_u}$ data-assisted decoupling signal over a decoupling layer $\mathscr{G}_d$ whose topology is indeed the same as

$\mathscr{G}_a$, to be designed in Subsection III-D. Note that $u_{di} = \mathbf{0}$ if $i \notin \mathscr{S}_a$. We rewrite the agent model (1) as follows:

$$\dot{x}_i = Ax_i + B(u_{ci} + u_{di}) + B \sum_{j \in \mathscr{N}_i^a} a_{ij}^a (I_{n_u} \otimes x_j^T) \theta_i^\star \tag{4}$$

where $\theta_i^\star = \text{vec}(C_i^T) \in \mathbb{R}^{n_u n_x}$ denote the unknown constant parameters for all $i \in \mathscr{S}_a$. We propose the following fixed-gain cooperation and data-assisted decoupling protocols:

$$\begin{aligned} u_{ci} &= K\Big(\textstyle\sum_{j \in \mathscr{N}_i^c} a_{ij}^c (x_i - x_j) + s_i^c x_i\Big) \quad \forall i \in \{1,2,\dots,N\} \\ u_{di} &= -\textstyle\sum_{j \in \mathscr{N}_i^a} a_{ij}^a (I_{n_u} \otimes x_j^T) \hat{\theta}_i \qquad \forall i \in \mathscr{S}_a \end{aligned} \tag{5}$$

in which $\hat{\theta}_i(t) = \text{vec}(\hat{C}_i^T(t)) \in \mathbb{R}^{n_u n_x}$ denote the data-assisted time-varying estimates of the unknown constant parameters $\theta_i^\star$, and $\hat{C}_i(t)$ the estimated matrices of C_i in (1) for all $i \in \mathscr{S}_a$. Accordingly, in addition to the main objective (2), we must address a side objective for the exact parameter estimation to be used in u_{di} of (5). We re-state the control objectives as follows:

$$\lim_{t \to \infty} x_i(t) = \mathbf{0} \qquad \text{and} \qquad \lim_{t \to \infty} \hat{\theta}_i(t) = \theta_i^\star \tag{6}$$

To facilitate the theoretical derivations of this paper, we go one step further and find the dynamics of the closed-loop agents (4) with the cooperation and decoupling protocols (5):

$$\begin{aligned} \dot{x}_i = Ax_i &+ B\textstyle\sum_{j \in \mathscr{N}_i^a} (I_{n_u} \otimes x_j^T) \theta_i^\star \\ &+ BK\big(\textstyle\sum_{j \in \mathscr{N}_i^c} a_{ij}^c (x_i - x_j) + s_i^c x_i\big) \\ &- B\textstyle\sum_{j \in \mathscr{N}_i^a} a_{ij}^a (I_{n_u} \otimes x_j^T) \hat{\theta}_i \end{aligned} \tag{7}$$

to model all agent layer (first row), cooperation layer (second row), and data-assisted decoupling layer (third row). We further partition this multilayer interconnected MAS:

$$\begin{aligned} \dot{x}_i = Ax_i \quad &+BK\big(\textstyle\sum_{j \in \mathscr{N}_i^c} a_{ij}^c (x_i - x_j) + s_i^c x_i\big) \\ &-B\textstyle\sum_{j \in \mathscr{N}_i^a} a_{ij}^a (I_{n_u} \otimes x_j^T) \tilde{\theta}_i \end{aligned} \tag{8}$$

where $\tilde{\theta}_i(t) = \hat{\theta}_i(t) - \theta_i^\star$ represents the the ith agent's parameter estimation error.

Remark 1: (Cyber-physical systems) We note that (7) represents a three-layer interconnected MAS with a data-assited control layer $\mathscr{G}_d$ whose topology is identical to the agent layer topology $\mathscr{G}_a$, and a cooperation layer $\mathscr{G}_c$ whose topology can be completely different from the agent layer topology $\mathscr{G}_a$. This framework enables us to distinguish the cyber (communication) malfunctions from the abnormalities of the physical components.

Definition 1: (Collective FE) A collection of bounded signals $x_j \in \mathbb{R}^n$, $j \in \mathscr{N}_i^a$, satisfies the collective finite excitation (FE) condition if there exist finite scalars $n_{Di} \in \mathbb{N}^+$, $t_l^s > 0$ and $t_l^e > 0$ for $l \in \{1,2,\dots,n_{Di}\}$, and $\gamma_i > 0$ such that:

$$\sum_{l=1}^{n_{Di}} \int_{t_l^s}^{t_l^e} \sum_{j \in \mathscr{N}_i^a} a_{ij}^a x_j(\tau) d\tau \int_{t_l^s}^{t_l^e} \sum_{j \in \mathscr{N}_i^a} a_{ij}^a x_j^T(\tau) d\tau \geq \gamma_i I_{n_x} > \mathbf{0}$$

where n_{Di} denotes the number of possibly discontinuous integration intervals based on the data collected by the ith agent. Also, $t_l^s \geq 0$ and $t_l^e > t_l^s$ refer to the *finite* start and end points of the lth integration time interval, respectively.

Remark 2: (Collective FE vs. PE, FE, and collective PE) The exact parameter convergence condition in (6) plays a key role in relaxing the need for an upper-bound on unknown parameters of the interconnected MAS (vs. [10] and [11]). This requires a persistency of excitation (PE) condition [15] to be satisfied by all regressors across the interconnected MAS. A bounded signal $x_j \in \mathbb{R}^n$ satisfies a PE condition, if there exist constant scalars $T_j, \gamma_j > 0$ such that the $\int_t^{t+T_j} x_j(\tau) x_j^T(\tau) d\tau \geq \gamma_j I_{n_x} > \mathbf{0}$ holds for all $x_j \neq \mathbf{0}$ and for all $t \geq 0$. We consider the following *modified PE condition* which is comparable to Definition 1:

$$\int_t^{t+T_j} x_j(\tau) d\tau \int_t^{t+T_j} x_j^T(\tau) d\tau \geq \gamma_j I_{n_x} > \mathbf{0}$$

Using this modified definition, we note that a bounded signal $x_j \in \mathbb{R}^n$, $j \in \mathscr{N}_i^a$, satisfies an *FE condition*, if there exist finite scalars $n_{Di} \in \mathbb{N}^+$, $t_l^s > 0$ and $t_l^e > 0$ for $l \in \{1,2,\dots,n_{Dj}\}$, $\gamma_j > 0$, such that the following inequality holds:

$$\sum_{l=1}^{n_{Dj}} \int_{t_l^s}^{t_l^e} x_j(\tau) d\tau \int_{t_l^s}^{t_l^e} x_j^T(\tau) d\tau \geq \gamma_j I_{n_x} > \mathbf{0}$$

where n_{Dj} denotes the number of possibly discontinuous integration intervals for the jth agent. We find that a collection of bounded signals $x_j \in \mathbb{R}^n$ for all $j \in \mathscr{N}_i^d$ satisfies a *collective (modified) PE condition*, if there exist constant scalars $T_i, \gamma_i > 0$ such that the following inequality holds for all $t \geq 0$:

$$\int_t^{t+T_i} \sum_{j \in \mathscr{N}_i^a} a_{ij}^a x_j(\tau) d\tau \int_t^{t+T_i} \sum_{j \in \mathscr{N}_i^a} a_{ij}^a x_j^T(\tau) d\tau \geq \gamma_i I_{n_x} > \mathbf{0}.$$

C. Fixed-gain cooperation protocol

Now, we focus on the cooperation protocol u_{ci} in (5). We rewrite the fixed part of (8) as follows:

$$\dot{x}_i = Ax_i + \kappa B v_i + BK\big(\textstyle\sum_{j \in \mathscr{N}_i^c} a_{ij}^c (x_i - x_j) + (s_i^c - \kappa) x_i\big) \tag{9}$$

where $\kappa > 0$ is a design scalar to be discussed in Design Procedure 1, and $v_i = Kx_i$ is a virtual (decoupled) control signal with the same gain K as in the actual (coupled) cooperation protocol u_{ci} in (5). We name the first two terms a "networked nominal dynamics" and the third term a "fictitious modeling uncertainty," and proceed with a set of decoupled dynamics:

$$\dot{x}_i'(t) = Ax_i'(t) + \kappa B v_i'(t) \qquad \forall i \in \{1,2,\dots,N\} \tag{10}$$

which, indeed, are the same as the networked nominal dynamics in (9) with the new variables $x_i' \in \mathbb{R}^{n_x}$ and $v_i'(t) = Kx_i'(t) \in \mathbb{R}^{n_u}$. Note that (10) is a stabilizable system because (A, B) represents stabilizable dynamics (by assumption) and $\kappa > 0$. For the design purpose, we recommend using a sufficiently large κ to avoid any singularity (poor controllability) in solving the design problem of this subsection. It can be easily done noting the fact that, unlike the agent layer interconnection topology $\mathscr{G}_a$, the cooperation communication topology $\mathscr{G}_c$ (thus, $\mathscr{H}_c$ and κ) is a design degree of freedom.

Let $\mathscr{U}_{vi}$ be the set of all admissible, static linear state feedback, stabilizing signals v_i' for the networked nominal dynamics (10). The following fact holds for any valid control layer topology $\mathscr{G}_c$ as defined in Section II.

Fact 1: [23] There exists a positive definite matrix $\Delta = \text{diag}\{\delta_i\} \in \mathbb{R}^{N \times N}$ such that $\Delta \mathscr{H}_c + \mathscr{H}_c^T \Delta \succ \mathbf{0}$, where $\delta_i = \frac{\delta_i^n}{\delta_i^d} > 0$ with $\text{col}\{\delta_i^n\} = (\mathscr{H}_c^{-1})^T \mathbf{1}_N$ and $\text{col}\{\delta_i^d\} = \mathscr{H}_c^{-1} \mathbf{1}_N$.

Design Procedure 1: The candidate $\mathscr{G}_c$ and K of the distributed cooperation protocol (5) are designed as follows:

1) Choose a nonsymmetric control layer topology $\mathscr{G}_c$ with $\mathscr{H}_c$ as its modified Laplacian matrix. Let $\kappa > 0$ be a real-valued scalar such that $\Delta \mathscr{H}_c + \mathscr{H}_c^T \Delta \succcurlyeq 2\kappa\Delta$. Let the state weighting matrix $W_x \in \mathbb{R}^{n_x \times n_x}$ and the

control input weighting matrix $W_v \in \mathbb{R}^{n_u \times n_u}$ be positive definite design matrices.

2) Find the solution $v_i' = Kx_i'$ of the following Linear Quadratic Regulator (LQR) problem. Then, K gives a candidate stabilization gain to be used in the cooperation protocol u_{ci} in (5).

$$V(x_i'(0)) = \min_{v_i' \in \mathscr{U}_{vi}} \int_0^\infty (x_i'^T(\tau)W_x x_i'(\tau) + v_i'^T(\tau)W_v v_i'(\tau))d\tau \quad \text{subject to} \quad (10)$$

This design procedure for structurally nonsymmetric control layer is modified from [12] such that, now, the state weighting matrix W_x of the LQR problem is chosen completely arbitrary. We note that the candidate stabilization gain K is characterized as follows [24]:

$$K = -\kappa W_v^{-1} B^T P \tag{11}$$

in which the positive definite matrix $P \in \mathbb{R}^{n_x \times n_x}$ is the unique stabilizing solution of the Algebraic Riccati Equation (ARE):

$$A^T P + PA + W_x - \kappa^2 PBW_v^{-1} B^T P = \mathbf{0} \tag{12}$$

The existence and uniqueness of P follow from the stabilizability and observability of $(W_x^{1/2}, A, \kappa B])$.

We use (11) and (12), and find the following equalities:

$$\begin{aligned} \Delta \otimes (A^T P + PA + W_x - \kappa^2 PBW_v^{-1} B^T P) &= \mathbf{0} \\ \Delta \otimes (K + \kappa W_v^{-1} B^T P) &= \mathbf{0} \end{aligned} \tag{13}$$

Fact 2: The following MAS-level equalities hold in an MAS of networked nominal dynamics and the candidate gains K and G of Design Procedure 1:

$$\begin{aligned} x^T \bar{W}_x x + v^T \bar{W}_v v + \bar{V}_x^T (\bar{A}x + \kappa \bar{B} v) &= 0 \\ 2v^T \bar{W}_v + \kappa \bar{V}_x^T \bar{B} &= \mathbf{0} \end{aligned} \tag{14}$$

where $x = [x_1^T, x_2^T, \ldots, x_N^T]^T$, $v = \text{col}\{v_i\} = \bar{K}x = (I_N \otimes K)x$, $V_x^T = \frac{\partial \bar{V}}{\partial x}$, $\bar{V} = x^T(\Delta \otimes P)x$, $\bar{W}_x = \Delta \otimes W_x$, and $\bar{W}_v = \Delta \otimes W_v$. (See [24] for single dynamical systems.)

Remark 3: The results of this section remain valid if we use a symmetric cooperation layer. In particular, $\mathscr{H}_c$ is a (symmetric) positive definite modified Laplacian matrix with strictly positive eigenvalues to be sorted as $0 < \mu_{c1} \le \mu_{c2} \le \ldots \le \mu_{cN}$ [10]. Then, Fact 1 holds with $\Delta = I_N$. Further, Step 1 of Design Procedure 1 is satisfied with $\kappa = \mu_{c1}$.

D. Data-assisted decoupling protocol

We start the design of u_{di} in (5) for agents $i \in \mathscr{S}_a$ by choosing an integration window length $\delta t_i > 0$ for each $i \in \mathscr{S}_a$, and integrating both sides of (4) from $t - \delta t_i$ to t as follows:

$$\Delta_{gi}(t) := x_i(t) - x_i(t - \delta t_i) - s_{gi}(t) = BR_{gi}(t)\theta_i^\star \tag{15}$$

where the subscript "g" distinguishes the integrated variables from the non-integrated ones, and the system-related signals $s_{gi} \in \mathbb{R}^{n_x}$ and regressor-related matrices $R_{gi} \in \mathbb{R}^{n_u \times n_x n_u}$ are defined as follows for $i \in \mathscr{S}_a$:

$$s_{gi}(t) = Ax_{gi}(t) + Bu_{gi}(t) \quad \text{and} \quad R_{gi}(t) = \sum_{j \in \mathscr{N}_i^a} a_{ij}^a (I_{n_u} \otimes x_{gj}^T(t))$$

$$x_{gi}(t) = \int_{\max(t-\delta t_i, 0)}^{t} x_i(\tau)d\tau \quad \text{and} \quad u_{gi}(t) = \int_{\max(t-\delta t_i, 0)}^{t} u_i(\tau)d\tau$$

We define data-collection matrices $D_i \in \mathbb{R}^{n_x n_u \times n_x n_u}$:

$$D_i(n_{Di}) = \sum_{l=1}^{n_{Di}} R_{gi}^T(t_l) B^T BR_{gi}(t_l) \tag{16}$$

to be updated at the time $t_{n_{Di}}$ of agent i if it is an "acceptable" excitation sample instance n_{Di}. This is defined as the sample $n_{Di} \in [0, n]$ that results in the following inequality:

$$\lambda_{min}(D_i(n_{Di})) > \lambda_{min}(D_i(n_{Di} - 1)) \tag{17}$$

when $n \in \mathbb{N}^+$ increases in time, as the integration window moves forward.

For each agent $i \in \mathscr{S}_a$, we use (15)-(17) and propose the following update rule for the unknown parameter estimation:

$$\begin{aligned} \dot{\hat{\theta}}_i(t) = \Gamma_i \Big(R_i^T(t) B^T Px_i \; & - \gamma_{Di} (D_i(t_{n_{Di}}) \hat{\theta}_i(t) \\ & - \textstyle\sum_{l=1}^{n_{Di}} R_{gi}^T(t_l) B^T \Delta_{gi}(t_l)) \Big) \end{aligned} \tag{18}$$

where $R_i = \sum_{j \in \mathscr{N}_i^a} a_{ij}^a (I_{n_u} \otimes x_j^T)$, and $\Gamma_i \in \mathbb{R}^{n_x n_u \times n_x n_u}$ and γ_{Di} are two design sets of positive-definite matrices and positive scalars, respectively, and $t_{n_{Di}}$ is the time associated to the sample instance n_{Di}.

The update law (18) can be rewritten as $\dot{\tilde{\theta}}_i(t) = \Gamma_i R_i^T(t) B^T Px_i - \gamma_{Di} \Gamma_i D_i(t_{n_{Di}}) \tilde{\theta}_i(t)$ which justifies the selection of the criterion (17) to characterize an acceptable excitation time. While the first part is similar to the traditional adaptive control laws, the second is a data-assisted one to obviate the need for the PE condition in parameter estimation.

Assumption 1: For each agent $i \in \mathscr{S}_a$, there exists a finite $n_{Di} \in \mathbb{N}^+$ such that the collective FE condition in Definition 1 is gradually satisfied over a finite time interval $[t_{si}^{start}, t_{si}]$.

The emphasis of the above assumption is on the existence of a "finite" time interval rather than its start point. Thus, while t_{si} is chosen as noted below, the start point t_{si}^{start} can be any number equal to or greater than zero. Indeed, a $t_{si}^{start} > 0$ may refer to the time when an external probing signal is turned on in order to sufficiently excite the ith agent.

E. Theoretical analysis

We follow similar steps as those of [19] for the analyses of this subsection.

Properties 1: The data-collection matrix (16) has the following guaranteed properties for all $i \in \mathscr{S}_a$:

1) $D_i(n_{Di}) \succeq \mathbf{0}$ for all $t \ge 0$,
2) $D_i(n_{Di}) \succ \mathbf{0}$ for all $t \ge t_{si}$ where $t_{si} > \delta t_i$
3) $\lambda_{min}(D_i(n_i')) \ge \lambda_{min}(D_i(n_{Di}))$ using each new sample $n_i' > n_{Di}$.

Proof: To prove the *first property*, we note that for any vector $z \in \mathbb{R}^{n_x n_u}$, $z^T D_i(n_{Di}) z = \sum_{l=1}^{n_{Di}} z^T R_{gi}^T(t_l) B^T BR_{gi}(t_l) z = \sum_{l=1}^{n_{Di}} \|BR_{gi}(t_l)z\|^2 \ge 0$ which means either $D_i(n_{Di})$ or each new arrived matrix $R_{gi}^T(t_l) B^T BR_{gi}(t_l)$ is a positive semidefinite matrix, even if the collective FE condition is not satisfied.

Regarding the *second property*, we start with

$$D_i(n_{Di}) = \sum_{l=1}^{n_{Di}} R_{gi}^T(t_l) B^T BR_{gi}(t_l) \ge \lambda_{min}(B^T B) \sum_{l=1}^{n_{Di}} R_{gi}^T(t_l) R_{gi}(t_l)$$

where $\lambda_{min}(B^T B) > 0$ because B is a full column rank matrix, and $\sum_{l=1}^{n_{Di}} R_{gi}^T(t_l) R_{gi}(t_l)$ is equal to

$$I_{n_u} \otimes \sum_{l=1}^{n_{Di}} \int_{t_l - \delta t_i}^{t_l} \sum_{j \in \mathscr{N}_i^a} a_{ij}^a x_j(\tau) d\tau \int_{t_l - \delta t_i}^{t_l} \sum_{j \in \mathscr{N}_i^a} a_{ij}^a x_j^T(\tau) d\tau$$

which, when the collective FE Assumption 1 is satisfied, means $\sum_{l=1}^{n_{Di}} R_{gi}^T(t_l)R_{gi}(t_l) \succ \mathbf{0}$.

The *third property* is guaranteed by the definition of acceptable excitation time (17) which acts as a criterion to decide whether we should consider new data in the update law (18) or not. Therefore, the proof is immediate. We note that at least one update exists for each data collection matrix if the collective FE conditional is met. This is because we start from $D_i = \mathbf{0}$ and $D_i(n_{Di}) \succ \mathbf{0}$ when the ith agent is sufficiently and collectively excited at time t_{si}. ∎

To facilitate the analysis of the main theorem, we aggregate the cooperation signal u_{ci} of (5), and find

$$u_c = (\mathscr{H}_c \otimes K)x$$

where $u_c = \mathrm{col}\{u_{ci}\}$ for all $i \in \{1,2,...,N\}$, and $\mathscr{H}_c$ is the modified Laplacian matrix associated to the nonsymmetric cooperation layer $\mathscr{G}_c$. We further find the following representation of the three-layer (closed-loop) interconnected MAS:

$$\dot{x} = \bar{A}x + \kappa\bar{B}v + \kappa\bar{B}\bar{E}_c v + \bar{B}u_a + \bar{B}\tilde{C}\bar{\mathscr{A}}_a x \tag{19}$$

where $\bar{E}_c = ((\frac{\mathscr{H}_c}{\kappa} - I_N) \otimes I_{n_u})$, $\bar{\mathscr{A}}_a = \mathscr{A}_a \otimes I_{n_x}$, $\bar{C} = \mathrm{diag}\{C_i\}$, and $u_a = \mathrm{col}\{u_{ai}\}$ for all $i \in \{1,2,...,N\}$ (if $i \notin \mathscr{S}_a$, we consider zero for the associated interconnection allocation matrix C_i and data-assisted decoupling signal u_{di}). We also define:

$$\Omega_b(t) = x^T(t)\bar{P}x(t) + \frac{1}{\lambda_{min}(\Gamma)}\|\tilde{\theta}(t)\|^2 \tag{20}$$

$$\rho_\omega = \min\left(\frac{\lambda_{min}(W_{xK})}{\lambda_{max}(P)}, 2\gamma_D^{min}\lambda_{min}(\Gamma)\lambda_{min}(D(n_D))\right) \tag{21}$$

where $\tilde{\theta} = \mathrm{col}\{\tilde{\theta}_i\}$ and $\Gamma = \mathrm{diag}\{\Gamma_i\}$ for all $i \in \mathscr{S}_a$, and $W_{xK} = W_x + K^T W_v K \succ \mathbf{0}$, $\gamma_D^{min} = \min_i\{\gamma_{Di}\}$ $\forall i \in \mathscr{S}_a$, and $\lambda_{min}(D(n_D)) = \min_i\{\lambda_{min}(D_i(n_{Di}))\}$.

Theorem 1: In a closed-loop interconnected MAS of agents (1), the two-layer data-assisted distributed stabilization protocol (3) and (5), and the update rule (18), the following is guaranteed under the collective FE Assumption 1:

1) All trajectories $x_i(t)$ and $\tilde{\theta}_i(t)$ are bounded $\forall t \geq 0$,
2) All trajectories $x_i(t)$ and $\tilde{\theta}_i(t)$ exponentially converge to the origin for $t \geq t_s = \max_i\{t_{si}\}$ where t_{si} are defined in Assumption 1,
3) All trajectories $x_i(t)$ and $\tilde{\theta}_i(t)$ are upper-bounded as in (22) and (23), respectively, where $\Omega_b(t_s) \leq \Omega_b(0)$.

$$\|x_i(t)\| \leq \begin{cases} \sqrt{\frac{1}{\lambda_{min}(P)}\Omega_b(0)}, & \forall 0 \leq t < t_s \\ \sqrt{\frac{\exp^{-\rho_\omega(t-t_s)}}{\lambda_{min}(P)}\Omega_b(t_s)}, & \forall t \geq t_s \end{cases} \tag{22}$$

$$\|\tilde{\theta}_i(t)\| \leq \begin{cases} \sqrt{\lambda_{max}(\Gamma)\Omega_b(0)}, & \forall 0 \leq t < t_s \\ \sqrt{\lambda_{max}(\Gamma)\exp^{-\rho_\omega(t-t_s)}\Omega_b(t_s)}, & \forall t \geq t_s \end{cases} \tag{23}$$

Proof: Step 1) We propose a Lyapunov function:

$$\Omega(x,\tilde{\theta}) = \bar{V}(x) + \sum_{i\in\mathscr{S}_a} \tilde{\theta}_i^T\Gamma_i^{-1}\tilde{\theta}_i \succ \mathbf{0}$$

where $\bar{V}(x) = x^T\bar{P}x$ was introduced in Fact 2 and $\gamma_i \succ \mathbf{0}$ in the update law (18). Along the unknown trajectories of the three-layer interconnected MAS (19), we find:

$$\dot{\Omega} = \dot{\bar{V}} + 2\sum_{i\in\mathscr{S}_a} \tilde{\theta}_i^T\Gamma_i^{-1}\dot{\tilde{\theta}}_i = \bar{V}_x^T\dot{x} + 2\sum_{i\in\mathscr{S}_a} \tilde{\theta}_i^T\Gamma_i^{-1}\dot{\tilde{\theta}}_i$$

The first part of $\dot{\Omega}$ results in the following inequality:

$$\bar{V}_x^T\dot{x} = \bar{V}_x^T(\bar{A}x + \kappa\bar{B}v) + \kappa\bar{V}_x^T\bar{B}\bar{E}_c v - \bar{V}_x^T\bar{B}\tilde{C}\bar{\mathscr{A}}_a x$$

in which $\tilde{C} = \bar{\hat{C}} - \bar{C}$, $\bar{\hat{C}} = \mathrm{diag}\{\hat{C}_i\}$, and $\bar{C} = \mathrm{diag}\{C_i\}$. Using the second equality in Fact 2, we know $\kappa\bar{V}_x^T\bar{B}\bar{E}_c v = -2v^T((\frac{\Delta\mathscr{H}_c + \mathscr{H}_c^T\Delta}{2\kappa} - \Delta) \otimes W_v)v \preccurlyeq \mathbf{0}$ where the negative semi definiteness is immediate by definition of κ and W_v in Step 1, Design Procedure 1.

Using $v = -\kappa\bar{W}_v^{-1}\bar{B}^T\bar{P}x$ and $\bar{W}_{xK} = I_N \otimes W_{xK}$, and based on the second equality in Fact 2:

$$\begin{aligned}\dot{\bar{V}} &\leq -x^T\bar{W}_x x - v^T\bar{W}_v v + \frac{2}{\kappa}v^T\bar{W}_v\tilde{C}\bar{\mathscr{A}}_a x \\ &\leq -x^T\bar{W}_{xK}x - 2\sum_{i\in\mathscr{S}_a} x_i^T PB\tilde{C}_i \sum_{j\in\mathscr{N}_i^a} a_{ij}^a x_j \\ &\leq -x^T\bar{W}_{xK}x - 2\sum_{i\in\mathscr{S}_a} x_i^T PB \sum_{j\in\mathscr{N}_i^a} a_{ij}^a(I_{n_u}\otimes x_j^T)\tilde{\theta}_i \\ &\leq -x^T\bar{W}_{xK}x - 2\sum_{i\in\mathscr{S}_a} \tilde{\theta}_i^T \sum_{j\in\mathscr{N}_i^a} a_{ij}^a(I_{n_u}\otimes x_j)B^T Px_i\end{aligned}$$

The second part of $\dot{\Omega}$ leads to the following inequality:

$$\begin{aligned}2\sum_{i\in\mathscr{S}_a} \tilde{\theta}_i^T\Gamma_i^{-1}\dot{\tilde{\theta}}_i =& 2\sum_{i\in\mathscr{S}_a} \tilde{\theta}_i^T \sum_{j\in\mathscr{N}_i^a} a_{ij}^a(I_{n_u}\otimes x_j)B^T Px_i \\ &-2\sum_{i\in\mathscr{S}_a} \gamma_{Di}\tilde{\theta}_i^T D_i(n_{Di})\tilde{\theta}_i\end{aligned}$$

Consequently, for the candidate Lyapunov function and closed-loop trajectories, we find

$$\dot{\Omega} \leq -x^T\bar{W}_{xK}x - 2\sum_{i\in\mathscr{S}_a} \gamma_{Di}\tilde{\theta}_i^T D_i(t_{n_{Di}})\tilde{\theta}_i \preccurlyeq \mathbf{0}$$

where the negative semidefiniteness is concluded because $D_i(n_{Di}) \succcurlyeq \mathbf{0}$ for all $t > 0$ (see the first item in Properties 1). Thus, all state trajectories and estimated parameter values remain bounded even in the transient time, when collective FE Assumption 1 is not satisfied [25]. (See Step 3 for the transient bounds.)

Step 2: When $t \geq t_s$, the latter inequality on $\dot{\Omega}$ can be rewritten as follows:

$$\dot{\Omega} \leq -\frac{\lambda_{min}(W_{xK})}{\lambda_{max}(P)}V(x) - 2\alpha\sum_{i\in\mathscr{S}_a} \tilde{\theta}_i\Gamma_i^{-1}\tilde{\theta}_i$$

where $\alpha = \gamma_D^{min}\lambda_{min}(\Gamma)\lambda_{min}(D(n_D)) > 0$ because $D_i(n_{Di}) \succ \mathbf{0}$ for all $t \geq t_s$ (see the second item in Properties 1). In fact, we know that the minimum $\lambda_{min}(D_i(n_{Di}))$ of each agent i occurs when at time t_{si} when it has been just sufficiently excited, and the future updates will either keep it constant or increase it (see the third item in Properties 1). Using the definition of $\rho_\omega > 0$, given prior to the main statement of this theorem, we find $\dot{\Omega} \leq -\rho_\omega\Omega$ which, based on the comparison lemma [25], indicates $\Omega(t) \leq \exp^{-\rho_\omega(t-t_s)}\Omega(t_s)$ where $\Omega(t) \triangleq \Omega(x(t),\tilde{\theta}(t))$. Thus, we find $\lim_{t\to\infty}\Omega(t) = 0$ which implies that all state and estimation error trajectories of the multilayer interconnected MAS exponentially converge to the origin ((6)).

Step 3) The Lyapunov function Ω of this theorem satisfies

$$\lambda_{min}(P)\|x(t)\|^2 \leq V(t) \leq \Omega(t)$$

$$\frac{1}{\lambda_{max}(\Gamma)}\|\tilde{\theta}(t)\|^2 \leq \sum_{i\in\mathscr{S}_a} \tilde{\theta}_i^T(t)\Gamma_i^{-1}\tilde{\theta}_i(t) \leq \Omega(t)$$

where $\tilde{\theta} = \text{col}\{\tilde{\theta}_i\}$ for $i \in \mathscr{S}_a$. Thus, $\|x(t)\| \leq \sqrt{\frac{1}{\lambda_{min}(P)}\Omega(t)}$ and $\|\tilde{\theta}(t)\| \leq \sqrt{\lambda_{max}(\Gamma)\Omega(t)}$.

Based on the first step of this proof, $\dot{\Omega} \preccurlyeq 0$ holds for all time including $0 \leq t \leq t_s$. Thus,

$$\Omega(t) \leq \Omega(0) = \bar{V}(0) + \sum_{i \in \mathscr{S}_a} \tilde{\theta}_i^T(0)\Gamma_i^{-1}\tilde{\theta}_i(0) \leq \Omega_b(0)$$

where $\Omega_b(0)$ can be found from (20). Consequently, for all $0 \leq t \leq t_s$:

$$\|x(t)\| \leq \sqrt{\frac{1}{\lambda_{min}(P)}\left(x^T(0)\bar{P}x(0) + \frac{\|\tilde{\theta}(0)\|^2}{\lambda_{min}(\Gamma)}\right)}$$

$$\|\tilde{\theta}(t)\| \leq \sqrt{\lambda_{max}(\Gamma)\left(x^T(0)\bar{P}x(0) + \frac{\|\tilde{\theta}(0)\|^2}{\lambda_{min}(\Gamma)}\right)}$$

Based on the second step of this proof, we know $\Omega(t) \leq \exp^{-\rho_\omega(t-t_s)}\Omega(t_s)$ holds for all $t \geq t_s$. Thus, $\Omega(t) \leq \exp^{-\rho_\omega(t-t_s)}(x^T(t_s)\bar{P}x(t_s) + \sum_{i \in \mathscr{S}_a}\tilde{\theta}_i^T(t_s)\Gamma_i^{-1}\tilde{\theta}_i(t_s)) \leq \exp^{-\rho_\omega(t-t_s)}\Omega_b(t_s)$ where $\Omega_b(t_s)$ can be found from (20). For all $t > t_s$, we have $\|x(t)\| \leq \sqrt{\frac{\exp^{-\rho_\omega(t-t_s)}}{\lambda_{min}(P)}\left(x^T(t_s)\bar{P}x(t_s) + \frac{\|\tilde{\theta}(t_s)\|^2}{\lambda_{min}(\Gamma)}\right)}$ and $\|\tilde{\theta}(t)\| \leq \sqrt{\lambda_{max}(\Gamma)\exp^{-\rho_\omega(t-t_s)}\left(x^T(t_s)\bar{P}x(t_s) + \frac{\|\tilde{\theta}(t_s)\|^2}{\lambda_{min}(\Gamma)}\right)}$. Recalling that $\|x_i\| \leq \|x\|$ and $\|\tilde{\theta}_i\| \leq \|\tilde{\theta}\|$, the bounds in (22) and (23) can be derived. It is also evident that $\Omega_b(t_s) \leq \Omega_b(0)$ based on the first step of this proof. Thus, these inequalities can be further upper-bounded using $\Omega_b(0)$ instead of $\Omega_b(t_s)$. ■

IV. Concluding Remarks

We develop a distributed protocol to guarantee the exponential convergence of state trajectories to the origin in an interconnected MAS with completely unknown interconnection allocation matrices. A nonsymmetric cooperation layer whose topology is completely independent of the agent and data-assisted decoupling layer is designed using a matrix algebraic approach. A data-assisted decoupling protocol compensates for the effect of unknown interconnections among agents' dynamics. A new finite excitation condition is proposed to relax the need for either persistency of excitation or the excitation of all agents in the interconnected multiagent system. We prove that all interconnection matrices are exponentially estimated under the proposed collective FE condition. Consequently, exponential convergence of the state trajectories of the interconnected multiagent system to the origin is also guaranteed. Extension of the collective FE-based idea to the output feedback problem is an interesting future topic [26].

References

[1] R. Olfati-Saber, J. A. Fax, and R. Murray, "Consensus and Cooperation in Networked Multiagent Systems," *Proc.of IEEE*, 95(1):215-233, 2007.

[2] K-K. Oh, K. Moore, and H-S. Ahn, "Disturbance Attenuation in a Consensus Network of Identical Linear Systems: An H_∞ Approach", *IEEE Trans. on Automatic Control*, 59(8):2164-2169, 2014.

[3] X. Ai, J. Yu, Z. Jia, Y. Shen, P. Ma, and D. Yang, "Adaptive Robust Consensus Tracking for Nonlinear Second-Order Multi-Agent Systems with Heterogeneous Uncertainties," *Int. Journal of Robust and Nonlinear Control* 27:5082-5096, 2017.

[4] V. Rezaei and M. Stefanovic, "Distributed optimal leaderless consensus of linear multiagent systems with polynomial state space models" *IEEE Conf. on Control Applications (CCA)*, Buenos Aires, Argentina, 2016.

[5] C. Rieger, K. Moore, and K. Baldwin, "Resilient Control Systems: A Multi-Agent Dynamic Systems Perspective," *Int. Conf. on Electro/Information Technology*, USA, 2013.

[6] M. Egerstedt, "From Algorithms to Architectures in Cyber-Physical Networks," *Cyber-Physical Systems*, 1(2-4):67-75, 2015.

[7] A. Cardenas, S. Amin, and S. Sastry, "Research Challenges for the Security of Control Systems," *3rd Workshop on Hot Topics in Security*, USA, 2008.

[8] V. Rezaei and M. Stefanovic, "Distributed Decoupling of Linear Multiagent Systems with Interconnected Nonlinear Uncertainties" *IEEE Conf. on Decision and Control*, USA, 2016.

[9] V. Rezaei and M. Stefanovic, "Distributed Decoupling of Linear Multiagent Systems with Mixed Matched and Unmatched State-Coupled Nonlinear Uncertainties," *American Control Conf.*, USA, 2017.

[10] V. Rezaei and M. Stefanovic, "Event-Triggered Robust Cooperative Stabilization in Nonlinearly Interconnected Multiagent Systems," *European J. of Control*, 48:9-20, Jul 2019.

[11] V. Rezaei and M. Stefanovic, "MultiLayer Distributed Protocols for Robust Cooperative Tracking in Interconnected Nonlinear Multiagent Systems," *Int. Journal of Robust and Nonlinear Control*, 29(12):3859-3891, Aug 2019.

[12] V. Rezaei and M. Stefanovic, "Distributed Stabilization of Interconnected Multiagent Systems using Structurally Nonsymmetric Control Layers," *IFAC World Congress*, Germany, 2020.

[13] S. Baldi, S. Yuan, and P. Frasca, "Output Synchronization of Unknown Heterogeneous Agents via Distributed Model Reference Adaptation," *IEEE Trans. on Control of Network Systems*, 6(2):515-525, 2018.

[14] G. Song and G. Tao, "An Adaptive Control Scheme for Consensus of Multi-Agent Systems with Parametric Uncertainties," *American Control Conference*, USA, 2017.

[15] P. Ioannou and J. Sun, *Robust Adaptive Control*, Dover, 2012.

[16] B. Anderson, "Adaptive Systems, Lack of Persistency of Excitation and Bursting Phenomena," *Automatica*, 21(3):247258, 1985.

[17] W. Chen, C. Wen, S. Hua, and C. Sun, "Distributed Cooperative Adaptive Identification and Control for a Group of Continuous-Time Systems with a Cooperative PE Condition via Consensus, *IEEE Trans. on Automatic Control*, 59(1):91106, 2014.

[18] C. Yuan, N. Xue, W. Zeng, and C. Wang, "Composite Consensus Control and Cooperative Adaptive Learning," *IEEE Conf. on Decision and Control*, USA, 2018.

[19] V. Rezaei and M. Stefanovic, "Distributed Stabilization of Interconnected Linear Multiagent Systems with Adaptive Decoupling under Cooperative Finite Excitation," *AIAA Conf. on Guidance, Navigation, and Control*, pp. 1-16, USA, 2020.

[20] A. Parikh, R. Kamalapurkar, and W. Dixon, "Integral Concurrent Learning: Adaptive Control with Parameter Convergence using Finite Excitation," *Int. J. of Adaptive Control and Signal Processing*, 33(12):1775-1787, Dec 2019.

[21] M. Mesbahi and M. Egerstedt, *Graph Theoretic Methods in Multiagent Networks*, Princeton University Press, 2010.

[22] B. Anderson and J. Moore, *Optimal Control: Linear Quadratic Methods*, Prentice-Hall, 1990.

[23] H. Zhang, Z. Li, Z., Qu, and F. Lewis, "On Constructing Lyapunov Functions for Multi-Agent Systems," *Automatica*, 58:39-42, 2015.

[24] F. Lin, *Robust Control Design: An Optimal Control Approach*, Wiley, 2007.

[25] H. Khalil, *Nonlinear Systems*, Prentice Hall, 2003.

[26] V. Rezaei and M. Stefanovic, "Distributed Decoupling of Partially-Unknown Interconnected Linear Multiagent Systems: State and Output Feedback Approaches," *IFAC World Congress*, France, 2017.

Projection-Based Inter-Agent Collision Avoidance in Dual Agent Systems

Vinod P. Gehlot and Mark J. Balas
Mechanical Engineering Department
Texas A&M University, College Station, Texas 77843, USA
email: {vinodgehlot, mbalas}@tamu.edu

Saptarshi Bandyopadhyay, Marco B. Quadrelli, and David S. Bayard
Jet Propulsion Laboratory
California Institute of Technology, Pasadena, California 91125, USA
email: {saptarshi.bandyopadhyay, marco.b.quadrelli, david.s.bayard}@jpl.nasa.gov

***Abstract*—Inter-agent collisions can occur in otherwise dynamically-stable (i.e., Lyapunov stable) dual-agent leader-follower systems. These inter-agent collisions between the leader and the follower happen during the transient phase of the system's evolution, although the steady-state behavior of the system is asymptotically/exponentially stable. Therefore, to avoid such inter-agent collisions, it is essential to control the relative error trajectory between the leader and the follower during the transient phase of the system's evolution. In this paper, we introduce a novel projection operator based model-reference control architecture that can mitigate impending inter-agent collisions by modifying the transient dynamics of relative trajectories. This controller augments the follower's baseline controller and consists of two essential components: a collision-free reference model based on the projection operator and a model reference tracking controller to guide the follower to follow the reference-model. This paper defines the concept of transient-instability in leader-follower systems, introduces collision mitigation controller architecture, and presents an illustrative example demonstrating its effectiveness.**

***Keywords*—Inter-agent collision avoidance; Collision mitigation; Multi-agent systems; Swarms; Interconnected systems; Motion planning; Projection operator.**

I. INTRODUCTION

In a dual agent leader-follower system, the leader is an independent entity; and the follower, as the name suggests, follows the leader at a specified separation distance. Relative position vectors and their associated dynamics are fundamental to the leader-follower formation maintenance. Therefore, the dynamic stability of the relative error dynamics is of paramount importance. We begin our discussion by introducing the mathematical preliminaries of dual agent leader-follower systems.

In the figure below, there are two identical agents — linear time-invariant (LTI) systems — identified by their indices **1**, and **2**, and their corresponding state vectors x_1, and x_2, respectively. They are in a leader-follower arrangement, with agent **1** as the leader, and agent **2** as the follower.

The trajectories of the agents evolve according to the dynamics defined in (1). Here, $i \in \mathcal{I} = \{1, 2\}$, is the index of the two agents, x_i is the state vector of the agents that

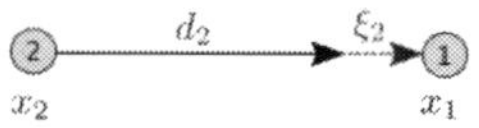

Fig. 1. Two Agent Leader-Follower Formation

evolves in the $n-$dimensional state space $\mathbf{X} \subseteq \mathbf{R^n}$, $u_i \in \mathbf{U} \subseteq \mathbf{R^m}$, and $y_i \in \mathbf{Y} \subseteq \mathbf{R^p}$ are the $m-$dimensional input and $p-$dimensional output vectors of the agents, respectively. The tuple (A, B, C) are the set of appropriately sized matrices that model the system dynamics.

$$\dot{x}_i = Ax_i + Bu_i \tag{1a}$$

$$y_i = Cx_i \tag{1b}$$

Although not necessary, assume that in (1), the matrix A has at least a one-dimensional null space. This assumption allows for the arbitrary assignment of constraints on a partial set of an agent's state vector; without the use of a constant control effort.

In this formation, agent **1** is an independent entity, and agent **2**, the follower, does not affect its dynamics. Agent **2** merely tracks agent **1** and maintains a spatial separation of $d_2 \in X$ using the control law

$$u_2 = G\,(y_1 - y_2 - Cd_2) = GC\xi_2. \tag{2}$$

Here, $\xi_2 \equiv x_1 - x_2 - d_2 \in \mathbf{R^n}$ is the relative error as measured from agent **2**, and $G \in \mathbf{R^{m \times p}}$ is a stable closed loop gain matrix that drives the relative error trajectory $\xi_2(t) \to 0$ as $t \to \infty$. Note that d_2 is a vector quantity, and it resides in the null space of the system matrix A ($d \in \ker(A)$), therefore, it can include many more constraints besides distance. Equation (3) is the relative error dynamics of the two agent formation, and a suitable value of the gain matrix G will render the closed loop matrix $A_C \equiv (A - BGC)$ Hurwitz, thereby meeting the formation control objective. We say that agent **2** is "looking" at agent **1** when it takes control actions based on its sensor observation of agent **1** — like in (2).

$$\dot{\xi}_2 = (A - BGC)\xi_2 + Bu_1 \tag{3}$$

The two agent formation discussed thus far is quite common in many applications, and it sets the stage for discussion on transient stability in this paper. Examples of the formation just described include adaptive cruise control in vehicles, autonomous convoy or platooning, autonomous mid-air refueling, and formation flying spacecraft among others. Whatever the application may be, it is important to ensure that the dynamics in (3) are dynamically stable (i.e. Lyapunov stable). In our previous work [1]–[3], we explored the stability and adaptive control of several general formation geometries with large number of agents and arbitrary network topologies. In this paper, we use the two-agent leader-follower formation from Figure 1 to introduce the concept of transient instability in leader-follower systems, and a novel control architecture that mitigates transient stabilities. We define transient instability for the leader-follower formation as follows:

Definition 1.1 (Transient Stability): The dynamics of a two agent leader-follower formation is transient-stable if the relative error trajectory $\xi_2(t) \to 0$ as $t \to \infty$, and

$$\|\xi_2(t)\| \leq \xi_2^{max} \equiv (1-\alpha)\|d_2\|, \tag{4}$$

for all $t \in \mathbf{R}^+$. The scalar $\alpha \in [0,1)$ describes a safety perimeter around agent **2**.

In other words, we say that the two agent system is transient-stable if 1) the relative error trajectory is asymptotically stable, and 2) the agent trajectories evolve collision free. The problem of collision avoidance in formation and swarms is a thoroughly studied subject in the control and robotics literature, but many questions, particularly that of transient stability, still remain unanswered.

When it comes to collision avoidance algorithms in autonomous systems, the paper by Ames et. al [4] is noteworthy. They present a control barrier function based Quadratic Programming (QP) algorithm, that the follower continuously executes to generate collision free trajectories, all the while meeting asymptotic stability of the relative trajectories. And, since the control inputs are generated optimally, we know that the trajectories will be unique. The recent survey by Rossi et. al [5] offers comprehensive outlook on the current state-of-the-art multi-agent coordination and control algorithms. Based on this survey, the vast array of coordination and control algorithms can be classified into two broad categories: predictive and reactive algorithms. In predictive algorithms, optimization based path planning algorithms determine collision free trajectories for the agents to follow. Well known predictive algorithms include Optimal Reciprocal Collision Avoidance (ORCA), and Model Predictive Control and Sequential Convex Programming (MPC-SCP). Reactive algorithms, on the other hand, accomplish collision avoidance on an ad-hoc basis; when a safety-perimeter violation occurs, imminent collision is avoided by recomputing the motion planning algorithm. Voronoi-based [6], and Artificial Potential Functions (APF) [7] are two examples of reactive algorithms. With regards to stability, predictive algorithms, in general, can guarantee asymptotic stability but not collision avoidance, and reactive algorithms, can guarantee collision avoidance, but not asymptotic stability. It is worth mentioning that no algorithm mentioned in [5] can guarantee transient-stability.

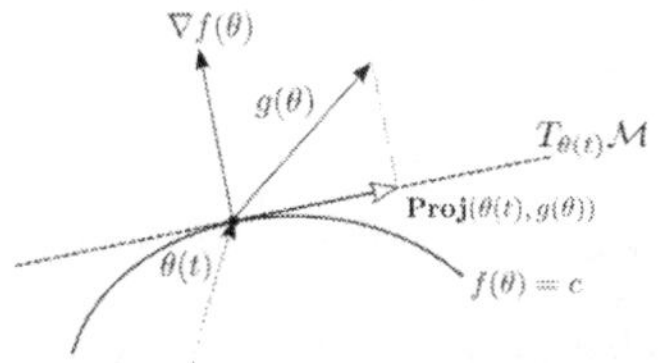

Fig. 2. Projection Operator in Action

Unlike the methods thus described, in this paper, we introduce a smooth, Lipschitz continuous method for collision avoidance that does not require the controller to solve optimization problems continuously in realtime. Moreover, this approach can satisfy dynamic stability and collision avoidance simultaneously. In the proposed method, we introduce a novel reference model for the follower that uses the projection operator to modify the drift vector field $(A - BGC)\xi_2 + Bu_1$ in (3) of the relative error vector $\xi_2(t)$ to generate transient-stable relative trajectories. Since directly differentiating $\xi_2(t)$ can induce unwanted noise into the feedback loop, we instead propose a Luenberger estimator of the form

$$\dot{\hat{\xi}}_2 = (A - BGC)\hat{\xi}_2 + L(\hat{y}_2 - y_2) \tag{5a}$$

$$\hat{y}_2 = C\hat{\xi}_2 \tag{5b}$$

to generate an estimate of the drift vector field in (3). This estimator is embedded within the projection operator to form the reference model, thereby generating relative error trajectories that satisfy the constraint (4). Finally, we augment the baseline control law in (2) with a type-1 tracking control law that tracks the transient stable trajectories generated by the reference model. It is the combination of the reference model, the reference model tracking controller, and the baseline relative error regulator that ensures transient stability in Definition 1.1. Figure 3 shows the proposed control methodology. We present our results in three sections. In Section II, we introduce the fundamentals of the projection operator and a few essential results without proof. In Section III, we introduce the transient instability mitigation architecture and discuss its various components, and present the main theoretical results. Finally, in Section IV, we use an illustrative example to demonstrate the effectiveness of the collision mitigation strategy presented in this paper.

II. The Projection Operator

The projection operator is among several methods in the convex analysis that can solve constrained convex optimization problems. In gradient descent iterations, the projection operator projects the gradient of the cost function onto the constraint manifold, limiting the solution to the convex set defined by the constraints. According to [8], Kreisselmeier and Narendra [9] were the first to use the projection operator to bound time-varying gains in adaptive control systems. And since then, it has been hugely popular in several adaptive control algorithms [10] [8] [11]. Let $\theta \in \mathbf{R}^n$ be a state vector that evolves according to

$$\dot{\theta}(t) = g(\theta), \tag{6}$$

and suppose that we want the trajectory $\theta(t)$ to stay within a convex set with the boundary $f(\theta) = c$. We can accomplish this by constraining the dynamics in (6) with the projection operator dynamics

$$\begin{aligned}\dot{\theta}(t) &= \mathbf{Proj}(\theta, g(\theta)) \\ &= \begin{cases} \left(I - \frac{\nabla f (\nabla f)^T}{\|\nabla f\|^2} f(\theta)\right) g(\theta) & \text{if } f > 0 \text{ and } \theta^T \nabla f > 0 \\ g(\theta) & \text{otherwise.} \end{cases}\end{aligned} \tag{7}$$

The modification of the dynamics in (6) by (7) guarantees that $\theta(t)$'s trajectory will stay within the convex set

$$\Theta = \{\theta \in \mathbf{R}^n : f(\theta) \leq 0\}. \tag{8}$$

The projection operator achieves this by subtracting from the drift vector field $g(\theta)$, the component of $g(\theta)$ that is parallel to the gradient vector $\nabla f(\theta)$ (see Figure 2). Therefore, drift vector $\mathbf{Proj}(\theta, g(\theta))$ lies on the tangent plane $T_\theta \mathcal{M}$, where $\mathcal{M} = \{\theta : f(\theta) = c\}$ is the constraint manifold. The following is a significant lemma that is useful in stability proofs involving the projection operator.

Lemma 2.1 (Projection Inequality): Let θ^* be point in the interior of the convex set Θ, and let $\Gamma > 0$ be some positive definite and symmetric matrix, then for any other $\theta(t) \in \Theta$,

$$(\theta - \theta_*)^T \left(\Gamma^{-1}\mathbf{Proj}\left(\theta, \Gamma g(\theta)\right) - g(\theta)\right) \leq 0. \tag{9}$$

For the proof of this inequality, please refer to [8]. In this section, we have given a concise summary of the application of the projection operator applied to dynamical systems. For a more thorough treatment on this subject, we ask the reader to refer to [12] [11] [8].

III. The Collision Avoidance and Dynamic Stability Architecture

As discussed earlier, the follower implements the output feedback control law (2) to maintain the separation vector d_2 from the leader, resulting in the closed-loop relative error dynamics (3). Also, as discussed before, we know that the trajectory $\xi_2(t)$ can violate the transient stability criteria in Definition 1.1, even though the closed-loop matrix $A_c \equiv A - BGC$ is Hurwitz, and the input $u_1(t)$ is bounded. Therefore, there is a need to manage and modify the transient dynamics of the vector $\xi_2(t)$ to prevent inter-agent collisions, and hence satisfy the transient stability criterion. One — and possibly the most straightforward — approach, would be to specify the transient stability criteria directly in terms of frequency or time domain specifications. Then, compute the feedback gain G using an appropriate method from classical/modern control theory. This approach can work quite well for multi-agent systems with low cardinalities, like the leader-follower system discussed in this paper. Still, as the number of agents gets more substantial, and communication and sensing topologies can get complicated, it can be challenging to compute gains for the individual agents.

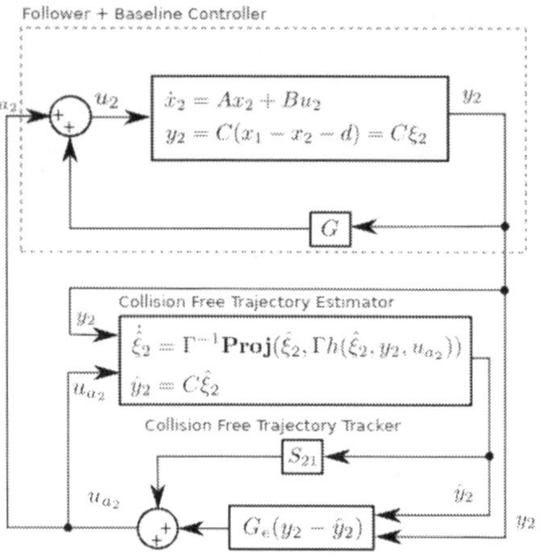

Fig. 3. Follower Collision Mitigation Architecture

Moreover, in [3], we show that eigenvalues of the Laplacian matrix of the network digraph of the formation can inadvertently scale the baseline feedback gains G, thereby causing stability issues in the formation geometry, and all the while degrading the controller performance. Motivated by these issues, and addressing the problem of transient stability in formations with a large number of agents, we introduce the control architecture shown in Figure 3, that can simultaneously satisfy dynamic stability as well as avoid inter-agent collisions. The proposed architecture consists of two essential controller subsystems: the collision-free (CF) estimator, and the collision-free (CF) trajectory tracker. Combined, the two controller subsystems augment the baseline control law (2) to guarantee transient stability. The CF subsystems generate the control vector u_{a_2}, and adds to the baseline control law as

$$u_2 = GC\xi_2 + u_{a_2}. \tag{10}$$

At its core, the CF estimator has a drift vector field

$$h(\hat{\xi}_2, y_2, u_{a_2}) = A_c\hat{\xi}_2 - Bu_{a_2} + L(\hat{y}_2 - y_2), \tag{11}$$

which is the structure of a standard Luenberger observer. Provided the pair (A_c, C) is observable, and the closed-loop estimator matrix $A_c + LC$ is Hurwitz, the estimated state $\hat{\xi}_2(t)$ will converge exponentially to the actual state $\xi_2(t)$. We enclose the estimator drift vector field $h(\hat{\xi}_2, y_2, u_{a_2})$ inside the projection operator. Therefore, we have

$$\begin{aligned}\dot{\hat{\xi}}_2 &= \Gamma^{-1}\mathbf{Proj}(\hat{\xi}_2, h(\hat{\xi}_2, y_2, u_{a_2})) \\ &= \Gamma^{-1}\begin{cases} (I - \frac{\nabla f (\nabla f)^T}{\|\nabla f\|^2} f(\theta))h & \text{, if } f > 0 \text{ and } \hat{\xi}^T \nabla f > 0 \\ h & \text{, otherwise.} \end{cases}\end{aligned} \tag{12}$$

Here,

$$f(\hat{\xi}_2) \equiv \frac{(1+\varepsilon)\|\hat{\xi}_2\|^2 - \|\hat{\xi}_2^{\max}\|^2}{\varepsilon\|\hat{\xi}_2^{\max}\|^2}, \tag{13}$$

which is the constraint vector for the projection operator, and $\xi_2^{\max}$ is the bound on the relative error trajectory from the transient stability criterion in Definition 1.1. $\varepsilon > 0$ is a scalar that creates a smooth boundary by defining two concentric convex sets

$$\Omega_0 \equiv \{\hat{\xi}_2 \in \mathbf{R}^n : \|\hat{\xi}_2\| \leq \frac{\|\hat{\xi}_2^{\max}\|}{\sqrt{1+\varepsilon}}\}, \text{ and} \tag{14a}$$

$$\Omega_1 \equiv \{\hat{\xi}_2 \in \mathbf{R}^n : \|\hat{\xi}_2\| \leq \|\hat{\xi}_2^{\max}\|\}. \tag{14b}$$

From Lemma 11.4 in [8], for any trajectory $\hat{\xi}_2(t_i) = \hat{\xi}_{t_i} \in \Omega_0$, the projection operator guarantees that for all $t > t_i$, $\hat{\xi}_2(t) \in \Omega_1$. Hence, the estimated state vector $\hat{\xi}_2(t)$ satisfies the transient characteristics and generates CF trajectories. Moreover, in the following result, we show that even though the estimator dynamics are enclosed within the projection dynamics, the estimated state $\hat{\xi}_2(t)$ exponentially converges to the actual state vector $\xi_2(t)$.

Theorem 3.1 (Collision Free Estimator Stability): The error trajectory $e(t) \equiv \hat{\xi}_2 - \xi_2$, of the estimator dynamics

$$\begin{aligned} \dot{\hat{\xi}}_2 &= \Gamma^{-1}\mathbf{Proj}(\hat{\xi}_2, \Gamma h(\hat{\xi}_2, y_2, u_{a_2})) \\ \hat{y}_2 &= C\hat{\xi}_2, \end{aligned} \tag{15}$$

with $h(\hat{\xi}_2, u_{a_2}, y_2) \equiv A_c\hat{\xi}_2 - Bu_{a_2} + L(\hat{y}_2 - y)$, is exponentially stable.

Proof: For notational convinence, let $z \equiv (\hat{\xi}_2, y_2, u_{a_2})$. Taking the time derivative of $e(t)$, we have

$$\begin{aligned} \dot{e}(t) &= \dot{\hat{\xi}}_2(t) - \dot{\xi}_2(t) \\ &= \Gamma^{-1}\mathbf{Proj}(\hat{\xi}_2, \Gamma h(z)) - h(z) + (A_c + LC)e. \end{aligned}$$

Let $V(e)$ be the positive definite and decresent Lyapunov function associated with the estimator error trajectory $e(t)$, and defined by

$$\lambda_{\min}(\Gamma)\|e\|^2 \leq V(e) \equiv \frac{1}{2}e^T\Gamma e \leq \lambda_{\max}(\Gamma)\|e\|^2.$$

By taking the time derivative of $V(e)$ and using Lemma 2.1, we obtain

$$\begin{aligned} \dot{V}(e) &= e^T\Gamma\dot{e} \\ &= \underbrace{e^T\Gamma\left(\Gamma^{-1}\mathbf{Proj}(\hat{\xi}_2, \Gamma h(z)) - h(z)\right)}_{\leq 0} \\ &\quad + e^T\Gamma(A_c + LC)e \\ &\leq e^T\Gamma(A_c + LC)e. \end{aligned}$$

The closed-loop estimator matrix $A_c + LC$ is Hurwitz, therefore, for a given $Q > 0$, there exists a matrix $\Gamma > 0$ that solves the Lyapunov matrix equation

$$\Gamma(A_c + LC) + (A_c + LC)^T\Gamma = -Q.$$

Therefore,

$$\dot{V}(e) \leq -\frac{1}{2}e^TQe \leq -\frac{1}{2}\lambda_{\min}(Q)\|e\|^2 \leq -\underbrace{\frac{\lambda_{\min}(Q)}{2\lambda_{\max}(\Gamma)}}_{=\mu}V(e)$$

$$\Rightarrow \dot{V}(e) + \mu V(e) \leq 0.$$

Using the integrating factor $e^{\mu t}$, we have

$$\int_0^\tau e^{\mu t}(\dot{V} + \mu V) \leq \int_0^\tau e^{\mu t}\, 0 \Rightarrow V(e(\tau)) \leq e^{-\mu\tau}V(0)$$

Further,

$$V(0) \leq \lambda_{\max}(\Gamma)\|e(0)\|^2, \text{ and}$$

$$\sqrt{\lambda_{\min}(Q)}\,\|e(\tau)\| \leq V^{\frac{1}{2}}(e(\tau)) \leq e^{-(\mu/2)\tau}\,V^{\frac{1}{2}}(0).$$

Therefore,

$$\|e(\tau)\| \leq \underbrace{\sqrt{\frac{\lambda_{\max}(\Gamma)}{\lambda_{\min}(\Gamma)}}}_{=K_0}e^{-(\mu/2)\tau}\,\|e(0)\| = K_0e^{-(\mu/2)\tau}\|e(0)\|$$

■

The CF tracker subsystem generates the input vector u_{a_2} so that the follower can track the transient stable relative error trajectories produced by the CF estimator. Fundamentally, the CF tracker is a servomechanism problem, and there are several options for its structure. A PID/LQR controller based type-1 tracker is a perfectly reasonable option. With a view on applying the CF tracker/estimator to more extensive and complex swarms, we opt for an output-feedback model-reference based tracking architecture. A model-reference based approach can readily accept time-varying adaptive gains, which allows for the automation of gain determination in complex formation structures.

Assumption: The output state vector $\hat{\xi}_2(t)$ of the CF estimator can be expressed as a linear combination of basis vectors $\phi_i(t)$ with some coefficient matrix L.

With this assumption, we can write the CF estimator output in the command generator form

$$\begin{aligned} \hat{\xi}_2(t) &= L\phi(t) \\ \hat{y}_2 &= C\hat{\xi}_2(t) \end{aligned} \tag{16}$$

where, $\phi(t) = (\phi_1(t), \ldots, \phi_p(t))^T$, is a column vector of tracking signal basis functions. According to [13], (16) is equivalent to the dynamical system

$$\begin{aligned} \dot{\eta}(t) &= F\eta(t) \\ \hat{y}_2 &= C\eta(t). \end{aligned} \tag{17}$$

The following result is the stability proof of the CF tracker subsystem based on the output-feedback model-reference tracking controller.

Theorem 3.2 (Reference Model Tracking): The follower LTI system

$$\dot{x}_2 = Ax_2 + Bu_2 \tag{18a}$$

$$y_2 = C(x_1 - x_2 - d_2) = C\xi_2, \tag{18b}$$

with the tracking control law

$$u_{a_2} = G_e(y_2 - \hat{y}_2) + S_2\hat{y}_2, \tag{19}$$

for appropriately sized gain matrices G_e, and S_2, will track the command generator reference (CGR) system

$$\hat{\xi}_2(t) = L\phi(t) \tag{20a}$$

$$\hat{y}_2 = C\hat{\xi}_2(t), \tag{20b}$$

such that, both the output relative error vector $e_y(t) \equiv \hat{y}_2(t) - y_2(t)$, and the error between the relative error vectors $e(t) \equiv \hat{\xi}_2(t) - \xi_2(t)$, are driven to the origin exponentially. Provided, the transmission zeros and the poles of the relative error dynamics $\xi_2(t)$ are distinct.

Proof: Let ξ_2^*, u_2^*, and y_2^*, be the ideal trajectory, ideal inputs, and ideal output, respectively. The ideal trajectory, and its associated vectors evolve according to the dynamics

$$\dot{\xi}_2^* = A_c\xi_2^* + Bu_2^* \tag{21a}$$

$$y_2^* = C\xi_2^* = \hat{y}_2. \tag{21b}$$

That is, the ideal trajectory ξ_2^* evolves so that it tracks the CGR system output exactly. Let S be a matrix that relates the ideal trajectories to the CGR system, defined by

$$\begin{pmatrix} \xi_2^* \\ u_i^* \end{pmatrix} = S\begin{pmatrix} \hat{y}_2 \\ 0 \end{pmatrix} = \begin{pmatrix} S_{11} & S_{12} \\ S_{21} & S_{22} \end{pmatrix}\begin{pmatrix} \hat{y}_2 \\ 0 \end{pmatrix}. \tag{22}$$

The CGR system can also be expressed in the form of an equivalent LTI system

$$\dot{\eta}(t) = F\eta(t) \tag{23a}$$

$$\hat{y}_2 = C\eta(t) \tag{23b}$$

Using (21), and (23), and taking the time derivative of (22), we have matrix equations

$$(A_cS_{11} - BS_{21})C = S_{11}CF \tag{24a}$$

$$CS_{11} = I, \tag{24b}$$

which are the matching conditions for the tracking problem. The implementation of the tracking control law requires the solution to the matrices S_{11} and S_{21}. According to [14], the solution to the matrices S_{11} and S_{21} exists, provided the transmission zeros of the reference model, and the poles of the plant are distinct, which by assumption is true. We now define the tracking error $\Delta\xi_2 \equiv \xi_2^* - \xi_2$. Taking its time derivative, we have

$$\Delta\dot{\xi}_2 = A_c\Delta\xi_2 - B\Delta u_{a_2} \tag{25a}$$

$$\Delta y_2 = C(\xi_2^* - \xi_2) = y_2^* - y_2 = \hat{y}_2 - y_2, \tag{25b}$$

where, $\Delta u_{a_2} = u_{a_2}^* - u_{a_2}$. Let $\Delta u_{a_2} = G_e\Delta y$, so that, the closed-loop tracking error system

$$\Delta\dot{\xi}_2 = (A_c - BG_eC)\Delta\xi_2 = \tilde{A}_c\Delta\xi_2 \tag{26a}$$

$$\Delta y_2 = C\Delta\xi_2 \tag{26b}$$

is exponentially stable. Therefore, $\Delta\xi_2 \to 0$ as $t \to \infty$, which implies $\xi_2(t) \to \hat{\xi}_2(t)$ as $t \to \infty$. Also, since

$$\Delta u_{a_2} = G_e\Delta y$$

$$\Rightarrow u_{a_2}^* - u_{a_2} = G_e(\hat{y}_2 - y_2)$$

$$\Rightarrow u_{a_2} = G_e(y_2 - \hat{y}_2) + S_{21}\hat{y}_2$$

■

The proposed CF tracking controller tracks the collision-free trajectory generated by the CF estimator. But, only if the follower dynamics are deterministic. In practice, an adaptive control law would determine the gain matrices G_e and S_{21}, which would result in robust tracking performance similar or better to that of integral action in type-1 servomechanisms.

IV. Simulation Result

We use the two simulation runs: Run 1 with CF tracker disabled, and Run 2 with CF tracker enabled, to demonstrate the functioning, and also highlight a few limitations of the CF estimator and tracker subsystem. For the two simulation runs, the leader and follower are double integrator agents with the model $\ddot{x} = u$. The leader and the follower initially rest at their specified separation of 5 meters. After a specified time of about 20 seconds, a position and velocity disturbance is applied to the leader using the input vector u_d, as shown in Figure 5. $\dot{x}_1 = Ax_1 + Bu_1 + u_d$ is the structure of the leader's dynamics with the disturbance vector input u_d. In Figures 6 and 7, the solid horizontal lines named Relative Error Upper limit, and Relative Error Lower limit, reflect the relative error bounds in (3). The dashed lines represent the beginning of the soft constraint boundary for the projection operator; the estimates from the projection operator are allowed to exceed the soft boundary temporarily. Figure 4 shows timed sequence of the leader and follower positions for the two simulation runs. Stiffness in the Ordinary Differential Equations (ODEs) can arise from the projection-based dynamics in the follower reference model, and it can lead to slow convergence when using popular explicit ODE solvers such as the Dormand-Prince RK5(4) [15]; usually, an implicit solver is a better solution. For the simulation runs in this paper, we used the LSODA solver (which is roughly equivalent to ode15s in MATLAB) from SciPy [16], which is a scientific library for Python, and it can automatically switch between implicit and explicit methods to handle stiff ODEs.

Figure 6 shows the results for the simulation run with the CF tracker turned off. There are two important outcomes. First, as expected, the relative error trajectory violates the upper and lower limits for collision avoidance. Second, the CF estimator generated trajectory saturates and never exceeds the transient stability bounds. However, when the actual relative error is within the bounds, the estimator perfectly tracks the actual trajectory. The outcomes of this simulation demonstrate the predictions of Theorem 3.1.

Figure 7 shows the results for the simulation run with the CF tracker turned on. Right away, we see that both the true and the estimated relative trajectories never exceed the transient instability bound; therefore, no collisions occur. Since the CF estimator on the follower does not have access to the leader's input information, whenever the vector u_d is non-zero, a near constant bias/DC component exists between the actual and estimated relative trajectories. The magnitude of the disturbance vector components is deliberately limited to 2 [m] or [m/s]. If the magnitude of the disturbance is any higher, the bias between the actual and estimated trajectories increases and degrades the tracking performance, which can result in inter-agent collisions. It can be shown that the sharing of control information (i.e., $u_1(t)$) from the leader to the follower will resolve the aforementioned issues.

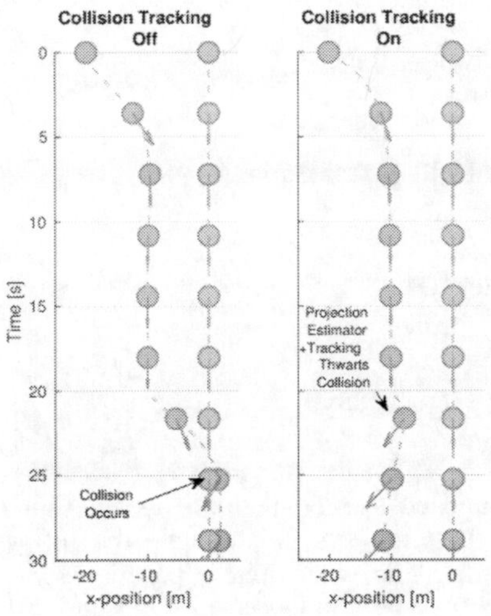

Fig. 4. Sequences of Leader-Follower Motion from Simulation Runs

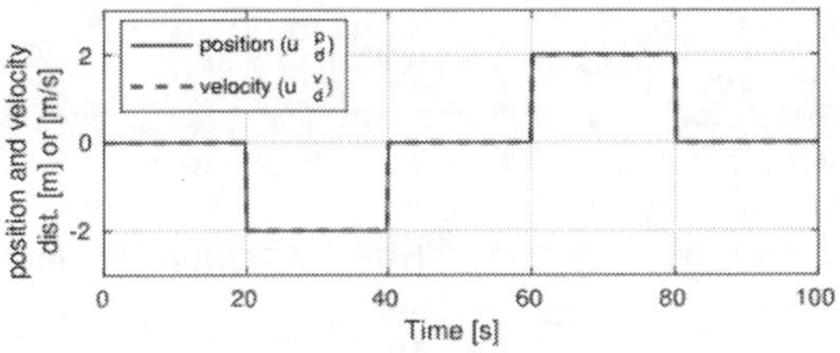

Fig. 5. Leader Disturbance Vector

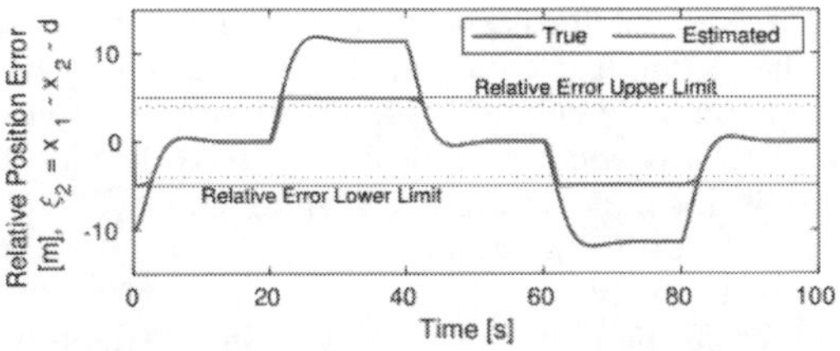

Fig. 6. Follower Trajectory with Tracking Off

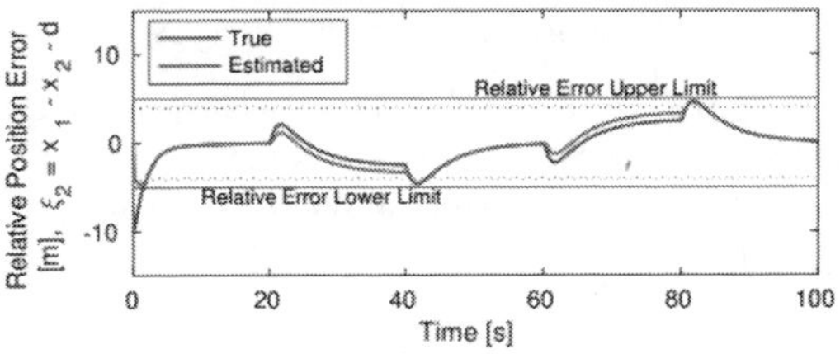

Fig. 7. Follower Trajectory with Tracking On

V. Conclusion

We have developed a novel controller architecture that addresses the problem of transient instabilities in dual-agent formations. We also presented the preliminary theoretical results on the stability of the collision-free estimator and the tracker subsystems. The proposed controller is particularly attractive due to its simplicity and its ability to guarantee both dynamic and transient stability. Future work will focus on 1) developing a comprehensive analytical framework that will investigate robustness to external noise and disturbances. And 2) on generalizing the architecture to larger and more complex formation structures.

Acknowledgment

Part of this research was carried out at the Jet Propulsion Laboratory, California Institute of Technology, under a contract with the National Aeronautics and Space Administration. ©2020 California Institute of Technology. Government sponsorship acknowledged.

References

[1] V. P. Gehlot and M. J. Balas, "An evolving systems approach to the stable operation of dynamic formations and swarms of autonomous vehicles in a disruptive environment," in *2018 AIAA SPACE and Astronautics Forum and Exposition, AIAA SPACE Forum*. American Institute of Aeronautics and Astronautics, 2018.

[2] ——, "A theoretical framework for the stable operation of autonomous spacecraft formations in the hill-clohessy-wiltshire frame," in *IEEE Southeast Conference*. IEEE, 2019.

[3] V. P. Gehlot, M. J. Balas, and S. Bandyopadhyay, "Dynamic stability and adaptive control of networked evolving formations with weak nonlinearities," in *AIAA Scitech Forum*. AIAA, 2020.

[4] A. D. Ames, J. W. Grizzle, and P. Tabuada, "Control barrier function based quadratic programs with application to adaptive cruise control," in *53rd IEEE Conference on Decision and Control*, 12 2014, pp. 6271–6278.

[5] F. Rossi, S. Bandyopadhyay, M. Wolf, and M. Pavone, "Review of multi-agent algorithms for collective behavior: a structural taxonomy," *IFAC-PapersOnLine*, vol. 51, no. 12, pp. 112 – 117, 2018, iFAC Workshop on Networked & Autonomous Air & Space Systems NAASS 2018.

[6] D. Zhou, Z. Wang, S. Bandyopadhyay, and M. Schwager, "Fast, on-line collision avoidance for dynamic vehicles using buffered voronoi cells," *IEEE Robotics and Automation Letters*, vol. 2, no. 2, pp. 1047–1054, 2017.

[7] O. Khatib, "Real-time obstacle avoidance for manipulators and mobile robots," in *Proceedings. 1985 IEEE International Conference on Robotics and Automation*, vol. 2, 1985, pp. 500–505.

[8] E. Lavretsky and K. Wise, *Robust and Adaptive Control: With Aerospace Applications*, ser. Advanced Textbooks in Control and Signal Processing. Springer London, 2012.

[9] G. Kreisselmeier and K. Narendra, "Stable model reference adaptive control in the presence of bounded disturbances," *IEEE Transactions on Automatic Control*, vol. 27, no. 6, pp. 1169–1175, 1982.

[10] N. Hovakimyan and C. Cao, *L1 Adaptive Control Theory: Guaranteed Robustness with Fast Adaptation*, ser. Advances in Design and Control. Society for Industrial and Applied Mathematics, 2010.

[11] P. A. Ioannou and J. Sun, *Robust Adaptive Control*. Mineola, New York: Dover Publication, Inc., 2012, p. 586.

[12] P. Ioannou and B. Fidan, *Adaptive Control Tutorial*, ser. Advances in Design and Control. Society for Industrial and Applied Mathematics, 2006.

[13] C. D. Johnson, "Disturbance-accommodating control; an overview," in *1986 American Control Conference*, 1986, pp. 526–536.

[14] M. J. Balas and S. A. Frost, "Adaptive Tracking Control for Linear Infinite Dimensional Systems," ser. Smart Materials, Adaptive Structures and Intelligent Systems, vol. Volume 2: Modeling, Simulation and Control; Bio-Inspired Smart Materials and Systems; Energy Harvesting, 09 2016. [Online]. Available: https://doi.org/10.1115/SMASIS2016-9098

[15] J. Dormand and P. Prince, "A family of embedded runge-kutta formulae," *Journal of Computational and Applied Mathematics*, vol. 6, no. 1, pp. 19 – 26, 1980.

[16] P. Virtanen et al., "SciPy 1.0: Fundamental Algorithms for Scientific Computing in Python," *Nature Methods*, vol. 17, pp. 261–272, 2020.

Area Inspection by Robot Swarms through Exploitation of Information Gain

Carlos Carbone*, Dario Albani†*, Daniele Nardi*, Dimitri Ognibene‡ and Vito Trianni§

*La Sapienza University of Rome, Rome, Italy
Email: [surname]@diag.uniroma1.it

†Technology Innovation Institute, Abu Dhabi, United Arab Emirates
Email: dario.albani@tii.ae

‡University of Essex, Colchester, UK
Email: dimitri.ognibene@essex.ac.uk

§National Research Council of Italy, Rome, Italy
Email: vito.trianni@istc.cnr.it

***Abstract*—We propose a decentralized, collaborative approach for area coverage and mapping by means of a swarm of robots. The approach is hinged on Information Theory, and builds over a Reinforced Random Walk (RRW) specifically tailored for a precision agriculture scenario, but general enough to accommodate different applications. Here, we improve by considering the estimated uncertainty about the features present in a target area, and by the expected reduction in uncertainty that visiting the target area could provide, that is, the information entropy and information gain, respectively. The latter is exploited to weight the random selection of the next area to explore, taking also into account the presence of nearby agents that could visit the same target area. The proposed approach features no configuration parameters related to the number of agents employed and the size of the field, opening to direct implementation without preliminary tuning and configuration steps.**

Keywords–Swarm Robotics; Entropy; Information Gain; Random Walk

I. INTRODUCTION

Many monitoring and mapping applications require to fully cover a wide region of space detecting the presence of points of interest and mapping their exact position. This is a common task, especially for precision agriculture, which has been approached in many different ways: pheromone-based approaches [1] [2], evolutionary path planning [3], and random walk based approach [4] [5] to cite some. In this research, we rely on Information Theory and propose a new algorithm for coverage and mapping of large areas. We consider precision agriculture as the target application, whereas a swarm of Unmanned Aerial Vehicles (UAVs) is required to detect the presence of weeds in the field, but the proposed algorithm is general enough to accommodate a variety of scenarios. The swarm inspection strategy is informed by a heuristic computed according to Information Theory concepts such as Entropy and Information Gain (IG). Moreover, we exploit the presence of multiple robots scattered throughout the field and propose a decentralized collaborative approach that improves accuracy and reduces the time needed for exploration. Indeed, by quantifying and including the knowledge of an agent about the area, it is possible to develop a cooperative behavior that focuses on points of interest and reduce the mapping time, i.e., the time needed to recognize all the relevant features within the field. In this work, we assume the following simplified world model. The work area is partitioned in a 4-connected grid which can be configured to represent spaces of different complexity. Agents are not limited to orthogonal motion and can move in continuous space. A grid cell $c_k \in C$ represents a region of the field, where a robot can move, and might contain a certain number of points of interest (e.g., weeds). All robots are identical and each robot is identified by its unique id i and its position in the environment. The robots move at constant speed and are able to avoid collision thanks to an on-board collision avoidance algorithm [6]. Robots can communicate with each other by using broadcast communication that might be subject to range limitations.

II. INFORMATION GAIN FOR EXPLORATION

The swarm strategy aims at maximizing the expected information that could be gathered from an area after inspection: the IG, that is, the expected reduction in entropy. When used for exploration and mapping tasks, the IG can be used to quantify how much knowledge would be obtained if an observation in a certain location occurs [7]. To this end, we exploit the IG to quantify the information that could be gathered from a new observation performed by the agents in a specific cell c_k and to represent the utility of visiting it. In its simplest form, at a specific time instant, the agent i can compute the IG of a cell c_k according to the following equation:

$$\mathrm{IG}_i(c_k) = H_i(c_k) - H_i(c_k|o_k(i)) \tag{1}$$

where $H_i(c_k)$ express the residual uncertainty that robot i has about cell c_k, and $H_i(c_k|o_k(i))$ is the conditional entropy of the same cell given the observation o_k performed by robot i at a specific time instant. The residual uncertainty of a cell is computed as follows.

$$H_i(c_k) = -\sum p_i(c_k) log(p_i(c_k)), \tag{2}$$

with $p_i(c_k)$ representing the knowledge of robot i—i.e., the current knowledge about the number of points of interest existing in cell c_k, which are in a discrete number and are represented by a vector that associates to each value $c \in [0, C]$

the probability of having c points of interest. Lastly, replacing $o_k(i)$ with $\tilde{o}_k$, the conditional entropy is:

$$H_i(c_k|\tilde{o}_k) = -\sum_o p_i(\tilde{o}_k) \sum_c \left[p_i(c_k|\tilde{o}_k) \log\left(p_i(c_k|\tilde{o}_k)\right)\right]. \tag{3}$$

The knowledge vector is calculated by means of the probability of having a certain observation as $p_i(c_k|\tilde{o}_k) = p_i(c_k)p_i(\tilde{o}_k|c_k)/p_i(\tilde{o}_k)$, where $p_i(c_k|\tilde{o}_k)$ is the probability of robot i performing an observation o for the cell c_k. Thus, each new observation increases the confidence about the points of interest present in a cell. When the uncertainty decreases below a fixed threshold, the cell is considered as mapped and no further observation is required. Note that observations can also be shared by neighbouring robots, allowing to update the residual uncertainty about a cell also when others have visited it. In this way, the robots keep a local model of the entire area exploiting both own and others' observations.

III. Information Theory Enriched Random Walk

The IG of a cell can now be used as a proxy of the expected quantity of information gathered from a new observation of a cell. This is computed separately from each agent in the swarm and in a completely decentralized way since the units in the swarm only rely on their local knowledge for the computation of these values—e.g., the knowledge vector $p(c_k)$. Computed values are then used for next target selection. In particular, we propose a distance-aware collaborative strategy that assigns higher probabilities of inspection to closer cells—avoiding big jumps that proved to be detrimental for exploration [4]—and that weights the decisions according to other agents expected behaviors. We start by assigning probabilities to each cell thanks to (1):

$$P_i(c_k) = \frac{\mathrm{IG}_i(c_k)}{\sum_z \mathrm{IG}_i(c_z)} \tag{4}$$

where P_i is the probability of selecting cell c_k computed from the perspective of agent i with respect to all cells considered for inspection at this stage. Nonetheless, (4) alone is not enough since it does not consider the presence of other agents, hence, collaboration. To this end, we rewrite (1) has:

$$P_i(c_k) = \frac{\mathrm{IG}_i(c_k)}{\sum_z \mathrm{IG}_i(c_z)} \prod_{j \neq i} \left[1 - \frac{\mathrm{IG}_j(c_k)}{\sum_z \mathrm{IG}_j(c_z)}\right] \tag{5}$$

where, the probability $P_i(c_k)$ is now weighted by the probability that the cell c_k will be selected by inspection by another agent $j \neq i$. This allows for direct inclusion of other agents operations and in a completely decentralized way since all the probabilities in the right-most term are computed relying only on the local knowledge of agent i. Lastly, we introduce distance and upgrade (5) as:

$$P_i(c_k) = \frac{d_i(c_k)^{-1}\mathrm{IG}_i(c_k)}{\sum_z d_i(c_z)^{-1}\mathrm{IG}_i(c_z)} \prod_{j \neq i} \left[1 - \frac{d_j(c_k)^{-1}\mathrm{IG}_j(c_k)}{\sum_z d_j(c_z)^{-1}\mathrm{IG}_j(c_z)}\right] \tag{6}$$

with the terms $d_i(c_k)$ representing the euclidean distance between agent i and the cell c_k. From a computational point of view, (5) is expensive and does not scale well with hundreds of agents. To mitigate this issue, the choices are constrained to the local neighbourhood of the agent (see Figure 1). At first, the algorithm computes the probabilities only for immediate neighbors cells—i.e., those composing the 3×3 neighbourhood. If no valid cell is found—i.e., all cells are already mapped or targeted by other agents—the algorithms proceeds with the 5×5 neighbourhood. In case there is still no valid cell, a random choice is made among the cells of the outer border that are not targeted by other agents. Note that the set of agents taken into account in (6) is constrained to those agents that can potentially move to the target cell c_k, hence those that are within a 5×5 neighbourhood of c_k.

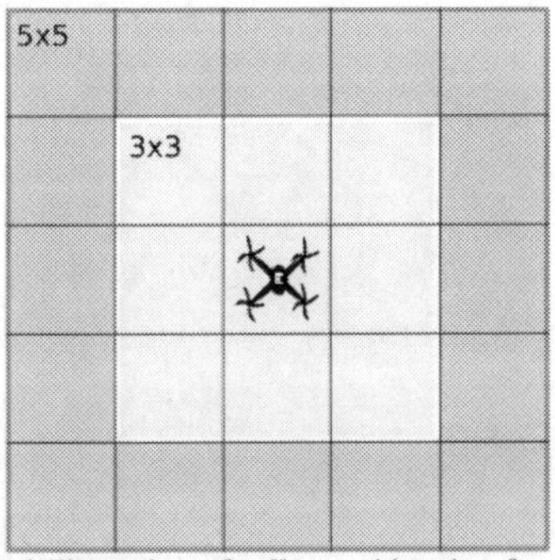

Figure 1. Graphical illustration of cells consideration for random selection based on IG.

IV. Conclusion and Future Work

We presented an algorithm for area inspection that relies on IG to chose the next area to inspect. It does not present free parameters, exempting the user from pre-operational tuning and making it suitable for application such as search and rescue and precision agriculture, where the deployment speed is an important requirement. Next, it is completely decentralized, robust to failure and noisy communication since the cell selection procedure relies only on local knowledge. Nonetheless, the latter is built over information received during operation and local communications are required for good performance. To this end, we are currently working on introducing direct sharing of the IG through belief propagation. We believe that this would help reducing the overall communication overhead and will greatly boost the performances. Last, the algorithm scales up to swarm size of hundreds and, if limiting the agents considered in (6) to local neighbors, even more.

References

[1] B. Hrolenok, S. Luke, K. Sullivan, and C. Vo, "Collaborative foraging using beacons." in AAMAS, vol. 10, 2010, pp. 1197–1204.

[2] M. Paradzik and G. İnce, "Multi-agent search strategy based on digital pheromones for uavs," in 2016 24th Signal Processing and Communication Application Conference (SIU). IEEE, 2016, pp. 233–236.

[3] M. Popovic, G. Hitz, J. Nieto, I. Sa, R. Siegwart, and E. Galceran, "Online informative path planning for active classification using uavs," arXiv preprint arXiv:1609.08446, 2016.

[4] D. Albani, D. Nardi, and V. Trianni, "Field coverage and weed mapping by uav swarms," in Intelligent Robots and Systems (IROS), 2017 IEEE/RSJ International Conference on. IEEE, 2017, pp. 4319–4325.

[5] D. Albani, T. Manoni, A. Arik, D. Nardi, and V. Trianni, "Field coverage for weed mapping: Toward experiments with a uav swarm," in Bio-inspired Information and Communication Technologies, A. Compagnoni, W. Casey, Y. Cai, and B. Mishra, Eds. Cham: Springer International Publishing, 2019, pp. 132–146.

[6] J. Van Den Berg, S. J. Guy, M. Lin, and D. Manocha, "Optimal reciprocal collision avoidance for multi-agent navigation," in Proc. of the IEEE International Conference on Robotics and Automation, Anchorage (AK), USA, 2010.

[7] E. Palazzolo and C. Stachniss, "Effective exploration for mavs based on the expected information gain," Drones, vol. 2, no. 1, 2018, p. 9.

Imitating Task-oriented Grasps from Human Demonstrations with a Low-DoF Gripper

Timothy Patten and Markus Vincze

Automation and Control Institute
TU Wien
Vienna, Austria
Email: {patten, vincze}@acin.tuwien.ac.at

***Abstract*—Task-oriented or semantic grasping is important in robotics because it enables objects to be manipulated appropriately and used for their intended purpose. Many objects are human designed, therefore, we address the problem of learning task-oriented grasps by directly observing human behaviour. A person simply demonstrates the appropriate grasp, which is quick and convenient for any user in the real world. Our approach uses RGB images to track the object and hand pose, then employs a neural network to translate the human hand configuration to a robotic grasp with fewer degrees of freedom. Analysis shows that a variety of low-dimensional representations of the hand enable the mapping to be learned and that the model better generalises to new demonstrators handling new objects when the training data is augmented. Experiments with a mobile manipulator show that a robot successfully observes grasps and imitates the action on objects in various poses. This is accomplished immediately, without additional learning and is robust in real-world conditions.**

Keywords–Robotic grasping; task-oriented grasping; learning from demonstration; imitation learning; deep learning.

I. Introduction

Grasping is an important capability for robots operating in industry or in homes. The human world is very complex: objects have a variety of characteristics and the environment imposes unpredictable constraints. As such, learning generalisable grasping strategies that are robust in real-world conditions is an ongoing and active field of research.

Significant advances have been made by applying deep learning, which has been enabled by the introduction of large datasets that are annotated by hand [1] [2], compiled with 3D object models and analytical metrics [3] [4] or generated using grasp planners in simulation [5]–[7]. Grasping methods trained on these datasets ignore the semantics of the grasp and only measure success if an object is securely lifted or transported. Semantic or task-oriented grasping introduces the concept that objects should be grasped to enable task-related manipulation actions [8]. For example, grasping the handle and not the blade enables a knife to be used for cutting. Existing approaches exploit manually annotated examples [9] [10], constrain grasps to parts that afford the task [11]–[13] or perform self-supervised learning in simulation [14].

In this paper, we address task-oriented grasping by Learning from Demonstration (LfD) in which a robot learns to replicate a grasp demonstrated by a human, as shown in Figure 1. In contrast to previous work, we contribute a convenient human-robot interface that requires no special instrumentation [15], manual annotation [16], physical interaction with the robot [13] or an offline learning process [17]. Our system uses only the onboard camera to observe a single example of a human grasp to understand how the grasp is performed, which makes it easy to be adopted by untrained users in the real world. Furthermore, we explicitly address the problem of transferring the human grasp to a robot gripper with fewer Degrees of Freedom (DoF). We employ a neural network to learn the mapping between the joints of the human hand and the parameterisation of the robot grasp to effectively transfer the observed human grasp to a robotic parallel-jaw gripper.

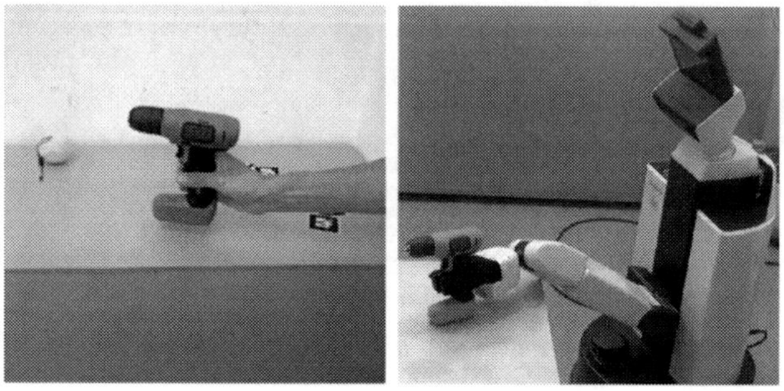

Figure 1. Human demonstrates how to semantically grasp an object by lifting a drill by the handle (left). Robot imitates the semantic grasp (right).

An analysis of the neural network shows that it has the capacity to successfully transfer human grasps to the robot platform. In an ablation study, we show that it is sufficient to learn from a subset of hand joints to yield high quality robot grasp pose predictions. Furthermore, learning from interactions with one object better transfers to other objects when the training data is augmented. In experiments with a mobile manipulator, people demonstrate semantic grasps by grasping the handles of objects, such as mugs and drills. The robot shows the ability to observe the human and instantly imitate the demonstrated grasp on the same object when it is presented in any new pose.

In summary, we make the following contributions:

- A neural network architecture to regress the grasp parameterisation for a low-DoF robotic gripper from the human hand configuration;
- evaluation of the grasp regression network for transferring between different demonstrators and objects;
- a grasp imitation learning pipeline using state-of-the-art object pose estimation and hand tracking with our regression network to transfer demonstrated human grasps to robot grasps for the observed objects; and
- experiments of real-world task-oriented grasp learning from demonstration with a mobile manipulator.

The remainder of the paper is organised as follows. Section II discusses related work. Section III outlines our approach for learning to transfer human grasps to robot grasps and Section IV describes the imitation learning framework. Section V presents the experimental results. Section VI concludes the paper.

II. Related Work

Learning from demonstration or imitation learning is a paradigm in which a robot learns skills by imitating the actions shown by an expert [18] [19]. The approach is popular because it enables robots to learn complex tasks that are otherwise difficult to program. In the robotics context, recent work has shown successful learning of highly advanced skills such as dispensing water from a thermos [20], making coffee [21], preparing a food platter [22] and transferring small items with a kitchen ladle [23].

Human expertise is also a fruitful source of knowledge for learning robotic grasping. This is especially useful for robots operating man-made objects designed for human manipulation. Human knowledge is exploited by physically moving the robot arm and kinesthetic teaching [24], controlling the robot by teleoperation [25] or virtual reality [26], or using a hand-held replica of the robot end-effector [27]. It is cumbersome and time consuming to annotate or physically interact with hardware, therefore, learning from observation [28] is more appropriate because the human involvement is kept to a minimum. But despite this advantage, learning from observation introduces other issues. Most prominent is how to track the human arm and hand while the grasp is performed and secondly how to overcome the disparity between the human and robot hand kinematics. For tracking the hand, many approaches use data gloves or markers with a motion capture system [29] [30] but this is inflexible because the tracking apparatus must be set up and calibrated. This prevents the easy and quick use of the systems by people in real-world home or office settings. Some approaches directly use vision and thus do not require extra hardware to learn and transfer grasps. Do et al. [31] use a single camera to estimate the joints of the human body but simplify the task of estimating the state of the hand. They use a proxy in which the orientation and grasp type are estimated to predict a robot grasp. Therefore, they do not estimate the full hand pose. Palli et al. [32] estimate the wrist and finger tip locations to transfer the demonstrated human grasp to the DEXMART anthropomorphic hand. Due to the high kinematic similarity, the transfer is simplified; it only requires an additional scaling factor between the length of the demonstrator's fingers and the robot fingers. The current solution to transfer grasps to robot end-effectors with significantly different kinematics is to use a predefined mapping between known human and robotic grasp shapes [29]. No work thus far learns a mapping between arbitrary human grasp poses and robotic grasps for grippers with fewer DoF.

Semantic grasping is a special case of grasping in which the grasp enables task-related manipulation [8]. The most common approach is to compute grasps and then introduce constraints or affordances to select grasps that satisfy the task [11]–[13]. Learning semantic grasps directly from observation has been studied in [15]–[17] but these transfer the demonstrated grasps to anthropomorphic hands and some use data gloves to localise hand joints. In this work, we address the problem of observing and imitating semantic grasps only using a camera and provide a learning-based solution to map the human hand to a low-DoF robotic gripper configuration.

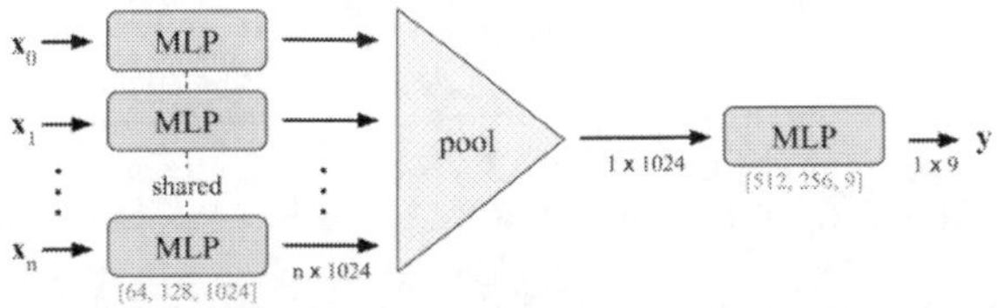

(a) Each point passes through a separate MLP (all with shared weights). Feature maps transformed to a global feature with a pooling operation (*maximum* or *average*). Global feature passes through another MLP.

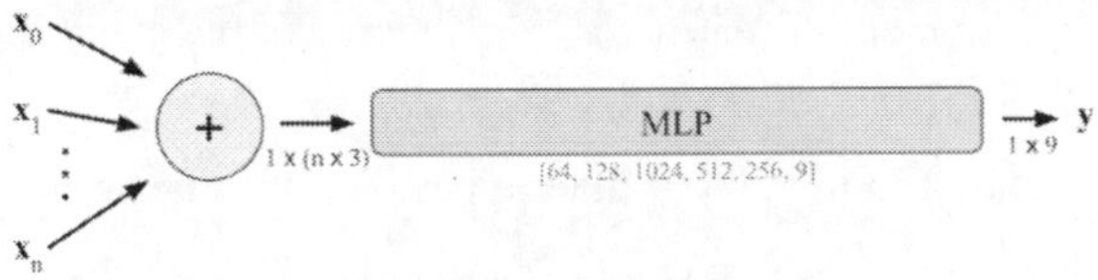

(b) Input points are sorted and concatenated. The concatenated feature vector passes through a single MLP.

Figure 2. Network architectures for regressing robot grasp from human grasp. Layer sizes are shown beneath the MLP blocks.

III. Learning Robotic Grasp Poses from Human Hand Configurations

Imitating a human demonstrated grasp by a robot equipped with a parallel-jaw gripper requires the mapping between the human hand and the gripper's degrees of freedom to be determined. This mapping is represented as a function $\mathcal{F}$ that transforms a human grasp $\mathbf{H} \in \mathbb{R}^H$ to a robot grasp $\mathbf{G} \in \mathbb{R}^G$, i.e., $\mathbf{G} = \mathcal{F}(\mathbf{H})$, and where $H > G$. We choose to model this function as a neural network. The architecture for the network, the loss function and the training procedure are discussed in the following.

A. Network Architecture

An overview of the network architecture is shown in Figure 2a. This architecture is based on the PointNet architecture [33] that is developed for classification or point-wise segmentation of unstructured 3D point cloud data. We modify PointNet to instead regress a 6-DoF pose that represents a grasp for a parallel-jaw gripper. PointNet also includes a spatial transformer network that makes the learned representations invariant to geometric transformations. This is necessary for classification since transformations of the points should not result in different class predictions. For our work, different poses in the input should generate different poses of the grasp, therefore, the spatial transformer network is removed.

The input to the network is a set of points representing the joints of the hand in the camera coordinate system. The joint coordinates are shifted and scaled to fit in the unit sphere. They are then fed to a Multilayer Perceptron (MLP) with layer output sizes [64, 128, 1024]. The output is max-pooled to create a global feature descriptor with 1024 units. The global feature is passed to the second stage of the pipeline to generate the output. This is an MLP that progressively reduces the global feature to the desired size. Our goal is to estimate the 6-DoF pose for a gripper, i.e., translation and rotation. The translation is represented by the x, y and z coordinates of the centroid of the grasp pose. The rotation is represented as unit vectors of the approach and closing directions. The output, therefore, consists of nine values by passing through the MLP with layer output sizes $[512,\ 256,\ 9]$. Batch norm and ReLu activation function are used for all layers except the last that uses linear activation. Dropout with a rate 0.7 is applied to the second last layer (i.e., layer before the pose prediction).

The output $\mathbf{y} = [\mathbf{t}, \mathbf{a}, \mathbf{c}]$ represents the robot grasp pose. The first three components $\mathbf{t} = (x, y, z)$ is the translation of the gripper with respect to the centre of the hand. The next three, $\mathbf{a} = (a_x, a_y, a_z)$ where $||\mathbf{a}|| = 1$, represent the grasp approach direction as a unit vector. The last three, $\mathbf{c} = (c_x, c_y, c_z)$ where $||\mathbf{c}|| = 1$, represent the closing angle of the gripper as a unit vector. The rotation of the gripper pose is obtained by

$$\mathbf{R} = \left[(\mathbf{c} \times \mathbf{a})^T, \mathbf{c}^T, \mathbf{a}^T \right], \tag{1}$$

and the final transformation matrix is thus $\mathbf{G} = [\mathbf{R}|\mathbf{t}^T]$. This represents the transformation of the gripper to the grasp pose in the camera coordinate system.

Since the input for the regression is a consistent configuration of finger joints, it is in fact unnecessary to account for unordered input with a symmetric function (i.e., pooling operation). Therefore, we also investigate a simplified network, as shown in Figure 2b. The joint values are concatenated and processed by a single MLP with layer output sizes $[64, 128, 1024, 512, 256, 9]$ to be consistent with the baseline approach.

B. Loss

For regression, the l_2 loss is used between the vectors of the estimated, $\mathbf{y}$, and the ground truth, $\mathbf{y}^{\text{GT}}$, gripper poses according to

$$\mathcal{L}\left(\mathbf{y}^{\text{GT}}, \mathbf{y}\right) = \frac{1}{n} \sum_{i=1}^{n} \left(\mathbf{y}_i^{\text{GT}} - \mathbf{y}_i\right)^2. \tag{2}$$

A grasp pose for a parallel-jaw gripper is 180° symmetric around the axis of the approach direction. This has two implications. First, grasps rotated by 180° around the axis should not be penalised but treated the same. Second, annotation does not need to be perfectly consistent for this degree of freedom. To account for the symmetry, the loss is computed for the output $\mathbf{y}$, as well as the same output with the negative of the closing angle, i.e., $\mathbf{y}^{\text{flipped}} = [\mathbf{t}, \mathbf{a}, -\mathbf{c}]$. The symmetric loss function is thus the minimum of the two,

$$\mathcal{L}_{\text{sym}}\left(\mathbf{y}^{\text{GT}}, \mathbf{y}\right) = \min\left(\mathcal{L}\left(\mathbf{y}^{\text{GT}}, \mathbf{y}\right), \mathcal{L}\left(\mathbf{y}^{\text{GT}}, \mathbf{y}^{\text{flipped}}\right)\right). \tag{3}$$

C. Training

The HO-3D dataset [34] is used to train the network. This dataset consists of multiple sequences of people manipulating an object in their right hand. The dataset consists of many different subjects and objects, as well as different perspectives from multiple cameras. The objects used for the data collection are a subset of the YCB object set [35]. The joints of the hand and the pose of the objects are accurately annotated using a joint optimisation procedure (see [34] for more details). A sample of the dataset is shown in Figure 3.

To learn the robot gripper pose corresponding to hand configurations, gripper poses are annotated for the corresponding

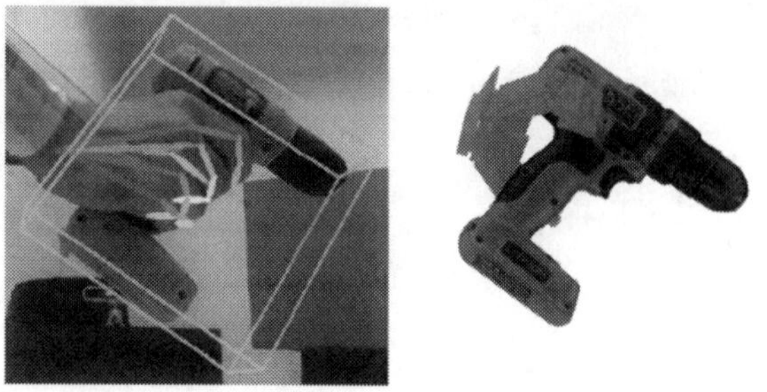

Figure 3. Example of the annotated data for training the gripper pose regression network. Annotation of the hand pose and object from [34] (left). Annotation of the corresponding robot grasp pose (right).

hand pose, as shown in Figure 3. The transformed object model and hand mesh, as well as the gripper model are loaded into Blender. The gripper model is manually adjusted to align its centre with the wrist position and its direction to approximate the angle between the thumb and the other fingers of the human hand. Fine adjustments are made such that the closure of the gripper tips coincides with the centre of the human grasp. Grasp poses from a single camera perspective (i.e., one subject-object pair) are annotated and the poses are transformed to the other camera perspectives.

Augmentation is applied to the input. This consists of a global rotation applied to both the input 3D coordinates of the hand joints and to the ground truth pose. The purpose of this augmentation is to generalise the predictions to a larger variety of input pairs. Local augmentation is also applied to the 3D coordinates of the hand joints. This applies both a small rotation, as well as random jitter to individual joints. The purpose of this augmentation is to robustify the network to noisy hand pose estimates.

IV. Imitating Grasp Demonstrations

To imitate grasps with the robot requires the human hand to be estimated online, the hand pose to be translated to a gripper pose and then the gripper pose to be associated with the object of interest. In this work we assume the target objects are known and have a designated local frame of reference. Therefore, every observed grasp is transformed to the local reference and retrieved for new positions of the object.

Pseudo-code for the grasp estimation procedure is given in Algorithm 1. During a demonstration, the pose of the object and the human hand are estimated in each camera frame, I_t, until the pose of the object is observed to move above a set threshold θ_o; in other words, until the object is moved by the human demonstrator; or when the object is not detected and thus the pose cannot be estimated due to the occlusion created by the grasp (line 13). This frame, at time t_{end}, establishes the end of the demonstration.

The hand pose at t_{end} is ideal to estimate the robot grasp because it represents the time instant when the human has a solid hold of the object. However, the quality of the estimated pose may be low due to the occlusion that occurs during the physical interaction. Therefore, throughout the demonstration, the hand pose is estimated in every frame (line 7). The nearest frame to the final frame with a valid hand pose, at time t_{est} where $t_{\text{est}} < t_{\text{end}}$, is used to generate the robot grasp pose using the regression network with the relevant hand joints (line 18). The validity of the hand pose depends on the implementation.

Algorithm 1: Robot Grasp Pose Estimation

Result: Robot grasp $\mathbf{G}^o$ in object's frame of reference

1 $\mathbf{P} \leftarrow$ Object pose in first frame
2 $\mathbf{H} \leftarrow$ Computed hand pose
3 $\mathbf{v} \leftarrow$ Grasp pose offset
4 **Loop**
5   Get current image I_t
6   Estimate object pose $\mathbf{P}_t$
7   Estimate hand joints $\mathbf{H}_t$
8   **if** $\mathbf{H}_t$ *is valid* **then**
9         $\mathbf{H} \leftarrow \mathbf{H}_t$
10   **else**
11         $\mathbf{v} \leftarrow$ Update using valid joints in $\mathbf{H}$ and $\mathbf{H}_t$
12   **end**
13   **if** $\mathbf{P}_t = \emptyset$ *or* $|\mathbf{P}_t - \mathbf{P}| > \theta_o$ **then**
14         $\mathbf{P} \leftarrow \mathbf{P}_t$
15   break
16   **end**
17 **EndLoop**
18 $\mathbf{G} \leftarrow$ Estimate robot grasp pose from hand $\mathbf{H}$
19 $\mathbf{G} \leftarrow$ Adjust position of grasp by offset $\mathbf{v}$
20 $\mathbf{G}^o \leftarrow$ Transform $\mathbf{G}$ to object reference frame
21 **Return:** $\mathbf{G}^o$

In this work, we estimate the hand pose using [36] and the residual of the inverse kinematics optimisation, that lifts the 2D keypoints detections to 3D, scores the quality of the hand pose estimate. Please see [36] for more details.

In the case that the hand is only valid in a frame before the final grasp is made (because the hand is less occluded by the object), the predicted gripper pose needs to be adjusted. This is because the hand may be located away from the object and no longer be in an ideal position to associate the robot grasp. To account for this offset, the estimated robotic gripper pose is re-positioned according to the distance and direction between the hand in frames t_{est} and t_{end} (line 19). The vector of the movement in the camera coordinate system for all hand joints between the two frames are computed and then averaged (line 11). For robustness, only the vectors of joints that are visible in every frame between t_{est} and t_{end} are used. This removes spurious estimates that occur due to the occlusion.

Finally, the demonstrated grasp is transformed to the object's frame of reference by $\mathbf{G}^o = \mathbf{P}^{-1}\mathbf{G}$. Once a demonstration is observed, the robot is expected to replicate the grasp for any new pose of the target object. When the object is re-observed, its pose is estimated and the known grasp pose is transformed using the estimate. More concretely, in a new frame, where the object has a different pose $\mathbf{P}'$, the grasp pose that is executed by computing $\mathbf{G}' = \mathbf{P}'\mathbf{G}^o$.

V. EXPERIMENTS

The performance of the presented method for grasp imitation is evaluated in this section. We first give implementation details. We then report results of offline experiments to quantitatively analyse the robot grasp pose prediction. Lastly, we present results for real-world grasping experiments with a mobile manipulator.

A. Implementation Details

The regression network for robot grasp pose estimation is implemented in PyTorch. All models are trained for 120 epochs with an initial learning rate of 0.001 that is divided by 10 every 50 epochs. A batch size of 64 is used. Training is performed on an NVIDIA GTX TitanX.

Object poses are estimated with Pix2Pose [37], which uses only RGB images as input. The network is trained with the YCB-Video dataset and is therefore compatible with the data from HO-3D. The pose of the hand is estimated using the method in [36] and the keypoints of individual joints to compute the movement offset between the final and valid frame are determined with the OpenCV implementation of [38], where the predictions in the RGB image are lifted to 3D using the corresponding depth image.

Hardware experiments use the Toyota Human Support Robot [39] [40]. Observation of the demonstrations and the stand-alone objects for the grasping experiments use the head-mounted ASUS XTion Pro Live RGB-D camera. The estimated grasp poses are executed by generating a trajectory using MoveIt [41]. This plans trajectories that avoid obstacles within the scene. All code runs on the robot in Ubuntu 16.04 with ROS [42]. Inference for the pose estimation when running on the robot runs on an external PC with an NVIDIA GTX 1050 Ti.

Note that since HO-3D contains examples with the right hand, the applied hand tracking algorithms also use the right hand model and live demonstrations use the right hand. Adapting to the left would require flipping the images in HO-3D and using different models for [36] and [38].

B. Grasp Estimation Analysis

We analyse the quality of the grasp pose estimation using the data from six subjects (ABF, BB, GPMF, GSF, MDF and ShSu) in HO-3D. Separation between the data used for training and testing is maintained by training networks on the data from five subjects and testing on the sixth subject that was not seen in training.

The accuracy of grasp pose predictions is measured by the average distance between all vertices of a 3D mesh (ADD) when transformed by the prediction in comparison to the ground truth. This is a common metric for general object pose estimation [43] because it conveniently unifies translation and rotation error into a single metric. Similar to (3), the accuracy is reported for the minimum of the predicted pose and the 180° rotation around the approach vector to account for the symmetry of the gripper. Points are extracted from the gripper model to compute the metric.

1) Architecture and training procedure: The performance of different architectures and the inclusion of data augmentation is compared in Figure 4a, where results are averaged over all subjects. Considering the different architectures, the best performing is when the joint positions are concatenated into a high-dimensional input that is processed by a single MLP (Figure 2b). This results in 8.8% (at 16% diameter threshold) improvement over the baseline architecture, that applies separate MLPs to each point (Figure 2a). Furthermore, removing the pooling operation and instead processing the the $n \times 1024$ feature vector improves over the baseline architecture. Having separate heads to predict the translation and rotation does not introduce any performance gain, which has been shown in

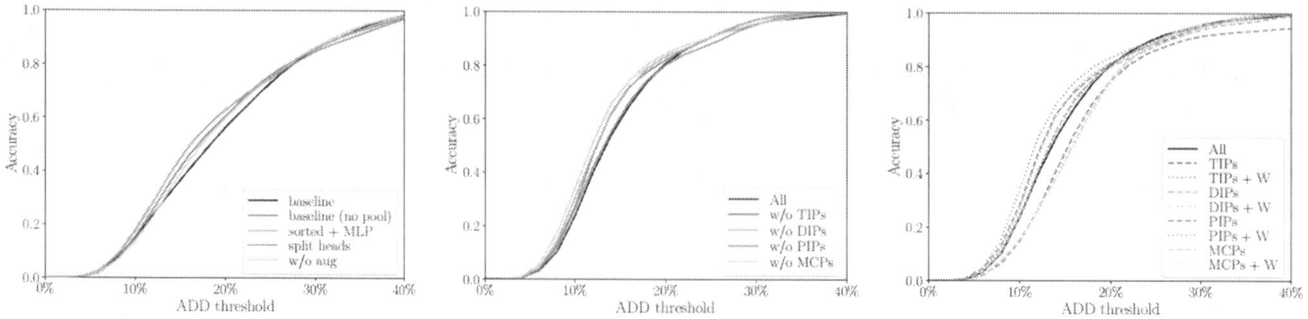

(a) Architectures and data augmentation. (b) Missing joint sets. (c) Only individual joint sets (and wrist).

Figure 4. Grasp pose estimation accuracy at varying ADD thresholds for different architectures, data augmentation and configurations of hand joint inputs.

similar work such as [44]. The data augmentation provides a substantial performance boost. At the 12% diameter threshold, the accuracy drops by 5.5% without data augmentation.

2) Hand configuration: We investigate the relative importance of different joints for learning grasps from human hand poses. The joints are grouped into their corresponding occurrence on the finger. Starting from the ends of the fingers, these groups are the tips (TIPs), distal interphalangeal joints (DIPs), proximal interphalangeal joints (PIPs), metacarpophalangeal joints (MCPs) and the wrist (W). We train three types of networks for each group "X": only with a joint group (X), only with a joint group and the wrist (X + W) and all inputs without the joint group (w/o X). The comparison is conducted for subject ABF (i.e., tested on ABF, trained on all subjects except ABF). The results in Figure 4b show that the removal of a single group of joints in fact improves performance. This is promising for learning grasps from simplified hand poses, especially considering the strong performance without the finger tips, which are often difficult to accurately estimate. In Figure 4c, we show the performance when only specific sets are input to the network. Surprisingly, the performance can be better when only using the DIPs or PIPs. Learning only from the TIPs or MCPs has a noticeable performance loss. This can be explained by the high level of noise in the TIP joint estimates and the relative inflexibility of the MCPs in different hand poses causing a large amount of ambiguity for learning. Including the wrist improves the performance; most notably, the performance of learning from TIPs improves the most when the wrist joint is included and the average performance is slightly better than learning from all 21 joints.

3) Sensitivity to hand pose estimation: The relationship between the robot grasp pose accuracy and the estimate of the hand pose is shown in Figure 5. The hand pose is estimated using [36] and the error of the estimate is computed as the average distance between the estimated joints and the ground truth positions. The robot grasps are predicted from the estimated joints. As the figure shows, there is a clear correlation between the accuracy of the robot grasp and the hand pose. Therefore, the final grasp pose estimate strongly depends on the quality of the input.

C. Real-World Grasp Imitation

Qualitative results of the full grasp imitation pipeline are given in Figure 6. We use the sorted-input single-MLP regression network and train it on all six subjects in HO-3D. The threshold for detecting object movement, θ_o, is set to 5cm.

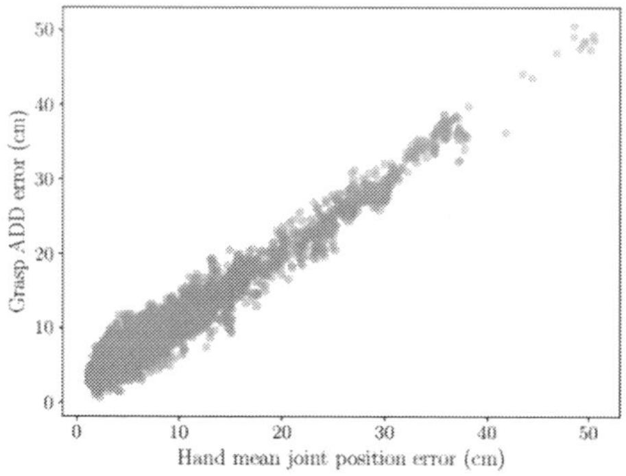

Figure 5. Grasp error (ADD metric) for the estimated hand poses using [36]. Frames in which the hand pose could not be estimated are not included.

TABLE I. GRASP SUCCESS RATE FOR DIFFERENT TARGET OBJECTS FOR THREE DIFFERENT DEMONSTRATIONS. RIGHT-MOST COLUMN SHOWS THE AVERAGE FOR ALL OBJECTS.

	Demo 1	Demo 2	Demo 3	Average
sugar_box	0.6	0.8	0.8	0.73
tomato_soup_can	0.8	0.8	1.0	0.87
mustard_bottle	1.0	0.8	1.0	0.93
mug	1.0	0.4	0.2	0.53
power_drill	0.6	1.0	0.8	0.80

The first column in Figure 6 shows the human demonstration, the second column shows the estimated hand and object pose, the third column shows the estimated robot grasp in the object reference frame, and the remaining columns show successful grasps executed by the robot with the object in different poses. The examples show that the demonstrations of semantic grasps, that is, grasps on the handles of the `mug` (second row) and `power_drill` (third row) are directly transferred to the robot. The robot is able to grasp the relevant part of the object in a similar pose that the person performed.

Table I reports quantitative results of grasps using the full pipeline. For each object, three demonstrations are performed and five grasps are attempted for the object in new poses. The `mug` has the lowest grasp success rate due to the grasps being placed on the thin handle. Consequently, small pose errors cause grasp failures. Surprisingly, the `sugar_box` is also difficult to grasp. This can be attributed to the poor pose estimation that occurred when the front side of the box was not visible. For the other objects, our pipeline achieves a high scoring grasp success rate of over 80%.

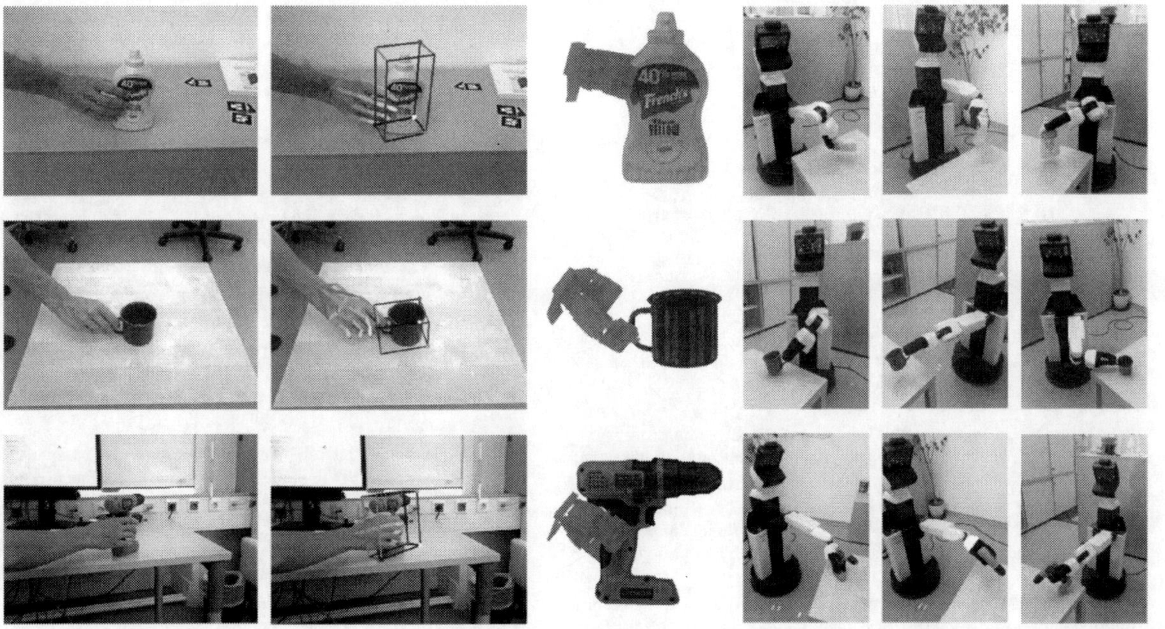

Figure 6. Qualitative results of imitating task-oriented grasp demonstrations for a the mustard_bottle, mug and power_drill. Columns show: (1) observation, (2) estimated object and hand pose, (3) predicted robot grasp, and (4-6) executed grasps for the object presented in new poses.

VI. Conclusion

This work presented an end-to-end system for imitating human-demonstrated task-oriented grasps with a mobile manipulator. Our main contribution is a vision-based imitation learning framework in which the pose of a target object and a demonstrator's hand are tracked to estimate the relevant robot grasp. The robot grasp is derived from the output of a neural network that learns the mapping from a human grasp pose to the configuration of a grasp with a low-DoF gripper. Results show that the predictions of grasps successfully transfer to new demonstrators and that lower-dimensional representations of the hand are sufficient for learning. Experiments with a mobile manipulator demonstrate that a robot is capable of observing a demonstration and immediately grasping the same object when presented in new poses in real-world conditions.

Our analysis showed that the error in the hand pose estimation degrades the quality of the grasp pose. Future work will overcome this issue by directly estimating the robot grasp from the observation without the intermediate hand pose estimation stage. We will also investigate the utility of including an auxilliary task, such as classifying the grasp type, to learn richer features and therefore strengthen the grasp pose estimation task. Lastly, we plan to generalise the framework to transfer grasps from a demonstration to objects that belong to the same class or have similar shape (e.g., grasp all mugs after observing the demonstration for one mug instance) using class-based pose estimation or geometric correspondence prediction.

Acknowledgement

The research leading to these results has received funding from the Austrian Science Fund (FWF) under grant agreement No. I3969-N30 (InDex).

References

[1] Y. Jiang, S. Moseson, and A. Saxena, "Efficient grasping from RGBD images: Learning using a new rectangle representation," in Proc. of IEEE International Conference on Robotics and Automation, 2011, pp. 3304–3311.

[2] I. Lenz, H. Lee, and A. Saxena, "Deep learning for detecting robotic grasps," The International Journal of Robotics Research, vol. 34, no. 4-5, 2015, pp. 705–724.

[3] J. Mahler *et al.*, "Dex-net 2.0: Deep learning to plan robust grasps with synthetic point clouds and analytic grasp metrics," in Proc. of Robotics: Science and Systems, 2017.

[4] A. ten Pas, M. Gualtieri, K. Saenko, and R. Platt, "Grasp pose detection in point clouds," The International Journal of Robotics Research, vol. 36, no. 13-14, 2017, pp. 1455–1473.

[5] C. Goldfeder, M. Ciocarlie, Hao Dang, and P. K. Allen, "The Columbia grasp database," in Proc. of IEEE International Conference on Robotics and Automation, 2009, pp. 1710–1716.

[6] D. Kappler, J. Bohg, and S. Schaal, "Leveraging big data for grasp planning," in Proc. of IEEE International Conference on Robotics and Automation, 2015, pp. 4304–4311.

[7] A. Depierre, E. Dellandréa, and L. Chen, "Jacquard: A large scale dataset for robotic grasp detection," in Proc. of IEEE/RSJ International conference on Intelligent Robots and Systems, 2018, pp. 3511–3516.

[8] Z. Li and S. S. Sastry, "Task-oriented optimal grasping by multifingered robot hands," IEEE Journal on Robotics and Automation, vol. 4, no. 1, 1988, pp. 32–44.

[9] Y. Bekiroglu, D. Song, L. Wang, and D. Kragic, "A probabilistic framework for task-oriented grasp stability assessment," in Proc. of IEEE International Conference on Robotics and Automation, 2013, pp. 3040–3047.

[10] T. Patten, K. Park, and M. Vincze, "DGCM-Net: Dense geometrical correspondence matching network for incremental experience-based robotic grasping," arXiv preprint arXiv:2001.05279, 2020.

[11] R. Detry, J. Papon, and L. Matthies, "Task-oriented grasping with semantic and geometric scene understanding," in Proc. of IEEE/RSJ International Conference on Intelligent Robots and Systems, 2017, pp. 3266–3273.

[12] M. Kokic, J. A. Stork, J. A. Haustein, and D. Kragic, "Affordance detection for task-specific grasping using deep learning," in Proc. of

IEEE-RAS International Conference on Humanoid Robotics, 2017, pp. 91–98.

[13] S. H. Kasaei, N. Shafii, L. S. Lopes, and A. M. Tomé, "Interactive open-ended object, affordance and grasp learning for robotic manipulation," in Proc. of IEEE International Conference on Robotics and Automation, 2019, pp. 3747–3753.

[14] K. Fang *et al.*, "Learning task-oriented grasping for tool manipulation from simulated self-supervision," in Proc. of Robotics: Science and Systems, 2018.

[15] J. Aleotti and S. Caselli, "Part-based robot grasp planning from human demonstration," in Proc. of IEEE International Conference on Robotics and Automation, 2011, pp. 4554–4560.

[16] M. Hjelm, C. H. Ek, R. Detry, and D. Kragic, "Learning human priors for task-constrained grasping," in Proc. of International Conference on Computer Vision Systems, 2015, pp. 207–217.

[17] D. Antotsiou, G. Garcia-Hernando, and T.-K. Kim, "Task-oriented hand motion retargeting for dexterous manipulation imitation," in Proc. of European Conference on Computer Vision Workshops, 2018.

[18] B. D. Argall, S. Chernova, M. Veloso, and B. Browning, "A survey of robot learning from demonstration," Robotics and Autonomous Systems, vol. 57, no. 5, 2009, pp. 469–483.

[19] H. Ravichandar, A. S. Polydoros, S. Chernova, and A. Billard, "Recent advances in robot learning from demonstration," Annual Review of Control, Robotics, and Autonomous Systems, vol. 3, no. 1, 2020, pp. 297–330.

[20] P. N. Hung and T. Yoshimi, "Programming everyday task by demonstration using primitive skills for a manipulator," in Proc. of IEEE 7th Annual International Conference on CYBER Technology in Automation, Control, and Intelligent Systems, 2017, pp. 321–325.

[21] L. Smith, N. Dhawan, M. Zhang, P. Abbeel, and S. Levine, "AVID: Learning multi-stage tasks via pixel-level translation of human videos," arXiv preprint arXiv:1912.04443, 2019.

[22] T. Yu *et al.*, "One-shot imitation from observing humans via domain-adaptive meta-learning," in Proc. of Robotics: Science and Systems, 2018.

[23] Y. Liu, A. Gupta, P. Abbeel, and S. Levine, "Imitation from observation: Learning to imitate behaviors from raw video via context translation," in Proc. of IEEE International Conference on Robotics and Automation, 2018, pp. 1118–1125.

[24] M. Kopicki, R. Detry, M. Adjigble, R. Stolkin, A. Leonardis, and J. L. Wyatt, "One-shot learning and generation of dexterous grasps for novel objects," The International Journal of Robotics Research, vol. 35, no. 8, 2016, pp. 959–976.

[25] T. Zhang *et al.*, "Deep imitation learning for complex manipulation tasks from virtual reality teleoperation," in Proc. of IEEE International Conference on Robotics and Automation, 2018, pp. 5628–5635.

[26] J. S. Dyrstad, E. R. Øye, A. Stahl, and J. R. Mathiassen, "Teaching a robot to grasp real fish by imitation learning from a human supervisor in virtual reality," in Proc. of IEEE/RSJ International Conference on Intelligent Robots and Systems, 2018, pp. 7185–7192.

[27] S. Song, A. Zeng, J. Lee, and T. Funkhouser, "Grasping in the wild: Learning 6DoF closed-loop grasping from low-cost demonstrations," IEEE Robotics and Automation Letters, vol. 5, no. 3, 2020, pp. 4978–4985.

[28] V. Krüger, D. L. Herzog, S. Baby, A. Ude, and D. Kragic, "Learning actions from observations," IEEE Robotics Automation Magazine, vol. 17, no. 2, 2010, pp. 30–43.

[29] J. Tegin, S. Ekvall, D. Kragic, J. Wikander, and B. Iliev, "Demonstration-based learning and control for automatic grasping," Intelligent Service Robotics, vol. 2, no. 1, 2009, pp. 23–30.

[30] Y. Lin and Y. Sun, "Robot grasp planning based on demonstrated grasp strategies," The International Journal of Robotics Research, vol. 34, no. 1, 2015, pp. 26–42.

[31] M. Do *et al.*, "Grasp recognition and mapping on humanoid robots," in Proc. of IEEE-RAS International Conference on Humanoid Robots, 2009, pp. 465–471.

[32] G. Palli *et al.*, "The DEXMART hand: Mechatronic design and experimental evaluation of synergy-based control for human-like grasping," The International Journal of Robotics Research, vol. 33, no. 5, 2014, pp. 799–824.

[33] C. R. Qi, H. Su, M. Kaichun, and L. J. Guibas, "PointNet: Deep learning on point sets for 3D classification and segmentation," in Proc. of IEEE/CVF Conference on Computer Vision and Pattern Recognition, July 2017, pp. 77–85.

[34] S. Hampali, M. Oberweger, M. Rad, and V. Lepetit, "HOnnotate: A method for 3D annotation of hand and object poses," in Proc. of IEEE/CVF Conference on Computer Vision and Pattern Recognition, 2020, pp. 3196–3206.

[35] B. Calli *et al.*, "Yale-CMU-Berkeley dataset for robotic manipulation research," The International Journal of Robotics Research, vol. 36, no. 3, 2017, pp. 261–268.

[36] P. Panteleris, I. Oikonomidis, and A. Argyros, "Using a single RGB frame for real time 3D hand pose estimation in the wild," in Proc. of IEEE Winter Conference on Applications of Computer Vision, 2018, pp. 436–445.

[37] K. Park, T. Patten, and M. Vincze, "Pix2Pose: Pixel-wise coordinate regression of objects for 6D pose estimation," in Proc. of IEEE International Conference on Computer Vision, 2019, pp. 7668–7677.

[38] T. Simon, H. Joo, I. Matthews, and Y. Sheikh, "Hand keypoint detection in single images using multiview bootstrapping," in Proc. of IEEE/CVF Conference on Computer Vision and Pattern Recognition, 2017, pp. 4645–4653.

[39] T. Yamamoto, K. Terada, A. Ochiai, F. Saito, Y. Asahara, and K. Murase, "Development of the research platform of a domestic mobile manipulator utilized for international competition and field test," in Proc. of IEEE/RSJ International Conference on Intelligent Robots and Systems, 2018, pp. 7675–7682.

[40] T. Yamamoto, K. Terada, A. Ochiai, F. Saito, Y. Asahara, and K. Murase, "Development of human support robot as the research platform of a domestic mobile manipulator," ROBOMECH Journal, vol. 6, no. 4, 2019, pp. 1–15.

[41] http://moveit.ros.org.

[42] https://www.ros.org.

[43] S. Hinterstoisser *et al.*, "Model based training, detection and pose estimation of texture-less 3D objects in heavily cluttered scenes," in Computer Vision – ACCV 2012, 2013, pp. 548–562.

[44] G. Gao, M. Lauri, Y. Wang, X. Hu, J. Zhang, and S. Frintrop, "6D object pose regression via supervised learning on point clouds," in Proc. of IEEE International Conference on Robotics and Automation, 2020, pp. 3643–3649.

Semantic Segmentation for the Estimation of Plant and Soil Parameters on Agricultural Machines

Peter Riegler-Nurscher
Josephinum Research
Wieselburg, Austria
Email: p.riegler-nurscher@josephinum.at

Johann Prankl
Josephinum Research
Wieselburg, Austria
Email: johann.prankl@josephinum.at

Markus Vincze
Automation and Control Institute
Vienna University of Technology
Vienna, Austria
Email: vincze@acin.tuwien.ac.at

***Abstract*—Many machine vision problems in agriculture, like plant classification, soil cover estimation or agronomic process evaluation in general, can be solved with semantic segmentation approaches. Naturally growing non-rigid organic and inorganic materials and plants are often characterized by blurred class transitions and high intra-class variance. Especially outdoor uncontrolled plant growth and plant decomposition lead to strong occlusions, cluttered scenes and strong illumination variances in images. An agricultural vision system has to cope with these challenges. This work presents four different applications for semantic segmentation in agriculture: (1) soil cover estimation, (2) estimation of grass-legumes ratio, (3) grassland swath detection and (4) grassland cut segmentation. For training, TensorFlow and a convolutional neural network are used. We investigate the influence of different pre-training methods to improve the overall classification performance with a limited number of training samples. The best test accuracy was achieved by initializing the weights from a model based on a semi-artificial clover and grass data set. The use cases with images from closer perspectives, (1) and (2), resulted in less accuracy compared to use cases (3) and (4). In general, all use cases can be solved with sufficient accuracy.**

Keywords–Semantic Segmentation; Agriculture.

I. Introduction

Most research in the field of computer vision for agriculture focuses on plant and weed detection, pest detection and plant health. However, with increasing autonomy of agricultural machines, the need for process monitoring and evaluation, especially for seeding and harvesting, increases. Many of these applications use semantic segmentation to classify non rigid objects, like plants and soil, or at a higher level, to detect field areas worked of different processing stages.

Development in recent years in semantic segmentation focuses mostly on Convolutional Neural Network (CNN) based methods [1]. CNNs for semantic segmentation consist of an encoder followed by a decoder network. Current works focus on solving the degradation problem, where detailed shape information is discarded by the encoder. Circumventing the degradation problem increases accuracy of the output mask.

We applied semantic segmentation in four use cases on arable fields and grassland. During tillage and seeding, soil cover (1) is an important parameter for soil conservation. The ability to distinguish grasses and legumes (2) during harvesting of grassland is the basis for site specific application of fertilizer and targeted feeding. In harvesting of grassland, detection of swaths (3) and areas of cut grass (4) are the basis for automation of machines and yield estimation. This is work in progress and we want to present preliminary findings in this short paper. The main contribution of this work is the investigation of the influence of pre-training in these use cases in different perspectives and resolutions. Additionally, we adapted the ERFNet CNN [2] for the use cases and tested the inference speed with different hardware. The following Section II gives an overview of the four agronomic use cases for semantic segmentation and its challenges. Section III presents the method applied for the segmentation task. In Section IV, the accuracy and Intersection over Union (IoU) of the different trained models and the inference speeds are shown and discussed.

II. Use Cases

We investigated four different use cases for semantic segmentation on agricultural fields. The images were captured with color cameras mounted on different agricultural implements and annotated manually.

The first use case is soil cover estimation. Soil cover is an important parameter to measure the danger of soil erosion. To objectively quantify the amount of soil cover on a field, camera images are classified into the classes soil, living organic matter, dead organic matter and stones. Studies like [3] and [4] have investigated the problem of segmenting soil cover in images, but often fail because of environmental influences, such as direct sunlight or motion blur. The work in [5] uses CNNs for soil cover estimation, but on a very limited test data set. The image in Figure 1 depicts all four classes. Higher amount of soil cover increases the ability to protect against erosion, where soil cover includes all classes except soil. The percentage of soil cover calculated from the segmentation mask can directly be used to quantify erosion protection.

Figure 1. Soil image for soil cover segmentation (left), test mask (middle), ground truth map (right). Living organic matter •, dead organic matter •, soil • and stone •.

A related problem to soil cover classification is distinguishing plant species. Our special use case is to distinguish between soil, grasses and legumes in grassland. An example image is shown in Figure 2. This segmentation can be the basis for optimized cow feeding and it can serve as an additional parameter for grassland yield estimation.

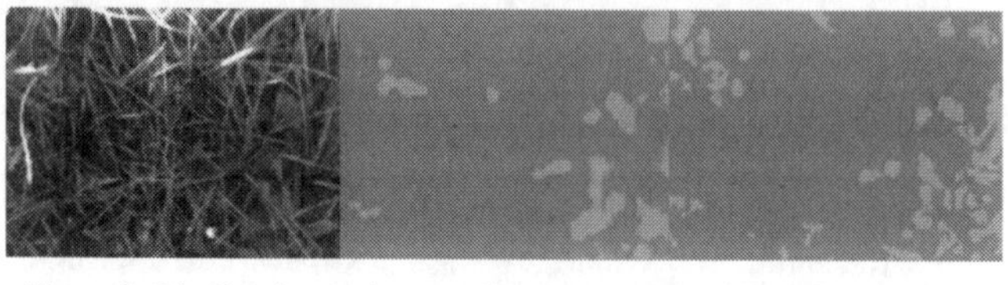

Figure 2. Meadow image for grass/legumes segmentation (left), test mask (middle), ground truth map (right). Grass ● and legumes ●.

In contrast to use cases (1) and (2), the last two have a more global perspective where the classification is not on plant level, but on field area level. The method presented in [6] shows the potential for segmentation of swaths based on stereo depth data and texture information. Our attempt to segment the swath purely on color images in a natural environment makes this problem more difficult, but allows to rely on simpler hardware setups with a single camera. Figure 3 shows an example image for the detection of grassland swaths. This approach can be used for navigation within the field or for yield estimation. The pixels of the images are binary classified into swath or no swath.

Figure 3. Grassland swath image (left), test mask (middle), ground truth map (right). Swath ● and no swath ●.

The last use case, segmentation of areas of cut grass, is a very similar task to swath detection. The segmentation information can be used for machine control or yield estimation. The image is segmented into the different states of grass during mowing: standing grass, grass turf and mown grass. Due to the camera mounting position, an additional class is introduced to mask the machine. Figure 4 shows an example image from the test data set. Cropped parts of areas with standing grass are included in the grasses and legumes use case.

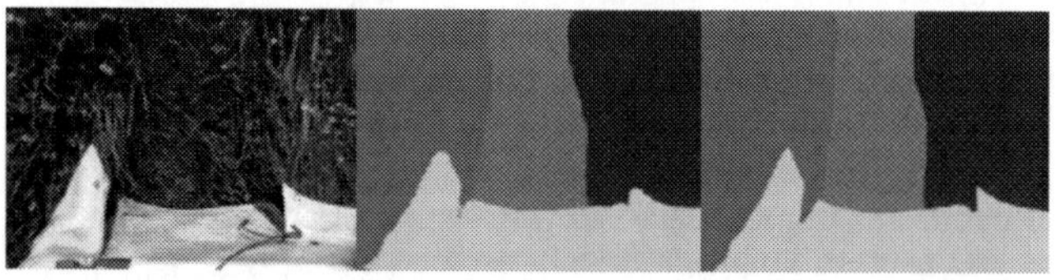

Figure 4. Image for segmentation of areas of cut grass (left), test mask (middle), ground truth map (right). Standing meadow ●, grass turf ●, machine ● and mown grass ●.

CNNs for semantic segmentation are trained in a supervised way. Basis for the training are labelled training samples. Table I shows the number of samples for each use case.

To increase the variance of the training data set, image augmentations were added. Usually, images are taken in any orientation, therefore we added horizontally and vertically flipped images. To accommodate for distance changes between soil and camera, with fixed focus cameras, blurring was added randomly. The application on mobile machines with fast optical flow requires short exposure times. At higher speeds, the image brightness decreases. Strong lighting variations in outdoor operations are simulated with linear and non-linear (gamma) brightness changes.

TABLE I. DATASETS FOR EACH USE CASE

Use case	*Number of images*
(1) soil cover estimation	3621
(2) grass/legumes ratio estimation	1030
(3) swath detection	189
(4) cut segmentation	382

III. SEMANTIC SEGMENTATION WITH CNN

The task of semantic segmentation is to classify each pixel of an image into predefined classes. A CNN for semantic segmentation consists of an encoder block followed by a decoder block. During training, the weights of the network are incrementally adapted to fit the labelled training data. Afterwards, new test images are fed into the network to generate the corresponding classification mask as output of the decoder. The encoder extracts discriminative features from the image to get semantic information for classifying objects. The decoder network reconstructs a class label map, where information from high dimensional encoder layers bypasses the bottle-net in skip connections. This allows to sustain detailed contour information. These CNNs are called U-nets. One variant of a U-net is the ERFNet [2]. The work in [7] compared different state of the art semantic segmentation network architectures. The authors showed that ERFNet provides a good compromise between speed and accuracy and is further used in the proposed work. ERFNet introduces non-bottleneck-1D (non-bt-1D) layers, which combine benefits of bottleneck and non-bottleneck layers. Table II shows the layer architecture of the implemented ERFNet. The implementation is based on an adapted version of the bonnet framework [8].

A major problem in agricultural image processing is that it is quite difficult to generate data, so most data sets are quite small. Different approaches have been introduced, which are able to deal with small data sets. One option is to use data augmentation, where image processing steps, like blurring, affine transformations etc., are performed randomly on the training images. This enriches the training data set. Another possibility is to artificially render a large number of training images. Artificial training images often result in a certain bias; they do not cover the high variance of natural images. Hence, the performance is often weak. Pre-training, on the other hand, uses model weights from similar problems as initial weights for training [9]. We tested combinations of all these approaches and investigated the aspect of pre-training in detail.

Pre-training allows for transferring model parameters from a similar problem. We use model weights of the encoder as initial parameters in the new model. This allows for reusing encoder features and transferring semantic information. The decoder weights are trained from scratch, due to different final classes. The last column of Table II shows which layers are initialized with weights from the pre-trained models.

The publicly available sugar beet data set [10] consists of

TABLE II. LAYERS OF THE ERFNET [2] AS IMPLEMENTED IN THE BONNET FRAMEWORK [8]. THE NUMBER OF OUTPUT FEATURES AND RESOLUTION ARE FOR INPUT IMAGES OF 512X384.

	Layer	Layer Type	# output features	output resolution	initia-lization
Encoder	1	Downsampler block	8	256x192	pre-trained model
	2-3	2 x Non-bt-1D	8	256x192	
	4	Downsampler block	16	128x96	
	5-8	4 x Non-bt-1D	16	128x96	
	9	Downsampler block	64	64x48	
	10-13	4 x Non-bt-1D	64	64x48	
	14	Downsampler block	64	64x48	
	15-18	4 x Non-bt-1D	64	64x48	
Decoder	19	Deconvolution (upsampling)	32	128x96	random
	20-23	4 x Non-bt-1D	32	128x96	
	24	Deconvolution (upsampling)	16	256x192	
	25-28	4 x Non-bt-1D	16	256x192	
	29	Deconvolution (upsampling)	8	512x384	
	30-31	2 x Non-bt-1D	8	512x384	

images of sugar beets and different weeds on various soils. The data set consists of 12,714 images with a resolution of 1296 x 966 pixel, which are resized to 512 x 384 pixel for training. Figure 5 (left) shows an example image of the sugar beet data set. Another publicly available data set is the semi-artificial GrassClover data set from Aarhus University [11]. It consists of artificially generated collages of real cut out clover and grass images. We used 2,600 of the 8,000 images in the data set. The semi-artificial images have a higher resolution than the images in our data set, therefore we resized them by 60% and cut out parts. This resulted in 33,000 image patches with a size of 512 x 384 pixel. Figure 5 (right) shows an example image of the data set.

Figure 5. Example image from the sugar beet data set [10] (left), example image of the semi-artificial GrassClover data set [11] (right).

Both data sets contain images, or are based on images, captured under controlled lighting with no direct sunlight. The images are not blurry and contain no impurities. However, the images in our data sets are captured on moving agricultural implements without parasol or additional lighting and, therefore, contain all these environmental influences. Figure 6 shows two examples from the grass/legumes ratio use case with motion blur (top), saturated parts caused by the limited dynamic range under direct sunlight (bottom) and with strong shadows. However, these issues can be overcome to some extent by varying the exposure time of the camera dependent on lighting conditions and driving speed of the machine.

IV. EVALUATION

Each use case was trained in three variants. The weights were either initialized with the sugar beet data set, with the clover grass data set or randomly (without pre-training).

After training convergence, the models were evaluated with a separate test data set. The metrics, IoU and accuracy, were estimated, as presented in Table III. The mean IoU

Figure 6. Challenging example images from the grass/legumes use case. The corresponding manually annotated label maps are shown on the right.

was calculated as shown in (1). Each class, of all C classes contributes equally to the overall IoU, therefore, scarce classes equally influence the IoU.

$$IoU = \frac{1}{C}\sum_{i=1}^{C}\frac{TP}{TP+FP+FN} \quad (1)$$

The best model was selected by the best accuracy in the validation data set.

TABLE III. MODEL ACCURACY AND IOU, WITH AND WITHOUT PRE-TRAINING ON THE TEST DATA SETS

Application	*Pre-training*	*Accuracy*	*IoU*
(1) soil cover estimation	sugar beet dataset	0.7993	0.4974
	clover grass dataset	**0.8746**	**0.6640**
	none	0.8546	0.6172
(2) grass/legumes ratio estimation	sugar beet dataset	0.8522	**0.5374**
	clover grass dataset	**0.8859**	0.4480
	none	0.8462	0.5288
(3) swath detection	sugar beet dataset	0.9653	0.9313
	clover grass dataset	**0.9734**	**0.9470**
	none	0.9604	0.9221
(4) cut segmentation	sugar beet dataset	0.9106	0.7903
	clover grass dataset	**0.9340**	**0.8312**
	none	0.9286	0.8241

The results show that all use cases can be solved with satisfactory accuracy. In general, pre-training improves model accuracy. Especially, pre-training with the semi-artificial clover grass data set is beneficial for all use cases. This can be attributed to several factors. In general, the scenes in the sugar beet data set have less soil cover. All four use cases, especially the grassland use cases (2-4), have more soil cover, up to 100%. Additionally, the linear and circular structures within the image data are more similar to the clover grass data set, than to the sugar beet data set. Especially grass and clover are very common in our grassland use cases. The improved performance can be explained by encoder features, taken from the pre-training, which more accurately describe our scenes. The initial weights from the sugar beet data set worsen the accuracy for the cut segmentation even more than no pre-training. This might be attributed to strongly differing requirements and ill-fitting features.

TABLE IV. INFERENCE SPEEDS OF ERFNET ON DIFFERENT DEVICES WITH AN IMAGE RESOLUTION OF 512X384 PX.

Device	Inference time
UP AI Core X Myriad™ X 2485	268 ms
Intel® Core™ i7-3630QM CPU	190 ms
NVIDIA® Jetson Nano™	166 ms
NVIDIA® GeForce RTX 2080 Ti	6.1 ms

As expected, the best accuracy gain was accomplished with the clover grass data set for the grass/legumes ratio estimation problem. Our data set differs mainly in higher naturalness of the images to the semi-artificial clover grass data set.

The use cases swath detection and cut segmentation resulted in better segmentation accuracy and IoU. This can be explained by lower variance within the samples and less conflicting annotations in the data set because of the simpler, less cluttered, scenery. In addition, the effect of motion blurring is more apparent on the soil and plant images, compared to images from more global perspectives. There are more annotation errors, and in general poorer quality, in the data sets with fine grained resolution.

For application on mobile agricultural machines, edge hardware for inference of the models is needed. Depending on the use case, inference times must be guaranteed, especially for real time machine control, and on the other hand, connection to cloud computing is often not an option in rural areas. We investigated the inference speeds on four different devices, as shown in Table IV. The inference on the NVIDIA® GeForce graphics card is shown for reference, but is not eligible for the use on agricultural machines due to active cooling and high power consumption. The Jetson Nano™ is the most promising edge device for our application, based on inference speed and power consumption, and will be integrated into a vision system.

Results from previous works are published for the common use case of soil cover estimation (e.g., in [4]). In order to show the improvements of CNN methods compared to classic methods, we compared the soil cover estimation results using the established grid method to the results presented in [4]. In the grid method, points are selected in a regular grid pattern from the image and the share for each class is calculated in percent. A regression line between the manual annotation values and the computed results shows the quality of the estimation. The random forest method used in [4] had a regression of $y_{RF} = 0.7573x + 0.233$ ($R^2 = 0.7627$) to the manually annotated test samples x for the class soil and $y_{RF} = 0.5095x + 0.0363$ ($R^2 = 0.7221$) for class dead organic matter. The proposed method in this paper accomplishes a relation of $y_{CNN} = 0.944x + 0.0878$ ($R^2 = 0.8085$) for soil and $y_{CNN} = 0.7687x + 0.0002$ ($R^2 = 0.7467$) for dead organic matter. This shows a significant improvement, especially for the challenging task of distinguishing soil from dead organic matter.

V. CONCLUSION

Semantic segmentation is an important task for many applications in agronomic image analysis. Especially for soil and plant segmentation, CNN based approaches look very promising.

In order to get good results with a low number of training samples, we investigated the influence of pre-training on four different use cases, soil cover estimation, estimation of grass-legumes ratio, grassland swath detection and grassland cut segmentation.

In general, pre-training improves model accuracy. Especially, pre-training with the semi-artificial clover grass data set [11] is beneficial for all use cases. This can be attributed to the similarity of the textures and the consequently well-fitting of the encoder features emerged from the pre-training.

In the further course of the project, we will integrate the use cases into applications and record and annotate additional labelled data. This will allow for validation of the presented models integrated on agricultural machines based on high level agronomic metrics.

ACKNOWLEDGMENT

Parts of this study were financially funded by the Austrian Research Promotion Agency (FFG) under the program BRIDGE 1 between March 2018 and February 2021.

REFERENCES

[1] I. Ulku and E. Akagunduz, "A survey on deep learning-based architectures for semantic segmentation on 2d images," arXiv preprint arXiv:1912.10230, 2019.

[2] E. Romera, J. M. Alvarez, L. M. Bergasa, and R. Arroyo, "Erfnet: Efficient residual factorized convnet for real-time semantic segmentation," IEEE Transactions on Intelligent Transportation Systems, vol. 19, no. 1, 2017, pp. 263–272.

[3] T. Bauer and P. Strauss, "A rule-based image analysis approach for calculating residues and vegetation cover under field conditions," Catena, vol. 113, 2014, pp. 363–369.

[4] P. Riegler-Nurscher, J. Prankl, T. Bauer, P. Strauss, and H. Prankl, "A machine learning approach for pixel wise classification of residue and vegetation cover under field conditions." Biosystems Engineering, vol. 169, 2018, pp. 188 – 198.

[5] A. K. Mortensen et al., "Semantic segmentation of mixed crops using deep convolutional neural network." in CIGR-AgEng Conference, 26-29 June 2016, Aarhus, Denmark. Abstracts and Full papers. Organising Committee, CIGR 2016, 2016, pp. 1–6.

[6] M. R. Blas and M. Blanke, "Stereo vision with texture learning for fault-tolerant automatic baling," Computers and Electronics in Agriculture, vol. 75, no. 1, 2011, pp. 159 – 168.

[7] S. Mehta, M. Rastegari, A. Caspi, L. G. Shapiro, and H. Hajishirzi, "Espnet: Efficient spatial pyramid of dilated convolutions for semantic segmentation," CoRR, vol. abs/1803.06815, 2018. [Online]. Available: http://arxiv.org/abs/1803.06815

[8] A. Milioto and C. Stachniss, "Bonnet: An open-source training and deployment framework for semantic segmentation in robotics using cnns," in 2019 International Conference on Robotics and Automation (ICRA), 2019, pp. 7094–7100.

[9] J. Yosinski, J. Clune, Y. Bengio, and H. Lipson, "How transferable are features in deep neural networks?" arXiv, no. 1411.1792, 2014.

[10] N. Chebrolu et al., "Agricultural robot dataset for plant classification, localization and mapping on sugar beet fields," The International Journal of Robotics Research, vol. 36, no. 10, 2017, pp. 1045–1052.

[11] S. Skovsen et al., "The grassclover image dataset for semantic and hierarchical species understanding in agriculture," in 2019 IEEE/CVF Conference on Computer Vision and Pattern Recognition Workshops (CVPRW), 2019, pp. 2676–2684.

Computation of Suitable Grasp Pose for Usage of Objects Based on Predefined Training and Real-time Pose Estimation

Muhammed Tawfiq Chowdhury, Shuvo Kumar Paul, Monica Nicolescu, Mircea Nicolescu,
David Feil-Seifer and Sergiu Dascalu
Department of Computer Science and Engineering, University of Nevada, Reno
1664 North Virginia Street, Reno, Nevada 89557, USA
Email Addresses: {mtawfiqc@nevada.unr.edu, shuvo.k.paul@nevada.unr.edu, monica@cse.unr.edu, mircea@cse.unr.edu,
dave@cse.unr.edu, dascalus@cse.unr.edu}

***Abstract*—Existing grasping mechanisms focus on executing accurate grasps which are not always suitable for the usage of objects. We developed a system that can be used to train humanoid robots with different types of grasp poses. We present a grasping mechanism using homogeneous transformation that allows a humanoid robot to grasp objects in such a way that is suitable for the usage of the objects. The system captures the relative poses of an object and a robot's wrist for training such that when the object's pose changes, the robot's gripper attached to the wrist adjusts its pose accordingly and lines up with the object. For detecting the objects and estimating their poses, we developed and used a color-based pose detection and estimation system and a homography-based planar pose detection and estimation system. We conducted experiments using a humanoid PR2 robot. We used the Robot Operating System as the primary framework of the system and MoveIt Interface for manipulation of grasps. The grasping system showed robust results for different poses of the objects using both arms of the robot. Our experiments involved human validation in which the robot successfully grasped objects such as a screwdriver, a wrench and books from human hands in different grasp poses that are appropriate for usage of the objects.**

Keywords–Robotics; Homogeneous Transformation; Pose Estimation; Grasping; Objects Usage.

I. Introduction

Grasping is an important aspect of a robot's capabilities. Since different objects come in different shapes, it is often difficult for robots to grasp objects accurately. In order to use tools, such as a screwdriver and a wrench, a robot needs to grasp them with high level of precision as they need to be grasped at specific locations and also in appropriate orientations. This is not the case for a tennis ball for which the grasp pose can be more flexible. A human grasps a screwdriver from the top of its base and this is an ideal grasp. If a robot attempts to grasp it for usage, it needs to do the same. Thus, an approach is required so that robots can grasp tools in ideal grasp poses. This requires a robust system that can train the robots to grasp objects in required poses so that regardless of the objects' orientations, robots can grasp it properly and use.

In this paper, we have designed a grasping technique for humanoid robots that will enable the humanoid robots to grasp objects of diverse shapes precisely based on predefined grasp poses. We are using a homogeneous transformation matrix to record the relative poses between the end-effector of a robot and an object so that when the position and orientation of the object changes, the end-effector follows it accordingly based on the recorded relative pose. Since this system allows users to train the initial poses of objects and robot's end-effectors, the robots can be trained with different types of grasp poses. We used a humanoid PR2 [1] robot for conducting experiments. In our experiments, we used linear shaped tools, such as a wrench and used a color-based pose detection and estimation system for these tools. We also used rectangular-shaped objects for the experiments. We used a planar pose estimation system for running experiments with such objects. During the experiments, the robot could robustly grasp objects in different grasp poses which are suitable for the usage of the objects.

The major outcomes of this research are (i) developing a system that can train a humanoid robot different types of grasps, (ii) finding predefined grasp poses that would allow a robot to use tools such as screwdrivers, hammers, etc., (iii) enabling the robot to grasp objects accurately from human hands, (iv) introducing a homography-based planar pose detection and estimation technique for objects that have complex shapes (v) implementing a color-based pose detection and estimation system using mathematical formulas for objects with linear shapes

The rest of the paper is structured as follows: Section II discusses the related works in grasping, Section III presents an analysis of the grasps for humanoid robots, Section IV elaborates the vision systems that were used for pose estimation of objects, Section V provides an overview of the system, Section VI discusses the results and Section VII draws the conclusion of the paper and discusses future works.

II. Related Work

There has been a wide range of research on robot grasping. Designing a grasping system is challenging due to the infinite nature of the shapes of objects. Kehoe et al. [2] used a candidate grasp from a set of grasps based on feasibility analysis conducted by a grasp planner and a humanoid PR2 robot was used for their experiments. For stable horizontal poses of objects, objects such as a mustard bottle is close to the width of the PR2's gripper so the grasps were not very accurate in such orientations of the object. Huebner et al. [3] also took a similar approach as they performed grasp candidate simulation. They created a sequence of grasps and then computed a random grasp evaluation for each model of objects. In both works, a grasp was chosen from a list of candidate grasps. Their research focused on finding a grasp that would be successful while we focus on training a robot to grasp objects in a way that is not only successful but also suitable for usage of the objects.

Aleotti et al. [4] proposed a grasping model that involves programming by demonstration for teaching proper grasps with automatic 3D shape segmentation for object recognition and semantic modeling. They developed a virtual grasping algorithm for object picking and computing the part of the object which is grasped. Pinto et al. [5] trained a Convolutional Neural Network (CNN) for predicting grasp locations without vast overfitting. Graspit was used as a grasp simulator [6][7] to predict grasping. Supervised learning was used [8][9] to predict grasp locations from RGB images. These works emphasised on developing and using learning models for obtaining accurate grasps. In our work, we designed a training mechanism based on mathematical concepts which not only generated accurate grasps but also the grasps could follow a predefined training.

Related methods were also developed on autonomous grasping [10] based on estimated shapes and poses of the segmented objects. Weng et al. [11] proposed a system which recognizes objects and estimates the pose of the objects using deep neural network and then allows grasping objects using the centers of their defined pose classes. Robots were also trained to choose optimum grasp from a set of grasps using machine learning models based on human demonstration [12]. In order to ensure robust grasp of unknown objects, a new algorithm using Bayesian optimization was developed for simulation [13]. Their work did not focus on the usage of the objects but rather focused on finding a grasp that enabled the robots to appropriately hold the objects.

III. Analysis of Grasps

When a human works with a screwdriver, the ideal grasp is to grasp it from the top of its base. We classify this type of grasp as top grasp. There are also objects, such as a hammer and a wrench for which it is necessary to grasp them from side. We classify it as side grasp. Figure 1 illustrates top grasp and side grasp.

Figure 1. Top Grasp and Side Grasp.

For a 7-DOF robot such as the PR2, a robot's planner could successfully plan in various complex poses of the objects in our experiments with redundancy. Planning is inherently more challenging to plan for a top grasp. Some poses of the linear shaped tools are only suitable for grasp using the right arm while some other poses are only suitable for grasp using the left arm. Although our system is capable of recording the relative poses of objects and the robot's gripper in any relative pose, we used top grasp and side grasp in our experiments as these are the most suitable grasps for the usage of the objects.

IV. Pose Estimation

In order for robots to operate effectively, it needs to be aware of its surrounding environment. One aspect of this awareness is the knowledge of the 3D positions and orientations of the objects in the scene in real-time. In order to achieve this we need to locate the objects and find their orientations so that robots can interact with these objects seamlessly. While object classification, detection, and segmentation have become relatively easier, pose estimation remains a challenging problem as the large number of complex shapes of objects found in real life makes it hard to come up with a general pose estimation technique. Although, some recent pose estimation methods, named PoseCNN [14] and DOPE [15], show promising results in terms of accuracy; generating synthetic data for each newly introduced object requires additional preprocessing tasks that may require other expertise and can take a lot of time. Moreover, as these methods utilize neural networks, training and running these models necessitate high computing resources. Keeping these difficulties in mind, we applied directional cosines to estimate the pose for objects with simple linear shapes that extend along a straight or nearly straight line using color cues, and introduced a homography-based planar pose estimation technique for other objects that have more complex shapes.

A. Color-based Pose Detection and Estimation

We used two different colors such as yellow and green on the two edges of the linear objects. This method can be applied to any linear shaped tools. We computed the position of the object with respect to one of the edges of the objects. We calculated the roll, pitch and yaw rotational angles of the pose using directional cosine equations shown below.

$$\begin{cases} \gamma = \cos^{-1}(\frac{\vec{u_x}}{|\vec{u}|}) \\ \beta = \cos^{-1}(\frac{\vec{u_y}}{|\vec{u}|}) \\ \alpha = \cos^{-1}(\frac{\vec{u_z}}{|\vec{u}|}) \end{cases} \quad (1)$$

Figure 2 shows the directional cosine in 3D space

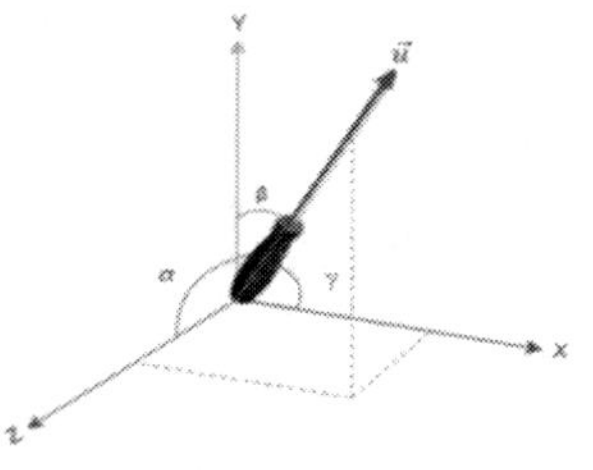

Figure 2. Directional Cosine.

B. Planar Pose Estimation Using Homography

For more complex shapes, we used a descriptor based detection system that utilizes homography and the depth data to estimate the pose of the plane of an object. First, for each object, we acquired an undistorted image of the object's plane that we wanted to detect and take as a reference for homography computation. Then we applied feature detector to find keypoints [16] and used descriptor to retrieve the feature vectors. Then, we did the same for the image frames received from the camera and find the matches using FLANN [17] and compute the homography using RANSAC [18]. We applied a perspective transform to find the corresponding points on the frame using the homography matrix and approximate the location of the two axes on the plane on the object. Finally, we used depth information to estimate the third orthogonal axis by taking the cross product and recover the pose. Figure 3 demonstrates the planar based pose estimation system and Figure 4 shows the pose detection and visualization.

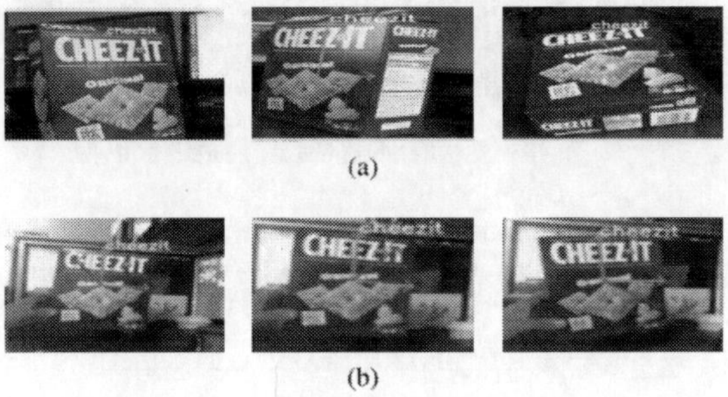

Figure 3. (a) Homography for Different Planar Rotation. (b) Computed Third Directional Axis Projected onto Image Plane.

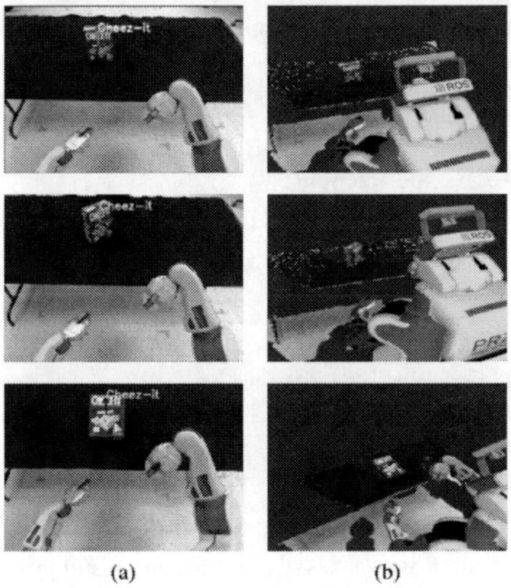

Figure 4. (a) Pose Detection in Robot's Camera (b) Visualization of Corresponding Poses in Rviz.

V. System Overview

We used Robot Operating System (ROS) [19] as the primary framework for the system as it is used by humanoid robots such as PR2 and Baxter. We also used MoveIt Interface [20] for manipulation of the arms and the grippers of the robot. We had two different phases: the training phase and the testing phase. During the training phase, we placed the object and the robot's gripper close to each other in our desired training poses. We got the poses of the objects from our vision systems while we recorded the pose of the robots' wrist to which the gripper is attached using a wrist pose recording system for the PR2 robot. Then we computed the transformation matrix using the two poses and used the matrix in testing phase. We used the ROS Python API for developing the functionality of the transformation matrix. The transformation matrix captures the relative poses of the object and the wrist. During testing phase, we placed the objects in different poses and our system used mathematical equations to generate a new grasp pose for the robot's end-effector. The 3D coordinate frame for the vision system and the robot's wrist during the training and testing phase need to be the same. Once a grasp pose was computed, we used the C++ API of the MoveIt Interface for the manipulation of the robot's arm and the wrist to grasp objects. Figure 5 shows the high level system architecture.

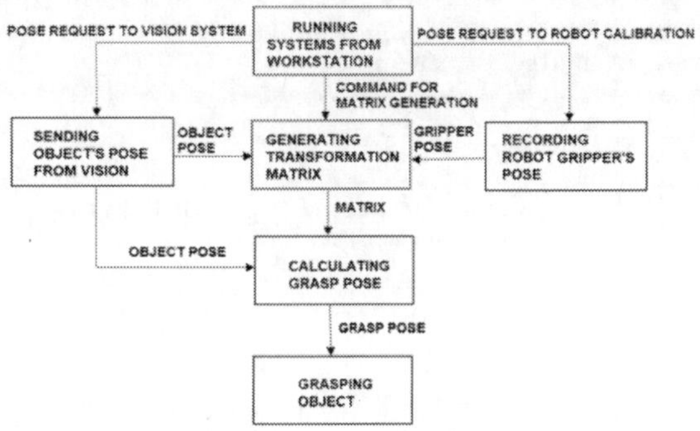

Figure 5. System Architecture.

A. Training

The system allows us to train a wide range of grasp poses, allowing the robot to use various grasps for different object uses. During the training phase, we placed the object and the robot's gripper close to each other and recorded the relative pose. Figure 6 illustrates the training process in which the robot's gripper and a screwdriver were placed in close proximity and the relative poses were recorded for grasping the objects from top which is the general grasping approach for a screwdriver. Figure 6 shows a training scenario.

Figure 6. Recording Relative Pose for Top Grasp.

B. Matrix Calculation

We used the following homogeneous transformation matrix [21]:

$$ {}^{A}T_{B} = \begin{bmatrix} {}^{A}R_{B} & {}^{A}P_{B} \\ 0 & 1 \end{bmatrix} = \begin{bmatrix} c_{11} & c_{12} & c_{13} & x_t \\ c_{21} & c_{22} & c_{23} & y_t \\ c_{31} & c_{32} & c_{33} & z_t \\ 0 & 0 & 0 & 1 \end{bmatrix} \quad (2) $$

${}^{A}T_{B}$ refers to the transformation of the coordinate frame B with respect to the coordinate frame A. ${}^{A}R_{B}$ and ${}^{A}P_{B}$ refer to the rotation and translation respectively of the coordinate frame B with respect to the coordinate frame A. We then used (3) to record the relative pose.

$$ {}^{O}T_{G} = {}^{O}T_{B} \times {}^{B}T_{G} \text{ where } {}^{O}T_{B} = ({}^{B}T_{O})^{-1} \quad (3) $$

In the equation, O refers to the object, B refers to the robot's base and G refers to the wrist of the robot to which the gripper is attached.

C. Pose Calculation

Once we have a training matrix saved in a file, we can get a new pose of the object from vision and generate the final matrix that has the new position and orientation of the robot's wrist in matrix form using (4):

$$ {}^{B}T_{G} = {}^{B}T_{O} \times {}^{O}T_{G} \quad (4) $$

We then calculate rotational angles of the grasp pose using the calculated matrix from (4) with (5)

$$ \begin{cases} \gamma = tan^{-1}(c_{32}/c_{33}) \\ \beta = tan^{-1}(-c_{31}/\sqrt{c_{32}{}^{2} + c_{33}{}^{2}}) \\ \alpha = tan^{-1}(c_{21}/c_{11}) \end{cases} \quad (5) $$

VI. Results and Discussion

We tested our system on a comprehensive set of estimated poses that included different types of orientations of the object. We conducted 75 experiments in total. We used two types of grasps-top grasp and side grasp. We conducted two types of experiments: general validation experiments and human validation experiments. For the general validations experiments, the objects were attached to a tripod and for human validations experiments, a human held the objects in hand and then the robot grasped it. We placed the objects in various locations in front of the robot and in various orientations in the 3D space. For the experiments using the color-based pose detection and estimation system, we used a screwdriver and a wrench. Figure 7 shows the objects used in the experiments.

Figure 7. Objects for Experiments.

For running experiments using the homography based planar pose estimation system, we used a sticker-book and a cartoon book. The pose estimation systems showed robust performance. Figure 8 shows the pose estimation in ROS Visualizer (RViz) for color-based pose estimation system. In the figure, the green axis is parallel to the object and touches its base which indicate that the pose estimation is accurate.

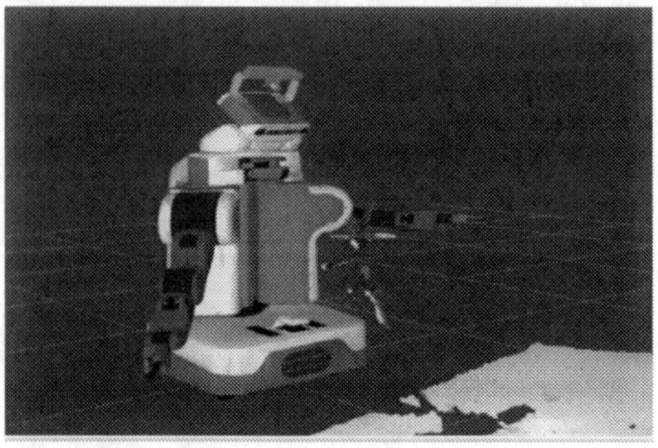

Figure 8. Checking Pose Estimation in Rviz.

We ran 45 experiments in general scenario. We conducted 30 and 15 experiments respectively using the right and left arm. Table I shows the general validation results.

TABLE I. GENERAL VALIDATION RESULTS

Objects	Top Grasp	Side Grasp	Successful Grasp (Top | Side)	Accuracy (Top | Side)
Wrench	12	24	12 | 22	100% | 91.67%
Screwdriver	6	N/A	6 | N/A	100% | N/A
Books	N/A	5	N/A | 5	N/A | 100%

The results from the human validation experiments indicate that the training and pose estimation have been precise enough for the robot to accurately grasp objects from human hands. We ran 24 and 6 experiments using the right and left arm, respectively. Table II shows the experimental results for human validation experiments.

TABLE II. HUMAN VALIDATION RESULTS

Objects	Top Grasp	Side Grasp	Successful Grasp (Top | Side)	Accuracy (Top | Side)
Wrench	9	7	9 | 6	100% | 85.72%
Screwdriver	9	N/A	9 | N/A	100% | N/A
Books	N/A	5	N/A | 5	N/A | 100%

The robot could successfully grasp the objects in 72 out of 75 experiments in different grasp poses which are suitable for the usage of the objects. In 3 experiments, pose estimation during testing was not accurate enough for a successful grasp. Poses of the objects could be detected instantly after they were placed in the scene. The grasps could be initiated in about a second after the poses were estimated and be completed in about 5 seconds. This makes the pose estimation and grasping a real-time operation. In successful experiments, the robot grasped the objects perfectly with respect to the training. It demonstrates that both the grasping system and the pose estimation systems are robust and they can handle rotations of objects in multiple axes and in different angles. It also shows that this system is ideal for training robots to grasp linear shaped tools, such as screwdrivers, wrenches, saws, hammers, etc. as well as objects with more complex shapes, such as box, book, magazine, etc. The pose estimation and the grasping had been robust and accurate enough for the robot to grasp objects from human hand. Grasping from human hand is sensitive as if the robot tries to grasp in incorrect locations, it will place its grippers on human hand but in our experiments, that issue did not occur. There are some poses which are not reachable by a 7-DOF robot. For instance, when the object is pointing inward or back in x-axis in the robot reference frame, it is not possible for the end-effector to make a top grasp. There are also poses for which right arm is reachable but left arm is not reachable and vice versa. Thus, in our experiments, we used both arms so that we could cover all segments in a 3D coordinate system. Figure 9 shows the side grasp of a wrench tied to a tripod which displays that the gripper lined up with the wrench and the grasp pose is similar to the way human grasps a wrench.

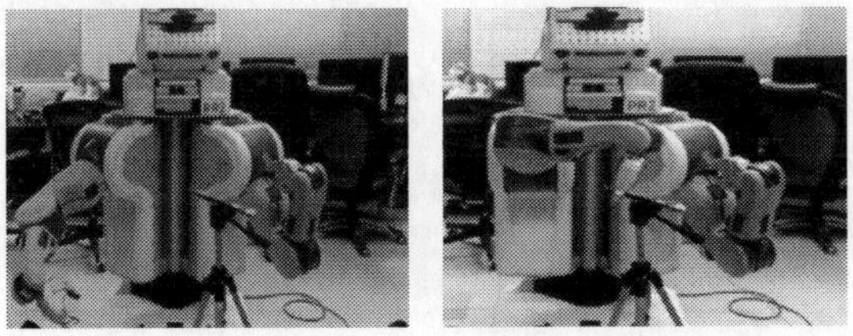

(a) (b

Figure 9. (a) Initial Pose of the Right Gripper and a Wrench. (b) Side Grasp of the Wrench Using the Right Gripper.

This grasp then can be used to work with the tool. The training ensures that the gripper lines up with the objects in rotations in all axes in the 3D coordinate. Thus, the system shows capability of handling complex rotations and the resultant grasp pose is always suitable for usage of the objects. The robot grasped objects in a very accurate manner from human hand. The color-based pose estimations system worked robustly while the human held the objects in hand and we were able to receive very accurate pose estimations from the vision systems for complex rotations of the tools. Figure 10 and Figure 11 show grasps of a screwdriver from human hand in which the robot was able to grasp the screwdriver from the top of its base.

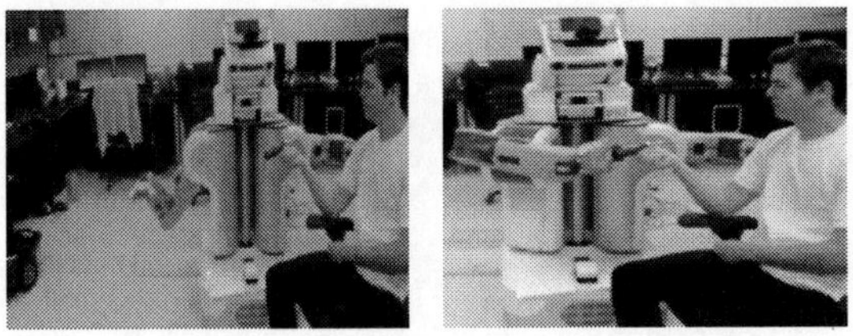

(a) (b

Figure 10. (a) Initial Pose of the Right Gripper and a Screwdriver. (b) Top Grasp of the Screwdriver Pointing Towards the Robot.

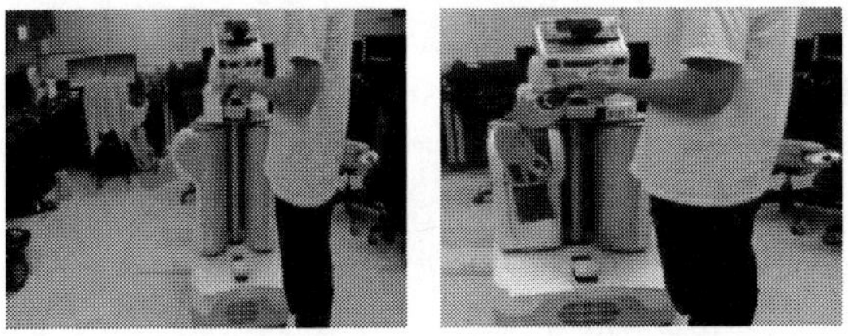

(a) (b

Figure 11. (a) Initial Pose of the Right Gripper and a Screwdriver. (b) Top Grasp of the Screwdriver Pointing Towards the Human.

The system had also been successful in using both of the robot's arms. The use of the left arm allows the robot to grasp objects in poses that are not feasible to grasp with the right arm. Figure 12 shows the side grasp of a wrench using the left arm. The robot also successfully grasped books from human hand. Figure 13 and Figure 14 show the results.

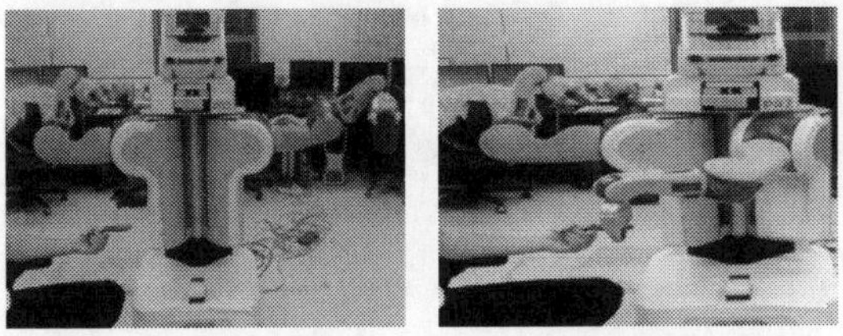

(a) (b

Figure 12. (a) Initial Pose of the Left Gripper and a Wrench. (b) Side Grasp of the Wrench Using the Left Gripper.

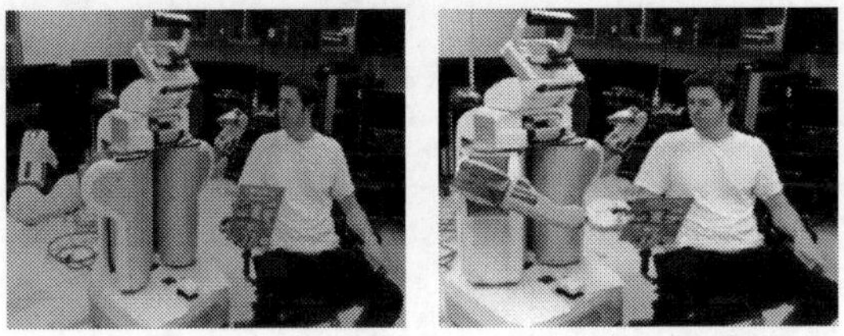

(a) (b

Figure 13. (a) Initial Pose of the Right Gripper and a Sticker-book. (b) Side Grasp of the Sticker-book.

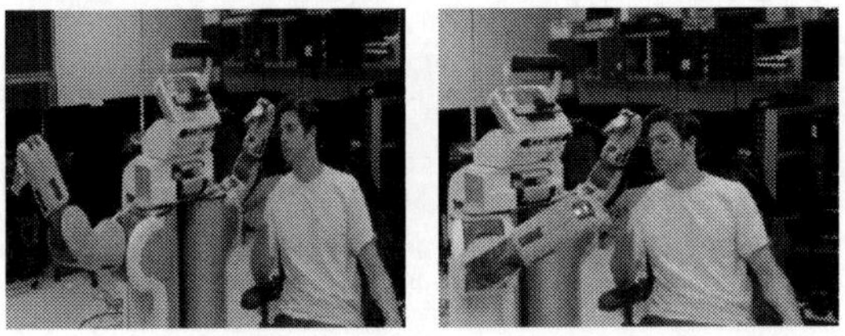

(a) (b

Figure 14. (a) Initial Pose of the Right Gripper and a Cartoon-book. (b) Side Grasp of the Cartoon-book.

VII. Conclusion and Future Work

This paper discussed an approach that enables humanoid robots to grasp objects for usage using two different vision systems for object pose detection and estimation. Application of mathematical theories and development of software systems were integrated in our work. The system had been robust enough for grasping objects such as a screwdriver and a wrench from human hand and a comprehensive set of poses had been tested for grasping with human validation. The predefined training generated accurate grasps which are suitable for usage of the objects. The accuracy of the results indicate that the system is robust.

We plan to extend the project to add more features to it. An important addition to the project would be an introduction of the movement of both arms of the robot simultaneously. If we receive two different poses coming from the vision system simultaneously then the robot could grasp both the objects at the same time. We would like to introduce a dialogue feature in the work for collision avoidance [22]. If a robot attempts to grasp an object, it would initiate a dialogue with humans in its surrounding environment. If it gets positive response from the humans, it will execute the grasp. Otherwise, it will not move its arm. The dialogue will enhance the safety in the movement of the robots' arms and will ensure that the robot avoids obstacles in its surrounding environment while grasping an object. We would also like to add an automated planning system for robots so that if the robot planner fails to plan for a grasp pose using one arm, it would automatically try with the other. This would increase the robustness of the grasping system.

ACKNOWLEDGMENTS

We acknowledge the financial support for this work by the Office of Naval Research (ONR) award #N00014-16-1-2312, N00014-14-1-0776.

REFERENCES

[1] S. Cousins, "ROS on the PR2 [ROS topics]," *IEEE Robotics & Automation Magazine*, vol. 17, no. 3, pp. 23–25, Sep. 2010. [Online]. Available: https://doi.org/10.1109/mra.2010.938502

[2] B. Kehoe, A. Matsukawa, S. Candido, J. Kuffner, and K. Goldberg, "Cloud-based robot grasping with the google object recognition engine," in *2013 IEEE International Conference on Robotics and Automation*. IEEE, May 2013. [Online]. Available: https://doi.org/10.1109/icra.2013.6631180

[3] K. Huebner, S. Ruthotto, and D. Kragic, "Minimum volume bounding box decomposition for shape approximation in robot grasping," in *2008 IEEE International Conference on Robotics and Automation*. IEEE, May 2008. [Online]. Available: https://doi.org/10.1109/robot.2008.4543434

[4] J. Aleotti and S. Caselli, "Part-based robot grasp planning from human demonstration," in *2011 IEEE International Conference on Robotics and Automation*. IEEE, May 2011. [Online]. Available: https://doi.org/10.1109/icra.2011.5979632

[5] L. Pinto and A. Gupta, "Supersizing self-supervision: Learning to grasp from 50k tries and 700 robot hours," in *2016 IEEE International Conference on Robotics and Automation (ICRA)*. IEEE, May 2016. [Online]. Available: https://doi.org/10.1109/icra.2016.7487517

[6] A. Miller and P. Allen, "Graspit! a versatile simulator for robotic grasping," *IEEE Robotics & Automation Magazine*, vol. 11, no. 4, pp. 110–122, Dec. 2004. [Online]. Available: https://doi.org/10.1109/mra.2004.1371616

[7] A. Miller, S. Knoop, H. Christensen, and P. Allen, "Automatic grasp planning using shape primitives," in *2003 IEEE International Conference on Robotics and Automation (Cat. No.03CH37422)*. IEEE. [Online]. Available: https://doi.org/10.1109/robot.2003.1241860

[8] A. Saxena, J. Driemeyer, and A. Y. Ng, "Robotic grasping of novel objects using vision," *The International Journal of Robotics Research*, vol. 27, no. 2, pp. 157–173, Feb. 2008. [Online]. Available: https://doi.org/10.1177/0278364907087172

[9] L. Montesano and M. Lopes, "Active learning of visual descriptors for grasping using non-parametric smoothed beta distributions," *Robotics and Autonomous Systems*, vol. 60, no. 3, pp. 452–462, Mar. 2012. [Online]. Available: https://doi.org/10.1016/j.robot.2011.07.013

[10] A. Uckermann, C. Elbrechter, R. Haschke, and H. Ritter, "3d scene segmentation for autonomous robot grasping," in *2012 IEEE/RSJ International Conference on Intelligent Robots and Systems*. IEEE, Oct. 2012. [Online]. Available: https://doi.org/10.1109/iros.2012.6385692

[11] J. Yu, K. Weng, G. Liang, and G. Xie, "A vision-based robotic grasping system using deep learning for 3d object recognition and pose estimation," in *2013 IEEE International Conference on Robotics and Biomimetics (ROBIO)*. IEEE, Dec. 2013. [Online]. Available: https://doi.org/10.1109/robio.2013.6739623

[12] O. Kroemer, R. Detry, J. Piater, and J. Peters, "Active learning using mean shift optimization for robot grasping," in *2009 IEEE/RSJ International Conference on Intelligent Robots and Systems*. IEEE, Oct. 2009. [Online]. Available: https://doi.org/10.1109/iros.2009.5354345

[13] J. Nogueira, R. Martinez-Cantin, A. Bernardino, and L. Jamone, "Unscented bayesian optimization for safe robot grasping," in *2016 IEEE/RSJ International Conference on Intelligent Robots and Systems (IROS)*. IEEE, Oct. 2016. [Online]. Available: https://doi.org/10.1109/iros.2016.7759310

[14] Y. Xiang, T. Schmidt, V. Narayanan, and D. Fox, "Posecnn: A convolutional neural network for 6d object pose estimation in cluttered scenes," 2018.

[15] J. Tremblay, T. To, B. Sundaralingam, Y. Xiang, D. Fox, and S. Birchfield, "Deep object pose estimation for semantic robotic grasping of household objects," in *Conference on Robot Learning (CoRL)*, 2018. [Online]. Available: https://arxiv.org/abs/1809.10790

[16] S. K. Paul, M. T. Chowdhury, M. Nicolescu, M. Nicolescu, and D. Feil-Seifer, "Object detection and pose estimation from rgb and depth data for real-time, adaptive robotic grasping," in *International Conference on Image Processing, Computer Vision Pattern Recognition*, Las Vegas, NV, July 2020.

[17] M. Muja and D. G. Lowe, "Fast approximate nearest neighbors with automatic algorithm configuration," in *International Conference on Computer Vision Theory and Application VISSAPP'09)*. INSTICC Press, 2009, pp. 331–340.

[18] M. A. Fischler and R. C. Bolles, "Random sample consensus: A paradigm for model fitting with applications to image analysis and automated cartography," *Commun. ACM*, vol. 24, no. 6, p. 381–395, Jun. 1981. [Online]. Available: https://doi.org/10.1145/358669.358692

[19] M. Quigley, K. Conley, B. P. Gerkey, J. Faust, T. Foote, J. Leibs, R. C. Wheeler, and A. Y. Ng, "Ros: an open-source robot operating system," in *ICRA 2009*, 2009.

[20] S. Chitta, "MoveIt!: An introduction," in *Studies in Computational Intelligence*. Springer International Publishing, 2016, pp. 3–27. [Online]. Available: https://doi.org/10.1007/978-3-319-26054-9_1

[21] K. Lynch and F. Park, *Modern Robotics: Mechanics, Planning, and Control*. Cambridge University Press, 2017. [Online]. Available: http://hades.mech.northwestern.edu/images/7/7f/MR.pdf

[22] B. A. Anima, J. Blankenburg, M. Zagainova, S. P. H. Alinodehi, M. T. Chowdhury, D. Feil-Seifer, M. Nicolescu, and M. Nicolescu, "Collaborative human-robot hierarchical task execution with an activation spreading architecture," in *Social Robotics*. Springer International Publishing, 2019, pp. 301–310.

Reference Detection for Off-road Self-Driving Vehicles Using Deep Learning

Marcelo Eduardo Pederiva

School of Electrical and
Computer Engineering
University of Campinas, Brazil
Email: marcelopederiva@gmail.com

Ely Carneiro de Paiva

School of Mechanical Engineering
University of Campinas, Brazil
Email: elypaiva@fem.unicamp.br

***Abstract*—This paper proposes the application of deep neural network models to detect references in off-road driving for autonomous vehicles. Due to the absence of traffic signs in non-urban areas, the work searched for a low-cost sensory-based solution for autonomous localization in this environment. Given the advancement of Machine Learning techniques, we used Object Detection algorithms to solve the localization problem. For this reason, we trained three existing object detection models (Fast YOLOv2, SSD300 and Faster R-CNN) to detect a reference at the road boundary. The project analyzed these three architectures performance after training with a small dataset (around 300 images), regarding the detection distance, the number of detection and image processing time. Through two experiments, one in the same environment as the training step and another with a different background, we evaluate the pros and cons of each model and the possible application scenario for each one in autonomous cars.**

Keywords*–*YOLO; Faster RCNN; SSD; Object Detection; Autonomous Vehicles.

I. Introduction

In the last years, autonomous driving in signposted roads is a research field that has received increasing interest, both from academy and industry. Different solutions and strategies have been proposed to provide the right information and actions to make a robot vehicle drive autonomously. The main objective is to use different sensors and algorithms to map and identify traffic signs, traffic lights, obstacles, pedestrians and cars on the street, in real-time. However, off-road environments still present challenges that need attention. In the absence of lane lines and traffic signs, uneven terrain and the presence of animals, off-road environments require careful driving with different approaches to extract the information of the road and make the right decisions.

Nowadays, the use of Deep Learning in autonomous vehicles is one of the most common solutions, becoming the state-of-the-art approach for a host of problems in perception area, such as image classification and semantic segmentation [1]. Based on how humans accelerate, brake, identify the signs and the limits of the road, the machine can learn and respond in the same fashion. One important research line focuses on the different ways to train the machine on how to detect lane lines [2] or the road itself [3][4]. Another investigation field related to the off-road driving used Semantic Segmentation to identify tracks in the middle of a forest [5]–[7]. The Semantic Segmentation method presents a perfect choice to train a robot how to drive on an off-road track because this method does not use any kind of line or reference on the road. The technique uses a mask as a reference to train the machine for identifying each place or object in the scene [8]. Nowadays, there are some techniques that can achieve more than 70% accuracy processing more than 70 frames per second [9][10]. However, it requires a powerful Graphics Processing Unit (GPU) to train the machine. Consequently, this is one of the main motivations for the work presented in this paper, where we use a different approach for reference detection.

Learning-based Object Detection is a fast method to train a robot to detect specific objects (car, dog, cat, person, etc.). Many models in the literature, with different architectures, compete to be the fastest and most accurate method [11]. The evolution, in the last decade, regarding fast processors and efficient object detection algorithms allows for the use of these models to train and identify specific objects, increasing their application to autonomous systems.

The concept of detecting patterns through images has been studied for decades and used in detecting faces, people and simple objects [12]. Nowadays, with the advantage of fast processing CPU's (Central Processing Unit) and GPU's, the complexity of artificial intelligence allows us to train a machine to detect and classify any pattern with a predetermined data set. Furthermore, new techniques, such as transfer learning, allow the use of a small amount of data to achieve good results [13].

The detector algorithms are usually composed of two parts, a backbone, that aims to identify the main characteristics of the image and, the head, which uses the backbone information to predict classes and bounding boxes of objects. The backbone component is usually represented by the VGG model [14], ResNet [15], MobileNet [16][17] or DarkNet [18]. On the other hand, the head component uses different approaches and, based on that, the detector algorithm can be categorized as a two-stage detector or an one stage detector.

The two-stage detectors are composed of two parts: the first part uses the input image to propose a set of regions of interest, with select search or Region Proposal Network (RPN) and the second part performs the classification of the candidate regions. The models that use this approach are the Regions with Convolutional Neural Network (R-CNN) features [19], Fast R-CNN [20] and Faster R-CNN [21].

On the other hand, one-stage detectors do not use the region proposal step, but rather go straight to the detection of a limited number of predefined bounding boxes. This method makes the model processing faster, however, it decreases the accuracy. The most known models that use this one-stage detector are You Only Look Once (YOLO) [18][22][23], Single Shot Detector (SSD) [24] and RetinaNet [25].

This paper is organized as follows. Section II presents the background related to the object detection models that were used in this work. Section III proposes the training method and two experiments to evaluate the model's performance. Finally, Section IV presents the conclusion about the experiments and discusses improvements to the project in the future.

II. Background

In this section, we will present the main Learning-based Detecion algorithms used for image recognizing applications.

A. *Faster R-CNN*

In 2014, Ross Girshick proposed a simple and scalable detection algorithm, an approach that combines the high-capacity of convolutional neural networks with proposed regions to localize and segment objects [19]. The model, called Regions with CNNs features (R-CNN), receives the input image and extracts around 2000 region proposals. Each region is warped to a fixed-size and computed by a large CNN, where it is classified by label probabilities (Figure 1).

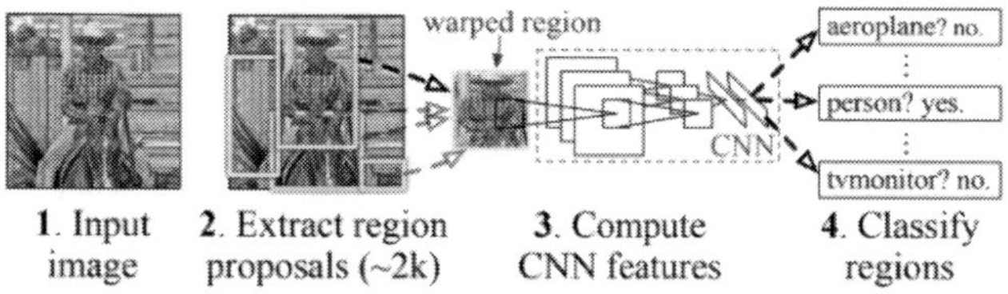

Figure 1. R-CNN architecture [19].

However, the R-CNN method presents some problems in real-time implementation. It needs a huge amount of time to train the network by classifying 2000 region proposals per image. Thus, in 2015, Girshick presented Fast R-CNN, a new model evolved from the previous one and intended to be faster and more accurate [20].

The approach of Fast R-CNN is similar to the R-CNN algorithm, however, instead of feeding the region proposals to the CNN, it sends the image into the CNN to generate a convolutional feature map. From this map, the regions proposals are identified and warped into bounding boxes. Using a Region of Interest (RoI) pooling layer, the regions are reshaped into a fixed size to be fed into a sequence of fully connected layers, each one with two outputs. The first output is a softmax classification layer, where it decides which object class was found in the prediction. The second output is the Bounding Box Regressor (BBox Regressor), a popular technique to refine or predict localization boxes in recent object detection approaches. This technique approximates the nearby bounding boxes to the region proposals (or *Anchors*). In other words, the BBox Regressor outputs the bounding box coordinates for each object class [20].

Both algorithms (R-CNN and Fast R-CNN) use Selective Search. This involves sliding a window over the image to generate region proposals where objects could possibly be found [26]. However, this method is a slow and time-consuming process that affects the performance of the network. For this reason, in 2017 Shaoqing Ren et al. proposed a different object detection design, called Faster R-CNN, that eliminates the selective search algorithm and makes a network learn the region proposals [21].

The Faster R-CNN head part is composed of two modules. First, there is a deep fully convolutional neural network that proposes regions, the RPN and, second, a network that uses these proposals of RPN to detect objects (Figure 2a). The second module works with the same detector used in Fast R-CNN.

The RPN takes an image of any size and, with a Convolutional Neural Network (VGG-16 was used in [21]), it proposes a set of region boxes (Anchors) and gives the probability of those region boxes being an object class or a background. To generate these regions, an $n \times n$ window slides over the feature map. Each sliding-window predicts multiple region proposals (*Anchors*), where the maximum number of possible regions is denoted by k ($k = 9$ [21]) (Figure 2b).

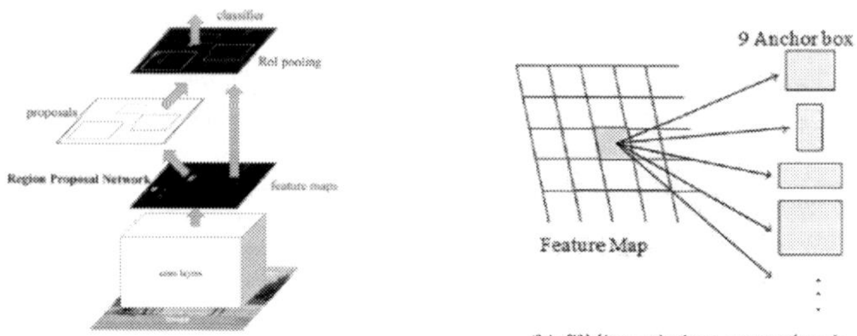

(a) Faster R-CNN Architecture [21].

(b) Sliding-window generating k ($k = 9$) *Anchors*.

Figure 2. Faster R-CNN.

As a final step, the model unifies the RPN with the Fast R-CNN detector. The algorithm applies a RoI to reduce all *Anchors* to the same size and, for each region proposal, the model flattens the input, passing it through two fully-connected layers with Rectified Linear Unit (ReLU) activation. Finally, these fully-connected layers generate the prediction of the class and the box of each object.

B. *YOLO*

The YOLO architecture, differently from Faster R-CNN, has no RPN. It uses a single feed-forward convolutional network to predict classes and bounding boxes.

The YOLO algorithm divides the input image into a $S \times S$ grid, where each grid cell is responsible for detecting the object in its area. Each one predicts B bounding boxes and it scores the confidence to be an object or not. The confidence score reflects the probability of the predicted box to contain an object $P_r(Object)$, as well as how accurate is the predicted box by evaluating its Intersection over Union value (IoU^{truth}_{pred}). In this sense, the confidence score becomes:

$$\text{Confidence Score} = P_r(Obj) * IoU^{truth}_{pred} \quad (1)$$

$$P_r = \begin{cases} 1 & \text{If object exists} \\ 0 & \text{Otherwise} \end{cases} \quad (2)$$

Each bounding box consists of 5 values, 4 representing its coordinates (x,y,w,h) and one representing the confidence score.

Regarding the grid cell, each one also predicts the number of C Conditional Class Probabilities, where C represents the number of classes and the Conditional Class Probabilities represent the chance of an object to belong to class *i* (Equation 3).

$$\text{Conditional Class Probabilities} = P_r(Class_i|Object) \quad (3)$$

At the test time, the model multiplies the Conditional Class Probabilities and the individual box Confidence score:

$$P_r(Class_i|Object) * P_r(Obj) * IoU_{pred}^{truth} = P_r(Class_i) * IoU_{pred}^{truth} \quad (4)$$

Consequently, the above equation yields the score of the probability of the class appearing in the box and how the predicted box fits the object (Figure 3)[22].

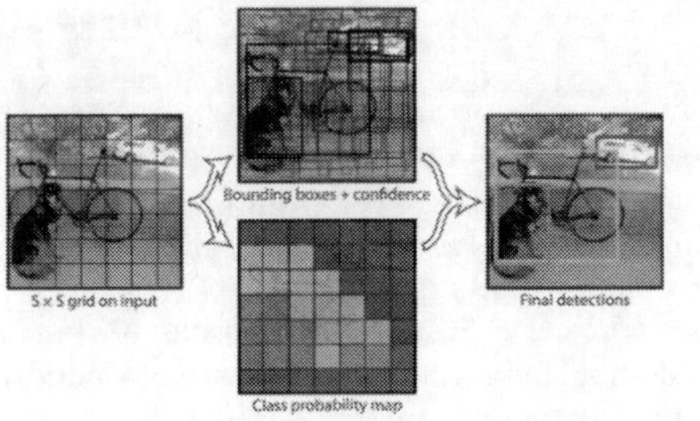

Figure 3. The representation of the two YOLO steps, identifying the objects and defining the probabilities of the classes in each grid [22].

The predictions results into a $S \times S \times (B * 5 + C)$ tensor. For example, if it takes $S = 7$, $B = 2$ and $C = 20$, we have a $(7, 7, 2 * 5 + 20) \rightarrow (7, 7, 30)$ tensor. This tensor provides the information about the Bounding Boxes and each class probabilities.

There are two types of YOLO algorithms: Regular YOLO and Fast (Tiny) YOLO. The Regular model consists of 24 convolutional layers followed by 2 fully connected layers (Figure 4). On the other hand, the Tiny model has 11 layers, 9 convolutional and 2 fully connected. As this architecture is much smaller compared to other detecting methods, it presents a fast response in object predictions, allowing the detection in real-time speed.

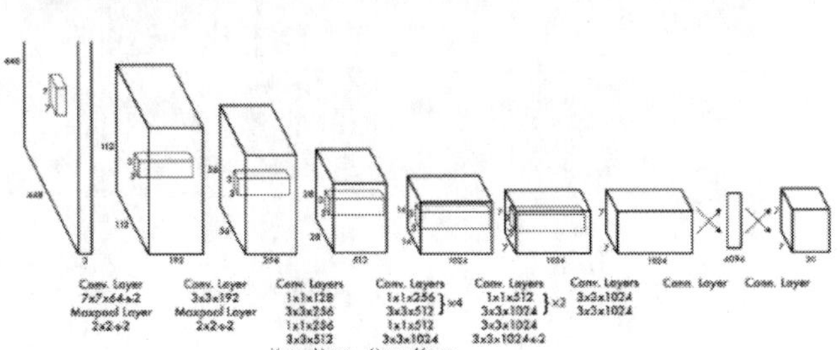

Figure 4. YOLO architecture [22].

The YOLOv2 represents the second version of YOLO where the objective is to improve the accuracy while making it faster. To achieve these features, the second model adds new features to improve the previous model performance. Among them, there are the adding of Batch Normalization in convolution layers, the high resolution classifier, convolutional with *Anchors* boxes, dimension clusters, direct location prediction, fine-grained features and a multi-scale training.

C. SSD

Single Shot Detector (SSD), like YOLO, takes only one shot to detect multiple objects present in an image using multibox. Furthermore, similar to Faster R-CNN, SSD model is built on a network architecture (backbone), e.g., the VGG-16 architecture [14], a high quality image classification model, without the final classification layers (fully connected layers). Instead, a set of convolutional layers are added, decreasing the size of the input to each subsequent layer, enabling to extract features at multiple scales. Thus, predictions for bounding boxes and confidence for different objects are done by multiple feature maps of different sizes (Figure 5).

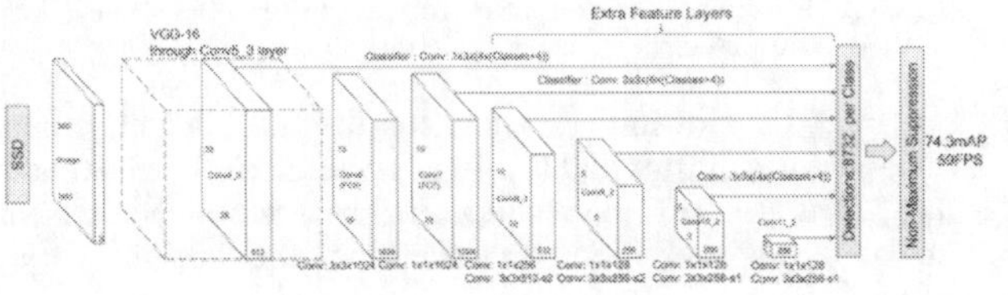

Figure 5. SSD architecture [24].

During the training process of SSD model, each added feature layer produces a detection prediction using convolutional filters (the "Extra Feature Layers" in Figure 5). For a layer of size $m \times n$ (number of locations) with p channels, the predicting map is a $3 \times 3 \times p$ kernel that produces a score for a category. For each location, the predicting map generating k bounding boxes. These boxes have different sizes (e.g., a 4 size box as in Figure 6). Furthermore, for each bounding box, there are computed c class score and 4 offsets relative to the original default box shape. At the training time, the default boxes are matched to the ground truth boxes, where the maching cases are treated as positives and the remaining as negatives. In this way, it results in a $(c+4)k$ filters that are applied around each location in feature map, resulting in a $(c+4)kmn$ outputs for an $m \times n$ map. Using the Figure 5 as an example, the result will be an 8732 bounding boxes.

During the training process, it is necessary to determine which boxes correspond to a ground truth detection. With this purpose, SSD model matches each ground truth box to the default box by their IoU ratio and, the boxes with an IoU value over than 0.5 are selected, simplifying the learning problem and allowing the network to predict high scores for multiple overlapping boxes.

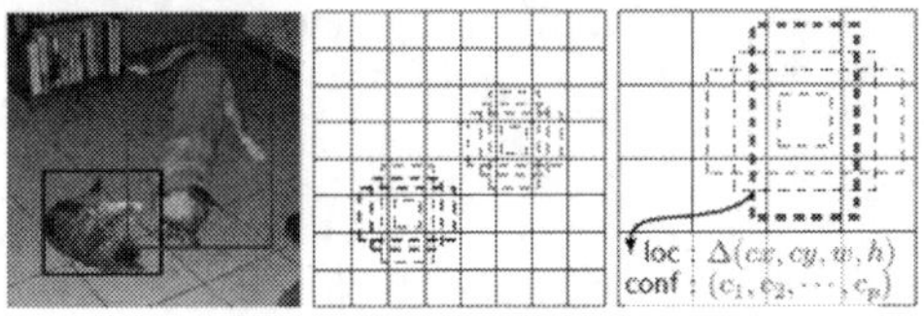

Figure 6. SSD Framework [24].

The SSD model is distinguished by two categories SSD512 and SSD300, working with images 512×512 and 300×300 respectively. SSD512 provides the best accuracy by detecting objects in large images, however the SSD300 model process the image almost twice as faster as SSD512 (Figure 7) [24].

To conclude, the SSD uses VGG-16 network as a backbone to extract features of images. However, different bases

Method	mAP	FPS	# Boxes	Input resolution
SSD300	74.3	46	8732	300 × 300
SSD512	76.8	19	24564	512 × 512

Figure 7. Comparison of SSD models [24].

(GoogleNet, MobileNet, AlexNet, Inception, etc.) can be used for better performance.

Network	Top 1	Params	MAdds	CPU
MobileNetV1	70.6	4.2M	575M	113ms
ShuffleNet (1.5)	71.5	**3.4M**	292M	-
ShuffleNet (x2)	73.7	5.4M	524M	-
NasNet-A	74.0	5.3M	564M	183ms
MobileNetV2	**72.0**	**3.4M**	**300M**	**75ms**
MobileNetV2 (1.4)	**74.7**	6.9M	585M	**143ms**

Figure 8. Performance on ImageNet, comparison for different networks [17]. MAdds represents the counting of total number of Multiply-Adds.

In 2017, Howard presented the first MobileNet, a network that performs faster and nearly as accurate as VGG-16 network [16]. And in 2018, the second version of MobileNet has shown to be faster and more accurate than the last network [17] (Figure 8).

III. Proposal work and Experimental Results

In this work, we seek for high speed and accurate detection of landmarks on the off-road track. To obtain the best result, we chose three models (Faster R-CNN, Fast YOLOv2 and the MobileNetv2 SSD300) and analyzed the result of each one for a real application.

This section presents the Training Stage, where all methods are trained considering the same conditions, as wall as the experiments comparing the different object detection models. Furthermore, the training and detection process were done with a GPU Nvidia Geforce 1060 3GB and CPU Intel i5 8500u on Windows 10 operational system.

A. Training Stage

To start the training process, it was chosen a white cone as the object for the reference detection to represent the limits of the road (Figure 9a). The training of this object was presented in Dhall work (June 2019). A monocular camera was used to detect and estimate the localization of a traffic cone in 3D world coordinates [27]. As the work aims to observe the performance of the models by detecting an object at the road boundary, the models were trained and tested to recognize the reference in this area.

The training was made using a set of different images with a single cone in different backgrounds and off-road tracks with cones spaced by 3 meters, which makes up most of the dataset (Figure 9).

To provide a fair comparison between the accuracy of the models, all object detection methods were adapted to train with the same dataset, 296 images (608 × 608 pixels).

The models were trained until the convergence of the Localization Loss value of each model. The Loss represents the quantitative measure of how much the predictions differ from the actual output (label). As an evaluation method, the localization loss value shows the difference of each model accuracy.

The loss of each model is represented by different equations [21][22][24]. To compare the predicted box localization

(a) Object reference. (b) Training example image.

Figure 9. Training process.

accuracy, it will be used only the *Localization Loss* which shows the errors of the predicted box localization when compared to the ground truth (Table I).

TABLE I. Model Loss comparative

Model	Loss	Training images
Faster R-CNN	0.017	296
MobileNetv2 SSD300	0.258	296
Fast YOLOv2	1.500	296

It is possible to observe from Table I that at the end of the training stage, the Fast Yolov2 presents a bigger error between the predictions and the real label with 1.5 of loss value. Furthermore, the Faster R-CNN and MobileNetv2 SSD300 showed small loss values, representing a good precision from these two methods.

B. Experiment 1

The first experiment was done by post-processing of an off-road driving video with similar characteristics of the dataset training. To compare the results of each model, it was chosen video frames of the off-road ride (Figure 10).

(a) Faster R-CNN Model. (b) SSD300 Model. (c) Fast YOLOv2 Model.

Figure 10. Comparative of three Detection Methods.

As can be observed from Figure 10, the Faster R-CNN model and the SSD300 presented comparable detection. The Faster R-CNN presents an advantage in accuracy, detecting the reference up to 12 meters ahead of the car (Figure 10a), while the SSD300 keeps the identification around 9 meters from the car (Figure 10b).

On the other hand, the Fast YOLOv2, which presented the biggest *Localization loss* value, showed the worst detector accuracy among the three models. The model resulted in a maximum detection of ~ 4 meters ahead from the car during all trajectory, failing sometimes to detect near references (Figure 10c).

Looking at the accuracy of each model, the Faster R-CNN showed the best choice for an autonomous driving application in off-road environments. However, besides a high precision in its detection, it is necessary a fast response of the reference identification. To estimate this, we tested 10 images, using different angles of the reference on the off-road street and, then the Mean Time Process (MTP) of each method was calculated (Table II).

TABLE II. COMPARATIVE OF MODELS. MTP: MEAN TIME PROCESSING; FPS: FRAMES PER SECOND

Model	Loss	Training images	MTP (seconds)	FPS
Faster R-CNN	0.017	296	3.14	00.3
MobileNetv2 SSD300	0.258	296	1.41	00.7
Fast YOLOv2	1.500	296	0.07	14.3

Through these results, it is possible to observe that the Faster R-CNN proved to be the slowest detector. It takes around 3 seconds to process each image, resulting in an unfeasible application for autonomous driving. On the other hand, the Fast YOLOv2, which showed a low precision in the detection, identified the references in less than 0.1 seconds. For this reason, it is expected to be a good detector for prevention moments, detecting nearby warnings, like animals or holes, or even tight curves.

Finally, the MobileNetv2 SSD300 showed an intermediary MTP. It detects all references in an image at around 1.4 seconds. The advantage of this model is that its accuracy was near to that of the Faster R-CNN, though SSD processing the image twice faster. For autonomous driving application, 1.4 seconds to detect the limits of a road in a curve presumably would result in a car off the track. On the contrary, in a straight road, such a fast steer correction may not be necessary and, this model can be useful.

C. Experiment 2

For the purpose of observing eventually overfitting in the models, in the second experiment, the detection architectures were tested to identify the same reference in a different background from those they were trained.

The experiment was done by post-processing video of a car driving in a different environment from the training step (Figure 11).

The experiment presented a decrease in the detection of the Faster R-CNN and SSD300, where the models presented some failures in near detection. However, even with a small number of training images (296) from a different background, the methods did not present many false positives detection.

The Fast YOLOv2 had the smallest performance decrease. As in the first experiment, the model could only detect close references, failing sometimes to recognize them.

(a) Faster R-CNN Model. (b) SSD300 Model. (c) Fast YOLOv2 Model.

Figure 11. Comparative of three Detection Methods in a different environment.

Ten images were used in the new background scenario to observe the change in time detection. However, the models provided the same time process observed in the first experiment.

IV. CONCLUSION AND FUTURE WORKS

This work showed a Deep Learning application to identify reference marks on a road. The technique was implemented by training three existing Object Detection models with transfer learning, to identify a new object as a reference and comparing their results, Faster R-CNN, Fast YOLOv2 and MobileNetv2 SSD300.

While Faster R-CNN and SSD300 showed similar accuracy, detecting references in close and far ahead distances, Fast YOLOv2 model did not detect references when it was more than 4 meters ahead. Despite the precision of Fast YOLOv2, it processes the detection in less than 0.1 seconds, providing the faster detection among the three models.

While the Fast YOLOv2 presented a fast detection, the Faster R-CNN showed the slowest detector. It spent more than 3 seconds to detect the references in each image. On the other hand, the SSD300 with an accuracy similar to that of the Faster R-CNN, processes the image twice faster, detecting objects in about 1.5 seconds.

Each model presented a particularity in accuracy and speed that is important for autonomous cars to drive safely on a road without line lanes. The Faster R-CNN presented the best accuracy of all, though it is considerably slow for an autonomous drive application. The SSD300 with a similar precision was proven to be a good model to identify the limits on straight roads. With a low process time to detect references, the model could only analyzes and determine the action to keep the vehicle in the middle of the road at every 1.5 seconds.

In addition, the Fast YOLOv2 only detected close references which can be useful for fast detection, e.g., tight curves or emergency situations, allowing the machine to make fast decisions on a drive.

For an autonomous driving application, that uses a powerful GPU and CPU, the implementation of SSD and Fast YOLOv2 should result in a safe drive. The first one for detecting the main limits of the road and the second one to work as a warning system for fast actions.

Future works in this project are aimed to explore alternative architectures, including the recent versions of the models presented at this work. Additionally, the work pretends to label a test dataset to provide a quantitative evaluation of the models or to conduct statistical tests known from the literature [28][29].

Searching for generalizing the ideas of this project, the work will extend the detection from the reference object described in the text to real objects that can be used to represent the road boundary in an off-road environment.

ACKNOWLEDGMENT

The authors acknowledge the funding received from: Project INCT-SAC - Aut. Collaborative Systems - (CNPq 465755/2014-3, FAPESP 2014/50851-0) and Fapesp Auto-VERDE (p. 2018/04905-1).

REFERENCES

[1] A. Krizhevsky, I. Sutskever, and G. E. Hinton, "Imagenet classification with deep convolutional neural networks," in Advances in Neural Information Processing Systems 25, F. Pereira, C. J. C. Burges, L. Bottou, and K. Q. Weinberger, Eds. Curran Associates, Inc., 2012, pp. 1097–1105.

[2] S. Lee et al., "Vpgnet: Vanishing point guided network for lane and road marking detection and recognition," in 2017 IEEE International Conference on Computer Vision (ICCV), 2017, pp. 1965–1973.

[3] G. Ros, L. Sellart, J. Materzynska, D. Vazquez, and A. M. Lopez, "The synthia dataset: A large collection of synthetic images for semantic segmentation of urban scenes," in 2016 IEEE Conference on Computer Vision and Pattern Recognition (CVPR), Los Alamitos, CA, USA, jun 2016, pp. 3234–3243.

[4] J. M. Alvarez, Y. LeCun, T. Gevers, and A. M. Lopez, "Semantic road segmentation via multi-scale ensembles of learned features," in Computer Vision – ECCV 2012. Workshops and Demonstrations. Springer Berlin Heidelberg, 2012, pp. 586–595.

[5] T. P. Breckon, "From On-Road to Off : Transfer Learning within a Deep Convolutional Neural Network for Segmentation and Classification of Off-Road Scenes," pp. 1–14.

[6] S. Adhikari, C. Yang, K. Slot, and H. Kim, "Accurate natural trail detection using a combination of a deep neural network and dynamic programming," Sensors, vol. 18, no. 2, Jan. 2018, p. 178.

[7] C. Caraffi, S. Cattani, and P. Grisleri, "Off-road path and obstacle detection using decision networks and stereo vision," IEEE Transactions on Intelligent Transportation Systems, vol. 8, no. 4, 2007, pp. 607–618.

[8] G. Ros, L. Sellart, J. Materzynska, D. Vazquez, and A. M. Lopez, "The SYNTHIA Dataset: A Large Collection of Synthetic Images for Semantic Segmentation of Urban Scenes," Proceedings of the IEEE Computer Society Conference on Computer Vision and Pattern Recognition, vol. 2016-Decem, no. 600388, 2016, pp. 3234–3243.

[9] P. Chao, C.-Y. Kao, Y.-S. Ruan, C.-H. Huang, and Y. Lin, "Hardnet: A low memory traffic network," 2019 IEEE/CVF International Conference on Computer Vision (ICCV), 2019, pp. 3551–3560.

[10] W. Chen, X. Gong, X. Liu, Q. Zhang, Y. Li, and Z. Wang, "Fasterseg: Searching for faster real-time semantic segmentation," ArXiv, vol. abs/1912.10917, 2020, accessed on 31.08.2020.

[11] M. Everingham, L. Van Gool, C. K. Williams, J. Winn, and A. Zisserman, "The pascal visual object classes (VOC) challenge," International Journal of Computer Vision, vol. 88, no. 2, 2010, pp. 303–338.

[12] C. Papageorgiou and T. Poggio, "Trainable system for object detection," International Journal of Computer Vision, vol. 38, no. 1, 2000, pp. 15–33.

[13] C. Tan, F. Sun, T. Kong, W. Zhang, C. Yang, and C. Liu, "A survey on deep transfer learning," CoRR, vol. abs/1808.01974, 2018, accessed on 31.08.2020. [Online]. Available: http://arxiv.org/abs/1808.01974

[14] K. Simonyan and A. Zisserman, "Very deep convolutional networks for large-scale image recognition," CoRR, vol. abs/1409.1556, 2015.

[15] K. He, X. Zhang, S. Ren, and J. Sun, "Deep residual learning for image recognition," 2015, accessed on 31.08.2020. [Online]. Available: http://arxiv.org/abs/1512.03385

[16] A. Howard, M. Zhu, B. Chen, D. Kalenichenko, W. Wang, T. Weyand, M. Andreetto, and H. Adam, "Mobilenets: Efficient convolutional neural networks for mobile vision applications," vol. abs/1704.04861, 2017, accessed on 31.08.2020.

[17] M. Sandler, A. Howard, M. Zhu, A. Zhmoginov, and L. C. Chen, "MobileNetV2: Inverted Residuals and Linear Bottlenecks," Proceedings of the IEEE Computer Society Conference on Computer Vision and Pattern Recognition, 2018, pp. 4510–4520.

[18] J. Redmon and A. Farhadi, "YOLO9000: Better, faster, stronger," Proceedings - 30th IEEE Conference on Computer Vision and Pattern Recognition, CVPR 2017, vol. 2017-January, 2017, pp. 6517–6525.

[19] R. Girshick, J. Donahue, T. Darrell, and J. Malik, "Rich feature hierarchies for accurate object detection and semantic segmentation," Proceedings of the IEEE Computer Society Conference on Computer Vision and Pattern Recognition, 2014, pp. 580–587.

[20] R. Girshick, "Fast R-CNN," Proceedings of the IEEE International Conference on Computer Vision, vol. 2015 Inter, 2015, pp. 1440–1448.

[21] S. Ren, K. He, R. Girshick, and J. Sun, "Faster R-CNN: Towards Real-Time Object Detection with Region Proposal Networks," IEEE Transactions on Pattern Analysis and Machine Intelligence, vol. 39, no. 6, 2017, pp. 1137–1149.

[22] J. Redmon, S. Divvala, R. Girshick, and A. Farhadi, "You only look once: Unified, real-time object detection," accessed on 31.08.2020. [Online]. Available: http://arxiv.org/abs/1506.02640

[23] J. Redmon and A. Farhadi, "Yolov3: An incremental improvement," accessed on 31.08.2020. [Online]. Available: http://arxiv.org/abs/1804.02767

[24] W. Liu et al., "SSD: Single shot multibox detector," Lecture Notes in Computer Science (including subseries Lecture Notes in Artificial Intelligence and Lecture Notes in Bioinformatics), vol. 9905 LNCS, 2016, pp. 21–37.

[25] T. Lin, P. Goyal, R. Girshick, K. He, and P. Dollár, "Focal loss for dense object detection," in 2017 IEEE International Conference on Computer Vision (ICCV), 2017, pp. 2999–3007.

[26] J. R. Uijlings, K. E. Van De Sande, T. Gevers, and A. W. Smeulders, "Selective search for object recognition," International journal of computer vision, vol. 104, no. 2, 2013, pp. 154–171.

[27] A. Dhall, D. Dai, and L. Van Gool, "Real-time 3D Traffic Cone Detection for Autonomous Driving," 2019, pp. 494–501.

[28] G.-F. Fan, L.-L. Peng, W.-C. Hong, and F. Sun, "Electric load forecasting by the SVR model with differential empirical mode decomposition and auto regression," Neurocomputing, vol. 173, Jan. 2016, pp. 958–970. [Online]. Available: https://doi.org/10.1016/j.neucom.2015.08.051

[29] Z. Zhang, S. Ding, and Y. Sun, "A support vector regression model hybridized with chaotic krill herd algorithm and empirical mode decomposition for regression task," Neurocomputing, vol. 410, Oct. 2020, pp. 185–201. [Online]. Available: https://doi.org/10.1016/j.neucom.2020.05.075

In the Depths of Hyponymy: A Step Towards Lifelong Learning

Tommaso Boccato*, Timothy Patten†, Markus Vincze† and Stefano Ghidoni*
*Department of Information Engineering, Università degli Studi di Padova, Padova, Italy
Email: tommaso.boccato@studenti.unipd.it, stefano.ghidoni@unipd.it
†Automation and Control Institute, TU Wien, Vienna, Austria
Email: {patten, vincze}@acin.tuwien.ac.at

***Abstract*—This paper proposes a novel framework for lifelong learning of semantic classes in order to extend the operational time of robots deployed in real-world and uncontrolled environments. In contrast to the common approach that assumes fixed object classes, the proposed framework keeps track of the intra-class variability over time in order to refine the class definition encoded into a classifier. A carefully designed metric is also presented to quantify the intra-class variability, which leads to automatic triggering of the class restructuring. Experiments performed with the CIFAR-100 dataset validate the framework and the measure of intra-class variability.**

Keywords–Classification; Lifelong learning; Open set learning.

I. INTRODUCTION

The applications in which a robot should be able to understand what it sees are countless: human-robot interaction, healthcare, service robotics, industrial robotics, logistics, connected and autonomous vehicles. A deep knowledge of the visual properties and functionalities that characterize the objects is vital in the application of the robot itself, allowing for better manipulation, navigation or exploration. Very often, this knowledge is manually encoded into the deployed computer vision algorithms during their training process. Lifelong learning capabilities [1], however, represent a desirable feature.

The last decade of advancements in deep learning have led to astonishing results in the applications that respond to the so called closed-world assumption (i.e., the assumption that the object classes encountered during the operational life of a robot are known and fixed a-priori) [2]. Robots, however, operate in dynamic and uncontrolled environments. As such, the use of standard approaches in these environments usually reveals performance drops. A continuous update of the semantic structure on which a classifier works requires the introduction of additional complexity in the system [3] [4] [5]. Moreover, the update should be efficient and downtimes minimized.

In the presented work, with reference to the classification task, a step is taken towards relaxing the aforementioned assumption by introducing a novel framework capable of allowing the refinement of the classes encoded into a classifier during its operational life. Specifically, the framework keeps track of the intra-class variability temporal evolution linked to the various categories in such a way as to trigger meaningful class reconfiguration. In other words, classes characterized by high intra-class variabilities should be divided into sets of subclasses whose labels are related to the original ones through hyponymy relationships (i.e., words of more specific meaning than general or superordinate terms applicable to them). An example of such a scenario is shown in Figure 1. Clearly, a

Figure 1. Randomly sampled batches extracted from 4 different CIFAR-100 [6] classes (poppies, sunflowers, orchids, tulips). All classes belong to the same super-class of flowers. Images in the top rows show homogeneous visual properties while images in the bottom rows are characterized by very different visual properties. Yet, all the batches belong to specific categories. A question arises: *How does the intra-class variability impact a classifier, and how can an agent (e.g., a robot) recognize and exploit this phenomenon?*

metric capable of quantifying the abstract intra-class variability concept plays a key role within the framework. Therefore, we also propose a suitable metric design.

The remainder of the paper is organized as follows. Section II discusses related work. Section III outlines the lifelong learning framework and Section IV describes the metric for intra-class variability. Section V presents the experiments and results. Section VI concludes and discusses future work.

II. RELATED WORK

According to survey [7], the classification task introduced within the proposed framework can be categorized as hierarchical. In particular, the so called "flat classification approach" is pursued. The class hierarchy, a tree data structure representing hyponymy relationships, is indeed ignored by the classifier, that only acts on its leaves. A possible class hierarchy implementation can follow the WordNet [8] [9] hyponymy network. However, most of the hierarchical classification literature assumes subsets of directed acyclic graphs to be trees in order to simplify their manipulation. We are currently unaware of works that exploit incremental or online hierarchical classification for lifelong learning purposes. On the other hand, parallel paths have been explored in robotics. This section continues with an overview of relevant literature addressing the open set recognition problem as well as measuring intra-class variability.

The Open World Recognition (OWR) framework is formally defined in [3], with the introduction of the Nearest Non-Outlier algorithm and the design of a suitable evaluation protocol; the algorithm is able to incrementally add object categories while detecting outliers. The OWR framework represents a starting point for [4] that proposes a deep extension of a non-parametric model that learns additional categories without retraining the whole system from scratch. The possibility of retrieving annotated images by autonomously mining the web constitutes a major contribution of the work. An attempt to extract label uncertainty from state-of-the-art object detection systems via dropout sampling is performed in [10]. Novel objects are also introduced to robots by means of pointing gestures and verbal communication [11]. Finally, an incremental version of the Regularized Least Squares for Classification algorithm is tested in [12]. The authors also address the problem of having an unbalanced proportion of training samples during the algorithm operational life. The work addressing the open set recognition problem all assume a definitive set of training classes. In contrast, we propose a framework capable of managing concept drifts introduced in all the classes encoded into the considered classifier.

The treatment of intra-class variability in the literature is scattered across several diverse fields, none that are specific to robotics or machine vision. For example, the intra-class variability affecting winter wheat mapping from multi-temporal Moderate Resolution Imaging Spectroradiometer (MODIS) Enhanced Vegetation Index (EVI) images is addressed by generating multiple training sub-classes to decrease the intra-class differences for the crop type detection [13]. The separability of the generated sub-classes exploits the Jeffries-Matusita (JM) Distance; such separability reflects the intra-class variability of the associated original class. A similar approach is used for liver lesion detection [14] where a multi-class convolutional neural network (CNN) categorizes image patches into sub-categories, which are then fused to obtain a binary lesion/non-lesion classification. A novel offline approach, instead, is proposed in [15] to model biometric data intra-class variability and typicality. The method consists of a two stage algorithm: the former is represented by the clustering of the input images while the latter performs a template extraction from the clustered data. Finally, [16] reports a few functions to represent the covariance matrix of a multi-variate distribution as a scalar. While these works consider intra-class variability, it has mainly been investigated from a qualitative and high-level point of view. Additionally, the concept is applied in domains different to our study: they do not specifically address lifelong learning for a robotic system.

III. Lifelong Learning Framework

Our work builds on the *Open Set Learning* paradigm and its framework [3] [4] in order to explore an alternative path towards the development of an agent characterized by lifelong learning capabilities. The objective pursued by the definition of the framework is to theoretically describe the operational life of a classifier trained on a set of semantic categories or classes labeled by the positive integers $\mathcal{K}_1 = \{1, \ldots, N_1\}$, with $|\mathcal{K}_1| = N_1$. The considered model thus refines its semantic categories every time the intra-class variability associated to a specific category proves to be sufficiently high according to a pre-defined criterion; this concept, as well as the whole framework definition, is presented generically in order to allow the framework to enclose a large variety of future works. It is therefore natural to define $\mathcal{K}_t \subseteq \mathbb{N}^+$ as the set of classes encoded into the classifier at time t. Moreover, $|\mathcal{K}_i| = N_i \leq |\mathcal{K}_j| = N_j$ when $i < j$. An example of class structure temporal evolution is shown in Figure 2.

Let $\boldsymbol{x} \in \mathbb{R}^d$ be the features associated to a new sample seen by the classifier. Let $\mathcal{T}_t \subseteq \mathbb{R}^d \times \bigcup_{j=1}^{t} \mathcal{K}_j$ be the set containing all the samples, with the respective labels, seen by the classifier up to time t (the definition of $\mathcal{T}_t$ does not allow the repetition of a specific pair, but such scenario can be verified in the operational life of a real classifier; the problem can be overcome by adding an auxiliary dimension to the space of features used to enumerate the samples). The set cardinality can be expressed as $|\mathcal{T}_t| = M_t + t$: the former term refers to the model training (ground truth labels) while the latter refers to the model operational life (labels provided by the classifier). A model, to function within the defined framework, must be characterized by the following main ingredients.

A. Multi-class Recognition Function

The *multi-class recognition function* $F_t : \mathbb{R}^d \longrightarrow \mathcal{K}_t$ exploits the vector function

$$\psi_t(\boldsymbol{x}) = [f_t^i(\boldsymbol{x})], \ \forall i \in \mathcal{K}_t, \tag{1}$$

where the generic *per-class recognition function* $f_t^i : \mathbb{R}^d \longrightarrow \mathbb{R}$ belongs to a suitable space $\mathcal{H}$. Typically, $f_t^i(\boldsymbol{x})$ reports the likelihood of being in class i, the values of $f_t^i(\boldsymbol{x})$ are normalized across the respective semantic categories and the multi-class recognition function is implemented as:

$$F_t(\boldsymbol{x}) = \arg\max_{i \in \mathcal{K}_t} f_t^i(\boldsymbol{x}). \tag{2}$$

B. State Update Function

For each semantic category, the corresponding element of the set should contain all the necessary information to compute its intra-class variability after the classification performed in the previous time step. The nature of the generic element s_t^i is not specified: it could represent a scalar, a matrix or any other kind of data structure depending on the needs. Every time a new sample is classified, the *state* $\mathcal{S}_t = \{s_t^i\}, \ \forall i \in \mathcal{K}_t$ must be updated accordingly. The *state update function* $U : \mathcal{S}_t \times \mathbb{R}^d \longrightarrow \mathcal{S}_{t+1}$ is exploited for the purpose. Specifically,

$$s_{t+1}^i = U(s_t^i, \boldsymbol{x}), \tag{3}$$

if $\boldsymbol{x}$ is recognized as belonging to class i. Clearly, $s_{t+1}^j = s_t^j, \ \forall j \neq i$.

At this point, the intra-class variability computation can finally be formalized through the function $V : \mathcal{S}_{t+1} \longrightarrow \mathbb{R}$. Intuitively, the intra-class variability of class i at time t should depend on $\mathcal{T}_t^i = \{(\boldsymbol{x}, k) \text{ s.t. } k = i\}$; s_{t+1}^i encapsulates this information allowing an efficient sequential update of the metric. Indeed, it could not be feasible to store the entire $\mathcal{T}_t^i$ or to use the set for a direct intra-class variability computation. The additional state $\mathcal{S}_t$ is also motivated by the fact that the V function, in general, is not invertible; this means that $V(s_{t+1}^i)$ may not be obtainable starting from $V(s_t^i)$.

Hence, a *trigger* $T : \mathbb{R} \longrightarrow \{0, 1\}$ is defined in accordance with a criterion selected by the designer in order to establish whether class i needs to be split or not; it returns 1 if the considered semantic category has to be replaced by more specific sub-classes, 0 otherwise.

C. Labeling Process and Data Retrieval Functions

The *labeling process function* $L_t : \mathcal{P}(\mathcal{T}_t^i) \longrightarrow \mathcal{P}(\mathbb{N}^+ \setminus \bigcup_{j=1}^t \mathcal{K}_j)$, where $\mathcal{P}(\bullet)$ denotes the power set, aims to retrieve the sub-class labels of class i when its split is triggered (i.e., $T(V(s_{t+1}^i)) = 1$). It is important to remember that the used labels are excluded from the function codomain. Again, a subset $\mathcal{T}_t^i$ can be exploited to overcome possible limitations in the available spatial and temporal computational resources.

Once the new categories are collected, the classifier class structure has to be updated. The following rule is exploited:

$$\mathcal{K}_{t+1} = \mathcal{K}_t \setminus i \cup \mathcal{N}_{t+1}, \quad (4)$$

where i is the label of the considered class and $\mathcal{N}_{t+1}$ represents the set of labels returned by the labeling process after the classification of the t-th sample.

The *data retrieval function* $R : \mathcal{P}(\mathcal{K}_{t+1}) \longrightarrow \mathcal{P}(\mathbb{R}^d \times \mathcal{K}_{t+1})$ is responsible for retrieving the new data $\mathcal{D}_{t+1} \in \mathcal{P}(\mathbb{R}^d \times \mathcal{K}_{t+1})$ for the incremental training of the model. The function domain is chosen as to allow approaches capable of mitigating the effect of catastrophic forgetting [5]. Additionally, it is worth noting that the L_t and R functions must rely on an external source of information (e.g., the web) and the performance of their implementations could not be error free.

D. Incremental Learning Function

The *incremental learning function* is defined as $I_t : \mathcal{P}(\mathbb{R}^d \times \mathcal{K}_{t+1}) \times \mathcal{H}^{N_t} \longrightarrow \mathcal{H}^{N_{t+1}}$, where $N_{t+1} - N_t = |\mathcal{N}_{t+1}| - 1$. The objective of the function is to incrementally update the model by replacing the obsolete per-class recognition function $f_t^i(\boldsymbol{x})$ with the ones related to the new $|\mathcal{N}_{t+1}|$ semantic categories. The retrieved data $\mathcal{D}_{t+1}$ is exploited for the purpose. Hence, the state $\mathcal{S}_{t+1}$ has to be expanded and the added entries must be initialized properly. If possible, the model should gradually adapt to the new class structures without completely retraining.

Every time $T(V(s_{t+1}^i)) = 0$, a simple implicit update of the $\mathcal{K}_t$, F_t, f_t^i subscripts (time steps) has to be performed.

IV. Metric for Intra-class Variability

This section describes the design of a suitable metric for quantifying the intra-class variability. This can then be used to trigger the splitting event and therefore the update of the classification model.

Let $\boldsymbol{X}$ be the matrix whose columns are the vectors belonging to the set $\{\boldsymbol{x} \text{ s.t. } (\boldsymbol{x}, k) \in \mathcal{T}_t^i\}$. In other words, $\boldsymbol{X}$ contains all the samples, belonging to or classified as belonging to class $i \in \mathcal{K}_t$, seen by the considered model up to time t. The matrix can be thought of as the repeated sampling of a probability distribution over $\mathbb{R}^d$ associated with the environment in which the model is immersed (when the d-th dimension is reserved for the sample enumeration, the underlying probability distribution should be defined over the first $d-1$ dimensions).

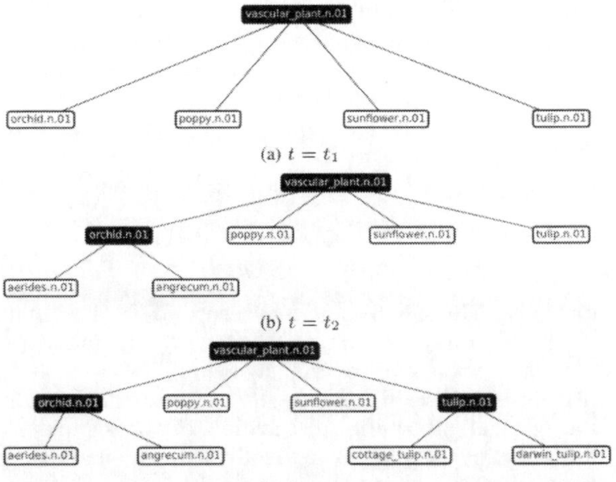

(a) $t = t_1$

(b) $t = t_2$

(c) $t = t_3$

Figure 2. Example of class structure temporal evolution for the semantic categories in Figure 1. The leaves (i.e., white nodes) of the trees represent the classes encoded into the classifier at the considered time steps, where $t_1 < t_2 < t_3$. Clearly, classes that are present at time t are labeled by the elements of $\mathcal{K}_t$. The `orchid` class is the first to be split ($t = t_2$), the `tulip` class follows ($t = t_3$). Trees follow the hyponymy in [8] [9].

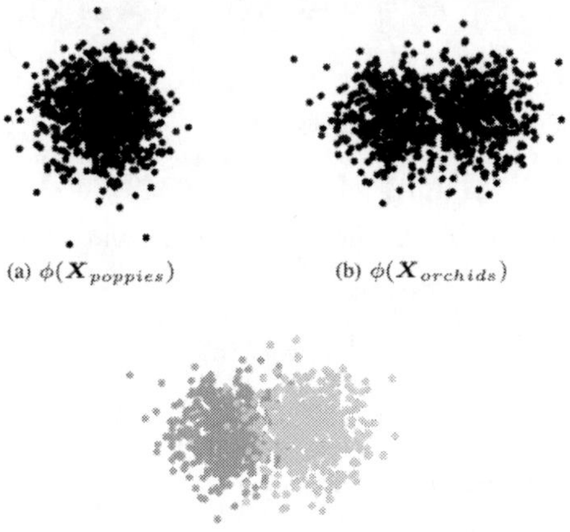

(a) $\phi(\boldsymbol{X}_{poppies})$ (b) $\phi(\boldsymbol{X}_{orchids})$

(c) $\phi(\boldsymbol{X}_{aerides})$, $\phi(\boldsymbol{X}_{angrecums})$

Figure 3. Our formulation of intra-class variability. The setup is the same reported in Figure 1 and 2. The intra-class variability of the category shown in (a) is low while the intra-class variability of the category shown in (b) is high (sub-classes are shown in (c) for comparison). The shape of the deep representations reflects the hypothesis: $\phi(\boldsymbol{X}_{poppies})$ approximates a hyperball better than $\phi(\boldsymbol{X}_{orchids})$.

If the used classifier belongs to the category of deep models, $\phi : \mathbb{R}^d \longrightarrow \mathbb{R}^n$ can be defined as the function responsible for extracting deep representations (e.g., the output of the last layer before the linear ones in ResNet [17] or VGG [18]) from the generic sample features $\boldsymbol{x} \in \mathbb{R}^d$. For simplicity, the ϕ notation is overloaded by defining $\phi(\boldsymbol{X})$ as the matrix obtained applying function ϕ to $\boldsymbol{X}$ columnwise. Also, $\phi(\boldsymbol{X})$ can be thought of as the repeated sampling of a new probability distribution derived from the original one by applying ϕ to the multivariate random variable $\boldsymbol{x}$ (depending on the context, $\boldsymbol{x}$

can be regarded as the features of a generic image sample or the associated random vector).

The intuition, therefore, is to link the abstract concept of intra-class variability to the shape of the $\phi(\boldsymbol{X})$ sampling in the space of the deep representations. The formulated hypothesis follows: *The lower the intra-class variability of class i, the better the sampling $\phi(\boldsymbol{X})$ approximates a hyperball.* Given the metric space $(\mathbb{R}^n, d)$, with the distance function set to be

$$\begin{aligned} d : \mathbb{R}^n \times \mathbb{R}^n &\longrightarrow \mathbb{R}^+ \cup \{0\} \\ (\boldsymbol{x}, \boldsymbol{y}) &\longmapsto d(\boldsymbol{x}, \boldsymbol{y}) = \|\boldsymbol{x} - \boldsymbol{y}\|, \end{aligned} \tag{5}$$

the hyperball of radius $r > 0$ centered in $\boldsymbol{p}$ is defined as $B_r(\boldsymbol{p}) = \{\boldsymbol{x} \in \mathbb{R}^n \text{ s.t. } d(\boldsymbol{x}, \boldsymbol{p}) < r\}$. Figure 3 provides a visual explanation of this hypothesis. It is worth noting that the sampling shape depends on key important elements: the original probability distribution of the sample features, the sampling $\boldsymbol{X}$ and, consequently, the exploited dataset; and function ϕ, hence, the considered model. Clearly, the concept of approximation introduced in the formulated hypothesis needs to be formalized.

A first proposal consists of analyzing the per-component variances of the random vector $\phi(\boldsymbol{x})$. Assuming that $\phi(\boldsymbol{x})$ is a zero mean vector (otherwise, the mean can be subtracted), its (sample) covariance matrix can be computed as

$$\boldsymbol{C}_{\phi(\boldsymbol{X})} = \frac{1}{|\mathcal{T}_t^i| - 1} \phi(\boldsymbol{X}) \phi(\boldsymbol{X})^T. \tag{6}$$

Hence, the considered variances can be identified in the diagonal terms of $\boldsymbol{C}_{\phi(\boldsymbol{X})}$; let

$$\boldsymbol{\sigma} = [\sigma_1^2, \ldots, \sigma_n^2], \tag{7}$$

be the vector containing these terms and

$$\begin{aligned} \tilde{\boldsymbol{\sigma}} &= [\tilde{\sigma}_1^2, \ldots, \tilde{\sigma}_n^2] \qquad (8) \\ &= \left[\frac{\sigma_1^2}{\sum_{i=1}^n \sigma_i^2}, \ldots, \frac{\sigma_n^2}{\sum_{i=1}^n \sigma_i^2} \right], \qquad (9) \end{aligned}$$

be its normalized counterpart. Two borderline cases can therefore emerge from the analysis of $\tilde{\boldsymbol{\sigma}}$:

$$\tilde{\sigma}_i^2 = \frac{1}{n}, \ \forall i \in [1, n], \tag{10}$$

is the best approximation of the introduced hyperball and

$$\exists i \in [1, n] \text{ s.t. } \tilde{\sigma}_j^2 = \begin{cases} 1 \text{ if } j = i, \\ 0 \text{ otherwise}, \end{cases} \tag{11}$$

is the worst one. The former case characterizes samples that are homogeneously spread across the n dimensions while the latter characterizes samples that are spread along a preferential dimension. At this point, an aggregate score of the $\tilde{\boldsymbol{\sigma}}$ terms needs to be computed in accordance with the approximation introduced in (10) and (11). Consequently, the concept of entropy is borrowed from Information Theory for the purpose. Let $H(\boldsymbol{p}) = -\sum_{i=1}^n p_i \log_2 p_i$ be the entropy of the generic distribution $\boldsymbol{p} = [p_1, \ldots, p_n]$. With reference to the framework of Section III, the proposed metric is defined to be

$$V(\boldsymbol{C}_{\phi(\boldsymbol{X})}) = H(\tilde{\boldsymbol{\sigma}}), \tag{12}$$

where the state s_{t+1}^i is set to be $\boldsymbol{C}_{\phi(\boldsymbol{X})}$ and the vector $\tilde{\boldsymbol{\sigma}}$ can be straightforwardly obtained from the diagonal of matrix $\boldsymbol{C}_{\phi(\boldsymbol{X})}$. It is easy to prove that (10) leads to the maximum value reachable by metric (12),

(a) $\boldsymbol{C}_{\phi(\boldsymbol{X})_{0°}} = \begin{bmatrix} 1 & 0 \\ 0 & 0.01 \end{bmatrix}$ (b) $\boldsymbol{C}_{\phi(\boldsymbol{X})_{45°}} = \begin{bmatrix} 0.505 & 0.495 \\ 0.495 & 0.505 \end{bmatrix}$

Figure 4. Rotated versions of the same set of samples. The two cases lead to different aggregated scores.

$$\begin{aligned} H\left(\left[\frac{1}{n}, \ldots, \frac{1}{n}\right]\right) &= -\sum_{i=1}^n \frac{1}{n} \log_2 \frac{1}{n} \qquad (13) \\ &= \sum_{i=1}^n \frac{1}{n} \log_2 n \qquad (14) \\ &= \log_2 n, \qquad (15) \end{aligned}$$

while (11) leads to the minimum one, 0. Note that, in the presented scenario, the original entropy meaning is abandoned. The measure, indeed, is only exploited in order to quantitatively describe the shape of the considered samples.

Here, a subtle problem arises. The basis in which the set of deep representations is expressed could not be the most meaningful one according to the way in which the proposed metric is computed. In other words, rotated versions of the same sampling could lead to different aggregated scores; certainly, such behavior is not desired. Figure 4 shows a concrete example of the mentioned scenario. The samples in Figure 4b, $\phi(\boldsymbol{X})_{45°}$, are obtained from the ones in Figure 4a, $\phi(\boldsymbol{X})_{0°}$, through $\phi(\boldsymbol{X})_{45°} = \boldsymbol{R}_{45°} \phi(\boldsymbol{X})_{0°}$, with

$$\boldsymbol{R}_{45°} = \frac{1}{\sqrt{2}} \begin{bmatrix} 1 & -1 \\ 1 & 1 \end{bmatrix} \tag{16}$$

Consequently, $\boldsymbol{C}_{\phi(\boldsymbol{X})_{45°}}$ can be computed as $\boldsymbol{C}_{\phi(\boldsymbol{X})_{45°}} = \boldsymbol{R}_{45°} \boldsymbol{C}_{\phi(\boldsymbol{X})_{0°}} \boldsymbol{R}_{45°}^T$. As reported by the captions, $\sigma_{0°}{}_x^2 \gg \sigma_{0°}{}_y^2$ while $\sigma_{45°}{}_x^2 = \sigma_{45°}{}_y^2$ leading to two different aggregated scores.

A possible solution to overcome the issue is inspired by Principal Component Analysis (PCA) [19]. The linear relationship shown in Figure 4b is measured by the off-diagonal terms of $\boldsymbol{C}_{\phi(\boldsymbol{X})}$ (i.e., the covariances). The larger the magnitudes of the terms, the higher the redundancy associated to the data. The goal, therefore, becomes to re-express the original sampling $\phi(\boldsymbol{X})$ into $\boldsymbol{Y} = \boldsymbol{R}\phi(\boldsymbol{X})$ according to a new orthonormal basis (i.e., a rotation) in which the covariance magnitudes related to $\boldsymbol{C}_{\boldsymbol{Y}}$ are minimized: matrix $\boldsymbol{C}_{\boldsymbol{Y}}$ should be diagonal. For a symmetric matrix $\boldsymbol{A}$, the following decomposition holds [19]:

$$\boldsymbol{A} = \boldsymbol{E} \boldsymbol{\Lambda} \boldsymbol{E}^T, \tag{17}$$

where $\boldsymbol{E}$ is a matrix whose columns are the orthogonal eigenvectors of $\boldsymbol{A}$ and $\boldsymbol{\Lambda}$ is a diagonal matrix. Recognizing that $\boldsymbol{C}_{\phi(\boldsymbol{X})}$ is symmetric [19] and setting $\boldsymbol{A} = \boldsymbol{C}_{\phi(\boldsymbol{X})}$, $\boldsymbol{R} = \boldsymbol{E}^T$ can be identified as the required solution (the orthogonal eigenvectors stored in $\boldsymbol{E}$ can always be normalized in order to obtain an orthonormal change of basis):

$$\boldsymbol{C}_{\boldsymbol{Y}} = \frac{1}{|\mathcal{T}_t^i| - 1}\boldsymbol{Y}\boldsymbol{Y}^T \quad (18)$$

$$= \frac{1}{|\mathcal{T}_t^i| - 1}(\boldsymbol{E}^T\phi(\boldsymbol{X}))(\boldsymbol{E}^T\phi(\boldsymbol{X}))^T \quad (19)$$

$$= \frac{1}{|\mathcal{T}_t^i| - 1}\boldsymbol{E}^T\phi(\boldsymbol{X})\phi(\boldsymbol{X})^T\boldsymbol{E} \quad (20)$$

$$= \boldsymbol{E}^T\left(\frac{1}{|\mathcal{T}_t^i| - 1}\phi(\boldsymbol{X})\phi(\boldsymbol{X})^T\right)\boldsymbol{E} \quad (21)$$

$$= \boldsymbol{E}^T\boldsymbol{C}_{\phi(\boldsymbol{X})}\boldsymbol{E} \quad (22)$$

$$= \boldsymbol{E}^T(\boldsymbol{E}\boldsymbol{\Lambda}\boldsymbol{E}^T)\boldsymbol{E} \quad (23)$$

$$= (\boldsymbol{E}^T\boldsymbol{E})\boldsymbol{\Lambda}(\boldsymbol{E}^T\boldsymbol{E}) \quad (24)$$

$$= \boldsymbol{\Lambda}, \quad (25)$$

where (17) is exploited in (23). It is important to highlight how the diagonal terms of $\boldsymbol{\Lambda}$ (i.e., the eigenvalues of $\boldsymbol{C}_{\phi(\boldsymbol{X})}$), denoted as

$$\boldsymbol{\lambda} = [\lambda_1, \ldots, \lambda_n], \quad (26)$$

represent the variances associated to the sampling $\phi(\boldsymbol{X})$ expressed in the new selected basis.

Let

$$\tilde{\boldsymbol{\lambda}} = [\tilde{\lambda}_1, \ldots, \tilde{\lambda}_n] \quad (27)$$

$$= \left[\frac{\lambda_1}{\sum_{i=1}^n \lambda_i}, \ldots, \frac{\lambda_n}{\sum_{i=1}^n \lambda_i}\right], \quad (28)$$

be the distribution extracted from $\boldsymbol{\lambda}$. The final proposal, therefore, consists of modifying (12) into

$$V(\boldsymbol{C}_{\phi(\boldsymbol{X})}) = H(\tilde{\boldsymbol{\lambda}}). \quad (29)$$

Again, the borderline cases (10) and (11) can be trivially translated into the new setup, as well as the metric minimum and maximum values.

V. Experiments & Results

The presented experiments, and the respective results, aim to verify the hypothesis formulated in Section IV, and preliminarily investigate the employability of the defined metric in a real application scenario.

A. Dataset

The experiments exploit the CIFAR-100 dataset [6], a popular benchmark for testing Computer Vision algorithms. The dataset consists of 100 "fine" classes (or sub-classes) containing 600 32×32 pixel color images each. All the sub-classes are grouped into 20 "coarse" classes (or super-classes). Moreover, CIFAR-100 is divided into 50000 training images and 10000 testing images.

B. Classifier

The DeepNCM classifier [20] is selected for the experiments. The model is a distance-based classifier that assigns a sample to the class with the closest mean:

$$F_t(\boldsymbol{x}) = \arg\max_{i \in \mathcal{K}_t} -d(\phi(\boldsymbol{x}), \boldsymbol{\mu}_{t-1}^i) \quad (30)$$

$$= \arg\min_{i \in \mathcal{K}_t} d(\phi(\boldsymbol{x}), \boldsymbol{\mu}_{t-1}^i), \quad (31)$$

where

$$d(\phi(\boldsymbol{x}), \boldsymbol{\mu}_{t-1}^i) = (\phi(\boldsymbol{x}) - \boldsymbol{\mu}_{t-1}^i)^T(\phi(\boldsymbol{x}) - \boldsymbol{\mu}_{t-1}^i), \quad (32)$$

and

$$\boldsymbol{\mu}_{t-1}^i = \frac{1}{|\mathcal{T}_{t-1}^i|}\sum_{\boldsymbol{x} \text{ s.t. } (\boldsymbol{x},i)\in\mathcal{T}_{t-1}^i} \phi(\boldsymbol{x}). \quad (33)$$

The incremental update of the model is granted by (33). The exploited implementation of DeepNCM relies on ResNet for the extraction of the deep representations. Hence, function ϕ corresponds to the network layers that precede the classification one, as anticipated in Section IV.

It is important to highlight that the class means $\{\boldsymbol{\mu}_t^i\}$ and covariance matrices $\{\boldsymbol{C}_{\phi(\boldsymbol{X}_t^i)}\}$ can be updated sequentially [21] according to:

$$\boldsymbol{\mu}_t^i = \frac{|\mathcal{T}_{t-1}^i|\boldsymbol{\mu}_{t-1}^i + \boldsymbol{x}}{|\mathcal{T}_{t-1}^i| + 1}, \quad (34)$$

$$\boldsymbol{C}_{\phi(\boldsymbol{X}_t^i)} = \frac{|\mathcal{T}_{t-1}^i| - 1}{|\mathcal{T}_{t-1}^i|}\boldsymbol{C}_{\phi(\boldsymbol{X}_{t-1}^i)} + \frac{1}{|\mathcal{T}_{t-1}^i| + 1}(\boldsymbol{x} - \boldsymbol{\mu}_{t-1}^i)(\boldsymbol{x} - \boldsymbol{\mu}_{t-1}^i)^T. \quad (35)$$

Therefore, with reference to the framework of Section III, the additional state information of the model can naturally be set to $s_{t+1}^i = \boldsymbol{C}_{\phi(\boldsymbol{X}_t^i)} = U(\boldsymbol{C}_{\phi(\boldsymbol{X}_{t-1}^i)}, \boldsymbol{x}) = U(s_t^i, \boldsymbol{x})$. Recomputing class means and covariance matrices by scratch, indeed, is prohibitively computationally expensive for large amounts of samples.

Hence, the choice of the classifier is motivated by the ease with which the DeepNCM framework can be extended in order to incorporate $\mathcal{S}_t$, U and V.

C. Qualitative Hypothesis Verification

To verify the presented hypothesis, DeepNCM is trained (200 epochs, further details on the training procedure can be found in [20]) on 20 modified CIFAR-100 super-classes, 250 samples per super-class, made of only one randomly selected sub-class. This change is introduced to start the metric computation from an initial set of super-classes that have a low intra-class variability. Subsequently, 5000 unseen samples belonging to the same sub-classes exploited during the model training (i.e., 250 samples per super-class) are supplied to the classifier. After each classification, the experiment assigns the samples to the respective ground truth categories in order to evaluate the metric regardless of the accuracy achieved during the classifier training. The model state is updated and the score produced by the metric computation is stored. Then, the model state is re-initialized. Again, 5000 unseen samples (i.e., 250 per super-class), from randomly chosen sub-classes, different from the ones of the training phase, are supplied to the classifier and the corresponding metric scores are computed and stored.

Note that misclassifications can impact the intra-class variability. The consequence, however, could be mitigated by the labeling process function L_t. For example, the function might be able to recognize if the images in $\mathcal{T}_t^i$ belong to the hyponyms of the considered super-class label i in accordance with the exploited external source of information.

The first part of the experiment analyzes the metric behavior in a scenario in which the intra-class variability is expected to remain constant (referred to as "constant"), while the second

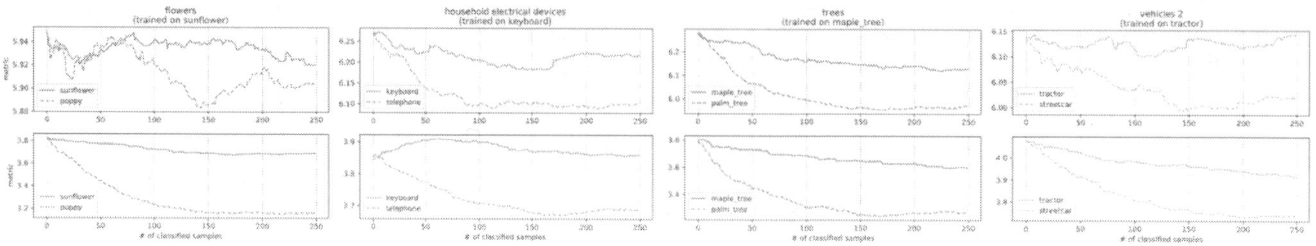

Figure 5. Metric scores for 4 randomly chosen example classes. Top row reports computations with the $V(\boldsymbol{C}_{\phi(\boldsymbol{X})}) = H(\tilde{\boldsymbol{\sigma}})$ definition while the bottom row reports computations with the $V(\boldsymbol{C}_{\phi(\boldsymbol{X})}) = H(\tilde{\boldsymbol{\lambda}})$ definition. Solid lines show the "constant" scenario and dashed lines show the "drift" scenario.

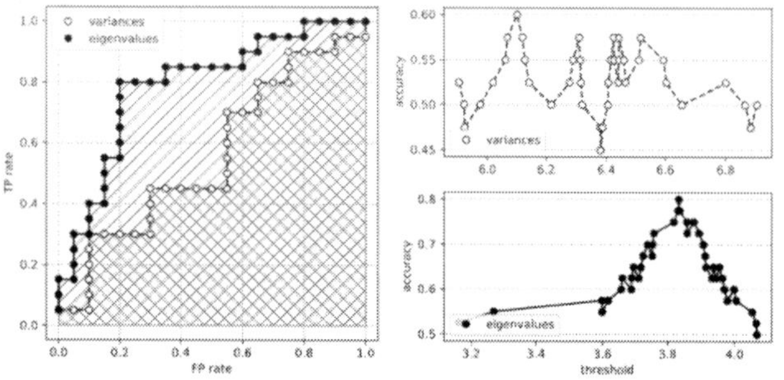

Figure 6. Quantitative evaluation of the considered scores/trigger pairs. The plot on the left reports the produced ROC curves while the plots on the right report the computed accuracies. White dotted lines refer to the $V(\boldsymbol{C}_{\phi(\boldsymbol{X})}) = H(\tilde{\boldsymbol{\sigma}})$ definition while black dotted lines refer to the $V(\boldsymbol{C}_{\phi(\boldsymbol{X})}) = H(\tilde{\boldsymbol{\lambda}})$ definition.

part investigates a scenario in which the intra-class variability is expected to increase (referred to as "drift"). Moreover, the metric scores are computed in accordance with both definition (12) and (29); this is necessary to understand the benefits introduced with the computation of the eigenvalues.

Figure 5 shows the obtained results for some example classes. Considering each super-class separately, most cases present lower metric values, under the same number of classified samples, for the "drift" scenario confirming the correctness of the formulated hypothesis with respect to the considered dataset/classifier pair. With reference to the $V(\boldsymbol{C}_{\phi(\boldsymbol{X})}) = H(\tilde{\boldsymbol{\lambda}})$ final metric definition, it is interesting to notice that the "constant" scenario is also characterized by slightly decreasing trends. The limited amount of training samples, indeed, leads to an adjustment of the scores during the testing phase. However, the initial values of the metric are spread into a large interval resulting in a partial overlapping of the curves related to the different tested scenarios; such data represents the legacy of the criterion with which the CIFAR-100 authors decided to collect the images in the different classes. Additionally, the initial scores assume intermediate values between 0 and $\log_2 n = 9$. Hence, it is immediate to infer that the considered initial configuration is placed in an intermediate position between the borderline cases described in (10) and (11).

D. *Quantitative Metric Evaluation*

In order to quantitatively evaluate the performance of the defined metric, the separability of the scores associated to the "constant" and "drift" scenarios is investigated. Defining

$$T(V(s_{10001}^i)) = \begin{cases} 0 \text{ if } V(s_{10001}^i) \geq \theta \\ 1 \text{ if } V(s_{10001}^i) < \theta, \end{cases} \tag{36}$$

as the family of threshold triggers acting on the metric scores after the 10000 sample classifications of the experiment, with $i \in \mathcal{K}_{10000} = \mathcal{K}^{const} \cup \mathcal{K}^{drift}$ (the super-class labels must be doubled in order to keep track of the model states deleted with the re-initialization performed after the first experiment part) and $\theta \in \mathbb{R}$, a True Positive (TP) is denoted as $V(s_{10001}^i)$ s.t. $i \in \mathcal{K}^{drift} \wedge T(V(s_{10001}^i)) = 1$ while a True Negative (TN) as $V(s_{10001}^i)$ s.t. $i \in \mathcal{K}^{const} \wedge T(V(s_{10001}^i)) = 0$. The False Positive (FP) and False Negative (FN) definitions immediately follow. Hence, the investigation is performed by computing the Receiver Operating Characteristic (ROC) curves for both the $V(\boldsymbol{C}_{\phi(\boldsymbol{X})}) = H(\tilde{\boldsymbol{\sigma}})$ and $V(\boldsymbol{C}_{\phi(\boldsymbol{X})}) = H(\tilde{\boldsymbol{\lambda}})$ definitions, and the respective Area Under the ROC Curve (AUC) integrals.

Figure 6 shows the produced ROCs and two additional accuracy evaluations. The computation of the eigenvalues reveals to be necessary with a final AUC of 0.79, a net improvement over the direct use of the per-component variances, characterized by an AUC of 0.56. The statement is also confirmed by the binary accuracy plots, with an accuracy peek of 0.80 for the $V(\boldsymbol{C}_{\phi(\boldsymbol{X})}) = H(\tilde{\boldsymbol{\lambda}})$ definition. Definition $V(\boldsymbol{C}_{\phi(\boldsymbol{X})}) = H(\tilde{\boldsymbol{\sigma}})$, instead, reveals a performance similar to that of a random trigger.

It is important to emphasize the naivety of the family of triggers considered in the evaluation process. Therefore, the presented results leave room for a promising future application of the metric in a real scenario.

VI. Conclusion

This paper presented a novel lifelong learning framework and metric in order to manage and quantify the intra-class variability of a trained classifier. The proposed work is an important step to extend the life of robots, thus enabling them to operate longer in real uncontrolled environments without the luxury of the closed-world assumption. For future work, we intend to fully implement the introduced framework (i.e., F_t, $\mathcal{S}_t$, U, V, T, L_t, R and I_t) and test the full framework's real-world performance on a robot platform.

Acknowledgment

The research leading to these results has received funding from the Austrian Science Fund (FWF) under grant agreement No. I3969-N30 (InDex). This work was partly supported by MIUR (Italian Minister for Education) under the initiative Departments of Excellence (Law 232/2016).

References

[1] S. Thrun and T. M. Mitchell, "Lifelong robot learning," in The Biology and Technology of Intelligent Autonomous Agents, 1995, pp. 165–196.

[2] A. Krizhevsky, I. Sutskever, and G. E. Hinton, "Imagenet classification with deep convolutional neural networks," in Advances in Neural Information Processing Systems 25, 2012, pp. 1097–1105.

[3] A. Bendale and T. Boult, "Towards open world recognition," in Proc. of IEEE Conference on Computer Vision and Pattern Recognition, 2015, pp. 1893–1902.

[4] M. Mancini, H. Karaoguz, E. Ricci, P. Jensfelt, and B. Caputo, "Knowledge is never enough: Towards web aided deep open world recognition," in Proc. of IEEE International Conference on Robotics and Automation, 2019, pp. 9537–9543.

[5] V. Losing, B. Hammer, and H. Wersing, "Incremental on-line learning: A review and comparison of state of the art algorithms," Neurocomputing, vol. 275, 2018, pp. 1261–1274.

[6] A. Krizhevsky, "Learning multiple layers of features from tiny images," Department of Computer Science University of Toronto, Tech. Rep., 2009.

[7] C. Silla and A. Freitas, "A survey of hierarchical classification across different application domains," Data Mining and Knowledge Discovery, vol. 22, 2011, pp. 31–72.

[8] G. A. Miller, "WordNet: A lexical database for english," Communications of the ACM, vol. 38, no. 11, 1995, pp. 39–41.

[9] D. Jurafsky and J. Martin, Speech and Language Processing: An Introduction to Natural Language Processing, Computational Linguistics, and Speech Recognition. Upper Saddle River, N.J.: Pearson Prentice Hall, 2008.

[10] D. Miller, L. Nicholson, F. Dayoub, and N. Sünderhauf, "Dropout sampling for robust object detection in open-set conditions," in Proc. of IEEE International Conference on Robotics and Automation, 2017, pp. 3243–3249.

[11] S. Valipour, C. Perez, and M. Jagersand, "Incremental learning for robot perception through hri," in Proc. of IEEE/RSJ International Conference on Intelligent Robots and Systems, 2017, pp. 2772–2777.

[12] R. Camoriano *et al.*, "Incremental robot learning of new objects with fixed update time," in Proc. of IEEE International Conference on Robotics and Automation, 2017, pp. 3207–3214.

[13] Y. Yang *et al.*, "An improved approach considering intraclass variability for mapping winter wheat using multitemporal MODIS EVI images," Remote Sensing, vol. 11, no. 10, 2019, p. 1191.

[14] M. Frid-Adar *et al.*, "Modeling the intra-class variability for liver lesion detection using a multi-class patch-based CNN," in Proc. of International Workshop on Patch-based Techniques in Medical Imaging, 2017, pp. 129–137.

[15] A. J. Abboud and S. A. Jassim, "Image quality guided approach for adaptive modelling of biometric intra-class variations," in Proc. of SPIE 7708, Mobile Multimedia/Image Processing, Security, and Applications, 2010, pp. 189–198.

[16] D. Paindaveine, "A canonical definition of shape," Statistics Probability Letters, vol. 78, no. 14, 2008, pp. 2240–2247.

[17] K. He, X. Zhang, S. Ren, and J. Sun, "Deep residual learning for image recognition," in Proc. of IEEE Conference on Computer Vision and Pattern Recognition, 2016, pp. 770–778.

[18] K. Simonyan and A. Zisserman, "Very deep convolutional networks for large-scale image recognition," in Proc. of International Conference on Learning Representations, 2015.

[19] J. Shlens, "A tutorial on principal component analysis," ArXiv, vol. abs/1404.1100, 2014.

[20] S. Guerriero, B. Caputo, and T. Mensink, "DeepNCM: Deep nearest class mean classifiers," in Proc. of International Conference on Learning Representations - Workshop, 2018.

[21] D. Savransky, "Sequential covariance calculation for exoplanet image processing," The Astrophysical Journal, vol. 800, no. 2, 2015.

Towards a Unified Approach to Homography Estimation Using Image Features and Pixel Intensities

Lucas Nogueira, Ely C. de Paiva
School of Mechanical Engineering
University of Campinas
Campinas, SP, Brazil
[lucas.nogueira]|[ely]@fem.unicamp.br

Geraldo Silveira
Robotics and Computer Vision research group
Center for Information Technology Renato Archer
Campinas, SP, Brazil
Geraldo.Silveira@cti.gov.br

Abstract—**The homography matrix is a key component in various vision-based robotic tasks. Traditionally, homography estimation algorithms are classified into feature- or intensity-based. The main advantages of the latter are their versatility, accuracy, and robustness to arbitrary illumination changes. On the other hand, they have a smaller domain of convergence than the feature-based solutions. Their combination is hence promising, but existing techniques only apply them sequentially. This paper proposes a new hybrid method that unifies both classes into a single nonlinear optimization procedure, applies the same minimization method, and uses the same homography parametrization and warping function. Experimental validation using a classical testing framework shows that the proposed unified approach has improved convergence properties compared to each individual class. These are also demonstrated in a visual tracking application. As a final contribution, our ready-to-use implementation of the algorithm is made publicly available to the research community.**

Keywords–Robot vision; Homography optimization; Hybrid approaches; Vision-based applications.

I. Introduction

The homography matrix is a key component in computer vision. It relates corresponding pixel coordinates of a planar object in different images, and has been used in a variety of vision-based applications such as image mosaicing [1], visual servoing [2] and object grasping [3]. The homography estimation task can be formulated as an Image Registration (IR) problem. IR can be defined as a search for the parameters that best define the transformation between corresponding pixels in a pair of images. Solutions to this problem involve the definition of at least four important characteristics [4]: the information space, the transformations models, the similarity measures, and the search strategy.

With respect to the information space, the vast majority of vision-based algorithms use a Feature-Based (FB) approach. In this class, firstly an extraction algorithm searches each image for geometric primitives and selects the best candidates. Then, a matching algorithm establishes correspondences between features in different images. Afterwards, the actual estimation takes place. However, both the extraction and matching steps are error-prone and can produce outliers that affect the quality of the estimation. Additionally, by using only a sparse set of features, these algorithms may discard useful information.

In contrast, Intensity-Based (IB) methods have no extraction and matching steps. These methods are also referred to as direct methods since they exploit the pixel intensity values directly. This allows the estimation algorithm to work with more information than FB methods and does not depend on particular primitives. Thus, it leads to more accurate estimates and is highly versatile. However, an important drawback is that they require a small interframe displacement, i.e., a sufficient overlapping between consecutive images.

The algorithms presented in this work use multidimensional optimization methods as the main search strategy for the image registration problem. When formulated as such, an initial solution is iteratively refined using a nonlinear optimization method. Specifically, the algorithms presented here are derived from the Efficient Second-order Minimization method (ESM) [5]. Its advantages include both a higher convergence rate and a larger convergence domain than standard iterative methods. It allows for a second-order approximation of the Taylor series without computationally expensive Hessian calculations.

The use of the ESM framework has shown remarkable results for IB methods. However, its application within FB methods has been limited so far. As discussed, the two classes of estimation methods have complementary strengths. This work aims to develop a hybrid method that exploits their advantages and reduces their shortcomings. The proposed algorithm is made available as ready-to-use ROS [6] packages and as a C++ library. In particular, a homography-based visual tracking application is also developed. In summary, our contribution is the development of a vision-based algorithm that:

- unifies the intensity- and feature-based approaches to homography estimation into a single nonlinear optimization problem;
- solves that problem using the same efficient minimization method, homography parametrization, and warping function;
- can be applied in real-time settings, such as for homography-based visual tracking as experimentally demonstrated in this paper; and
- its ready-to-use implementation is made publicly available for research purposes as a C++ library and as a ROS package.

The remainder of this article is organized as follows. Section II presents the related works, whereas Section III describes the proposed unified approach. Section IV then reports the benchmarking experiments and the application of the proposed algorithm to visual tracking. Finally, the conclusions are drawn in Section V, and some references are given for further details.

II. Related Works

The main distinction between IB and FB methods regards their information space. Indeed, on one hand FB requires the extraction and association of geometric primitives in different images before the actual estimation can occur. These primitives can be, e.g., points and lines [1][7]. IB methods simultaneously solves for the estimation problem and pixel correspondences with no intermediate steps [8][9].

The transformation model dictates which parameters are estimated. For example, the original Lucas-Kanade [10] algorithm only estimated translations in the image space. This was later extended to more sophiscated warp functions [11]. Simultaneous Localization And Mapping (SLAM) algorithms commonly use IR to perform the pose and structure estimation [12]. The homography matrix is often used as a transformation model when dealing with predominantly planar regions of interest [13][14][15]. Illumination parameters may also be considered as a component of the transformation model, e.g., in [16].

The quality of the IR is defined by a similarity measure. When an optimization method is applied, this measure is often used as a cost function, such as the Sum of Squared Differences (SSD) [10][17]. Other possibilities include correlation-based metrics [18][19] and mutual information [20].

The last component of IR algorithms is the search strategy. Most real-time applications use a multidimensional optimization approach based on gradient descent. They use the first and second derivatives of the similarity measures with respect to the transformation parameters. The ESM algorithm is such an example, and is applied in the proposed method. Alternative optimization approaches include Gauss-Newton and Levenberg-Marquardt [21]. All of these techniques are most suited to applications with small interframe displacements. Indeed, global techniques are too computationally expensive to be applied in real-time settings. A more thorough review and comparison of image registration algorithms can be found in [22][23].

As for the existing techniques that combine IB and FB methods, their overwhelming majority only applies them sequentially, e.g., [24][25]. In sequential strategies, a FB technique is firstly considered and then its estimated parameters are fed as the initial guess to some IB optimization. This standard combination scheme is thus not optimal and is more time consuming. An exception to that sequential procedure is reported in [26]. However, it aims to estimate the pose parameters, which requires a calibrated camera. The objective of this paper is to estimate the projective homography, i.e., there is no calibrated camera. Furthermore, that existing technique applies a first-order minimization method, and the considered scaling factors do not take into account the convergence properties of the individual approaches, as will be proposed in the sequel.

III. Proposed Unified Approach

Consider that a *reference template* has been specified to an estimation algorithm. This is typically a region of interest with predefined resolution inside a larger reference image. Then, a second image, referred to as the *current image*, is given to that algorithm. The goal is to find the transformation parameters that, when applied to the current image, results in a current template identical to the reference template.

A. Transformation Models

The considered transformation models consist of a geometric and a photometric one. The geometric transformation model explains image changes due to variations in the scene structure and/or the camera motion. For a given pixel $\mathbf{p}^*$ in the reference template that corresponds to pixel $\mathbf{p}$ in the current image, we model the geometric motion using a homography:

$$\mathbf{p} \propto \mathbf{H}\mathbf{p}^* \tag{1}$$

$$= \left[\frac{h_{11}u^* + h_{12}v^* + h_{13}}{h_{31}u^* + h_{32}v^* + h_{33}}, \frac{h_{21}u^* + h_{22}v^* + h_{23}}{h_{31}u^* + h_{32}v^* + h_{33}}, 1 \right]^\top \tag{2}$$

$$= \mathbf{w}(\mathbf{H}, \mathbf{p}^*), \tag{3}$$

where $\mathbf{p}^* = [u^*, v^*, 1]^\top \in \mathbb{P}^2$ is the homogeneous pixel coordinates in the reference template, $\mathbf{w}$ is the warping operator, and $\mathbf{H} \in \mathbb{SL}(3)$ is the projective homography matrix with its elements $\{h_{ij}\}$. Such matrix has only eight degrees-of-freedom. In general, this situation leads to a reprojection step after each iteration of the minimization algorithm that takes the estimated homography into the Special Linear Group. To avoid this problem, the proposed algorithm parameterizes the homography using its corresponding Lie Algebra [2]. This is accomplished via the matrix exponential function, which maps a region around the identity matrix $\mathbf{I} \in \mathbb{SL}(3)$ to a region around the origin $\mathbf{0} \in \mathfrak{sl}(3)$. A matrix $\mathbf{A}(\mathbf{v}) \in \mathfrak{sl}(3)$ is the linear combination of eight matrices that form a base of the Lie Algebra. Therefore $\mathbf{v}$ has eight components. A homography is thus parameterized as

$$\mathbf{H}(\mathbf{v}) = \exp(\mathbf{A}(\mathbf{v})). \tag{4}$$

The homography matrix may be used to extract relative motion and scene structure information [27]. However, this decomposition is out of the scope of this work and is unnecessary for many robotic applications.

The photometric transformation model explains the changes in the image due to variations in the lighting conditions of the scene. Let us model in this work only global illumination variations, i.e., changes that apply equally to all pixels in the images. This model is defined as

$$\mathcal{I}'(\mathbf{p}) = \alpha \mathcal{I}(\mathbf{p}) + \beta, \tag{5}$$

where $\mathcal{I}(\mathbf{p}) \geq 0$ is the intensity value of the pixel $\mathbf{p}$, $\mathcal{I}'(\mathbf{p}) \geq 0$ denotes its transformed intensity, and the gain $\alpha \in \mathbb{R}$ and the bias $\beta \in \mathbb{R}$ are the parameters that fully define the transformation. These parameters can be viewed as the adjustments in the image constrast and brightness, respectively.

B. Nonlinear Least Squares Formulation

Consider that the reference template is composed of m pixels. Also, consider that a feature detection and matching algorithm provides n feature correspondences between the reference template and the current image. Ideally, it would be possible to find a vector $\mathbf{x}^* = \{\mathbf{H}^*, \alpha^*, \beta^*\}$ such that:

$$\alpha^* \mathcal{I}(\mathbf{w}(\mathbf{H}^*, \mathbf{p}_i^*)) + \beta^* = \mathcal{I}^*(\mathbf{p}_i^*), \qquad \forall i = 1, 2, \ldots, m, \tag{6}$$

$$\mathbf{w}(\mathbf{H}^*, \mathbf{q}_j^*) = \mathbf{q}_j, \qquad \forall j = 1, 2, \ldots, n, \tag{7}$$

by substituting (3) in (5), where $\mathcal{I}$ and $\mathcal{I}^*$ are the current and reference images, respectively, $\mathbf{p}_i^* \in \mathbb{P}^2$ contains the coordinates of the i-th pixel of the reference template, and $\mathbf{q}_j, \mathbf{q}_j^* \in \mathbb{P}^2$ are the representations of the j-th feature correspondence set in the current image and reference template, respectively. The perfect calculation of $\mathbf{x}^*$ is impossible due to a variety of reasons, including noise in the camera sensor and outliers in the feature matching. This leads to the reformulation of this task as a nonlinear least-squares problem.

Two separate cost-functions are defined: One for the IB part and another for the FB one. The i-th pixel of the reference template contributes to the following row to the IB cost function via the distance

$$a_i(\mathbf{x}) = \alpha \mathcal{I}(\mathbf{w}(\mathbf{H}, \mathbf{p}_i^*)) + \beta - \mathcal{I}^*(\mathbf{p}_i^*), \tag{8}$$

and an output vector $\mathbf{y}_{IB}$ can be constructed as:

$$\mathbf{y}_{IB} = \begin{bmatrix} a_1 & a_2 & \cdots & a_m \end{bmatrix}^\top. \tag{9}$$

The FB cost function is defined using the distance between the features coordinates in each image:

$$\mathbf{b}_j(\mathbf{x}) = \mathbf{w}(\mathbf{H}, \mathbf{q}_j^*) - \mathbf{q}_j = \begin{bmatrix} b_j^u & b_j^v & 0 \end{bmatrix}, \tag{10}$$

where b_j^u, b_j^v are distances between the features in the u and v directions, respectively. The third element is disregarded since it is always zero. Thus, a vector $\mathbf{y}_{FB}$ can be constructed as:

$$\mathbf{y}_{FB} = \begin{bmatrix} b_1^u & b_1^v & b_2^u & b_2^v & \cdots & b_n^u & b_n^v \end{bmatrix}^\top. \tag{11}$$

Using (9) and (11), a unified nonlinear least squares problem can be defined as

$$\min_{\mathbf{x}=\{\mathbf{H},\alpha,\beta\}} \frac{1}{2}\Big(w_{IB}\,\|\mathbf{y}_{IB}(\mathbf{x})\|_2^2 + w_{FB}\,\|\mathbf{y}_{FB}(\mathbf{x})\|_2^2\Big), \tag{12}$$

where w_{IB}, w_{FB} are carefully chosen weights given to the intensity- and feature-based components of the cost function, respectively, as will be proposed later on. For real-time systems, only local optimization methods can be applied since global ones are too costly. In this case, an initial approximation $\widehat{\mathbf{x}} = \{\widehat{\mathbf{H}}, \widehat{\alpha}, \widehat{\beta}\}$ of the true solution is required. This estimate can be integrated into the least-squares formulation as:

$$\min_{\mathbf{z}=\{\mathbf{v},\alpha,\beta\}} \frac{1}{2}\Big(w_{IB}\left\|\mathbf{y}_{IB}(\mathbf{x}(\mathbf{z})\circ\widehat{\mathbf{x}})\right\|^2 + w_{FB}\left\|\mathbf{y}_{FB}(\mathbf{x}(\mathbf{z})\circ\widehat{\mathbf{x}})\right\|^2\Big), \tag{13}$$

where the symbol '$\circ$' denotes the composition operation. For the scalars α and β, it corresponds to the addition, whereas for the homography that operation is the matrix multiplication. Furthermore, to take into account the different number of observations for IB and FB methods, we include normalization factors and define the unified output vector as

$$\mathbf{y}_{UN} = \left[\sqrt{\tfrac{w_{IB}}{m}}\,\mathbf{y}_{IB} \quad \sqrt{\tfrac{w_{FB}}{2n}}\,\mathbf{y}_{FB}\right]. \tag{14}$$

Hence, a more concise unified formulation is achieved:

$$\min_{\mathbf{z}=\{\mathbf{v},\alpha,\beta\}} \frac{1}{2}\left\|\mathbf{y}_{UN}(\mathbf{x}(\mathbf{z})\circ\widehat{\mathbf{x}})\right\|^2, \tag{15}$$

which can be efficiently solved using [17].

C. Weight Choices

The weights w_{IB} and w_{FB} should be carefully selected to ensure the best convergence properties for the algorithm. The following constraints apply to the weights:

$$w_{IB} + w_{FB} = 1, \tag{16}$$

$$w_{FB}, w_{IB} > 0. \tag{17}$$

The idea behind the proposed method for determining the weights is to let the feature-based error be more influential to the optimization when the current solution is far from the true one. As the FB error decreases, then the intensity-based component becomes increasingly more important. This is consistent with the idea that the FB method is better suited to handle large displacements, whereas IB methods have higher accuracy, but only work when the initial guess is sufficiently close to the true solution.

The main measurement used for calculating the weights is the feature-based error associated with the current estimated homography $\widehat{\mathbf{H}}$. It is calculated using the following root mean squared error (RMSD):

$$RMSD(\mathbf{y}_{FB}) = \sqrt{\frac{\sum_{j=1}^{n}\left\|\mathbf{w}(\widehat{\mathbf{H}}, \mathbf{q}_j^*) - \mathbf{q}_j\right\|_2^2}{n}} = d_{FB}. \tag{18}$$

The proposed weights are then defined from

$$w_{FB} = 1 - \exp(-d_{FB}) \tag{19}$$

and (16). This function allows for a continuous transition where the feature-based weight decreases as its error gets lower, and the intensity-based component becomes increasingly more important in the optimization.

D. Local versus Global Search

The processing times may be drastically increased if the feature detection and matching algorithms are allowed to process the entire current image. The proposed method processes only a small region in the current image to obtain good matches whenever possible.

Firstly, a current template is generated by warping the current image with the initial approximation $\widehat{\mathbf{H}}$. Then, this current template is assigned a score by comparing it with the reference template using the Zero-mean Normalized Cross-Correlated. If this score is higher than a predefined threshold, then the feature detection algorithm searches only within this current template. Otherwise, the current template and $\widehat{\mathbf{H}}$ are both discarded. In this case, the detection algorithm searches the entire current image for features. The first scenario is referred to as a "local" search, whereas the second one as a "global" search. When the global search is used, it is necessary to recalculate an initial approximation $\widehat{\mathbf{H}}$. This is done by calculating the homography solely from the features matches between the current image and the reference template.

IV. EXPERIMENTAL RESULTS

A. Validation Setup

The same testing procedure used in [28] is implemented to validate the algorithm. Firstly, a reference image of size 800×533 pixels is chosen, and a region of size 100×100 pixels is selected as the reference template. The coordinates of each corner are independently perturbed in the $\overrightarrow{u}$ and $\overrightarrow{v}$ directions with a zero mean Gaussian noise and standard deviation of σ pixels (see Figure 1). The relation between the original corner points and the perturbed ones defines a test homography. The reference image is then transformed by this test homography. The algorithm receives the reference template and the transformed image with the identity element as the initial guess for the photogeometric transformation. From this input, the algorithm produces an estimated homography. In turn, this homography is used to transform each reference corner point. If the average residual error between the actual perturbed corner points and the estimated perturbed ones is less than 1 pixel, the result is declared to have converged. 1,000 test cases are randomly generated for each value of the perturbation $\sigma \in [0, 20]$ and used as input for each evaluated algorithm. In all tests, 3 levels of a multiresolution pyramid are used. In each level, a maximum of 3 iterations of the algorithm are allowed to execute.

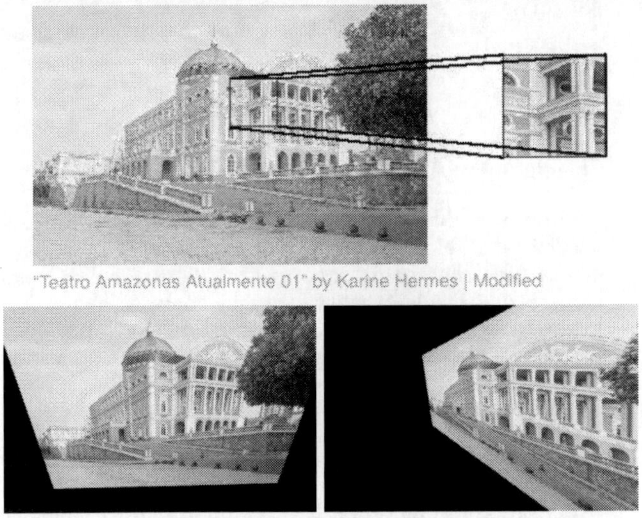

Figure 1. Validation setup. (Top) Reference image and selected reference template, resp. (Bottom) Examples of transformation with perturbations $\sigma = 5$ and $\sigma = 10$, resp.

This setup is used to compare different algorithms. Three criteria are analyzed: Convergence domain, convergence rate and timing analysis. The methods differ on whether they use only the IB or the FB component (SURF is here applied for feature detection and description) in the cost function, or both for the Unified case. Another difference is the use of a ZNCC predictor to improve the initialization in some methods. Finally, some algorithms do not consider the photometric part of the transformation space. These algorithms along with their characteristics are summarized in Table I.

TABLE I. HOMOGRAPHY ESTIMATION ALGORITHMS USED FOR COMPARISONS.

Method	IB	FB	Predictor	Photometric
ESM	✓	✗	✗	✗
IBG	✓	✗	✗	✓
IBG_P	✓	✗	✓	✓
FB_ESM	✗	✓	✗	✗
UNIF	✓	✓	✗	✓
UNIF_P	✓	✓	✓	✓

B. Convergence Domain

Figure 2 shows that the proposed Unified algorithms have a larger convergence domain than all pure FB or IB versions. It also shows that the use of the ZNCC predictor in the unified version does not affect its frequence of convergence, as well as that the IBG (i.e., IB with robustness to Global illumination changes) and ESM algorithms have a very similar performance. The latter is expected because there are no lighting changes in this validation setup.

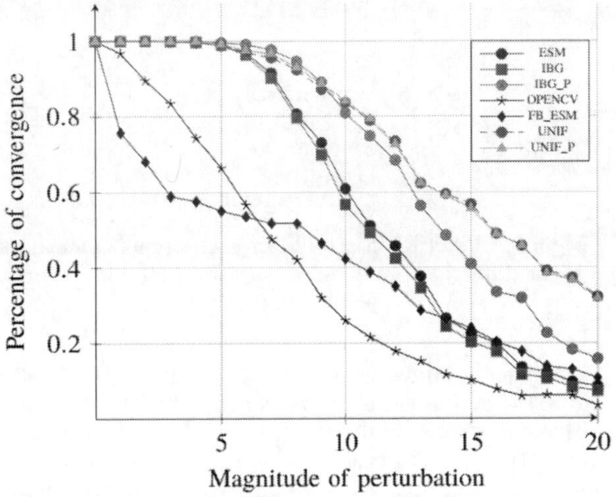

Figure 2. Percentage of convergence versus magnitude of perturbation for different homography estimation algorithms.

Another interesting observation is that the results of the algorithms in the FB class (FB_ESM and the algorithm available in OpenCV) were significantly worse than the ones in the IB class, although it was expected that they would have a higher convergence domain. This suggests that there is still room for improving the FB components of the estimation, which would in turn lead to a further improvement in the unified method as well.

C. Convergence Rate

Figure 3 compares the convergence rate of the homography estimation algorithms under a perturbation of magnitude $\sigma = 10$. This rate is displayed as the progression of the root mean squared (RMS) error between the coordinates of the 4 corners of the reference template and the estimated transformation of the current template. Out of the 1,000 test cases, only those where the estimation converged are considered here. Note that the results from the OpenCV algorithm is omitted because it was used as a black-box, and therefore the sequence of homographies at each iteration cannot be accessed. The x-axis of Figure 3 contains each important step in the optimization. The first step, which is labeled "predictor", is the result of the ZNCC prediction step. The second step, which is labeled "global", is the step where the algorithm decides to search for features in the entire current image, as described in Section III-D. Of course, these two steps are not performed by every algorithm. Afterwards, steps from the iterative optimization method follow. They are separated by pyramids level, such that the notation "X-Y" represents pyramid level X at iteration Y.

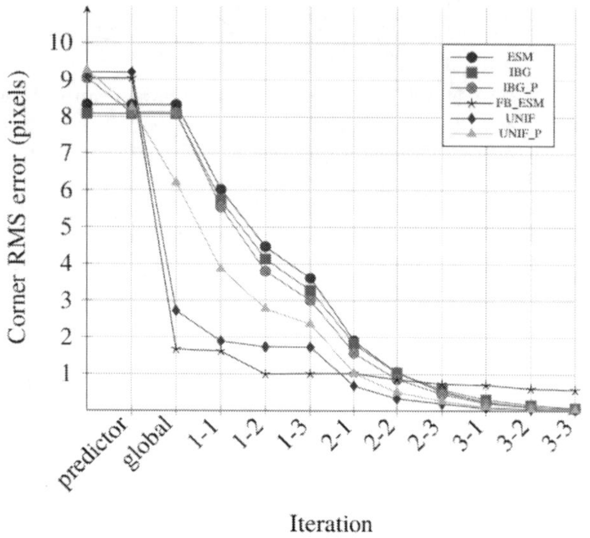

Figure 3. Pixel RMS error after each optimization iteration for different homography estimation algorithms under perturbation $\sigma = 10$.

Figure 3 allows for several observations. Firstly, the FB_ESM performance is very dependent on the "global" step. After this step, it is the algorithm with the best RMS value. However, it is not capable to improve this value too much in the subsequent optimization steps. When the other algorithms reach the third level of the pyramid, they all outperform its RMS. The behaviour of ESM, IBG and IBG_P is very similar as they share the same framework. A small difference between them is that IBG_P is able to converge even for cases with a slightly higher initial RMS error, due to the prediction step. After that step, however, all these three algorithms perform quite similarly.

Finally, let us note that the Unified algorithms have a behaviour that combines the FB and IB methods, as desired. The UNIF_P uses both the "predictor" and "global" steps. Interestingly, the global search is less applied in that version than the UNIF one because of the prediction step. This explains its smaller initial reduction in RMS value. On the other hand, less usage of the global step leads to a improvement in the processing times, as shown in the next section. After these steps, both the Unified algorithms behave similarly to IB ones, with the advantage of having a better initialization procedure.

D. Timing analysis

Figure 4 shows how the average time needed to run the estimation algorithms varies depending on the magnitude of perturbation. This time is measured in a Intel i7-6700HQ processor, and is averaged over the subset of the 1,000 cases only when the estimation has converged. The most noticeable aspect of this graph is that pure IB algorithms have nearly constant time, regardless of the perturbation level. In constrast, the algorithms that have a feature-based component need more time to process images with higher perturbation levels. This phenomenon can be explained by considering the effect of the global versus local feature search. As the perturbation level increases, the number of occasions where the algorithm applies the global search also increases. This step, however, is very computationally expensive. The UNIF_P manages to have a lower processing time because the prediction step increases the probability that the local search is used. Therefore, the UNIF_P can be seen as a compromise between having the advantage of being capable of performing global search, without taking a big penalty in the processing times.

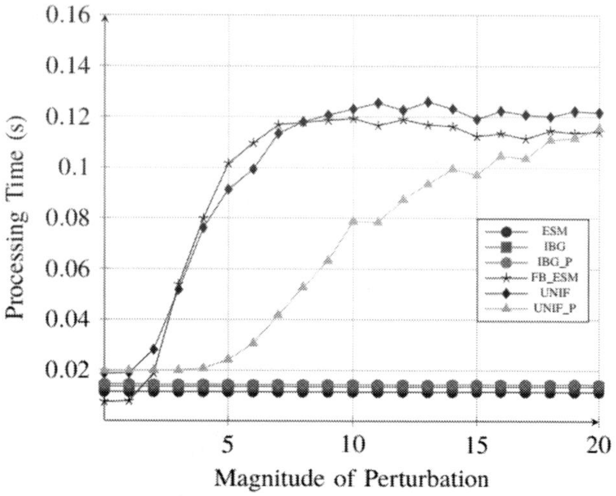

Figure 4. Processing times for different perturbation levels.

However, these results also show that more research is needed to develop a method that is able to reliably perform in real-time settings for large perturbations. The IB methods are already capable of that when they converge, requiring less than 0.02s/image. The FB and Unified methods may need up to 0.12s, which may be unacceptable for some applications.

E. Use Case: Visual Tracking

The proposed algorithm is publicly available for research purposes as a C++ library and as a ROS package [29], along with its technical report [30]. This section shows its application to homography-based visual tracking. Results are available at [31]. The prediction step is applied, as recommended for real-time tracking applications. Figure 5 shows some excerpts of this tracking experiment. An interesting result is that the proposed unified visual tracker can recover from full occlusions. Even after completely removing the tracked region from the current image, the tracker can recover given its feature-based ability to perform the "global" search. Additionally, it can be seen that the algorithm is robust to large global illumination changes, and that in some cases it can recover from complete failure even under severe lighting variations.

V. Conclusions

This paper proposes a first step towards a truly unified optimal approach to homography estimation. The results show that improved convergence properties are indeed obtained when combining both classes of feature- and intensity-based methods into a single optimization procedure. This can help vision-based applications to handle faster robot motions. Future work will focus on reducing the processing time of the unified algorithm, specially when very large interframe displacements lead to a global search for features.

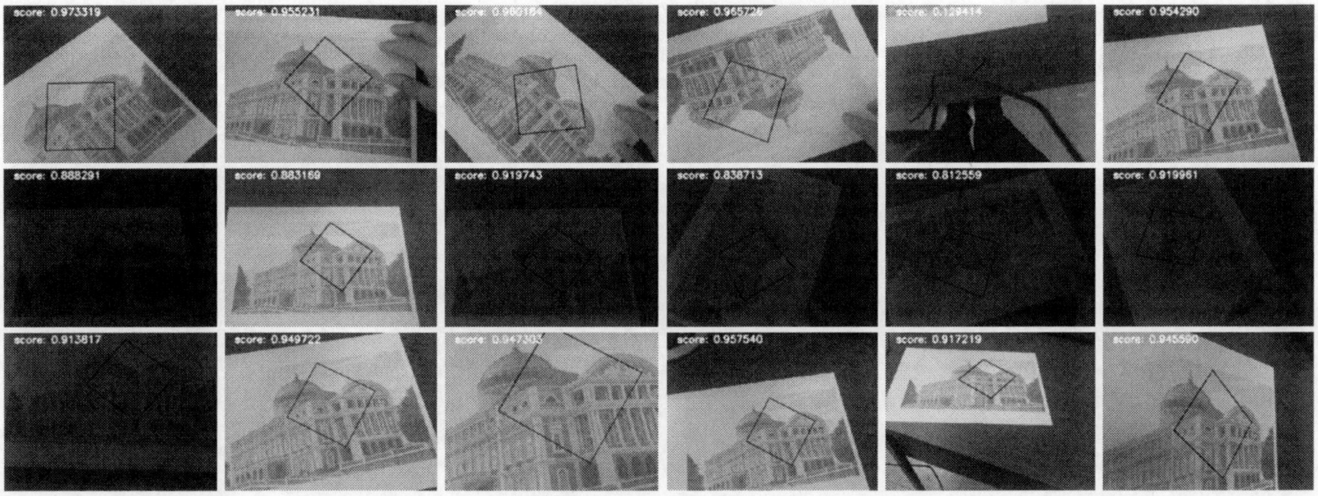

Figure 5. Excerpts of homography-based visual tracking (left-to-right then top-to-bottom) using the proposed unified approach.

Acknowledgment

This work was supported in part by the CAPES under Grant 88887.136349/2017-00, in part by the FAPESP under Grant 2017/22603-0, and in part by the InSAC project (CNPq under Grant 465755/2014-3, FAPESP under Grant 2014/50851-0).

References

[1] O. Faugeras, Q.-T. Luong, and T. Papadopoulo, The geometry of multiple images. The MIT Press, 2001.

[2] S. Benhimane and E. Malis, "Homography-based 2D visual tracking and servoing," The International Journal of Robotics Research, vol. 26, no. 7, 2007, pp. 661–676.

[3] B. Neuberger, G. Silveira, M. Postolov, and M. Vincze, "Object grasping in non-metric space using decoupled direct visual servoing," in Proc. Austrian Robotics Workshop & OAGM Workshop, 2019, pp. 99–104.

[4] L. Brown, "A survey of image registration techniques," ACM computing surveys, vol. 24, no. 4, 1992, pp. 325–376.

[5] S. Benhimane and E. Malis, "Real-time image-based tracking of planes using efficient second-order minimization," in Proc. IEEE/RSJ IROS, 2004, pp. 943–948.

[6] M. Quigley, K. Conley, B. Gerkey, J. Faust, T. Foote, J. Leibs, R. Wheeler, and A. Y. Ng, "ROS: An open-source robot operating system," in Proc. ICRA workshop on open source software, 2009.

[7] R. Szeliski, "Image alignment and stitching: A tutorial," Foundations and Trends in Computer Graphics and Vision, vol. 2, no. 1, 2007.

[8] M. Irani and P. Anandan, "All about direct methods," in Proc. Workshop on Vision Algorithms: Theory and practice, 1999.

[9] G. Silveira, "Contributions to direct methods of estimation and control from visual data," Ph.D. dissertation, Ecole des Mines de Paris, 2008.

[10] B. Lucas and T. Kanade, "An iterative image registration technique with an application to stereo vision," 1981.

[11] J. R. Bergen, P. Anandan, K. J. Hanna, and R. Hingorani, "Hierarchical model-based motion estimation," in Proc. ECCV, 1992, pp. 237–252.

[12] J. Zhang and S. Singh, "Visual-lidar odometry and mapping: Low-drift, robust, and fast," in Proc. IEEE ICRA, 2015, pp. 2174–2181.

[13] G. Silveira, E. Malis, and P. Rives, "An efficient direct approach to visual SLAM," IEEE transactions on robotics, vol. 24, no. 5, 2008, pp. 969–979.

[14] R. Mur-Artal, J. M. M. Montiel, and J. D. Tardos, "ORB-SLAM: a versatile and accurate monocular SLAM system," IEEE Transactions on Robotics, vol. 31, no. 5, 2015, pp. 1147–1163.

[15] D. DeTone, T. Malisiewicz, and A. Rabinovich, "Deep Image Homography Estimation," 2016.

[16] G. Silveira, "Photogeometric direct visual tracking for central omnidirectional cameras," Journal of Mathematical Imaging and Vision, vol. 48, no. 1, 2014, pp. 72–82.

[17] G. Silveira and E. Malis, "Unified direct visual tracking of rigid and deformable surfaces under generic illumination changes in grayscale and color images," International Journal of Computer Vision, vol. 89, 2010, pp. 84–105.

[18] G. D. Evangelidis and E. Z. Psarakis, "Parametric image alignment using enhanced correlation coefficient maximization," IEEE Transactions on Pattern Analysis and Machine Intelligence, vol. 30, no. 10, 2008, pp. 1858–1865.

[19] L. M. Fonseca and B. Manjunath, "Registration techniques for multisensor remotely sensed imagery," 1996.

[20] P. Viola and W. M. Wells III, "Alignment by maximization of mutual information," International journal of computer vision, vol. 24, no. 2, 1997, pp. 137–154.

[21] S. Baker and I. Matthews, "Lucas-kanade 20 years on: A unifying framework," International journal of computer vision, vol. 56, 2004.

[22] B. Zitova and J. Flusser, "Image registration methods: a survey," Image and Vision Computing, vol. 21, 2003, pp. 977–1000.

[23] A. K. Singh, "Modular tracking framework: A unified approach to registration based tracking," Master's thesis, University of Alberta, 2017.

[24] Y. Jianchao, "Image registration based on both feature and intensity matching," in Proc. IEEE International Conference on Acoustics, Speech, and Signal Processing, 2001, pp. 1693–1696.

[25] A. Ladikos, S. Benhimane, and N. Navab, "A real-time tracking system combining template-based and feature-based approaches," in Proc. VISAPP, 2007, pp. 325–332.

[26] P. F. Georgel, S. Benhimane, and N. Navab, "A unified approach combining photometric and geometric information for pose estimation," in Proc. BMVC, 2008.

[27] E. Malis and M. Vargas, "Deeper understanding of the homography decomposition for vision-based control," INRIA, Tech. Rep., 2007.

[28] S. Baker and I. Matthews, "Equivalence and efficiency of image alignment algorithms," in Proc. IEEE CVPR, 2001.

[29] L. Nogueira and G. Silveira, "GitHub - visiotec/vtec_ros: ROS packages from the VisioTec group," 2020, URL: https://github.com/visiotec/vtec_ros [Accessed 22 August 2020].

[30] L. Nogueira, E. de Paiva, and G. Silveira, "VTEC robust intensity-based homography optimization software," no. CTI-VTEC-TR-01-19, Brazil, 2019.

[31] L. Nogueira, "Unified Intensity- And Feature-Based Homography Estimation Applied To Visual Tracking," 2020, URL: https://www.youtube.com/watch?v=oArw449qp1E [Accessed 22 August 2020].